Islamism in the Modern World

Islamism in the Modern World

A Historical Approach

W. J. Berridge

BLOOMSBURY ACADEMIC
LONDON • NEW YORK • OXFORD • NEW DELHI • SYDNEY

BLOOMSBURY ACADEMIC
Bloomsbury Publishing Plc
50 Bedford Square, London, WC1B 3DP, UK
1385 Broadway, New York, NY 10018, USA

BLOOMSBURY, BLOOMSBURY ACADEMIC and the Diana logo are trademarks of
Bloomsbury Publishing Plc

First published in Great Britain 2019

Cover design by Holly Bell and Adriana Brioso
Cover image: © MarioGuti/iStock

A catalogue record for this book is available from the British Library.

A catalog record for this book is available from the Library of Congres

ISBN: HB: 978-1-4742-7283-4
PB: 978-1-4742-7282-7
ePDF: 978-1-4742-7285-8
eBook: 978-1-4742-7284-1

Typeset by Deanta Global Publishing Services, Chennai, India
Printed and bound in Great Britain

To find out more about our authors and books visit www.bloomsbury.com and
sign up for our newsletters.

CONTENTS

PREFACE

The following piece is intended primarily as a textbook for undergraduate and postgraduate modules on Islamism. It has grown out of my own third-year module taught to BA history students, and I hope it will be of considerable use to those who wish to approach Islamism as a historic phenomenon in an era where much of our analysis of this subject has a contemporary slant and is dominated by scholars working in fields such as political science, theology and area studies. While this text is primarily intended to make the subject history student-friendly, I also intend it to speak to the concerns of specialists in these other fields. The text is to some extent a survey of the historic development of Islamist ideology, but also seeks to foreground important academic debates about the provenance of various aspects in this ideology. I therefore hope that it will serve as a useful summary of a range of current scholarly positions on Islamism for those working at postgraduate level and beyond.

Each chapter concludes with a number of suggested primary source readings as well as secondary source readings, in addition to proposals for seminar debates and questions for students to consider when engaging in these debates. I have not provided any primary source excerpts here, and my intention would be for this textbook to be used in addition to a sourcebook such as *Princeton Readings in Islamist Thought* by Roxanne Euben and Qasim Zaman (Princeton: Princeton University Press, 2009) or John Calvert's *Islamism: A Documentary and Reference Guide* (Westport: Greenwood Press, 2008). In a number of cases I have suggested primary sources which are not accessible via either of these texts, but are either accessible online or could be scanned by a university library.

ACKNOWLEDGEMENTS

I would not have been able to produce this text without the support of a number of parties. First of all, Emma Goode and the production team at Bloomsbury have worked tirelessly at making the process of getting the book into print as smooth as possible. The anonymous reviewers of both my initial proposal and the final draft made many helpful suggestions that have added considerably to the quality of the final product. My colleague Dr Paul Jackson at the University of Northampton offered me many helpful clarifications on communism and fascism that helped me to explore the contentious relationship between Islamism and these two ideologies. The support I received from my line managers at the University of Northampton and Newcastle University – Cathy Smith and Sam Turner – assisted me greatly in completing this project. Finally, I must thank my father, Geoffrey Berridge, once again for his constant willingness to read and comment on my drafts.

GLOSSARY OF KEY ARABIC, FARSI AND URDU WORDS

Ansar	originally refers to the supporters of the Prophet in Medina; in a Sudanese context refers to the partisans of the Sudanese Mahdi and his descendants
asabiyya	tribal solidarity
ayatollah	a senior Shia scholar
ba'ya	oath of fealty
bazaari	a merchant in Iran
dar al-Islam	land of Islam
da'wa	calling to Islam
dawla	state
dhimmi	refers to religious minorities (usually Jews and Christians) who have 'protected' status within the Islamic community
effendis	originally an Ottoman Turkish term, denoting an upwardly mobile class which benefited from modern education. Collective plural – *effendiyya*
fard al-ayn	lit. individual duty; refers in Islamic jurisprudence to situations in which jihad is incumbent upon every able-bodied male within the Islamic community
fatwa	a jurisprudential ruling in Islam
fiqh	religious jurisprudence
fitna	a state of discord within the Islamic community
hadd	a fixed penalty applied to punish certain sins, including theft, drinking, adultery, fornication. pl. *hudud*
hadith	reports of the sayings of the Prophet Muhammad
hakimiyya	'divine sovereignty' in Islamist parlance
haram	forbidden
hijra	flight – originally refers to the flight of the Prophet Muhammad from Mecca to Medina

hizb	a political party – also connotes factionalism in early Islam. pl *ahzab*
hujjatalislam	a Shia scholar below the rank of ayatollah
ijma	consensus; refers to the practice of basing jurisprudence on the agreement of a number of scholars
intizar	awaiting the return of the twelfth Imam in Twelver Shi'ism
ijtihad	effort exerted by an Islamic scholar/jurisprudent to provide another interpretation of the classical religious sources
isti'ana bi'l-kuffar	seeking the assistance of non-believers
al-jahiliyya	the age of ignorance before the dawn of Islam in the seventh century; used by Islamists to describe the moral state of contemporary Muslim society
jihad	religious struggle
khilafa	man's vice-regency on earth
khudi	the mastery of one's self
kufr	unbelief
maslaha	public interest
marja'iyya	the Shia scholarly establishment in Iran and Iraq
mostafezin/ mustafzin	lit. 'the oppressed'
mujaddid	renewer
mujahidin	those who perform jihad
mujtahid	a religious scholar who performs *ijtihad*
pir	a sufi leader in South Asia
qawmiyya	nationalism
salafi	one who follows the *salaf*, or pious ancestors. In different contexts this has been used to refer to a theological school dating back to the ninth century, late-nineteenth-century/early-twentieth-century reform movement, or late-twentieth-century moral 'purists' influenced by Wahhabism/Islamism
shaikh	term of veneration for an elderly Muslim, including both religious scholars and notables
shari'a	literally the 'path' that Muslims must follow, also refers to Islamic law
shirk	attributing divine features to human beings; polytheism, associationism
shura	the practice of consultation in early Islam
sufi	a follower of Sufism, a form of Islamic mysticism
sunna	the practice of the Prophet; used as a source of Islamic jurisprudence

tafsir	Quranic exegesis
tajdid	renewal
takfir	denunciation of other Muslims as unbelievers
taqlid	lit. tradition; the practice of Islamic scholars relying on the judgements of previous scholars
taqiyya	dissimulation to hide one's true religious beliefs
tariqa	a sufi order. pl *turuq*
tathir	purging, cleansing
tawali	an innovation by al-Turabi; connotes 'mutual allegiance' in political life
tawhid	divine unity
velayet-i-faqih	'rule of the jurist'
al-wala wa-l-bara	loyalty to the Muslim community before all else
ubudiyya	obedience
ulama	religious scholars (sing. alim)
umma	the Islamic community
usul	fundamentals
uzla	separation

1

Introduction: Debates and terminology

It is often commented, with a fair degree of accuracy, that Islamist ideology presents an ahistoric view of society, offering those who adhere to it the choice between living in a pristine utopia modelled on seventh-century Mecca and Medina or miring themselves in the godless present, and ignoring everything in between. Yet, its Western critics are often equally ahistoric in their analysis of it, seeing Islamism as the timeless 'other' of a world divided between secularism and religion, authoritarianism and democracy, liberalism and totalitarianism – between the West and Islam. Nevertheless, since the founding of the Muslim Brotherhood by Hasan al-Banna in 1928, Islamism has had its own history. Why should we study this history? It is because we need to understand the social and political contexts in which Islamist ideology has evolved and the forces that have shaped it. We need to learn how to read the most prominent Islamist texts – such as Sayyid Qutb's *Milestones*, a key reading for contemporary militants – as we read other historical sources, as products of the sociopolitical environment in which they were written. We need to learn that Islamist ideology is not an undifferentiated whole. The methods and rhetoric of Islamic State in Iraq and Syria (ISIS) in Iraq and Syria in the 2010s are very different from those of the Muslim Brotherhood in Egypt in the 1930s or the Jama'at-i-Islami in Pakistan in the 1950s.

In emphasizing the historicity of Islamism, I am not seeking to impose (or indeed to reject) the argument that each movement has been defined more by the particular historic and geographical context that it emerged in than by a set of 'common denominators' that constitute the essence of Islamist ideology as a whole. From one viewpoint, Islamist ideology, while capable of adapting to a degree in each new era, is nevertheless underpinned by a set of core traits that include a monolithic and exclusivist view of society, as well as the desire for world domination.[1] Other accounts propose that such traits have never been core elements of Islamist ideology but are specific to historical eras in which totalitarian worldviews flourished and Islamism was radicalized by colonial and postcolonial authoritarianism. This brings us right to the core of contemporary debates about whether there can be a 'moderate' Islamism. As this volume is intended primarily as an introduction to the subject for students at the undergraduate and master's level, I have striven as far as possible to avoid didacticism – that is, I am not using this textbook to convey a particular intellectual perspective or advance a particular thesis. Rather, my aim here is to survey the many competing positions regarding the history of this controversial subject matter and thus to empower students to advance their own perspectives.

Terminological chaos

In recent times, scholars have been particularly inclined to write on Islamism as pundits and their language has become rather loose. Terms such as 'Islamic Revivalism', 'Islamic Fundamentalism', 'Salafism', 'Political Islam' and 'Islamism' are often used interchangeably. Here, expanding on an earlier effort by Guilian Denouex to 'navigat[e] the forgotten swamp',[2] I shall argue the case for preferring certain descriptors over others, attempt to define some of these terms, and indicate the context in which they will be used in this text.

'Islamic Fundamentalism'

Youssef Choueiri entitled his own survey text *Islamic Fundamentalism* 'for want of a better word', acknowledging that the second component of the term had its origins in the Protestant Reformation and, in consequence, made its use in an Islamic context problematic.[3] Islamists themselves tend to avoid the term, while many of Islamism's critics avoid it on the grounds that it takes Islamism's pretence of religious orthodoxy at face value.[4] The term 'Islamic fundamentalism' is most unsatisfactory when used to describe extremist groups such as al-Qa'eda and ISIS because the majority of religious Muslims think their disregard for human life violates the 'fundamentals' of their faith. It even fails to distinguish adequately between 'moderate' Islamists and those Muslims who remain attached to the 'fundamentals' of their faith and yet do not identify with an Islamist political programme.[5] Indeed referring to Islamists as 'fundamentalists' amounts to an implicit acceptance of the conceit of many such individuals that one cannot be a Muslim without being an Islamist.

On account of the difficulties identified above, especially those associated with the assumption that Islamism represents the one 'real' or 'fundamental' Islam, this text will avoid usage of the term 'Islamic fundamentalist'. In doing so, it does not seek to be so didactic as to impose the view that Islamism has no real basis in Islam at all. It will leave that question to the reader's judgement. However, one term that will appear later on in the text is 'neo-fundamentalism'. This is the expression coined by Olivier Roy for an ideology that evolved out of Islamism in the 1980s and 1990s and criticized the earlier Islamist movements for focusing too much on political at the expense of religious and moral transformation.[6] Although use of this term might lead us into a number of the same analytical pitfalls as have been identified above, it at least helps to mark out the separate ideological schools within the broader 'Islamist' trend.

'Political Islam'

A number of texts on Islamism employ the phrase 'Political Islam', both as part of their title and as their principal analytical category.[7] My own preference is to use this term only sparingly. It is not problematic in the same sense as 'Islamic fundamentalism', in that it can be accused of mispresenting the phenomenon that it is describes. So long as 'Islam' is understood as a wider cultural and civilizational phenomenon and not a monolithic religious phenomenon in this context we do not risk implicitly endorsing the ideological narrative of movements such as the Muslim Brotherhood or ISIS by using this term. Its principal analytical weakness comes from its lack of specificity. It is not necessary to accept the claim that 'Political Islam' is a pleonasm (i.e. that the adjective is redundant because Islam is inherently political) to maintain that there were many different political manifestations of Islam before the rise of Islamist movements such as the Muslim Brotherhood in the twentieth century – the Almoravid movement in medieval Morocco and the Wahhabiyya in eighteenth-century Arabia, to name just two. Yet, a number of the texts on 'Political Islam' dwell on the mass ideological movements of the twentieth century and, as a result, tend to overlook the characteristics that distinguish Islamism from movements like the Almoravids or the Wahhabis; for example, the exploitation of modern forms of propaganda and mobilization in modern, secular educational institutions.

'Islamism'

This term is now usually employed to refer to individuals, and movements seek to 'ideologize' Islam in a manner that transforms it into a tool of mass politics.[8] It is this specific theme of *ideologization* that distinguishes 'Islamism' from 'Political Islam' in the broader sense. Most commentators limit their use of the expression to the period following the founding of the Muslim Brotherhood – the first 'Islamist' movement – by Hasan al-Banna in 1928. This textbook will itself rely heavily on this term, as the majority of the movements on which it focuses emerged after 1928. However, a word of warning: the addition of the 'ism' potentially implies an assumption about the character of the movements under discussion – just as 'Islamic fundamentalism' risks accepting the claims of Islamists at face value, perhaps 'Islamism' concedes too much ground to those who maintain that Islamism is an ideology defined by the twentieth-century conditions that gave rise to it and has little organic connection to the Islamic past. Here is one definition of Islamism that offers such a perspective, from Guilian Denouex:

> Islamists usually aspire to reshape people's daily lives according to a more or less clearly defined political and cultural vision that harks back to a mostly mythical, invented Islamic past. While that vision draws on Islamic terms, symbols and events, it infuses them with new meanings that are typically alien to the actual historical and current experiences of Muslims. Islamists are engaged in a process of intellectual, political and social engineering which, through the familiar language of Islam, aims to legitimize a thorough restructuring of society and polity along lines that have no precedent in history.[9]

As will be seen below, there is a debate between those who maintain that Islamism represents a resurgence of the values and institutions of the precolonial Islamist past, and those who follow a line of analysis similar to Denouex or go even further and argue that it represents a mere rehashing of Western ideologies such as Marxism–Leninism and fascism. As mentioned above, I seek strenuously to avoid didacticism in this text, yet the barest definition of 'Islamism' need only imply (in Ruthven's words) 'the relationship between the pre-existing reality (in this case, a religion) and its translation into a political ideology'.[10] It is also a term (rendered in Arabic as *Islamiyyun*) that is accepted by a great number of Islamists themselves. A cautious working definition of Islamism might therefore understand it as 'an ideology that fuses political ideals from both Islamic history and the twentieth-century world in order to establish a revolutionary order'. As we will see throughout this text, debates as to the respective significance of the twentieth century and historic Islamic ideals are very much ongoing.

Islamic Revivalism

'Islamic Revivalism', like 'Political Islam', has been used to categorize a broad range of religio-political movements, from the medieval period till the present day, seeking to 'revive' Islam. For the purposes of this text I draw chiefly on the relatively narrow definition of 'Islamic Revivalism' offered by Youssef Choueiri: a cluster of eighteenth and nineteenth-century movements that sought to return to the original Islamic sources – the Quran, the Sunna and the Hadith – and which used them to challenge the existing religious and political establishment. For Choueiri, this was a movement of internal rejuvenation that made little reference to Western concepts.[11]

Confusingly, some scholars refer to twentieth-century movements that Choueiri would categorize as 'radical' as 'revivalist' – for instance, Nasr in his text *Mawdudi and the Making of Islamic Revivalism*. To ensure clarity, this text will avoid such use of the term. Eighteenth and nineteenth-century Revivalist movements, which include, for instance, the Wahhabiyya in Arabia and the Mahdiyya in Sudan, will be the principal subjects of Chapter 3, although the extent to which the 'Revivalist' phenomenon fed into twentieth-century Islamism will be the subject of much debate throughout the text.

Islamic Reformism/Islamic modernism

Choueiri defines 'Islamic Reformism' as principally a nineteenth and early-twentieth-century movement that sought to adapt Islam to the conditions imposed by Western colonialism. Thinkers such as Muhammad Abduh and Sayyid Ahmad Khan, who attempted to reconcile Islam with modern Western ideas such as nationalism and democracy, are identified as prominent reformists by Choueiri.[12] Other writers have termed these thinkers 'Islamic modernists' for the same reasons, seeing figures like Abduh as the intellectual forefathers of later 'modernists' such as Shaltut whom they differentiate from 'Islamists' and 'fundamentalists'.[13] In other regards, the 'reformists' might be regarded as the forerunners of the more 'moderate' Islamists in that they have a tendency to blend modern political ideals such as nationalism and democracy with seventh-century terminology. I shall mostly follow Choueiri's definition, although some of the problems associated with this term, such as challenges involved in differentiating it from 'Revivalism', will be discussed in Chapter 4.

Islamic Radicalism, Radical Islamism, Radical Islam

Each of these terms has been used to signify a more uncompromising form of Islamist ideology: one that has emerged in the latter half of the twentieth century that is more revolutionary, more totalitarian – and therefore less restrained in its advocacy of political violence. 'Radical Islam' is probably more prevalent than the first of these terms in the media and especially in political debate, where there is sometimes less concern about distinguishing between faith and ideology. For Choueiri, 'Islamic Radicalism' marks a qualitative break from 'Islamic Reformism', rejecting any potential for synthesis between Western and Islamic values and championing a pristine, undiluted form of Islam as the only saviour from secularism and imperialism.[14] Denouex proposes 'radical' Islamism as the possible 'other' of 'moderate' Islamism, suggesting that 'moderates' may be more willing to embrace democracy and compromise on the principle of 'divine sovereignty', while acknowledging that the distinction is a blurry and often unsatisfactory one and that there are both 'radicals' and 'moderates' within particular movements.[15] The controversies over the delineation of 'radical' and 'moderate' will be discussed throughout this text – for instance, arguments concerning the extent to which the ideology of the earlier, 'mainstream' Muslim Brotherhood can be differentiated from that of its later and more 'radical' offshoots will be a principal theme in Chapter 6.

Militant Islamism, Islamic Militancy, Militant Islam

As with 'radical Islam' and for similar reasons, the third of these terms is more prevalent in media and political circles. Collectively, they are in many regards interchangeable with 'Radical Islamism', although in themselves they convey the decision of a number of radical Islamist movements to take up arms against established Muslim regimes such as Egypt, Algeria and Syria in the last decades of the twentieth century. Militant Islamism converged to some extent with Jihadist Salafism (see below) at the turn of the century, when it became far more willing to consider attacks against Western governments – the 'Far Enemy'.[16] Militant Islamism and its Jihadist-Salafi variant will be the focus of Chapters 12 and 13.

Salafism

This is potentially the most misleading term in the whole academic literature on Islamism and pre-Islamist movements. Different scholars have applied it to different movements with quite divergent and indeed contradictory intellectual and political aims. At its core, 'Salafism' appears to signify a doctrine premised upon a revival of the values and practices of the 'pious forefathers' (al-salaf al-salih), the first three generations of Muslims. It advocates returning to these practices and values, rescuing them from centuries of subsequent distortion. Yet different thinkers have understood this principle in radically different ways. For instance, while many contemporary analysts understand 'Salafism' as a particularly puritanical, militant and conservative form of Islam, generations of historians of the later-nineteenth and early-twentieth-century Middle East have used 'Salafi' to label a number of the individuals described above as 'Islamic reformers' or 'Islamic modernists', notably the Egyptian scholar Muhammad Abduh. These individuals were 'Salafi' because they maintained that the pious ancestors possessed what post-Enlightenment scholars described as 'modern' values, yet these had been lost to the Muslim world because of the many years over which Muslim scholars had abandoned such values and retreated into traditionalism. Thus the Muslim world could 'modernize' by returning to the values of the salaf.[17] For the purposes of this definition, the category of the 'pious ancestors' was often broadened to include many of the philosophers of the first 300 years of Islamic history.[18] The conflation of 'modernism' and 'Salafism' has recently been challenged by Lauzière, who maintains that generations of scholars and political activists who adopted the term had been following the French Orientalist Massignon's mistaken reading of Abduh and the other reformers' doctrine and that they themselves would not have understood their ideology as 'Salafi'.[19] Although there have been efforts to rescue the concept of 'modernist Salafism' from Lauzière's critique,[20] for the purpose of this textbook I shall be avoiding this contentious use of the term and employing the less controversial language of 'Islamic Reformism'.

Part of the reason that analysts of the late-twentieth and twenty-first-century Middle East eschew the language of 'modernist Salafism' is the proliferation in this era of a far more intellectually and religiously conservative 'purist Salafism' that cannot easily be compared with the ideology of the Islamic reformists.[21] The emergence of this form of 'Salafism' is often attributed to the increasing global prominence of Saudi Arabia's Wahhabi religious movement, which has used its control over the holy places of Mecca and Medina as well as its vast oil wealth to diffuse its ideology all over the world. Scholars have often traced this form of 'Salafism' not just to the founder of the Wahhabi movement, Muhammad Ibn Abd al-Wahhab, but also to the medieval scholar Ibn Taymiyya, thus identifying it as a movement of some considerable historic pedigree.[22] However, for Lauzière, Salafism – as often understood today as an ideological movement that demands a total reform of Muslim religious, social, legal and even political life so as to enable it to more faithfully reproduce the practice of the *salaf* – can only trace its origins to the second half of the twentieth century and bears similarities with the 'total' ideologies that emerged in this era.[23] A more narrowly defined 'Salafi' theological school, to which individuals such as Ibn Taymiyya and Ibn Abd al-Wahhab would have adhered, and which was concerned with cleansing Islam of creedal innovations, probably existed since the Abbasid period, but would not have been as wide ranging and ambitious as the contemporary Salafi movement.[24]

Salafism is often distinguished from Islamism on the grounds that it is more genuinely 'fundamentalist', 'more interested in theology than politics' and less likely to advocate revolution against the established political order.[25] However, these distinctions are relative. As we shall see, many Islamists have sought to cultivate Salafi support and advocated – albeit perhaps less dogmatically – a revival of seventh-century mores in a manner similar to contemporary Salafis. A number of Islamist or proto-Islamist thinkers, such as Rida and the Qutb brothers, influenced Saudi Salafis of the late-twentieth-century era.[26] Meanwhile, the 'neo-fundamentalist' trend identified by Roy may be suggestive of the cross-fertilization of Islamist and Salafi thought.

In recent years, a clearer conceptual distinction has emerged between the various different strands of 'purist' Salafism – quietist, political and jihadi.[27] Quietist Salafis are the most critical of the Islamists' emphasis on revolution in its most narrow, political sense, and emphasize education as the most effective means of bringing the Muslim community back to the values of the *salaf*. Political Salafis, like 'moderate' Islamists, seek to participate in mainstream political life, including elections – a notable example being the al-Nur party in post-Arab Spring Egypt. Meanwhile, Jihadist Salafis or 'Salafi–jihadists' advocate jihad in its most narrow physical and military sense as the only means to force both Muslims and non-Muslims to adhere to their own interpretation of the pious forefathers' doctrine. They are thus more willing to advocate violence than quietist and political Salafis, yet at the same time they pay more attention to theology than militant Islamists. Unlike conventional militant Islamists, many Jihadist Salafis view their struggle as a holistic battle against both non-Muslims and deviant Muslims that transcends the confines of the nation state.[28] The concept of 'Salafi–jihadism', however, has come under attack on the grounds that it overprioritizes the doctrinal element in the agenda of the militants it describes, as the exact relationship between Salafism and the revolutionary violence they enact remains unclear. Hegghammer laments that 'Jihadi-Salafi' is used too frequently where terms that highlight their political rationale and methods would be more appropriate – 'nation orientated' militants, 'socio-revolutionary' militants and so forth.[29]

Islamism's origins: The debate

The question of Islamism's historic origins is one of the most contentious problems not just for academic specialists but also for journalists, policy makers and politicians all over the globe. I shall attempt to provide here a summary of six positions on the issue, albeit that each is broadly defined and in some cases they are overlapping.

1   Islamism represents a rejection of modernity

   This claim is prevalent in the media and public debate but is now somewhat less popular among scholars. It was more mainstream academically in the 1960s, when 'Modernization Theory' was a dominant intellectual trend. This theory held that Westernization was the only viable route to modernization for non-Western countries, and that anti-Westernism was thus anti-modernism by default. One text particularly associated with this thinking is Richard Mitchell's *The Society of Muslim Brothers*.

2   Islamism represents a rejection only of the Western, secular form of modernity, and offers 'Islamized' modernity in its place

   The rise of postcolonial theory and culture studies challenged a number of the key tenets of 'Modernization Theory'. It is now commonly accepted within culture studies and the various branches of area studies (notably Middle Eastern Studies) that the belief

that Westernization offers the only valid route to modernization
represents a hangover of colonial hubris. Ayubi suggests that while
Islamic reformists, living as they did in an era of colonial hegemony,
were seeking to 'modernize Islam', the Islamists of the twentieth
century sought to 'Islamize modernity'.[30] Hartung maintains that
Mawdudi's ideology constituted an effort to reshape Islam by
looking at it through what Brown called the 'prism of modernity'.[31]
At the same time, we should be wary of proposing that Islamism
represents the only culturally valid route to a non-Western form
of modernity. Movements as diverse as the Arab nationalists, the
Republican Brothers of Sudan and the followers of Turkey's Fetullah
Gulen have all sought to establish non-Islamist alternatives to
Westernization. Meanwhile, many of Islamism's critics maintain
that their ideology is in practice shaped just as much by Western
ideologies as that of the secular elites they decry.[32]

3 Islamism is a 'totalitarian' ideology that has more in common with
the other totalitarian ideologies of the twentieth-century Western
world than it does with historic Islamic values

This is an argument that grew in popularity in the decade after 9/11,
when neo-liberal writers identified militant Islamism as the one
remaining threat to the post-Cold War liberal capitalist world order.
A good example is to be found in Daniel Berman's *Terrorism and
Liberalism*, where he writes that

> the Baathists and the Islamists were two branches of a single
> impulse which was Muslim totalitarianism – the Muslim variation
> on the European idea. Their dreams bore the mark of the Muslim
> world, but their dreams were not exotic. The whole phenomenon
> of people wearing monochrome shirts and organizing phalanges
> and calling for the resurrection of ancient empires was definitely a
> trend of the moment.[33]

Mehdi Mozaffari argued in a provocative essay in 2007 that
Islamism, communism and fascism all shared common origins: they
were a response to the sense of civilizational crisis brought about by
the decline of the world empires following the First World War. He
maintains that, although each ideology has its own distinct features,
'nevertheless, their common denominators are at least as substantial
as their differences with regard to their origins, in a sense of
historical crisis, their utopian aspirations, their forms of leadership,
and their cult of violent action'.[34]

Other writers have compromised with position (5) below,
contending that the various ideologies of the twentieth century
merely gave shape to existing currents within Islam. For example,

Bernard Lewis – often identified as a key supporter of the Bush administration's invasion of Iraq – maintained in 'The Roots of Muslim Rage' that German philosophers of the Nazi era, in addition to Soviet ideologues, contributed a great deal to the Islamist (and Arab nationalist) *Weltanschaung*, but that 'though they helped to provide intellectual expression for anti-Westernism and anti-Americanism, they did not cause it'.[35] Others have attempted to compromise with point (6). Mirsepassi, for instance, maintains that Iranian Islamism was deeply immersed in the counter-Enlightenment philosophy of Martin Heidegger, whose ideas bore considerable totalitarian potential and helped to shape the ideology of the Nazi regime in Germany. At the same time, he acknowledges that were it not for the misguided policies of the Shah of Iran, who discredited Western post-Enlightenment modernity by combining a policy of aggressive Westernization with political and cultural subservience to America, this form of anti-Western ideology would never have become so influential.[36]

4   Islamism represents an effort to rediscover Islamic values that are just as advanced and progressive as Western post-Enlightenment values, or even superior to them

This is a position frequently taken by Islamists themselves. It was first fleshed out by the Islamic reformists Jamal al-Din al-Afghani and Muhammad Abduh, who argued that the classical Islamic concepts of *shura* and *ijtihad* had preceded the post-Enlightenment notions of democracy and free thinking respectively.[37] While individuals like Muhammad Abduh made such arguments in the context of expressing great admiration for Western civilization, later Islamists such as Mawdudi and al-Turabi used such claims to assert the distinctive character of the Islamic experience so as to assert a radical break with Western models. With the global rise of socialist ideology in the twentieth century, the Islamists made a number of comparable claims in order to challenge the political left, maintaining that the origins of social equality could be traced back to the original Islamic community of seventh-century Mecca and Medina, and that it had been lost as a result of subsequent Islamic rulers being seduced by the hierarchical and exploitative values of pre-Islamic society. As we shall see, these Islamists have often made little effort to substantiate such claims empirically.

5   Islamism represents a continuity with the precolonial Islamic past

The argument that Islamism represents a resurgence of 'historic' Islam is at its most controversial when made with reference to 'extremist' movements such as al-Qa'eda and ISIS. Ever since the organization known as ISIS or 'Daesh' proclaimed itself as the one true Caliphate, mainstream Muslims denounced its claims to represent 'true' Islam, and the BBC began to term the organization 'so-called' Islamic State. Yet, in a controversial article published by the *Atlantic* in 2015, Graeme Wood attempted to counter claims that the religious ideology of ISIS should not be taken at face value, maintaining that 'the reality is that the Islamic State is Islamic. *Very* Islamic. ... The religion preached by its most ardent followers derives from coherent and even learned interpretations of Islam.'[38] There were numerous critical responses to Wood's article, one author observing that while the ideologues of ISIS may frequently cite classical Islamic sources to justify their brutal actions, they often falls back on 'cherry-picking' unreliable *hadith* (records of sayings attributed to the Prophet) and do not apply the rigorous methods employed by more established Islamic scholars.[39]

Another relatively less contentious and more common claim is that mainstream Islamism represents a resurgence of the values of the Islamic past that were only briefly submerged during the period of colonial and postcolonial secularism. Beverley Milton-Edwards, for instance, argues that Islamist violence represents an inevitable response to the secularists' efforts to disrupt the ties between faith and politics that have always existed in the region and was successful because 'faith had been deeply embedded in the established institutions of Middle Eastern empires and states as well as social structures', and thus 'proved less easy to eject ... under the modernization process'.[40] This perspective can be challenged on a number of grounds – if Islamism represents a straightforward revival of precolonial Islam, why is it that so many Islamists express a desire to rediscover the seventh-century exemplar, and maintain that the first crisis experienced by the Islamic community was not the onset of Western colonialism but the end of the period of the Rightly Guided Caliphs in 661? Why is it that Islamists have apparently borrowed so assiduously from the rhetoric and practices of the various twentieth-century ideologies, such as nationalism and Marxism–Leninism?

6 Islamism is an ideology that has been directly shaped by historic Western colonialism and contemporary 'neocolonialism'

It is worth noting that few of the major figures in postcolonial theory – the majority of whom can be considered broadly left-wing and secular[41] – have expressed much sympathy with Islamism. Frantz Fanon, the Martinican psychiatrist and supporter of the Algerian liberation struggle against the French, wrote to the Iranian Islamist Ali Shariati explaining that he feared that his attempts to mobilize Islam for revolutionary ends would inevitably lead to regression.[42] Likewise, Edward Said rejected claims that the critique of Western colonial scholarship contained in his *Orientalism* was tantamount to a defence of 'Islamic fundamentalism'. Said observed that 'fundamentalism's epistemological mistake is to think that "fundamentals" are ahistorical categories, not subject to and therefore outside the critical scrutiny of true believers, who are supposed to accept them on faith'.[43]

While it would be contentious to maintain that Islamism *is* a postcolonial ideology, it certainly can be analysed from a postcolonial perspective. Fanon himself, while wary of the retrogressive potential of the evocation of imagined pasts, argued that such political behaviour was nevertheless a predictable psychological consequence of the erasure of the history of the colonized by the colonizers.[44] Islamists often claimed to be making a total break with the colonial and neocolonial world order, although such claims were often deceptive. This author's own research on Hasan al-Turabi, for instance, has shown that this Islamist's worldview was as much a product of his colonial education as it was of his efforts to combat colonialism.[45] The trend of postcolonial theory initiated by Homi Bhabha, which argues that colonial and postcolonial intellectuals inhabited a cultural 'third space', has considerable explanatory value.[46] At the same time, Mozaffari rejects outright the claim that colonialism was responsible for the rise of Islamism, maintaining instead that it was the cultural malaise of the Islamic world that led to colonialism's onset.[47]

2

Sufis, scholars and rebels:

Classical precedents for contemporary Islamism

Any effort to trace the origins of twentieth and twenty-first-century Islamism to the classical period of Islam is fraught with danger. Such endeavours are open to the challenge that they posit an 'essential' character to Islam and to Islamic history that generates political radicalism, and that they overlook more obvious contemporary factors such as Western colonialism and neocolonialism as well as socio-economic unrest. However, it is undeniable that Islamist groups have cited as sources of inspiration a variety of historical Islamic political figures, societies and religious texts – notably, the Prophet Muhammad, the original Islamic community of seventh-century Mecca and Medina, and the Quran as Islam's holy book. Historians should, of course, beware of taking Islamist rhetoric at face value. Islamists have often tended to draw upon a diverse range of political and intellectual influences while claiming that the seventh century provides them with their guiding framework.[1] As we will see in future chapters, these influences include postcolonialism and mass democracy, as well as twentieth-century political ideologies such as Marxism–Leninism, nationalism and fascism. It is open to debate whether Islamists used these political ideas to better understand the seventh-century prototype, or to reinvent it altogether.

It is also important to acknowledge that Islamists draw on a variety of reference points not just from the seventh century but from the classical Islamic epoch that followed it. In the case of radical Islamists and Salafis, the use of such references comes close to being paradoxical, since these two groups have sought to invalidate forms of Islam that emerged after the earliest period. Nevertheless, we will discuss here a range of classical precedents from the period subsequent to the seventh century, including messianists, anti-crusaders, scholars, Sufis and Shi'is, that have influenced later Islamists. In many cases Islamists have also expressed opposition to a number of these same groups – as we shall see, the distinction between Shi'i and Sunni Islamists is an important one. Mozaffari claims that these historical precedents are evidence of 'the endogenous ideological origins of contemporary Islamism in Islamic History'.[2] However, we might also consider them as a historical resource upon which Islamists have drawn, rather than an inspiration per se. At the same time, we need to remember that none of the forms of political radicalism that existed in the classical era necessarily express some essential quality of Islam, for each was shaped by a variety of political, socio-economic and at times ethnic contexts.

The era of the Prophet and Rightly Guided Caliphs

Islamists have invariably sought to emulate the sociopolitical ideals of the Islamic community (umma) as it existed during the Prophethood of Muhammad (610–632 CE) and the period of rule by his first four 'Caliphs', or successors (632–661 CE). Of course, emulation and inspiration are not necessarily one and the same – as we have seen, it is a common argument that Islamists use rhetoric about the seventh-century Islamic community to cloak a variety of more modern political ideals. The principal challenge in gauging the Islamists' relationship with the seventh-century prototype is the unreliability of the historical sources available to reconstruct the lived experience of the umma in this era. The vast majority of historical narratives concerning the 610–661 period date from after 800, when the shift from papyrus to paper within the Islamic world led to the proliferation of written sources.[3] The credibility of these sources is undermined both by the time that has elapsed since 661 and their bias towards the political and sociolegal order established under the Abbasid Caliphate.[4]

According to the standard Muslim narrative, Muhammad's prophecy began in 610, when he began to receive through the Angel Gabriel the revelations that would form the basis of the Islamic faith.[5] Muhammad himself was a caravaner and member of the commercially powerful Banu Hashim clan of the Quraysh, one of Mecca's leading tribes. The message he received via the Angel Gabriel was a monotheistic one that placed considerable emphasis on the unity (tawhid) of God, and thus alienated the principally pagan society of Mecca that persecuted Muhammad and his initial band of followers. In 622, Muhammad undertook the hijra (flight) from Mecca to the nearby city of Medina, where he believed that the local Jewish population would be more receptive to his monotheistic message. By acting as an arbitrator, Muhammad was able to unite the various tribes of Medina into a single sociopolitical unit which became known as the umma, or Islamic community. After a series of battles against his former persecutors, Muhammad then reconquered Mecca in 630, casting down the various pagan idols worshipped there.

Following the death of the Prophet in 632, four 'Rightly Guided' Caliphs emerged as his successors: Abu Bakr (632–634), Umar (634–644), Uthman (644–656) and Ali (656–661). The period was one of considerable political turmoil – the succession to the caliphate was a highly contentious affair, particularly in the cases of Abu Bakr and Ali, and three of the four caliphs were murdered. The murder of Uthman led to a period of conflict between Ali and his followers, and Uthman's Umayyad relatives led by Mu'awiya, which was itself ended by Ali's own assassination by a member of the Khariji sect (see below) in 661. Yet, almost paradoxically, this period was one of considerable territorial and religious expansion of the Islamic community. By the time the era of the Rightly Guided Caliphs had come to an end, the Muslims had conquered a vast swathe of territories in North Africa, Persia and the Near East. They had destroyed the Sassanid Persian Empire after victory at the Battle of Qadisiyya in 637, and driven the Byzantines back into Asia Minor and Europe.

Twentieth-century Islamists have frequently attempted to map this narrative onto their own political agendas. Revolutionary Islamists have maintained that their battle against Western colonialism/neocolonialism and its local proxies is the equivalent to that waged by the early Islamic community against the Byzantine and Sassanid Empires.[6] Others have used the concept of the umma as a body that transcended Medinan tribalism to support a pan-Islamist approach that seeks either to dissolve the current national boundaries within the Muslim world, or at least incorporate the existing nations into the political framework of a broader Islamic community.[7] Meanwhile, the more liberal Islamists have cited Muhammad's willingness to integrate members of Jewish tribes into the umma via the Covenant of Medina in 622 as evidence that an Islamic state can be genuinely multicultural.[8] Islamists attribute particular importance to the year 661, maintaining that the death of the last of the 'Rightly Guided' Caliphs and his replacement by Mu'awiya led to the disappearance of genuine Islamic governance and its replacement by the 'monarchical' rule of the Umayyads.

By casting the end of the period of the Rightly Guided Caliphs as a radical break, Islamists are able to represent the era between 622 and 661 in utopian terms, and maintain that a harmonious fusion of religion and state existed at this time. The problem – or perhaps the opportunity – for Islamists stems from the fact that we know so little about how Muslim society was governed in this era. While the available evidence suggests that there was most likely some form of state, its actual characteristics are very hard to delineate.[9] As a result, Islamists are forced to choose between either conceiving the Islamic state in highly idealistic terms or falling back on the adoption of models from the same states of the post-661 era that they condemn for abandoning the 'original' Islam.[10]

Many twentieth-century Islamists maintained that Islam's holy book provided a perfect blueprint for Islamic statehood, even going so far as to maintain that the Quran could be considered a constitution in its own right. However, while Islamists do often cite Quranic passages declaring that one must 'judge' (*hakama*, sometimes translated as 'rule') in accordance with 'what God has set down', Islam's central text contains little guidance on how exactly an Islamic state should manifest itself. Indeed, the Quran itself is written in a largely poetic style and contains little of the kind of empirical historical information from which the characteristics of an Islamic state might be discerned.[11] What can be said is that it contains several passages enjoining the believers to live in accordance with certain laws, even if it does not indicate what manner of state should enforce them. These injunctions cover matters as diverse as marriage, inheritance and criminal penalties – for instance, the *hudud* or amputation penalties and the stipulation that women may inherit one-third of a deceased relative's wealth can be traced back to the Quran. Whether these injunctions were directed only towards the society of the seventh century or should be considered as eternally binding is a matter of intense debate between Islamists and secularists.

Kharijis and Kharijism

The Kharijis (sometimes rendered as the Kharijites or Khawarij) formed a historic politico-religious movement often identified as a precursor to both the extremist and mainstream Islamists of the present day. Part of the reason that the comparison possesses such resonance is that the Kharijis dated right back to the period of the Rightly Guided Caliphs, thereby emerging even before the crystallization of conventional Sunnism and Shi'ism. However, in the case of the Kharijis, age and authenticity are not the same – the comparison between Islamism and Kharijism is usually a hostile one, made by critics of Islamism for propaganda purposes. Various Islamist tendencies (both alleged and real) held to date back to the period of the Kharijis include the belief that divine sovereignty (*hakimiyya*) must prevail at all times, the practice of denouncing other Muslims as non-believers (*takfir*), the legitimacy of fleeing (*hijra*) the corrupt society that has been accused of unbelief and the permissibility of fighting such unbelievers. Of course, the difficulty with validating the claim that the Kharijis acted as 'extremist' prototypes is that, as we have seen, first-hand sources for seventh-century history are extremely rare and we are often reliant on Abbasid-era historical and jurisprudential accounts that have a vested legal and political interest in representing the past in a certain way. The fact that the Kharijis were throughout this period rebels on the margins of the Umayyad and Abbasid Caliphates, never in power, means that – with old adages about winners and history books in mind – we must be particularly cautious. As Kenney has observed, medieval Sunni scholars caricatured the Kharijis as the classic 'other' of the Abbasid political order so as to highlight the fanaticism and destructiveness of those who sought to challenge the existing system.[12]

What do we know about the Kharijis? When did they first emerge? The narrative that emerges out of the mainstream Islamic tradition remembers them principally as the assassins of the last Rightly Guided Caliph, Ali Ibn Abi Talib. Their conflict with Ali stemmed from his decision to sign a truce with Mu'awiya at Siffin in 657, which the Kharijis (then known as 'Quran readers') maintained was an agreement reached between men who did not follow the judgement (*hukma*) of God and the Quran.[13] The Kharijis refused the truce, and subsequently suffered numerous casualties when Ali attacked their base at Nahrawan. Ali was then killed in retaliation by the Khariji Ibn Muljam outside the mosque of Kufa in 661.[14] Recent historical research suggests that the Kharijis may in fact have emerged during the reign of the third caliph, Uthman Ibn Affan, whose corrupt redistribution of the wealth of the umma to his close associates is believed to have provoked rebellion against his rule.[15] It is for reasons such as this that a number of leftist historians have sought to reinvent the Kharijis as social justice warriors.[16]

After Ibn Muljam brought an end to the period of the Rightly Guided Caliphs with his assassination of Ali, Khariji rebellions continued through the seventh and eighth Islamic centuries. We know more about these events as the later rebellions commenced in the era in which first-hand – albeit biased – accounts became available. One problem is discerning whether Kharijism represented a coherent movement or whether the label 'Khariji' was applied to a diverse range of rebellious groups with relatively few overlapping beliefs – the word Khariji itself can simply be translated as 'rebel'.[17] Khariji rebellions against the Umayyad Caliphate were often inspired by resentment of the rulers' misuse of wealth belonging to the Muslim community, as in the time of Uthman.[18] In the manner of later Islamist discourse, they also condemned the Umayyads for following Byzantine practices.[19] After the Umayyads defeated these rebellions, the Kharijis abandoned combat for preaching, and left the heartlands of the caliphate to settle in regions such as North Africa and Oman. The performance of *hijra* in this instance appears to have had tactical as much as religious motives.[20] One Khariji sect, the Ibadiyya, has survived in Oman to the present day, after making compromises with mainstream Sunnism.[21]

What do we know about Khariji doctrine? Given the nature of the sources available to us, it is easier to comment on the worldviews and agendas of particular Khariji groups in the eighth and ninth centuries than to trace a monolithic ideology back to the original Kharijis of the Rashidi age.[22] The most 'extreme' Khariji sect was the Azariqa, the members of which not only believed in denouncing the existing Muslim order as corrupt and fleeing from it but also maintained that all professed Muslims – including women and children – who did not join them were infidels and thus not entitled to live.[23] Anti-Khariji heresiographers often took the views of the Azariqa to be representative of Kharijism as a whole, following the familiar polemical technique of judging a movement by its most radical group.[24]

Khariji groups appear to have diverged from the Sunni orthodoxy of the time in a number of ways. One significant difference concerned the issue of the proper reaction to sin. Unlike mainstream Sunnis, many Kharijis did not actually distinguish between sin and unbelief; with the result that they would excommunicate Muslims who committed acts such as wine drinking and murder that were understood to be sins in Islam.[25] Another significant divergence was over the question of political disobedience. Thus, while the majority of orthodox Sunni scholars did not believe that rebellion against imperfect Muslim rulers could ever be sanctioned – unless they prevented the umma practising sharia – Kharijis maintained that it was justified by the Quranic verse which read 'whoso judges not according to what God has set down, they are unbelievers' (Q 5:48).[26] If the traditional narrative is even partly accurate, this doctrine of political disobedience was the position of the seventh-century Kharijis who rebelled against Ali: his agreement at Siffin, they believed, conferred the right to 'judge' on himself and Mu'awiya rather than on God.[27] This emphasis on divine *hukma* might even be regarded as the origin of the later Islamist doctrine of *hakimiyya*, which required Muslims to follow the principle of divine sovereignty in all political matters.[28]

While the *hakimiyya* principle would later encourage Islamists to disavow Western forms of electoral democracy on the grounds that they signified rule of man by man, the Kharijis themselves were more democratic and egalitarian in their outlook than the political system they railed against. Unlike the Sunni and the Shia, they believed that the caliph should be elected, and that candidature for this position should not be restricted on the basis of membership either of the Quraysh or the Prophet's family. They advocated that the status of the caliph was less important than the principle of rule by sharia,[29] a principle that most twentieth-century Islamists would later come to adopt. As we shall see, the Islamist Hasan al-Turabi would later make reference to the democratic credentials of the Kharijis, although the majority of the twentieth-century ideologues who sought to exploit their legacy have been secularists, including Arab nationalists and Marxists.[30] Most Islamists have sought to steer clear of this legacy. Given that their legitimacy is essentially religious, it is far too easy for their opponents to highlight the widely recognized divergences between Khariji beliefs and those of the conventional Sunni Muslims to whom Islamists appeal.[31] Whether or not the ideology of the latter-day Islamists has echoes of the Kharijis is a moot point, but it is a link their adversaries have been keener to trace than have the Islamists themselves.

The Abbasid and Umayyad periods

For Islamists, the ascent of the Umayyad Caliphate (661–750) marked the abandoning of Islamic political principles and a comprehensive surrender to the autocratic values of the Byzantine and Sassanid Empires, the territories of which had been incorporated during the first wave of Islamic conquests. In particular, Mu'awiya as the first Umayyad caliph is blamed for reintroducing the monarchical principle of hereditary succession by appointing his son Yazid as his successor. While the limited historical evidence makes it difficult to establish precisely how egalitarian the Islamic community was before 661, it is certainly true that the Umayyads and subsequently the Abbasids (750–1258) borrowed substantially from the hierarchical political systems of Ancient Persia and the Byzantine Empire. In Iran, the Abbasid state relied heavily on Persian administrators descended from the old Sassanid elites, and Ancient Persian 'advice for kings' literature was highly influential at the Abbasid Court in Baghdad, founded close to the old Sassanid capital of Ctesiphon.[32] Indo-Iranian patterns of social stratification helped to shape the post-Rashidi social order, marking a distinct break with the nomadic values of the early conquerors.[33] Meanwhile, the Umayyads and Abbasids also borrowed extensively from Byzantine legal and administrative systems.[34]

In general, the first few centuries of the post-Rashidi era marked a phase of considerable intellectual, cultural and scientific interaction between Islamic and non-Islamic civilizations, including the Greeks, Indians and Persians. In the early ninth century, the Abbasid Caliph Ma'mun established the House of Wisdom (*Bayt al-Hikma*) to translate the work of various Greek and Persian intellectuals.[35] The result was a flourishing of neo-Platonic philosophy and the rise of famous Muslim thinkers such as Ibn Sina, Ibn Rushd and al-Kindi. The neo-Platonic understanding of the ruler as a 'philosopher-king' overseeing a society divided between elites and masses combined with Indo-Iranian traditions of just leadership to produce the ideal of the caliph as an all-powerful ruler combining various religious, intellectual and political functions.[36] The fact that these understandings of the caliphate are a product of the ninth rather than the seventh century has not prevented them from influencing Islamist theorists of the state, notably Mawdudi and Khomeini (see Chapters 6 and 9).

It was during the Umayyad and particularly the Abbasid Caliphate that many of the institutions emerged that are central to Muslim life today. These include the esoteric Sufi orders (*tariqas*), the four schools of Islamic jurisprudence and the scholars (*ulama*) who act as the intellectual and religious custodians of sharia law. Islamist criticism of these institutions rests on the view that since they did not emerge in the period of the Prophet and four Rightly Guided Caliphs, they do not express the harmonious synthesis of religion and state that supposedly obtained at that time. Nevertheless, as we shall see, many Islamists have compromised with each of these institutions in order to further their influence.

The *ulama*, or religious scholars tasked with understanding the principal sources of the Islamic faith, first emerged in the Umayyad period but served a merely consultative function.[37] Until the early ninth century the foremost guardian of Islamic law was the caliph himself. At this point a power struggle broke out between the caliphate and the *ulama*. The Abbasid

Caliphs used one particular theological school, Mu'tazilism, to bolster their status. This decreed that the Quran was created and could thus be rationally interpreted by any prominent Muslim – a position that gave the caliph himself considerable latitude to determine what true Islam constituted.[38] Many *ulama*, meanwhile, maintained that as the Quran was eternal and uncreated it could not be subject to rational interpretation by human beings. As a result, they insisted that the various sources – including the *hadith* or sayings of the Prophet – that detailed the practice (*Sunna*) of Muhammad should be employed to determine Islamic law where the Quran was unclear.[39] The scholars were the intellectual guardians of these sources, and it was out of this principle that 'Sunni' Islam was born. The caliphs imprisoned those scholars who did not adhere to Mu'tazilite doctrine, among them the founder of the Hanbali law school, Ahmad Ibn Hanbal. It is for this reason that the most prominent Hanbalis of the contemporary Islamic world, the Wahhabis of Saudi Arabia, distrust rationalist scholars, whom they perceive to be 'neo-Mu'tazilites'.[40] For Mozaffari, Ibn Hanbal was the first Muslim thinker to foreshadow modern Islamists, in part because he was the first to characterize the 632–661 era as the sacrosanct 'Age of the Rigthly Guided Caliphs' and because he blamed the regimes that had followed this era for introducing the Greek rationalist philosophies that had inspired the Mu'tazilite ideas to which he was so violently opposed.[41] However, unlike later Islamists, Ibn Hanbal's focus was more narrowly theological, in that he was concerned with the post-661 failure to adhere to the correct practice of the Sunna. He was more devoted to establishing the correct Islamic beliefs (orthodoxy) than he was to setting a model for the correct Islamic practice (orthopraxy), and refused to condone either declaring Muslims unbelievers on the basis of sin, or rebellion against Muslim leaders, however imperfect.[42]

By the middle of the ninth century, the caliphs had relented and abandoned Mu'tazilite doctrine, and the caliphate was in any case subsequently emasculated by a variety of Turkic warlords invading from Central Asia. With the decline of the caliphs, the *ulama* emerged as the ultimate arbiters of sharia law, and established four different schools of jurisprudential thought: Maliki, Shafi'i, Hanbali and Hanafi. Thus, the form of Islam practised by around 90 per cent of Muslims today – Sunnism – did not emerge until well over two hundred years after the death of the Prophet. This is why the Islamists of the twentieth century were able to be so critical of the scholarly establishment. First, they argued that by seizing the religious role of the caliphs for themselves, the scholars created a de facto division between religion and state. The jurisprudence of these scholars thus came to be devoid of political content.[43] Meanwhile, although the *ulama* oversaw sharia courts that administered various forms of civil, criminal and family law, these had to compete with the worldly courts of the caliphs and various Turkic Sultans.[44] It was the Umayyads who first established *Mazalim* ('grievances') courts as a follow-on from Sassanid institutions performing a similar function.[45] These institutions drew on pre-Islamic custom as well as the historic prerogative of Near Eastern monarch to intervene in a number of civil and criminal disputes.[46] Islamists and their eighteenth- and nineteenth-century predecessors have also criticized the *ulama* for treating their own law schools as being more important reference points than the foundational sources, the Quran and Hadith. In the early years scholars fleshed out Islamic jurisprudence by attempting to directly interpret the Quran and Hadith through a practice known as *ijtihad*. However, the 'gate of ijtihad' was eventually shut, and scholars began to rely on imitation (*taqlid*) of previous jurisprudents.[47] Many Islamists characterized this as a retreat into traditionalism that threatened to make Islam irrelevant in a changing world.[48]

The mystical and ascetic Sufi orders (*tariqas*) were another Islamic institution that appeared in earnest in the Abbasid period. Sufism traces its origins to a number of eighth-century ascetics such as Hasan al-Basri and al-Hallaj, and indeed to an earlier tradition of asceticism and mysticism in the pre-Islamic monotheisms of the region.[49] Sufi mysticism required that its adherents seek union with the divine essence. This led in practice to the cultivation of esoteric approaches towards Islamic knowledge that diverged from the orthodoxy of the *ulama*. It also encouraged many Sufis to develop a latitudinarian outlook that enabled them to marry Islamic beliefs and customs with those of the many societies in Africa and Asia to which Islam spread in the first half of the second millennium. The Sufis increasingly began to organize themselves into formal brotherhoods, or *tariqas,* which began to serve a social and commercial as well as a religious purpose. Despite the chariness of the *ulama*, therefore, Sufis became increasingly integrated into mainstream Muslim society, offering a 'popular' variant of Islam that acted as an alternative to the scripturalist elitism of the formal religious establishment.[50] As we shall see in the coming chapters, the Islamist–Sufi relationship is complex. The first Islamist, Hasan al-Banna, was a Hasafi Sufi, and those Islamists who embraced mass politics valued the mobilizational potential of Sufism. At the same time, many Islamists – particularly those influenced by Salafism – have criticized the more heterodox forms of Sufism, as well as the more quietist trends which they hold to be responsible for widening the gap between religion and politics.

Religion, sectarianism and revolutionism in the classical era

In addition to the Kharijis, one of the principal dissenting 'sects' of the classical period was the Shia. With the death of Ali in 661 and the ascent of the Umayyads, there were many rebellions by groups that would eventually come to be referred to as the Shia, or 'partisans' of the family of the Prophet (*Ahl-i-Bayt*). They maintained that the Prophet had originally installed

Ali, his blood relative, as his successor and that consequently the first three caliphs – as well as the Umayyads themselves – were all illegitimate usurpers. Thus like their Sunni counterparts, Shia Islamists treat 661 as the dawn of an era of Muslim decline, but they hark back only to the five years of Ali's reign (656–661) and not the 'Age of the Rightly Guided Caliphs' as a whole.[51]

Throughout the Umayyad period the 'proto-Shi'i[s]'[52] continued to fight in the name of Ali's descendants, who were referred to as Imams and seen as the real leaders of the Muslim community. The most famous of these rebellions was led by Ali's nephew Hussein, and ended when he and his entourage were massacred by the forces of the Umayyad Caliph Yazid at the Battle of Karbala in 680.[53] Karbala is still a symbolic location in modern Iraq and the battle is commemorated annually by pilgrims to the city, which is also one of Shia Islam's holiest shrines and has continued to act as an important reference point for modern Shi'i political activists urging rebellion against an unjust political order.[54] Meanwhile, the Abbasid Caliphate itself, in spite of its later affiliation to Sunnism, emerged from a revolt against Umayyad rule led by an Iranian Shi'i named Abu Muslim. The Abbasids rode into power on this wave of rebellion, exploiting their status within the Ahl-i-Bayt as descendants of the Prophet's uncle Abbas.[55] However at this stage Shia identity was not fully formed, and an official line of succession had not been confirmed. It was Jafa'ar al-Sadiq who soon after the new regime emerged established the principle that the Shia Imams ought to be those descended from Ali through the martyred al-Hussein – thus invalidating the Abbasids. However, the majority of the followers of the Imams did not rebel against Baghdad, and the Abbasid Caliphs alternated between courting and repressing the Shia. It was in this period that the Shia adopted the practice of hiding their true beliefs (taqiyya) so as to avoid persecution.[56]

Classical Shi'ism was an extremely heterogeneous phenomenon, with a wide variety of sects competing for influence during the Umayyad and Abbasid eras. There are also many different schools of thought regarding the religio-political origins of Shi'ism. One suggestion is that the inspiration for Shi'i ideas may have come either from Iran or Yemen, in both of which the following of ruling dynasties had been the political norm for centuries. Another one is that the Quran and the Prophet established the principle that the relatives of Muhammad should rule.[57] Several Shi'i groups also transformed Shi'ism into a form of messianic ideology. Some Shi'i messianic prophecies propose that there will be a battle between a Mahdi or 'divinely-guided' saviour and the Sufyanid, a descendant of Abu Sufyan and ancestor of the Umayyad Caliphs, who had initially opposed Muhammad's preaching of his message before converting later in life.[58] Shi'i messianic beliefs have had the capacity to incubate revolutionary concepts, since they maintain that the Mahdi will make a break with existing Muslim law and introduce a new order based on the new messages that God has transmitted to him.[59] The Fatimid Caliphate, which emerged in Egypt in the tenth century, followed such a form of messianic ideology.[60] Yet, at times, messianism has also promoted political quietism, encouraging Muslims to await their saviour rather than fighting injustice in the present. This is particularly the case in Twelver Shi'ism, which is followed by the majority of the population of contemporary Iran (see Chapter 9).

Given the hegemony of Sunnism within the Abbasid Caliphate since the ninth century, adherents of the Sunni mainstream have fewer historic models for political radicalism than their Shi'i counterparts. Indeed, there are powerful anti-revolutionary messages within the scholarly tradition of Sunni Islam, which has used the Kharijis as a negative stereotype highlighting the dangers of religious fanaticism being tied to radical politics.[61] The scholars of the classical era tended to maintain that so long as the rulers of the Muslim community did not interfere with the practice of sharia overseen by the *ulama,* it was better to overlook their worldly flaws so as to avoid the *fitna,* or strife within the Muslim community, that would result from any effort to overthrow them. These classical rulings have posed a significant challenge to the efforts of Islamists who seek to justify rebellion against Muslim regimes in the current era.[62]

However, there are numerous exceptions to the rule that Sunnism did not legitimatize any form of political radicalism. While the consensus of the scholars may have deterred anti-Abbasid activism, Sunni radicalism was more of a possibility on the peripheries of the Islamic world.[63] One example was the emergence of the Almoravid and Almohad states in North Africa. The first of these manifested itself to the world as an apocalyptic movement but also represented the political mobilization of the marginalized Sanhaja Berber community of the Western Sahara.[64] The second was constituted after the founder of the Almohad dynasty, Ibn Tumart, declared himself the Mahdi.[65] Mahdism existed within Sunni Islam as well, with some Sunni prophecies casting the Sufyani in a more positive light and predicting that he would ultimately relent and deliver the caliphate to the Mahdi.[66] Sunni Mahdism tended to be more religiously conservative than its Shia equivalent, depicting the Mahdi as a figure who would revive the Sunna as it was originally practised in the time of the Prophet.[67] The Almohad and Almoravid states both called for strict adherence to the Sunna, although in practice they were unable to prevent heterodox Sufi groups – as well as rationalist philosophy – from continuing to flourish.[68] Most Islamists have tended to criticize Mahdist beliefs on religious grounds, as well as on the grounds that messianism encourages Muslims to avoid political action in the here and now while waiting for a saviour.[69] However, a number of Islamists – including forerunners such as Jamal al-Din al-Afghani – have seen the political utility of identifying with prominent Mahdis (see Chapters 3 and 10).

Political dissidence could also draw on conventional Sunnism in cases where the Islamic world was invaded by non-Muslims, or the ruling authorities – at least according to the dissidents – interfered with the rights of the Muslim community to practise sharia. Islamists have often taken Muslim generals such as Nur al-Din Zengi and Salah al-Din al-Ayyubi, who waged jihad against the invading crusaders of the twelfth and thirteenth centuries, as role models.[70] This is in spite of the fact that Zengi, a Turk, and al-Ayyubi, a Kurd, were not caliphs and embraced many of the same monarchical values that Islamists have understood as a resurgence of the *jahili* or pre-Islamic ideals that accompanied the post-661 malaise. Nur al-Din Zengi resembled 'every other Turkish prince' in that he 'regarded the conquest of Antioch to be the right of his family alone',[71] yet has still acted as a reference point for Abu'l-Hasan Nadawi,[72] Abu Musab al-Zarqawi and ISIS (see Chapter 13). Thus, in spite of Islamists seeing post-661 history as a 'perdition',[73] they have sought to exploit it nonetheless.

Ibn Taymiyya: A victim of misrepresentation?

No Sunni jurisprudent of the Islamic classical era has been cited more frequently as an inspiration to contemporary Islamist militancy than the Damascene scholar Ahmad ibn Taymiyya (1268–1328). Perhaps the reason his various fatwas and writings are quoted so often by Islamists is that he associated civilizational crisis with foreign invasion. Ibn Taymiyya was born ten years after the sacking of Baghdad by Genghis Khan brought an end to the Abbasid Caliphate, in an era in which both crusading Christians and shamanistic though nominally Muslim Mongols held sway in its former territories. This is what makes his writing so attractive to militant Islamists, who often equate the impact of Western colonialism on the modern Muslim world with that of the Crusades and the Mongol invasions. For scholars like Gilles Kepel and Stephen Schwartz, a genealogy of terror can be traced back to Ibn Taymiyya, through the writings of Bin Laden, Qutb and the eighteenth-century Arabian scholar Muhammad Ibn Abd al-Wahhab.[74] However, since Ibn Taymiyya was cited as an inspiration to al-Qa'eda in the report of the 9/11 commission, a wide body of scholarship has emerged which maintains that both twentieth and twenty-first-century militant Islamists, as well as their opponents, have distorted the writings of a far more nuanced and complex scholar.

Ibn Taymiyya is sometimes identified as a 'Salafi' for two reasons: first, because he aspired to revive the principles of the 'pious forefathers' and cleanse Islam of 'innovations' that emerged after their era; and second, because he criticized many of the same groups to which today's Salafis are vehemently opposed – Sufis, Shi'is and Christians. It is true that Ibn Taymiyya was a polymath who drew on a diverse range of theological and intellectual influences beyond those associated with the pious forefathers.[75] For example, his positions on matters of divorce – denying husbands the right to discard their wives instantaneously by declaring 'I divorce you three times' – challenge the image many have of him as an ultraconservative.[76]

Nevertheless, he explicitly identified himself as a follower of the pious forefathers when he was put on trial for his views.[77] It might be argued that in maintaining an ultraorthodox identification with the pious forefathers while in practice advancing views of a far more radical and innovative nature,[78] Ibn Taymiyya actually anticipated many of the 'Salafi' Islamists of the twentieth century, who were arguably no more consistent in following the *salaf*. One distinction that has been suggested is that while Ibn Taymiyya's Salafism was purely theological, the Salafis and Salafi–Islamists of the twentieth century applied Salafi methodology in a far more comprehensive fashion akin to the totalitarian ideologies of the day, using it to shape their understanding of law, politics and warfare.[79] This returns us to the question of whether the theological aspects of Islam should ever be regarded as entirely discrete.

Ibn Taymiyya's relationship with Sufism was more nuanced than that of most contemporary Salafis. He certainly never issued the kind of blanket condemnation of it associated with modern Wahhabi scholars. He objected most to those Sufi customs he believed led individuals towards polytheism,[80] but at the same time he lauded Sufi ethics as well as the Sufi quest for inner reformation, and was himself buried among Sufis.[81] However, his criticism of Shi'ism was more vehement and uncompromising. He maintained that Shi'i practices were close to those of Christians and Jews, linking the existence of Shi'ism to the wider decline of the Muslim faith.[82] Many of his criticisms were theological, but he did also participate in two Mamluk military campaigns against Shi'is, and penned a *fatwa* labelling Shi'ism a form of heresy so as to justify Muslims fighting against them.[83]

Whether or not we read the specifically 'Salafi' aspects of Ibn Taymiyya's creed as a purely theological phenomenon, many of his fatwas and other writings were explicitly political in content. He maintained that 'religion and the state are indissolubly linked. Without the power of coercion of the state, religion suffers.'[84] He was also a firm advocate of jihad in its most physical sense. He did not stray particularly far from the positions of the classical jurists on jihad, insofar as he maintained that it was only a voluntary duty (*fard kifaya*) when involving the expansion of Islam, but became incumbent on every capable Muslim as an individual duty (*fard al-'ayn*) when Muslim territories were invaded by unbelievers.[85] What made the fatwas Ibn Taymiyya directed against the Mongols different was that he faced a situation in which the non-Muslim invaders had nominally converted to Islam. Yet, for Ibn Taymiyya, the Mongols could not be considered genuine Muslims as they did not rule in accordance with sharia law but rather their own customary *Yasa* law code.[86] As we shall see in Chapter 12, twentieth-century militants cited Ibn Taymiyya's anti-Mongol fatwas in order to justify rebellion against regimes in the Muslim world that were not sufficiently committed to upholding sharia. Yet, many scholars have seen this as an ahistoric 'Mongolizing'[87] of later regimes that had not emerged in the same contexts.[88] The deviations from Islam of which Ibn Taymiyya accused the Mongols were far graver than those of contemporary regimes

– according to the Damascene scholar, they failed to support the pilgrimage and the majority of them refused to pray or pay alms.[89] Ibn Taymiyya even compared the Mongols themselves to the Kharijis, maintaining that like them they feigned religiosity in order to usurp genuine Islamic rule.[90] He argued that his own position was a 'middle way' between the position of the Kharijis and that of the Murji'ites who would obey rulers even if they were 'uncommitted to Islam'.[91]

Although he denounced the un-Islamic character of Mongol rule, in general Ibn Taymiyya was far warier of denouncing Muslims as non-believers than today's *takfiris*, knowing conventional Sunnism's wariness about condoning *takfir*. The *fatwa* he addressed in 1303 to the Muslim inhabitants of Mardin, who had been living under Mongol rule for twelve years, has been cited by some militants to maintain that true Muslims who live under un-Islamic systems are obliged to fight to overthrow those systems, or to flee from them.[92] According to one translation, Ibn Taymiyya declared that 'everyone who is with them under the state in which they rule ... is either an atheist (*zindiq*) and hypocrite who does not believe in the essence of the religion of Islam – or he belongs to that worst class of people who are the people of [heretical] innovations (*bid'ah*)'.[93] However, subsequent interpretations have suggested that Ibn Taymiyya meant only to condemn those who actively accepted the Mongols, rather those who chose to continue inhabiting the territories over which they ruled.[94] Indeed, he maintained that those who were able to continue practising their religion freely had no need to perform *hijra*.[95] Even though he did maintain that *hijra* was necessary if this was not the case, Michot suggests that he may have been recommending spiritual and moral as opposed to physical 'flight'.[96] This complex and nuanced response was necessary because, in Ibn Taymiyya's view, the Mongol conquest had not simply made Mardin a 'land of war' – rather, it had a 'composite status' in which elements of both the 'land of war' and 'land of peace' were present.[97]

Suggested readings: Secondary

Kenney, Jeffrey T., *Muslim Rebels: Kharijites and the Politics of Extremism in Egypt* (Oxford: Oxford University Press, 2006), Chapter 1

> Questions: What do representations of the Kharijites say about understandings of political and social order in the early Islamic period? How did Kharijite doctrine (according to the available sources) differ from that of the mainstream Muslim community? What does Kenney tell us about the problems of obtaining an accurate history of the Kharijites, and indeed the Islamic world in the seventh and eighth centuries in general?

Mona Hassan, 'Modern Interpretations and Misinterpretations of a Medieval scholar: Apprehending the Political Thought of Ibn Taymiyya', in Rapoport,

Yossef and Ahmed, Shahab (eds), *Ibn Taymiyya and his Times* (Oxford: Oxford University Press, 2010), 338–66.

Is Ibn Taymiyya a genuine source of inspiration for Islamist radicals? What is the significance of his understanding of a legitimate caliphate (*khilafa*)? Have his ideas been distorted by modern Islamists, and if so how?

Suggested readings: Primary

'Extract from a Legal Ruling (fatwa) Pronounced by Ibn Taymiyah on the Mongols, 702/1303', in Richard Bonney, *Jihad: From the Qu'ran to Bin Laden* (Basingstoke: Palgrave Macmillan, 2007) Appendix, 424–5.

Why does Ibn Taymiyya condemn the Mongols? What religious justification does he offer for fighting against them? What attitudes does Ibn Taymiyya express towards other Muslim groups? Can this text really serve as a blueprint for modern militancy?

3

The assault on tradition:

Islamic Revivalism in the eighteenth and nineteenth centuries

Here we will survey the 'Islamic Revivalist' movements that began to emerge throughout the Muslim world in the eighteenth century, and which – along with the later wave of 'Islamic Reformism' – prefigured the Islamist politics of the twentieth century. To some extent the revivalists recaptured the iconoclastic spirit of Ibn Taymiyya, although much had changed since the medieval scholar lamented the collapse of the Abbasid Caliphate in the thirteenth century. In the wake of the Abbasids' demise, the Ottoman dynasty asserted its suzerainty over large swathes of territory ruled by the caliphates of old, as well as new lands in Europe. The Ottomans incorporated a number of territories in the Balkans before taking over the Byzantine seat of Constantinople in 1453 and annexed most of the Levant, Egypt and the Hijaz at the beginning of the sixteenth century. After establishing himself as the sovereign of the two Holy Cities, the Ottoman sultan took on the title of caliph, which was transferred upon him by a descendant of the Abbasid rulers unseated in 1258. However, given that they were ethnic Turks and thus evidently not of Qurayshi descent the caliphal status of the Ottomans was often contested by those who could make claims to belong to the Prophet's lineage, such as the Alawite rulers of Morocco.[1] Elsewhere, Turkish migrations from Central Asia also led to the establishment of further Muslim imperial dynasties in Iran and the Indian subcontinent: those of the Safavids and the Mughals, respectively.

One feature of this period was the consolidation of the status of the Sufi orders and scholarly communities (*ulama*) as the principal institutions of the Islamic faith – institutions which revivalists, reformists and Islamists would later seek to challenge. The Ottoman, Safavid and Mughal Empires all incorporated the *ulama* into the framework of the state; for instance, the Ottoman sultan appointed a *Shaykh al-Islam* to oversee Islamic jurisprudence throughout his domain. This bureaucratization of the *ulama* represented a shift from the classical period during which scholars had tended to serve a variety of religious and legal functions independently of the state,[2] and set the stage for later religious movements to criticize the *ulama* as representatives of the establishment. Sufi orders continued to expand, spreading Islam along commercial routes in areas such as Africa, South East Asia and the Indian subcontinent.[3] The Ottoman state patronized a number of *tariqas*,[4] and the Sufi-influenced doctrine of *wahdat al-wujud* ('unity of being') remained popular.[5] In the Mughal Empire, the Sufi Chistiyya order played a substantial role in Emperor Akbar's efforts to synthesize Hinduism and Islam.[6]

Although the conquest of Constantinople in 1453 seemed to mark a significant shift in the balance of power between the Ottoman Empire and Western Christendom, Europe's discovery of the New World in the next century set the scene for its increasing commercial and economic hegemony over the Muslim states of Afro-Asia. As the Europeans brought gold and silver over from the New World and diverted trade that had previously passed through the Muslim heartlands around the Cape of Good Hope, Ottoman currency decreased in value. At the same time, a shift in the balance of power between the Ottomans and their European neighbours such as the Hapsburgs and the Russian Tsars brought about an end to Istanbul's conquests and the lucre that accompanied them. The Ottoman state thus came under increasing financial strain, and a number of regional potentates emerged that acted with increasing autonomy.[7] Meanwhile, the increasing purchasing power of European merchants enabled them to disrupt the South Asian trade in commodities such as indigo, pepper and silk by diverting it towards their own domestic markets, thus undermining the economy of the Mughal Empire and other major Muslim states in the Indian subcontinent.[8]

Revivalism: Core characteristics

This chapter largely follows Youssef Choueiri's definition of 'Islamic Revivalism' as a series of movements marked by the following features:

1 Belief that divine unity (*tawhid*) requires cleansing Islam of imported customs and traditions

2 Belief in *ijtihad* as 'independent reasoning' and hostility towards *taqlid* ('blind imitation')

3 Seeing the necessity of flight (*hijra*) from the *dar al-kufr* (abode of unbelief) to the to the *dar al-Islam* (house of Islam), and subsequent 'adoption of *jihad* ... whereby an open war would be declared against the enemies of Islam'

4 Following one leader, whether a *mujaddid* (renewer), Imam or Mahdi[9]

For Choueiri, Islamic Revivalism is markedly distinct from Islamic Reformism in so far as the latter was a 'modern movement' that emerged from direct engagement with the processes initiated by the global hegemony of Western colonialism, while Revivalism focused more on internal Islamic renewal.[10] Indeed, the emergence of Reformism in the nineteenth century led to Revivalism being eclipsed as an 'outdated reaction against European commercial expansion, agricultural stagnation and corrupt practices'.[11]

Choueiri's terminology is not universal. For instance, DeLong-Bas, in her controversial text on the emergence of the Wahhabi movement in the Arabian Peninsula, refers to the Islamic renewers of the eighteenth century as 'reformers', thus entirely subverting Choueiri's categorization.[12] While she recognizes that Muhammad Ibn Abd al-Wahhab as a 'reformer' differed in a number of ways from the later 'Islamic modernists', she does not distinguish between the two movements as radically as Choueiri, arguing that Ibn Abd al-Wahhab inspired thinkers such as Muhammad Abduh and Rashid Rida.[13] For DeLong-Bas, Ibn Abd al-Wahhab shared with the later modernists a defensive attitude towards jihad and an aspiration towards peaceful relationships with polytheists.[14] While her categorization thus matches that of Choueiri on a number of points – for instance, recognizing its internal character, and the attachment to *tawhid* and *ijtihad* and hostility towards *taqlid*[15] – she places less emphasis on hostility towards the 'enemies of Islam'. While this chapter and the next will rely on the Revivalism/Reformism distinction for their organizational framework, therefore, it is important to recognize that the exact degree of disparity between the two movements is contentious.

Indeed, the theoretical unity of the category of Islamic Revivalism is itself open to question.[16] Attitudes towards the various customs practised by Sufi orders were extremely varied, and it was certainly not the case that all Revivalist movements required their followers to perform *hijra* and subsequently jihad; as will be seen below, a number worked peacefully within the Ottoman and Mughal systems. Nevertheless, these movements shared an emphasis on challenging *taqlid* and promoting *ijtihad*, despite the fact that their interpretations of these concepts were far from identical. The reason for this was that they were all tied, directly or indirectly, to the movement of intellectual renewal that was underway in eighteenth-century Medina. It was the introverted hadith scholar, Muhammad Hayat al-Sindi (d. 1750 or 1752), who counselled the founders of the Wahhabiyya and the Sammaniyya as well as members of his own Naqshbandiyya order towards *ijtihad*.[17] His own teacher, Abu'l-Tahir al-Kurani, taught the Indian revivalist Shah Wali Allah.[18] Later in the eighteenth century, the Medinese scholar, Ahmad Ibn Idris, influenced the leaders of the Sanussiyya and Tijaniyya in the same fashion. We should beware of assuming that all revivalists shared the same inherent traits just because of their ties to intellectual developments at the heart of the Islamic world. This fallacy has led some scholars to describe all such movements as 'Wahhabi', thereby identifying them with the most famous and rigid of their type.[19] Indeed, al-Sindi counselled his other students against adopting the rigid worldview of Ibn Abd al-Wahhab.[20]

The origins of Revivalism

There are two principal perspectives on the origins of Islamic Revivalism. One understands its emergence as a reaction to a crisis, or at least a perceived crisis, within Islamic civilization brought about chiefly by the increasing commercial hegemony of Europe. In this regard, Islamic Revivalism is comparable to later waves of Political Islam, although it is recognized that it did not engage with European ideas in the manner of later movements.[21] The other perspective comprehends Revivalism as a process of consolidation, another phase in the expansion of Islamic civilization in which the earlier emphasis on syncretism and accommodation gave way to a more rigorous assertion of the core tenets of the Islamic faith.[22] Thus scholars have perceived Revivalism as either a response to an internal malaise or as a sign of the ongoing vitality of Islamic civilization. The salience of these perspectives probably varies with the region under study. In the Islamic heartlands of Anatolia, the Levant and the Arabian Peninsula, the emergence of Revivalist movements was to a certain extent a response to the regional collapse of the Ottoman Empire's authority; on the frontiers of the Islamic world in Asia and Africa it perhaps reflected a retrenchment of Islamic religious and civilizational ideals – what Voll terms 'Frontier Fundamentalism'.[23]

Although Mecca is often identified as the epicentre of the Revivalist wave and a number of the associated movements challenged an increasingly fragmented Ottoman authority, it was perhaps the increasing proximity between the Hijaz and Istanbul in the sixteenth and seventeenth centuries that enabled it to take the form that it did. The Ottomans invested heavily in Mecca and facilitated the growth of a resident scholarly class that would flesh out the new methodologies of hadith study and put *ijtihad* at the heart of Islamic Revivalism.[24] Arguably, the first 'Revivalist' movement emerged not in Mecca but in the Anatolian heartlands of the Ottoman Empire. This was the Kadizadeli movement, which was named after Kadizade Mehmed Efendi. Kadizade expanded the movement in the 1620s and 1630s, although its teachings were probably derived from the Bayrami Sufi, Imam Birgevi, two generations earlier.[25] Birgevi set the scene for Islamic Revivalism's synthesis of Sufi and orthodox beliefs with his famous text *al-Tariqa al-Muhammadiyya*, which sought to establish a more conventional set of practices for Sufi orders.[26] Kadizade translated one of Ibn Taymiyya's works on governance and seems in particular to have revived the latter's hostile attitude towards the visitation of saints' tombs (*ziyarat al-qubur*),[27] although the Kadizadeli doctrine differed from that of Ibn Taymiyya in a number of other regards.[28]

The influential generation of hadith scholars that emerged in eighteenth-century Mecca had a number of ties to the seventeenth-century Kadizadelis of Anatolia and the Levant. They were also the product of a cosmopolitan culture that was facilitated by Ottoman patronage and by Mecca's status as a destination for pilgrims from all over the Muslim world. These scholars came from diverse religious, cultural and national backgrounds. For instance, the pioneering revivalist Muhammad Hayat al-Sindi – himself from an Indian background – was taught by, and himself taught, *alims* who were variously Hanafi, Shafi'i and Hanbali, members of a variety of Sufi orders, and who hailed from a variety of different Muslim territories.[29]

Given that the Revivalist movement most famous in today's world, the Wahhabiyya, is uncompromisingly Salafi and anti-Sufi in orientation, it might seem counter-intuitive that Sufi orders such as the Nasqhbandiyya played a substantial role in the Islamic Revivalist movement – and yet they did. Revivalism is often associated with a number of 'neo-Sufi' thinkers who sought to retain the core elements of Sufi practice and organization while stripping it of the elements deemed un-Islamic by thinkers such as Ibn Taymiyya and Kadizade. For instance, the seventeenth-century Indian scholar Ahmad Sirhindi, who played a great role in entrenching religious conservatism in India, attempted to replace the prominent Sufi doctrine of 'unity of being' (*wahdat al-wujud*), often criticized by anti-Sufis for promoting pantheism, with the notion of 'unity of witness' (*wahdat al-shuhud*).[30] Many Revivalist Sufis attempted to distance themselves from classic Sufism's emphasis on individual unity with God, following the principles of *al-Tariqa al-Muhammadiyya*, and encouraged Sufis to connect with the 'spirit of the Prophet' instead.[31]

The emergence of Wahhabism

It is important to acknowledge that Wahhabism was not, as has been claimed,[32] the founding Revivalist movement. Nevertheless, given the prominence that has accrued to the Wahhabiyya since the conquest of Mecca by the Al Sa'ud in 1924, and its contentious links to both mainstream and extremist Islamism in the subsequent decades, particular attention will be given to the history of the movement here.

The movement sprang from the preaching of Shaykh Muhammad Ibn Abd al-Wahhab in the town of Huraymila in the Najd region of central Arabia. He denounced the polytheism (*shirk*) that he believed had become mainstream in Muslim society and sought support for his ultra-monotheistic doctrine by forming alliances with local rulers. An alliance with the Amir of Uyaynah ended after he was forced out of the town by opponents of his teachings, but he forged a more successful one in 1744 with Muhammad Ibn Sa'ud, the Amir of Dir'iyya.[33] Ibn Sa'ud promised to support Ibn Abd al-Wahhab's campaign against idolatry so long as the Shaykh supported his own worldly authority, and by the time Ibn Abd al-Wahhab died in 1792 the Sa'udi-Wahhabi emirate had come to dominate the Arabian Peninsula and enforce adherence to the Shaykh's doctrine throughout the entire area.[34] The alliance was maintained by the descendants of Ibn Sa'ud and Ibn Abd al-Wahhab, who helped to further expand Wahhabism, ruling Mecca itself from 1803 to 1818 and then from 1924 until the present day.

When considering the oft-debated question of Wahhabism's links to Islamism as a contemporary political ideology, it is worth noting that recent research on the movement by Khalid al-Dakhil has contended that the Wahhabiyya was chiefly a political as opposed to a religious ideology, and that the core purpose of its *tawhidi* message was to enable an early form of nation-building.[35] Challenging neo-Khaldunian arguments that present the Wahhabiyya emerging out of nomadic *asabiyya* (tribal solidarity), he argues that it was instead an urban (*hadari*) movement that sought to integrate semi-sedentarized tribes into the life of the town.[36] There is an evident parallel with analysis of twentieth-century Islamist parties here, as these have usually constituted urban movements that have sought to recruit rural–urban migrants.[37] Others have argued that the Wahhabi-Sa'udi Emirate emerged because it served the interests of the various *hadari* groups who wished to defend themselves against raids conducted by nomadic groups.[38]

In line with his argument, al-Dakhil stresses Ibn Abd al-Wahhab's roots as a member of the Banu Tamim, a tribe that had begun the process of urban settlement and had thus lost most of its 'solidarity', or *asabiyya*.[39] He brought his movement to prominence by forming an alliance with ruling families in the town of Dir'iyya that had provided generations of urban potentates.[40] This naturally opens the question as to whether Wahhabism can genuinely be seen as representing a 'radical' or 'counter-elite' movement. Sympathizers have certainly been keen to portray it as such. Some chroniclers of the Wahhabi movement have its founder living 'in poverty' before his rise to prominence.[41] DeLong-Bas's text also contends that Ibn Abd al-Wahhab himself was a rebel against the 'established social and political orders', identifying him with a reform movement composed of individuals who 'tended to either occupy the lower echelons of the religious establishment or stand outside it altogether, often enjoying mass popularity rather than government favour'.[42] However, given the partial nature of the existing sources, the extent of Ibn Abd al-Wahhab's marginality is open to question. DeLong-Bas herself observes elsewhere that the Najdi revivalist hailed from 'a prestigious family of Hanbali jurists and theologians', his grandfather being 'recognized as the greatest scholar and authority on Hanbali jurisprudence in his lifetime'.[43]

Ibn Abd al-Wahhab's historic ties to the Hanbali school leads us to consider the extent of his oft-mooted intellectual relationship with Ibn Taymiyya. That Ibn Abd al-Wahhab frequently cited Ibn Taymiyya in his works is well established.[44] However, as we have seen, Ibn Taymiyya's writings have been open to multiple interpretations. They were used against Ibn Abd al-Wahhab in his own lifetime by critics such as his brother Sulayman, who cited the thirteenth-century scholar's argument that the following of saints only constituted 'lesser idolatry' not tantamount to outright apostasy and who thus criticized his brother's views on *shirk*.[45] Ibn Abd al-Wahhab's opinions on what exactly constituted polytheism, or idolatry, were significant because he deemed the practice of 'calling upon' saints and visiting their shrines 'major idolatry' as it amounted to worshipping human beings as one should worship God.[46] Since a great number of Sunni Muslims, particularly the Sufis among them, pursued such practices, Ibn Abd al-Wahhab thus made a far more radical break with the existing social order than had Ibn Taymiyya.

Seeking to refute the narrative that Ibn Abd al-Wahhab parroted the medieval scholar's thought and passed it on to later radicals, DeLong-Bas argues that Ibn Taymiyya was 'a negligible source of inspiration' for him, and that his thinking synthesized a wide range of jurisprudential perspectives.[47] Indeed, Ibn Abd al-Wahhab's frequent travels before his rise to prominence gave him plenty of opportunity to expand his intellectual horizons. While the unreliability of the existing sources makes the precise extent of his peregrinations unclear, he certainly studied in Medina and Basra.[48] Much importance has been attached to his studies under the Medinese *hadith* scholars Abdullah Ibn Sayf and Muhammad Hayat al-Sindi,[49] as well as the important contributions of the Anatolia-based Kadizadeli school. Many of Ibn Abd al-Wahhab's own teachers had embraced Kadizadeli thought in early-eighteenth-century Damascus, and succeeded in passing its outlook – which as observed above was influenced, though not exclusively so, by Ibn Taymiyya – onto the Najdi renewer.[50] Indeed, Currie suggests that it was because Sufism and the Ottoman scholarly establishment were not as entrenched in the Arabian Peninsula as in Anatolia and the Levant that Ibn Abd al-Wahhab was able to put into practice the Kadizadelis' vision far more effectively than the original movement had been able to.[51]

Wahhabism, Islamism and violence: The controversy

Wahhabism requires more attention than any of the other 'Revivalist' movements since – on account of its ongoing significance as the principal ideological force underpinning the modern Saudi regime, protector of the holy places since 1924 – it is widely regarded as an inspiration for contemporary forms of Sunni Islamism. It has also been cited as an influence on the Muslim Brotherhood;[52] and, more controversially, on the more extremist organizations of the current era, including al-Qa'eda and Da'esh.[53] Scholars such as Benjamin Schwartz and Gilles Kepel have identified the Wahhabis as a link between Ibn Taymiyya, as the supposed forefather of contemporary Islamism, and modern militants from Sayyid Qutb to Osama bin Laden.[54] In particular, Wahhabism's critics maintain that its strict interpretation of the doctrine of *tawhid* and consequent justification of the principle of declaring professed Muslims as non-believers (*takfir*), and thus legitimate targets for the most militaristic form of jihad, has led it to act as an ideological incubator for contemporary extremism.[55] Within the Muslim world, such arguments date back to the early period of Wahhabi expansion – for instance, in the nineteenth-century denunciation of Wahhabi doctrine by its Ottoman opponents, who compared it to that of the Kharijis.[56]

DeLong-Bas's book *Wahhabi Islam: From Revival and Reform to Global Jihad*, published in 2004 in the wake of the 9/11 attacks on the United States three years earlier, seeks to challenge those who blamed Wahhabism for the rise of militant ideologies in the contemporary Islamic world. Instead, she maintains, the movement's founder, Muhammad Ibn Abd al-Wahhab, was a moderate reformer who sought to spread his ideal of *tawhid* through persuasion and not violence.[57] Although DeLong-Bas acknowledges that Ibn Abd al-Wahhab was willing to denounce Muslims whose actions did not respect the doctrine of *tawhid*, she also insists that he did not believe that this denunciation entailed the declaration of jihad against such non-believers. Rather, he advocated preaching the correct form of Islam to them, and negotiating a treaty relationship with all such individuals who continued to refuse to live within the true Islamic community. Only if preaching and negotiation both failed would military action be legitimate.[58] Furthermore, DeLong-Bas attacks the conventional narrative that Ibn Abd al-Wahhab lent his ideological support to Ibn Sa'ud's conquests in the Arabian Peninsula, maintaining that although he accepted the Saudi ruler's patronage, he abstained from public involvement and refused to sanction any of his campaigns by declaring them jihads.[59]

DeLong-Bas's text received much praise, but also hostile responses from a number of Wahhabism's detractors. The latter pointed to her unwillingness to quote Ibn Abd al-Wahhab directly, over-reliance on pro-Wahhabi chroniclers and disregard for texts that cast Ibn Abd al-Wahhab in a more negative light.[60] Firro, for instance, criticizes her over-reliance on Ibn Abd al-Wahhab's theological works, citing epistles to his followers that demonstrate his willingness to denounce his opponents as unbelievers with little justification.[61]

Nevertheless, what DeLong-Bas and her critics both appear to accept is that a more militant strain did enter Wahhabi religious ideology during the nineteenth century, as the descendants of Ibn Abd al-Wahhab and Ibn Sa'ud sought to extend their territorial hegemony in the Arabian Peninsula. It was only at the turn of the nineteenth century, when the

Saudi-Wahhabis sought reasons for throwing the Ottoman Empire out of Mecca, that they integrated the teachings of Ibn Taymiyya so as to justify rebellion against an established Muslim regime.[62] Ironically, DeLong-Bas's attribution to Ibn Taymiyya of responsibility for the radicalization of Wahhabism has led to further criticism from scholars who maintain that (as seen in the previous chapter) Ibn Taymiyya's fatwas do not justify such actions.[63]

As the Wahhabi–Ottoman conflict developed during the nineteenth century, its political exigencies led to the radicalization of the religious discourse of the Al al-Shaykh. When the Ottomans employed the ruler of Egypt, Muhammad Ali, to reconquer Mecca on their behalf, Sulayman al-Shaykh penned *al-Dala'il fi Hukm Muwalat Ahl al-Ishrak* (Evidence against loyalty to the polytheists), insisting that all those who displayed loyalty towards the polytheistic invaders would be considered guilty of polytheism themselves.[64] Although Sulayman's political instrumentalization of *takfiri* rhetoric could not prevent the downfall of the first Saudi state at the hands of the Ottoman-Egyptians, another Ottoman-Saudi conflict in the 1860s and 1870s led to further radicalization of the *takfir* doctrine. From the middle of the nineteenth century, a modernizing Ottoman state influenced by European developmentalist models attempted to exert a far more direct form of control over its Arabian provinces than it had before, even interfering in the politics of the Najd region, which it had previously left untouched.[65] When the Ottomans backed Abdullah Ibn Sa'ud in a struggle with his brother Sa'ud for power in Riyadh, Abd al-Latif al-Shaykh – as the senior Wahhabi scholar and a supporter of Sa'ud – denounced Abdullah for relying on the support of infidels. In doing so, he expanded the Wahhabi concept of *takfir* so that the denunciation of unbelief now applied to all those who lived outside of the Wahhabiyya, whether they were self-professing Muslims or not. This denunciation also legitimized jihad against the unbelievers in question, and was even extended to sections of the population of Najd when the Ottomans occupied Hasa with British support.[66]

The extent to which the Wahhabi doctrine – especially regarding *takfir* – can be considered responsible for contemporary militancy remains contentious. Writing in 2004, DeLong-Bas maintained that the principal militants of the contemporary period, Sayyid Qutb and Osama bin Laden, both drew inspiration from the medieval scholars Ibn Taymiyya and Ibn Qayyim al-Jawziyya and in particular their jurisprudential justifications for the unseating of un-Islamic rulers, rather than from Ibn Abd al-Wahhab.[67] DeLong-Bas therefore does not seek to refute the intellectual links between classical and contemporary jihadis – she merely denies that Ibn Abd al-Wahhab was a historical go-between. Whether or not the movement's founding father was a proto-extremist, the nineteenth-century *takfiris* such as Sulayman al-Shaykh and Abd al-Latif al-Shaykh have acted as important reference points for twentieth and twenty-first-century militants in Saudi Arabia and beyond. Their *takfiri* discourses were to some extent a response to a form of imperial expansion that, although it came from a Muslim and not a Western European power, can be understood as colonial.[68] The Ottomans since the Tanzimat reforms of the 1830s (of which more next chapter) had been greatly influenced by the scientific, cultural and political ideals of post-Enlightenment Europe and used modern armies and modern technology in attempting to assert their control over their far-flung provinces, including Arabia. This explains why the discourses of Sulayman and Abd al-Latif al-Shaykh would appeal to contemporary radicals battling what they perceive as contemporary Western colonialism.

While the contemporary Saudi state founded by Abd al-Aziz Ibn Sa'ud – which re-established its hegemony over Mecca and the rest of the Arabian Peninsula in the 1920s – has moderated its understanding of *takfir* and *al-wala wa-l-bara* for the purpose of pursuing its international relations, both internal and external critics have sought to use these doctrines against it. For instance, after the Gulf War the Jordanian jihadi Abu Muhammad al-Maqdisi, as well as members of the 'al-Shu'aybi' school in Saudi Arabia, cited the nineteenth-century *takfiris* to condemn the ruling dynasty's alliance with America during the 1991 Gulf War,[69] al-Maqdisi going as far as to label its reliance on American assistance as an act of *kufr* similar to that perpetrated by Abdullah in his own request for Ottoman aid.[70] This same reading of the American–Saudi alliance as engendering *kufr* subsequently inspired members of al-Qa'eda in the Arabian Peninsula, as well as figures in the mainstream organization as prominent as Ayman al-Zawahiri.[71]

Revivalism in Africa

Between the eighteenth and early twentieth centuries, the African continent witnessed Revivalist movements of diverse character. Some were militant movements that waged jihad against local opponents and attempted to establish an Islamic state; for example, Karamoko's jihad in the Futa Jallon region of Senegambia in 1726, and Uthman Dan Fodio's establishment of the Sokoto Caliphate in an area now covered by Nigeria, Niger and Chad.[72] Other Revivalist movements cooperated with the existing political authorities. For instance, in 1842 Muhammad Ali al-Sanusi created the Sanusiyya order and was able to establish a strong commercial, agricultural and religious presence in Libya and what is today Chad, while avoiding confrontation with the Ottoman state.[73] Ahmad al-Tijani spread his own Revivalist Sufi order, the Tijaniyya, throughout much of North and West Africa with the support of the Moroccan Sultan, Mawlay Sulayman.[74] A number of later Revivalist movements, such as the Mahdiyya of Muhammad Ahmad al-Mahdi in late-nineteenth-century Sudan, and Sayyid Muhammad Abdullah Hasan's jihad in early-twentieth-century Somalia, sought to resist European colonialism during the 'Scramble for Africa'.[75]

In practice, many of these movements were driven by mundane socio-economic concerns as much as religious ideology. The Fulani pastoralists who led the jihad that established the Sokoto Caliphate, for instance, used Islamic rhetoric to vocalize their resentment of the heavy cattle taxes imposed by the agricultural Hausa who ruled over them. It has been argued that theirs was in practice a movement of ethnic as much as religious solidarity.[76] In spite of the importance of local dynamics to each of these movements, they mostly shared a number of characteristics: first, close ties with the intellectual centres of Islamic revival in Mecca; second, the role of a more orthodox and less syncretic form of Sufism; third, hostility to local customs previously accepted by the more latitudinarian forms of Islamic authority that had prevailed in Africa; and fourthly, a number of these movements also had a strong messianic element.[77]

Understanding the role of Sufism in Revivalism is key to problematizing the dichotomy between Sufism and Islamism proposed by many analysts of twentieth-century Political Islam. One of the principal architects of the Meccan Revivalist movement was Ahmad Ibn Idris, himself a Moroccan Sufi. Idris strove hard to reconcile the devotional aspects of the Sufi tradition with adherence to the Quran and the Sunna, and thus influenced a new generation of more conservative Sufi orders, including the Sanussiyya in Libya and the Khatmiyya in Sudan.[78] Many of these revivalist Sufis shifted their devotional practices to conform with *al-Tariqa al-Muhammadiyya*.[79] These new *tariqas*, such as the Sanussiyya and Tijaniyya, were thus hostile to the forms of worship practised by earlier Sufi orders; that is, those that venerated individuals on account of their presumed closeness to God. In particular, they condemned visitations to the tombs of saints.[80]

The life of Sudan's Muhammad Ahmad al-Mahdi captures the essence of Islamic Revivalism's ambivalent relationship with the Sufi tradition. Al-Mahdi was a prominent member of the Sammaniyya, one of the new Sufi orders that had established itself in Sudan as the first waves of Islamic Revivalism passed through Africa. Yet this order had to some extent become 'Sudanized' as it integrated itself into the local society, adopting some of the syncretic practices of earlier Sufi orders.[81] In 1878 Muhammad Ahmad entered into conflict with Muhammad al-Sharif, the *Shaykh* of the Sammaniyya order, an event later attributed to al-Mahdi's anger at al-Sharif's permissive attitude towards music and dance.[82] In 1881 he declared himself the Mahdi (hence the addition of 'al-Mahdi' to his name), overthrew the British and Ottoman-backed Turco-Egyptian regime in Sudan, and founded the Mahdist State which persisted until the Anglo-Egyptian conquest of 1898. Like the Wahhabi *takfiris*, the Mahdists had rebelled against the rule of a Muslim colonial regime that had sought to emulate European developmentalism.

Muhammad Ahmad founded his own religious order, named the Ansar after the original supporters of the Prophet Muhammad in Mecca and Medina in the seventh century. However, despite his messianic pretensions, many of those who joined the Ansar or the rest of his forces did so for rather more prosaic motives. The Baqqara nomads of southern Kordofan, who represented one of the strongest elements in the Mahdist armies, joined up because they resented the taxes imposed by the Turco-Egyptian regime. Other prominent backers of the Mahdiyya included the riverain merchant groups that had profited heavily from the slave trade, which the British and the Turco-Egyptians had attempted to abolish.[83]

In spite of his evocation of the first Islamic community, the Mahdi's movement also deployed important Sufi concepts and ideals to appeal to the population of Sudan, where Sufism was the predominant expression of the Islamic faith. His exhortations to the Sudanese emphasized his closeness to Khidr, who was popular among Sufis, and his declaration that the Prophet had told him 'you are created from the light of the core of my heart' was rooted in Sufi symbology.[84] Muhammad Ahmad modelled the Ansar itself on a Sufi order[85] and, like previous Sufi shaykhs, demanded that his followers swear an oath of allegiance (ba'ya) to him.[86] His establishment of the Ansar might therefore be characterized as a case of the relatively new manifesting itself as the old. However, once the Ansar became an established movement, he formally abolished all of Sudan's Sufi orders[87] and banned a great number of practices that had been tolerated by its more lenient tariqas, including the playing of music at public festivals, consumption of alcohol and tobacco, and the wailing of women at funerals.[88] Yet, even the Mahdiyya itself was 'Sudanized' to a degree. Rudolf Slatin, an Austrian captive of the Ansar, recalled that when the Mahdi died in 1885, 'in spite of the strict and oft-repeated injunctions against loud lamentation, weeping and wailing arose from almost every house'.[89] The Mahdiyya's paradoxical relationship with the established Sufi culture shaped the policies of the British colonizers of Sudan, who supported the orthodox institutions of the ulama and gave little formal recognition to the Sufi orders, fearing that they had the capacity to generate another militant messianic movement.[90]

Revivalism in Asia

The Indian experience of Revivalism appears to encapsulate its contradictory heritage. On one level, the revivalist trends of eighteenth and nineteenth-century India marked a continuity with the vision of Ahmad Sirhindi, who – under the patronage of the Mughal emperor Aurangzeb – had promoted an 'intellectual renaissance' of Islamic Civilization in the sultanate marking a break with the syncretic outlook of the sixteenth-century emperor, Akbar.[91] In this regard, Indian Revivalism might fit well into Voll's 'Frontier Fundamentalism' model – yet, by the eighteenth century, it was also a response to internal crisis, as the Mughal Empire began to collapse in the face of regional dissent and the commercial and military expansionism of Britain's East India Company.

The rise and fall of the Mughal Empire, and the historical prominence of Sufism in the Asian subcontinent, were the two principal factors that shaped the unique character of Indian Revivalism. This is well illustrated by the case of the prominent revivalist thinker, Shah Wali Allah al-Dihlawi (also known as Ahmad Ibn Abd al-Rahim). Although Wali Allah was born around 1703 – only four years before the death of Aurangzeb caused a turning point in Mughal fortunes – his father, Shah Abd al-Rahim, had been one of those who helped to produce a famous collection of *fatawa* commissioned by the emperor to reinforce a more orthodox and less latitudinarian form of Islam.[92] Wali Allah had been influenced by the prominent hadith scholars under whom he had studied in Mecca,[93] and sought to forge closer links between the Islamic heartlands and their Asian peripheries.[94] He deliberately wrote in Arabic rather than Persian – the literary language of the Mughal Empire at the time – and expressed his satisfaction that Islam in the Arabian Peninsula had not been marred by the same 'accretions' as elsewhere.[95] Nevertheless, unlike Ibn Abd al-Wahhab, Wali Allah did not reject Sufi practices outright and he refused to practise *takfir*. This is unsurprising, given that his own mentor, Ahmad Sirhindi, had been a Sufi.[96] He denied that any of the Sufis in India should be labelled apostates and instead recommended reforming existing Sufi practices.[97]

Since Wali Allah distanced himself from *takfir* and refused to preach either jihad or migration from the land of unbelief, he does not fit neatly into Choueiri's model of revivalists as militant expanders of the Islamic faith. It is true that his son, Shah Abd al-Aziz, produced a *fatwa* in 1803 to the effect that the lands of the Mughal Empire were no longer within the Dar al-Islam.[98] However, whereas the Wahhabi *takfiris* had chosen to declare the Ottoman Empire – a sovereign Muslim state – to be outside the Dar al-Islam, the action of Shah Abd al-Aziz was a response to the ongoing encroachments of a Christian colonizer, and specifically the East India Company's declaration of a protectorate over the Mughal Empire.[99]

The Padri movement of Mingakabau in Western Sumatra was probably more directly influenced by the Wahhabi movement, its three founders having returned from Mecca only a year after it had first been conquered by the Al Sa'ud.[100] The term 'Padri' itself derives from a reference to area from which pilgrims departed to conduct the Hajj.[101] Probably the most influential Revivalist movement in South East Asia, the Padris expressed considerable hostility to the customs tolerated by the Sufi orders responsible for introducing Islam to Mingakabau at the beginning of the sixteenth century. They followed the Wahhabis in administering justice solely with reference to the Quran, and also adopted the Saudi model of the Imamate.[102] They took society in Wahhabi Mecca as a role model, forcing women to wear veils, encouraging men to grow beards, banning the smoking of opium and pushing the people of Mingakabua to move away from matrilineality.[103] Like the Mahdi and Shah Abd al-Aziz, the Padris took up arms against European colonizers, in this case the Dutch. However, the experience of colonialism did not define the Padri movement – if anything, their emergence facilitated colonialism, as the Dutch seized on the alienation of the customary leaders by the revivalists to turn them into local proxies.[104]

The legacy of Islamic Revivalism

Studying the subsequent historical development of Islamic Revivalism poses one significant challenge to those who wish to trace the origins of contemporary Islamist radicalism to the pre-twentieth-century era. While revivalist movements often sought a radical break with the existing sociopolitical order when they emerged in the eighteenth and nineteenth centuries, the descendants of the various movements' founders often became establishment figures: entrenched and more conservative. In Africa and the Middle East, these individuals even cooperated closely with the British Empire. For instance, when the British colonized Nigeria at the turn of the twentieth century, a number of the Sokoto Emirs chose to submit to them, following the principle that jihad was not incumbent upon them when it would inevitably lead to military defeat. The Sokoto Emirs then became the stalwarts of Britain's 'Native Administration' in northern Nigeria. The colonial state devolved a number administrative and legal responsibilities onto the emirs, who oversaw courts applying a modified form of sharia law.[105] This system appealed to the British because they saw Islam (or at least, the Islam of the Sokoto Emirs) as an 'appropriate' religion for sub-Saharan Africa;[106] and allowing the emirs to administer north of the country meant that they could avoid empowering secular elites, the members of which might embrace modern, anti-colonial nationalism.

The British pursued similar policies in Sudan during the era of the Anglo-Egyptian Condominium (1899–1956). In 1926 the governor-general bestowed a knighthood on the son of the Mahdi, Sayyid Abd al-Rahman al-Mahdi, following his public support during the First World War and the proto-nationalist White Flag Revolt of 1924.[107] Sayyid Abd al-Rahman acquired a significant stake in the colonial cotton economy, employing his neo-Mahdist religious followers on plantations along the White and Blue Niles.[108] The British saw Sayyid Abd al-Rahman and the Umma Party – which he bankrolled the founding of in 1945 – as useful proxies in their battle against the pro-Egyptian political forces who wished to unite the Nile Valley against the colonial order, as well as their struggle against the growing Sudanese left. There was no smooth transition from Revivalism to Islamism in Sudan – it was the Oxford-educated great-grandson of the Mahdi, Sadiq al-Mahdi, who was overthrown by the Islamist coup of 1989.

While, unlike Sudan and Nigeria, Saudi Arabia was never formally conquered by the British, the Wahhabiyya's Saudi protectors also established close relations with the Western governments in the first half of the twentieth century, signing a protection treaty with the British and granting substantial concessions to American oil firms.[109] Social, economic and political ties between the Saudi and American elites grew throughout the second half of the twentieth century as the United States took over from Britain as the principal informal hegemon in the Middle East. Meanwhile, the Wahhabi religious establishment supported these alliances. In 1990, after the royal family infuriated radical Islamists by allowing the American government to station its troops on Saudi soil during the Gulf War against Saddam Hussein, senior Wahhabi scholars issued fatwas declaring that a request for aid from a non-Muslim power could be permitted given the threat posed by Iraqi expansionism. One prominent *alim*, Abd al-Aziz bin Baz, even went so far as to declare Saddam an infidel.[110] Whether or not the eighteenth-century revivalists were the progenitors of the contemporary radicalisms, their more direct descendants were certainly far less militant.

Suggested reading: Secondary

DeLong-Bas, Natana J., *Wahhabi Islam: From Revival and Reform to Global Jihad* (Oxford: Oxford University Press, 2004), Chapter 1.

Is DeLong-Bas's account too sympathetic towards Muhammad Ibn Abd al-Wahhab? How convincing is her use of sources? Was Muhammad Ibn Abd al-Wahhab a 'traditionalist'? In what ways was he a 'reformer'? What was al-Wahhab's relationship with Sufism, Shi'ism and the *ulama*?

Ayoob, Mohammed and Kosebalaban, Hasan, *Religion and Politics in Saudi Arabia: Wahhabism and the State* (London: Lynne Rienner Publishers, 2009). Chapter 3, by Khalid S. Dakhil, 'Wahhabism as an Ideology of State Formation'.

Questions: How does al-Dakhil challenge existing representations of the Wahhabiyya? What was the significance of the concepts of *Tawhid* and *Shirk* for the Wahhabis? What was the social base of the Wahhabiyya?

Suggested reading: Primary

Sir Harford Jones Brydges, *An Account of His Majesty's Mission to the Court of Persia in the Years 1807-1811, to Which is Appended, a Brief History of the Wahauby*. 2 volumes (London: J Bohn, 1834).

Questions: Is it possible to glean any information of value from this source in spite of its 'Orientalist' character? How does it represent Wahhabi doctrine and the relationship between religion and politics in Wahhabi expansion?

4

Between Muslim rationalism and European colonialism:

The Islamic reformists

The focus of this chapter will be the trend defined by Youssef Choueiri as 'Islamic Reformism', which emerged within the Islamic world during the period from the mid-nineteenth to the early twentieth century. It signified a break with Islamic Revivalism's emphasis on internal revival, as generations of statesmen and intellectuals began to argue that the prosperity of the Muslim community would depend on its success in adapting to the specific form of modernity brought about by post-Enlightenment industrial Europe. Reformism represented both a state-led movement driven by progressive Ottoman viziers and provincial functionaries and a broader intellectual renaissance to which individual scholars and educationalists such as Jamal al-Din al-Afghani, Muhammad Abduh and Sayyid Ahmad Khan contributed. Since Reformism was not a cohesive movement, it is difficult to ascribe precise characteristics that defined each individual thinker or group, but among its most important characteristics identified by Choueiri are the following:

- the reformulation of certain classical Islamic concepts so as to equate them to the principles of post-Enlightenment Western rationalism; for example, the reinterpretation of the Quranic principle of *shura* ('consultation') as a form of parliamentary democracy;
- a belief that Western sciences and ideas must be used by Muslim nations as a means of bolstering the Islamic world against the European colonial threat;
- a continuation of the revivalists' assault on *taqlid*, linked to a more rationalistic usage of *ijtihad* in the interpretation of the Quran; and

- an increasing identification with urbanity and belief in the powers of modern state bureaucracy.[1]

This text will use Choueiri's characterization as a basic framework, although it is important to remember that the terms 'Islamic modernist' and 'Islamic modernism' are often used by scholars to describe the same phenomenon elsewhere.

The context that defined the emergence of Islamic Reformism was the increasing hegemony of colonial Europe in the Islamic world. In the eighteenth century this hegemony was largely commercial, as trading companies thriving off the influx of gold from the Americas and then the boom in production accompanying the Industrial Revolution sought out new markets in Africa and Asia. By the nineteenth century, the 'informal' empire constituted by the export of European culture and material goods grew,[2] but this process was accompanied by an increasing military expansionism helped by the boom in the European arms industry. In 1798 Napoleon conducted a brief expedition to Egypt, and France continued to expand into the region, establishing a settler colony in Algeria in 1830 and missionary-led educational institutions in Syria and Lebanon. For Britain's part, the East India Company slowly extended its grip on the Asian subcontinent until the Indian Mutiny of 1857, which led to the dismantling of the Mughal Empire and the annexation of India to the British crown; further conquests in Malaya, Egypt and Sudan came later in the nineteenth century. Meanwhile, the Russian Empire began gradually to push the Ottomans out of the Caucasus, and undermine their influence in the Balkans. European colonialism, in both its 'formal' and 'informal' manifestations, began to shape the character of social and economic development within the Islamic world. Modern educational institutions, whether the instructors were colonial Europeans or Muslims, increasingly began to rely on European-style curricula, and to teach in European languages. Meanwhile, economies in the Islamic world were restricted by the forces of the global market: Muslim territories in Africa and Asia exported primary resources such as silk and cotton to drive European industrialization, while local artisan production was undermined by the influx of cheap manufactured goods from Europe.

Was Islam itself the driving force behind Islamic Reformism? In light of the dominance of the specifically colonial form of modernity in the nineteenth-century Islamic world, this is a much-debated question. Many studies overlook the religious and cultural roots of Reformism and cast it instead as the direct by-product of the flow of knowledge, ideas and technology from Europe to the Orient.[3] Islam, in this view, is the object and not the subject in the reformist dynamic – to use Ayubi's term, al-Afghani and Abduh sought to 'modernize Islam'.[4] It is a common argument, pursued by Choueiri himself, that reformists sought to instrumentalize Islam for worldly political and intellectual purposes.[5] Elie Kedourie, in one markedly polemical monograph, pursued this logic to the extent of arguing that al-Afghani and Abduh were secret atheists manipulating religion for political ends.[6] This claim has received much criticism,[7] while Anscombe's recent research on the Ottoman Tanzimat reforms has contended that Islam provided more of an inspiration than the ideals of the Enlightenment *philosophes*.[8] Much scholarship on intellectuals such as al-Afghani and Abduh also challenges the presumed dichotomy between rationalist European-style political reform and faith-based Islamic politics, maintaining that these individuals were inspired as much by the Islamic rationalism of the classical era, particularly that of the Mu'tazilate school of theology and Neoplatonist philosophers such as al-Farabi, as by post-Enlightenment European ideas.[9]

A related area of contention is the relationship of Islamic Reformism to other significant trends within both Islamism and pre-Islamism. DeLong-Bas, already noted for having launched an implicit challenge to Choueiri's typology by identifying Muhammad Ibn Abd al-Wahhab as a progressive and reformer, insists that his theology – notably what she perceives to be his pacific interpretation of jihad – influenced both Abduh and Rida.[10] One mainstream assumption about Reformism is that it represented an evolution of the 'Salafi' doctrine of scholars like Ibn Taymiyya, in that it propagated the belief that modern values could be 'rediscovered' by returning to the Islam of the pious ancestors.[11] The belief that a concept of 'modernist Salafism' emerged in the late nineteenth century has recently been challenged by Henri Lauzière, who argues that the notion came about due to French scholar Massignon's misinterpretation of Abduh and Rida's views and was only later picked up by other Muslim intellectuals because of his mistake.[12] Meanwhile, it is also open to question whether Islamic Reformism should be treated as a unique product of a specific era of Western colonial hegemony, or instead as the initial sketch for the ideological template of Islamists after the 1920s. Choueiri himself argues that the establishment of the Muslim Brotherhood represented the 'culminating phase of Islamic reform and Salafism' in that it achieved the earlier activists' desire for a political party. Ayubi, nevertheless, maintains that al-Banna sought to 'Islamize modernity', and not to 'modernize Islam' in the manner of the reformers.[13] According to this logic, the fact that Islam itself was not the core driving force behind the reformists' activism distinguishes it from the Islamist movements of the twentieth century.

Sayyid Ahmad Khan, Aligarh and Reformism in India

It was no coincidence that Islamic Reformism developed most quickly where European and particularly British colonialism was at its strongest, as occupation and in some cases direct annexation by a foreign Christian power induced Muslims to adapt to the new challenge Western modernity posed to their culture. At the turn of the nineteenth century, Britain's East India Company had incorporated the Mughal Emperor and his domains into their informal empire in South Asia, provoking Sayyid Ahmad Barelvi to declare these lands part of the 'Dar al-Harb'.[14] In 1857 the Company's efforts to more directly incorporate the Mughal territories provoked a rebellion, following which both the Company and the Mughal Empire were removed by the British government, which annexed a number of India's provinces directly to the crown. More than in any of Britain's other non-settler colonies, the colonial regime in India made strenuous efforts to Westernize the country through the education system. Thomas Babington Macauley laid the groundwork in the 1830s for a network of schools that would produce a generation of 'brown Englishmen', and India's first universities emerged in 1857.[15] In the nineteenth century, Muslim elites, who had previously dominated the Mughal administration of India, were forced to compete for power and influence with Hindus educated by the British colonial system.[16]

It was thus in India that the emergence of a reformist trend was most directly linked to the context of colonial rule. Its foremost protagonist, Sayyid Ahmad Khan, was a lifelong servant of the British administration in India, first entering it as a functionary of the Judicial Department in 1838 at the age of twenty-one. It has been argued that Sayyid Ahmad Khan displayed only a 'real-politik loyalism', brought about by the need to protect the Muslim community following the dismantling of the Mughal Empire by the British after the Indian Mutiny in 1857.[17] Nevertheless, his writings frequently praised British and European culture, arguing that 'civilization in common parlance ... connotes the advanced, cultured and humanized form of the Europeans', and comparing their 'humanizing role' to that of ancient seafaring nations such as the Greeks and Phoenicians.[18] Indeed, explaining why the Muslim community in India should allow itself to be influenced by British civilization, Khan argued that it was the introduction of Greek arts and sciences that had led to the 'third stage of Islamic intellectual efflorescence' in the eighth and ninth centuries.[19]

Khan frequently attacked Muslim exceptionalism, insisting that different cultures could only survive through interchange with one another. This said, he did not enter the British colonial world as a tabula rasa; for instance, earlier Islamic revivalists such as Shah Wali Allah influenced his rejection of *taqlid* and critical attitude towards the *hadith*.[20] Unlike Jamal al-Din al-Afghani (see below), Khan never claimed that the Islamic faith had stood in the way of progress throughout history – rather, Islam was an inherently rational religion.[21] By suppressing the drinking of alcohol and other such harmful habits, Islam had facilitated the development of human civilization.[22] Moreover, while he encouraged cultural borrowing from the British, like previous revivalists he sought to reverse the process of cultural and religious syncretism that had defined the interaction between

Muslims and Hindus in the subcontinent for over eight hundred years. For example, his *Outline for Social and Cultural Change*, published in 1870, recommended the 'removal of Hindu influences from funeral and marriage ceremonies'.[23]

Khan's programme for modernization tied in with his accommodationist policies towards the British. Drawing inspiration from his visit to Cambridge University, Khan established the Muhammadan Anglo-Oriental College at Aligarh in 1874, which later became Aligarh University. This taught both Western and Islamic subjects to generations of students who would go on to staff the colonial administration in India.[24] Aligarh acted as a vehicle of cultural Westernization, teaching young men to play cricket and pursuing Khan's other recommendations from the *Outline for Social and Cultural Change*, such as the 'adoption of European table manners' and 'cultivation of polite manners – in the Western sense'.[25] Khan also began a journal, *Tahdhib al-Akhlaq*, to spread his modernist views.

Ottoman State Reformism

State-led Reformism in the Ottoman Empire provides a classic example of the process that James Gelvin has termed 'defensive developmentalism' – the tactical absorption of Western scientific, educational and military models to prevent European colonial encroachments.[26] The first instigator of the reformist programme was the Sultan Selim III, whose *Nizam-i-Cedid* (New Order) programme of military modernization soon lent its name to a much wider campaign of centralization, bureaucratization and financial regeneration. That the reformist campaign took its name from the new system of military organization is telling – the principal impetus for the state-led reforms appears to have come from the need to stave off advancing Austrian and Russian armies, and the Ottomans quickly learnt that they could not modernize their military without creating a better organized and financially sound state apparatus to support it.[27]

To what extent was Ottoman Reformism actually 'Islamic'? It is often argued that the next wave of reforms from the 1830s onwards, although inspired by efforts to fend off European encroachments, were tantamount to cultural Westernization. For instance, Hanioglu claims that the Gulhane decree of 1839, which initiated the period of restructuring known as the Tanzimat era, was inspired by the French *Declaration de Droits de Homme et du Citoyen*.[28] The reforms thus introduced a codified 'hybrid legal system' based on both Western and Islamic law, and a number of 'bureaucratic-legal institutions' including a Council of State.[29] Most importantly, by treating each individual inhabitant of the Ottoman Empire as a citizen rather than as a subject, they marked a break with the previous Ottoman policy of administering its subjects as members of separate denominational groups, or millets.[30] 'Super-Westernization' led to an increasing social and intellectual gulf between the educated elites and the wider public.[31] Thus the Islamic reform movement that appeared in the Arab territories of the Ottoman Empire did not significantly influence the Tanzimat process at the core of the Ottoman state.[32] Hanioglu's analysis chimes with that provided by the majority of historians of secular post-Ottoman Turkey, although the argument that the Tanzimat was a purely secular process has been challenged by Anscombe's research on Ottoman Reformism. Anscombe contends that 'Islam pervades the Gulhane' and that 'contrary to the assumption of both contemporary Europeans and later historians, the edict does not promise legal equality to all regardless of religion, but rather that all subjects had the right to be treated in accordance with law and that no-one was to be above the law'.[33]

It was one of the ironies of 'defensive developmentalism' that its exercises in self-strengthening often facilitated the European economic and cultural penetration they were designed to prevent. Thus, in attempting to promote state-led modernization of the Ottoman economy, in 1856 the Tanzimat reformers established a central bank – the Ottoman Bank – that was reliant on British capital and had its headquarters in London. Subsequently, a surge in borrowing from Europe caused the Ottoman state to accumulate a heavy debt and led to the establishment of a European-dominated Public Debt Administration; this outraged local intellectuals, who viewed it as an infringement of Ottoman sovereignty.[34] A similar process occurred in Egypt under Ismail Pasha.[35] It is worth observing in this context that the famous historians of the British Empire, Robinson and Gallagher, view rulers like the Ottoman sultans and the Egyptian khedives less as defensive developers and more as intermediaries on the periphery of an 'informal empire'.[36] It is true that when Abdulhamid II came to power in Istanbul in 1876 he promoted an Islamic identity more vigorously than the earlier Tanzimat reformers and consciously denounced imitation of 'Frankish civilization'. Yet, even Abdulhamid's government patronized literary endeavours that led in practice to a diffusion of Western ideas.[37]

While the progressive Ottoman reformers were able to expand and rationalize the Empire's legal system, they made frequent compromises with religious conservatives and autocratic sultans. In the 1870s the *ulama* defeated a proposal by the reformers to establish a Tanzimat Code on the French model, forcing them to base their new civil laws in sharia instead.[38] The 1876 constitution, although it brought the Empire closer to the principle of legal equality for all citizens, did little to challenge the status of the sultan as the supreme source of executive power, leaving to him the power to dismiss ministers and veto parliamentary legislation.[39] In 1878, the sultan brought to power by the reformers of 1876, Abdulhamid II, prorogued the parliament, suspended the constitution and ruled by decree. Yet, even Abdulhamid's rule promoted a form of developmentalism, rapidly expanding the state school system as well as telegraph and railway lines throughout the Empire.[40]

Reformism in North Africa

In North Africa, the Islamic reformists' pursuit of a policy of defensive development was accelerated by a far more immediate colonial threat: the expansion of imperial France across the Mediterranean, beginning with the invasion of Algeria in 1830. Khair al-Din al-Tunisi, the reformist prime minister of the nominally Ottoman province of Tunisia (1873–7), was unable to prevent the eventual occupation of the territory by the French in 1881 but had managed to transform a number of important sectors of Tunisian society, particularly education. During his premiership he established Sadiqi College, which followed a French-style curriculum and taught a number of modern subjects through the medium of the Arabic language. His *Surest Path to Knowledge Concerning the Conditions of Countries*, published in 1867, expressed the belief that progress for Muslim countries would come through the combination of historic Islamic religiosity and statecraft with modern Western knowledge and political values. Like many other Islamic reformers, al-Tunisi's relationship with the West was ambivalent. While he admired European ideas – the French apparently viewed him as one of their own, following the time he spent in Paris in the 1850s and 1860s – he also sought to stave off colonial encroachment and attempted to strengthen Tunisia's ties with the Ottoman sultan as a means of doing so. If the establishment of Sadiqi College was intended to provide the kind of education that would facilitate the emergence of a generation that might guarantee the country's independence, it is ironic that the French colonial government would continue to fund the literary projects of its alumni in the years that followed the occupation, hoping that by promoting a synthesis of French and Islamic values it might be able to justify its colonial presence.[41]

As for Morocco, although its Alawite dynasty was fully independent of the Ottoman Empire, it pursued the Ottoman model of state-led military Reformism more closely than any other regime in North Africa. It was after defeat by the French at the Battle of Isly in 1844 that the dynasty established a *Nizami* army. This was to be recruited on a professional basis and provided with uniforms and regular salaries. To fund this military reform, the Alawites followed the Ottoman, Egyptian and Tunisian model of encouraging European trade so as to benefit from increased customs revenue.[42] This was another example of 'defensive developmentalism' helping to facilitate European expansion rather than stall it. Moreover, the French offered the Moroccans artillery pieces and military instructors in treaties signed soon after Isly, and the *Nizami* army was used against Algerian resistance leader Abd al-Qadir al-Jazairi in 1847, although apparently to little effect.[43] In any case, the Moroccan sultanate suffered like other dynasties in North Africa, with increasing indebtedness to Europe and a consequent erosion of its independence; it was eventually occupied by France in 1912. During the colonial era, a more intellectual strand of Reformism appeared with the rise of Muhammad Alla al-Fasi, a nationalist leader who identified explicitly with the principles of Muhammad Abduh and claimed to be pursuing a modern form of Salafism.[44]

A different pattern emerged in Algeria. Here a *Nizami* model was adopted in the struggle of a resistance leader – Abd al-Qadir al-Jaza'iri – against an already entrenched colonial presence. After beginning his fight with the French in the 1830s with what was relatively traditional force, Abd al-Qadir hired European officers and French drummers, and reorganized his army into regular artillery, cavalry and infantry battalions. At the same time, he continued to stress its Islamic character. He frequently compared it to the first Islamic community of the Prophetic era and organized its daily routine in accordance with the five prayers, as well as ensuring that the entrance of each camp faced east towards Mecca.[45] After the *Nizami* resistance collapsed and Abd al-Qadir surrendered in 1847, later reformers pursued the more pragmatic path of seeking intellectual and religious reformation. In 1931 another 'modernist' Salafi, Abd al-Hamid Ibn Badis, founded the Association of Algerian Ulama. This organization followed Rashid Rida's principle that scholars should be provided with a modern education that had both religious and secular aspects.[46]

Al-Afghani and Abduh

One of the most remarkable facts about Jamal al-Din al-Afghani is that, despite being revered by today's Islamists as the pioneer of Islamic activism in the modern Sunni world, he was – contrary to the narrative of his life disseminated by him at the time – almost certainly born into a Shia background in Iran and educated as a Shia. Accounts of his early life now tend to emphasize that he was born to a family of *sayyids*, or descendants of the Prophet, in Asadabad, and that he was educated at Shia seminaries in Qazvin, Tehran and the holy cities of Ottoman Iraq.[47] Keddie argues that al-Afghani's education as a Shia was hugely significant in that it endowed him with a knowledge of philosophy and rationalist theology that he would not have obtained in the more religiously dogmatic Sunni world at the time. In particular, he became well versed in the writings of the classical Neoplatonist philosophers such as Ibn Sina, and was possibly influenced by the heterodox Shaikhi theological school of nineteenth-century Iran.[48] When al-Afghani's career as a peripatetic Islamic activist in predominantly Sunni lands such as India, Egypt and Anatolia began, he deliberately concealed his Shia background while remaining open about his passion for philosophy. He was still a teenager when he first travelled to India. Here he developed an ardent interest not just in the study of Western sciences, which he encountered for the first time, but also in the battle against Western colonialism, as he witnessed first hand the brutal suppression of the 1857 Indian Mutiny. Keddie suggests that at this point he may well have been inspired by the

Barelvi jihadist movement that followed the teachings of the eighteenth-century revivalist Wali Allah, but she acknowledges the evidence is limited.[49] Although after this point he allied himself to a broader Sunni movement advocating the renewal of Islam through the performance of *ijtihad* and the overcoming of *taqlid*, the crucial significance of his Shia education was that it led him to contribute a more rationalist interpretation of the duty to perform *ijtihad*.

Although his reputation was exaggerated by subsequent admirers, al-Afghani's career remains remarkable. He influenced many rulers, statesmen and political movements in a range of different locations in India, Afghanistan and the Ottoman Empire. He spent time in Afghanistan in the 1860s, Anatolia and then Egypt in the 1870s, France, India (again) and Russia in the 1880s, and Iran then finally Anatolia again before his death in 1897. He participated in anti-British and anti-Khedivial agitation in Egypt as well as the constitutional movement in Iran, and intrigued against the British Empire on his visits to the various other territories. In some regards, he attempted to play the role of the classic Sunni mujaddid who advised a worldly ruler on religious matters,[50] and in this capacity enjoyed the patronage of the amir of Afghanistan and the Ottoman sultan. Nevertheless, the fact that he was subsequently exiled by both of these rulers and machinated against others – among them the Khedive Ismail in Egypt and Nasir al-Din, the Shah of Iran, on account of their willingness to facilitate Britain's economic imperialism – shows that al-Afghani was perhaps more independent than the mujaddids of old. His networking methods were also decidedly more heterodox. He alienated the established scholarly elite in the Ottoman Empire, bringing about his expulsion from Istanbul after his speech on the merits of philosophy infuriated the *Sheyhulislam*.[51] When he fell on his feet in Egypt, it was his membership of the *Kawkab al-Sharq* (Eastern Star) Masonic lodge that enabled him to penetrate the ruling elite and influence senior statesmen such as Muhammad Sharif Pasha.[52] While al-Afghani's most famous protégé, the influential Egyptian reformist Muhammad Abduh, had a clerical training at al-Azhar, it was through a private study circle that he and a number of al-Afghani's other disciples first began to enjoy his patronage.[53]

As for Abduh, until first encountering al-Afghani, his own scholarly life was fairly unremarkable. Born in 1849 in the village of Mahallat al-Nasr in the Egyptian Delta, he had experienced a regular mosque-based education in Tanta before moving to Cairo to study at al-Azhar, one of the principle centres of Sunni Islamic learning in the entire Muslim world.[54] Under al-Afghani he studied Ibn Sina, al-Farabi and the later Iranian philosophers of the Isfahan school, and their influence was visible in the first book he published, *Risalat al-Waridat fi sir al-Tajaliyyat* ('An essay on mystical inspirations from the secrets of revelation'), which addressed debates about God's existence from a philosophical perspective.[55] Soon, his critics at al-Azhar began to claim that he was a follower of the classical Mu'tazilite school. This had advocated a rationalist interpretation of the Quran in the eighth and ninth centuries before the more conservative Asharite theological school came to define Sunni orthodoxy. Abduh denied being a Mu'tazilite; as a critic of *taqlid* he could not follow any one theological school more than another, he claimed. There is, however, little doubt that the rationalist theology he pursued was in many regards similar to that of the Mu'tazilites.[56]

Initially, Abduh joined in wholeheartedly with his mentor's anti-British, anti-Khedivial activism in Egypt. In 1879, he was exiled back to Mahallat al-Nasr, having been accused of involvement in agitation against Ismail as a member of al-Afghani's circle; and upon his return to Cairo he was once more banished – this time outside of Egypt – for supporting the military-led and proto-nationalist Urabist movement of 1882.[57] Between 1884 and 1885 he would join al-Afghani once more in Paris, where the two men co-published the anti-British, pan-Islamic journal *al-Urwa al-Wuthqa* ('the firmest bond'). Yet, in 1888 he made a clean break with his former tutor and his anti-imperialist activism, returning to Egypt and advocating, rather like Sayyid Ahmad Khan, an accommodation with the recently entrenched British colonial order. In the period between 1888 and his death in 1905, Abduh became a firm friend of the most senior British official in Egypt, the agent and consul general, Lord Cromer. With Cromer's blessing, he obtained a number of influential positions, becoming a judge, then a member of the administrative council at al-Azhar, and finally the Mufti of Egypt, whose job was to oversee sharia courts throughout Egypt.[58] He used these positions to develop a number of important proposals for reform of sharia and the education system at al-Azhar, and in doing so alienated many at the historic bastion of Sunni scholarship, an institution he considered to be docile and in need of rejuvenation.[59] In an ironic reversal of roles, he also infuriated the young pro-nationalist Khedive, Abbas Hilmi II, by giving support to the British proposal to replace Ottoman troops on the strategically placed island of Thasos with their own.[60] Abbas Hilmi disliked Abduh's proximity to Cromer. Nevertheless, while it is true that Abduh had become increasingly Europhile in the latter phase of his career, taking repeated vacations in Europe, like al-Afghani, he continued to stress that the European model of progress should not be imitated blindly by Muslims without reference to their own cultural background.[61]

Religion, irreligion and double discourses: A controversy

In 1965, Elie Kedourie published *Afghani and Abduh: An Essay on Religious Unbelief and Political Activism in Modern Islam*. This was controversial because it contended that, far from being revivers of Islam, al-Afghani and Abduh were in fact secretly irreligious and sought to subvert the established faith. Kedourie was a polemical writer and his argument would at least in part have been inspired by his general hostility to Islamism and Arab nationalism, both of which al-Afghani and Abduh influenced.[62] Yet, it is worth looking carefully at these claims, since they touch on some of the central controversies regarding the subject we are studying – namely, how *Islamic* was Islamism (or 'proto-Islamism'), in both a cultural and religious sense?

At times, Kedourie's claims are tendentious and the evidence can easily be dismissed. For instance, in order to demonstrate al-Afghani's 'sceptical relativism', at one point he leans on an account of the ridicule he directed at a group of passengers on a ship who believed he was a *fakir* capable of revealing the future.[63] Yet, a contempt for the customary and more superstitious elements of popular religion was something al-Afghani, like the twentieth-century Islamists, would have shared with strict Hanbali theologians. However, Kedourie's discussion of al-Afghani's debate with the French philosopher, Ernest Renan, during his time in Paris, is more provocative. Responding in the *Journal des Débats* to a lecture delivered by Renan in which he had claimed that Islam and science were fundamentally incompatible, al-Afghani defended Islam as a *civilization*, citing its proud history of fostering philosophers in its classical age. At the same time, he condemned it as a *religion*, conceding that 'wherever it has established itself, this religion has tried to stifle science and it has been marvellously served in its aims by despotism'.[64] Using freshly unearthed correspondence published in Tehran, Kedourie then claims that Abduh wrote to al-Afghani expressing his relief that he had managed to prevent the article being circulated in the Muslim world. Abduh went on to observe

> We regulate our conduct according to your sound rule: we do not cut the head of religion except with the sword of religion. Therefore, if you were to see us now, you would see ascetics and worshippers [of God] kneeling and genuflecting, never disobeying what God commands and doing all that they are ordered to do. Ah! How constricted life would be without hope!'[65]

The exact meaning of this passage is open to interpretation – Sedgwick contends that in referring to the 'head of religion', Abduh did not intend Islam as a whole.[66] He appears to be mocking the principle of 'never disobeying what God commands', although one might argue that in the wider context of the passage he is merely deriding the manner in which some of the more traditional worshippers of whom he and al-Afghani were contemptuous chose to express their obedience.

P.M. Holt criticized Kedourie's text for failing to distinguish between Islamic orthodoxy and Islam itself, and for failing to recognize that the notions of *ijma* and *ijtihad* enabled the Islamic community to reinterpret what they considered to be orthodox. He further observed that Kedourie's comparison of al-Afghani and Abduh to European revolutionary conspirators neglected pre-existing conspiratorial cultures in Islam dating back to those who inspired the Abbasid Revolution.[67] In the same vein Nikkie Keddie, while accepting al-Afghani's heterodoxy and instrumental use of religion, locates these attributes within the broader history of Islamic philosophy. Afghani was influenced by men such as Ibn Sina and al-Farabi, who held that it was pragmatic to offer separate discourses to the elite and the masses. For these men, as for al-Afghani, the religion served an important purpose in uniting the Islamic community, and literalist interpretations had the merit of leaving little room for the formation of potentially divisive sects. This might explain why al-Afghani apparently condemned the Islamic faith in his discussions with Renan, a philosopher, while using it as a mobilizational tool elsewhere in the Islamic world. For instance, in 1881 he published the treatise *Refutation of the Materialists*, in which he condemned the Indian reformer, Sayyid Ahmad Khan, for straying from true religion and collaborating with the British. Here, he emphasized the merits of religious faith as a means of spreading values that furthered human civilization – shame, trustworthiness and honesty.[68]

It was precisely because al-Afghani and Abduh valued the mobilizational capacity of conventional Sunnism that they sought to downplay the heterodox character of their own beliefs. Yet, it was the very heterodoxy of al-Afghani and Abduh that shaped their outlook and activism. Membership of masonic lodges introduced to Egypt from Europe enabled them to form networks of influence that would enable them to guide early Egyptian nationalism.[69] Both men were strongly influenced by the works of the nineteenth-century French statesman, Francois Guizot, particularly his *History of Civilization in Europe*.[70] Guizot's view that the Protestant Reformation had brought about the intellectual transformation that facilitated the rational philosophies as well as the social and political changes of the Enlightenment era influenced al-Afghani's belief that the Islamic world needed to experience a similar process.[71] Yet, the progressive ideology of the two men did not simply derive from European thought. Abduh's evolutionist outlook, although later encouraged by his engagement with Herbert Spencer, can also be traced to the worldview of the seventeenth-century Iranian philosopher Mulla Sidra, who argued that the world was constantly in motion towards a more perfect state.[72] It has been argued that the worldview that Abduh derived from the Iranian mystical philosophers contained 'a hidden impetus for socio-political action'.[73] The belief of al-Afghani and Abduh that prophecy was a product of intellectual genius rather than religious revelations reflects the influence of this same philosophical tradition.[74] Meanwhile, although Abduh attempted in his writings to reconcile the conflicting views of classical theologians who either posited or denied the existence of free will, in his political career he actively broke with the Ashari emphasis on predestination that prevailed in the Sunni world, arguing that Islam needed to rediscover its activist roots.[75]

Rashid Rida

Acting as a pupil to Abduh as Abduh had to al-Afghani before him, Rashid Rida is the intellectual most often credited with carrying on the reformist legacy of the two men into the twentieth century. It has often been argued that, in doing so, Rida took the intellectual tradition they had established in a more conservative and 'fundamentalist' direction, encouraging identification with the new Saudi-Wahhabi state that had emerged after 1924. However, it was the regional diffusion of the Afghani-Abduh brand of Reformism through *al-Urwa al-Wuthqa* that first inspired the young Rida, and drove him to travel from his native Lebanon to study under Abduh in Cairo. He continued al-Afghani and Abduh's legacy by publishing an influential reformist journal, *al-Manar*, between 1898 and 1935, and by establishing a new university, the *Dar al-Dawa wa'l-Irshad* in 1911. The founding of this institution is probably evidence that Rida had learnt from his mentor's relatively unsuccessful efforts to reinvigorate al-Azhar, recognizing that only a separate body could train *ulama* with the right balance of education in 'religious' and 'modern' subjects required to reform Islam in the modern era.[76]

Was Rida more 'fundamentalist' than al-Afghani and Abduh? Wood has concluded that such a characterization would hold only for the latter part of his career; that is, after he became an influential propagandist of the Wahhabi cause. For instance, he advocated the same utilitarian approach to jurisprudence as Abduh and his writing discussed allegorical interpretation of religious texts in depth.[77] His alliance with the Sa'udi-Wahhabi state, which had emerged as the foremost independent Muslim power after the downfall of the Ottoman Empire in 1923, was probably driven by the same pragmatic perspective that had led al-Afghani and Abduh to prioritize unification of the umma over doctrinal and theological differences. It is, nevertheless, true that between 1924 and 1935 Rida attempted to compromise with the more rigid outlook of the Wahhabis.[78]

Even in 1908, before his relationship with the Wahhabis, Rida re-edited Abduh's seminal *Risalat al-Tawhid*, moderating the tone of some of the more controversial passages and removing others altogether. He then re-edited his re-edition in 1934, further criticizing Abduh's views on the role of the *salaf*.[79] On the face of it, Rida was far more religiously orthodox than his predecessors, yet by advocating a more conservative form of Islam he was merely pursuing the same imperative as al-Afghani and the earlier Islamic philosophers in using a simplified version of religious faith to mobilize and unify the umma. Yet, in an era in which print culture was expanding and the reformist school was earning itself a wider reputation among the Muslim public, it was hard to maintain a division between the discourse addressed to the 'philosophers' and the discourse offered to the public at large. While the initial manuscript of the *Risalat al-Tawhid* was not widely distributed, the 1908 re-edition was reprinted on a number of occasions and translated into a variety of languages.[80] In excising controversial passages from Abduh's text, therefore, Rida seems to have been driven by the same motives that led Abduh to prevent the further distribution of al-Afghani's debate with Renan; that is, to keep the discussion of controversial rationalist positions restricted to the elite.

Were Islamic reformers 'Salafis'? The debate

For around the last hundred years, it has been a common assertion in the scholarship on Islamic Reformism or 'Islamic modernism' that the trend initiated by al-Afghani and Abduh represented a form of 'Salafism' or even 'modernist Salafism'. The prevalent interpretation has been that it sought to re-establish 'modern' values supposedly existing in the seventh century but lost because subsequent generations had strayed from the original values of the first generation of Muslims – the pious forefathers, or *salaf* – and blindly imitated the jurisprudence of the four Sunni legal schools. Thus al-Afghani, Abduh and later Rida followed earlier Salafis such as Ibn Taymiyya and Muhammad Ibn Abd al-Wahhab, except that they demanded a more rationalist and 'modern' interpretation of the original sources. The use of 'Salafi' to describe nineteenth-century intellectual modernists caused a degree of confusion in Middle Eastern Studies scholarship, particularly as the notion of modernist Salafism disappeared from broader public discourse in the latter half of the twentieth century and the 'purist' Salafism propagated by the Sa'udi-Wahhabis came to represent the best-known form of the doctrine.[81]

In an influential article from 2010 and his later monograph, *The Making of Salafism*, Henri Lauzière challenged the notion that al-Afghani and Abduh were 'modernist Salafis', arguing that the popularization of this notion occurred only as a result of the unintentional falsification of the historical record by Orientalists such as Louis Massignon and Ignaz Goldziher, the latter of whom had argued that Muhammad Abduh and Rashid Rida followed 'cultural Wahhabism'.[82] It was Massignon who in 1919 introduced the belief that Salafism was an intellectual movement that could be traced back to al-Afghani and Abduh and even the founder of the Indian *Ahl-i-Hadith* movement, Siddiq Hasan Khan, before them. Massignon did so in his attempt to analyse the blending of modern science with classical Islamic knowledge found in the 1917 journal *Majalla al-Salafiyya* or Salafiyya Review, published by an associate of Rida's via the Salafiyya Bookstore in Cairo.[83] Here, Lauzière argues, Massignon was unnecessarily projecting a loose contemporary notion of 'Salafiyya' – onto the nineteenth-century past. The idea of an historic 'modernist Salafism' largely came about as a result of Massignon's mistake. The notion is flawed, he argues, for a number of reasons. Whereas late-twentieth- and twenty-first-century Salafism denotes an all-encompassing cultural, jurisprudential, and theological movement influenced by the totalizing ideologies of the modern era, prior to this stage the term 'Salafi' merely denoted a school of creedal interpretation concerned with doctrine rather than jurisprudence.[84] Moreover, there is no evidence that al-Afghani, Abduh and others identified themselves as being Salafi by creed.[85]

Frank Griffel has countered Lauzière and maintained that the use of the term 'Salafi' to describe Abduh can be justified on the grounds that Abduh genuinely advocated recapturing the ideals of Islam's 'pious forefathers', even though – unlike later Salafis, who were more narrowly focused on the seventh century – Abduh included the great theologians and philosophers of the third and fourth Islamic centuries in his definition of the *salaf*.[86] He further justified the use of the term 'Salafi' to label individuals who did not describe themselves as such via analogy with the ex post facto coining of the term 'socialism'.[87] Lauzière responded to Griffel's criticism by arguing that a desire to emulate the *salaf* was commonplace in Sunni scholarship, and must be differentiated from identification with Salafism as a doctrine.[88] Nevertheless, Lauzière does acknowledge that Rida himself expanded the meaning of the term 'Salafi' beyond its original theological sense, arguing in 1914 that it signified 'nothing other than acting according to the Quran and the Sunna without any accretion'.[89] This prefigured the efforts of later 'purist' Salafis to transform the doctrine into a normative programme for Islamic living, and Rida facilitated the convergence of the late reformist and Wahhabi trend by dispatching a number of his own disciples to lecture in the universities established by Abd al-Aziz Ibn Sa'ud.[90] At the same time, a number of 'modernist Salafis' would emerge in mid-twentieth-century North Africa who derived their understanding of 'Salafism' from Massignon's flawed interpretation.[91]

Reformism and Sufism

As the revivalists' relationship with Sufism was ambivalent, so was that of the reformists. Being advocates of modernization, they were reacting to a context in which colonial economic transformations had undermined the commercial power base of traditional Sufism in the artisans' guilds and historic trading networks.[92] Like revivalists, reformists were hostile to the more popular, customary and 'superstitious' elements of Sufism, including the worshipping of saints.[93] Abduh would later attribute his escape from the sterility of traditional Islam to the influence of his uncle, Shaykh Darwish, a Sufi of the Shadhiliyya Tariqa, who probably came under the influence of the revivalist 'neo-Sufi' orders such as the Tijaniyya and Sanusiyya;[94] Rashid Rida was a Murid in the Nashqbandiyya Sufi order, also influenced by earlier revivalist currents.[95]

Nevertheless, for al-Afghani and Abduh in particular, there was another source of inspiration not found in mainstream Sunni Revivalism – the philosophically orientated Shia Sufi tradition which the former had embraced during his educational upbringing in Iran.[96] Indeed, Abduh acted towards his mentor as a Sufi disciple would towards his Shaykh. His 1874 treatise, *Risala al-Waridat*, using classic Sufi terminology, referred to the knowledge he took from al-Afghani as 'mystical inspirations' and 'revelations'.[97] After Abduh made a break with al-Afghani by making his peace with the British and returning to Egypt, he began to distance himself from his Sufi past and such symbology was far less evident in his later text, *Risalat al-Tawhid* (Theology of Unity).[98] Part of the reason that Abduh's Sufism has not been fully acknowledged by posterity is that Rashid Rida – who also gravitated away from the Sufism of his youth towards Wahhabism in the 1920s – downplayed the extent of his teacher's explicit identification with Sufism when he re-edited *Risalat al-Waridat* in 1925.[99]

Democracy

Although it was the Islamic reformers of the nineteenth century whose cross-identification of Islamic and Western concepts helped to inspire the equation of the Quranic value of *shura* (consultation) with modern mass democracy, many in the first wave of Reformism, such as al-Afghani, Abduh and al-Tunisi, employed a much more restricted and perhaps more literal understanding of the principle of *shura*. For al-Afghani and Abduh, *shura* required that rulers consult not the public at large but those who had sufficient expertise, either in matters of religion – the *ulama* – or the modern sciences, to decide what was in the public interest. In this context, autocracy was perfectly acceptable.[100] Abduh did not reject the principle of representative government outright but, like a number of European statesmen at the time, objected to the principle of mass enfranchisement, arguing that 'the lowest class of the workers ... perform the function of deaf instruments'.[101] The Ottoman reformists who drew up the constitution of 1876 were more committed to the principle of representative government, but structured the electoral system to ensure that the ensuing parliament would retain an elitist character: they introduced a two-tier structure in which local assemblies established through a limited democratic process would elect representatives to the Ottoman parliament in lieu of a direct popular vote.[102]

The first reformists' objections to democracy were not necessarily absolute, and were not rooted in the anti-humanism of later radicals. More often they were a product of the immediate context to which the reformists had to adapt. For instance, Abduh argued that, because Egypt was still in the very early phases of political growth, the emergence of constitutional governance must inevitably be a slow process guided by a small elite.[103] Sayyid Ahmad Khan opposed one-man, one-vote elections in India on the grounds that they would empower the Hindu majority over the Muslim minority, and feared that representative government and the withdrawal of the British colonial regime might lead to a destructive communal conflict.[104] The Islamic reformers of the first half of the twentieth century, including theorists such as Rashid Rida and leaders of mass political parties such as Muhammad Allal al-Fasi, were much more flexible in their interpretation of the relationship between Islamic and democratic concepts in an era of mass nationalism. Rida argued that the Islamic principle of *ijma* (consensus) could act as a framework to support political pluralism, and equated the *ahl al-hall wa'l-aqd* ('people who loose and bind') with the representatives of a modern parliament, with the exception that the greater virtue and wisdom of these individuals would make them superior to the representatives of a Western democratic system.[105] Rida even advocated revolution against tyrannical rulers who refused to allow political participation.[106]

Nationalism and jihad

Islamic Reformism was often defined as much by its mode of engagement with Western colonialism, whether rejectionist or accommodationist, than it was by any specific Western or Islamic ideology per se. This was why the most versatile and influential Islamic reformers, al-Afghani and Abduh, advocated linguistic, territorial or pan-Islamic nationalism according to the specific political context they encountered. In 1870s Egypt, they allied themselves to a movement that campaigned against British economic interventionism via the slogan 'Egypt for the Egyptians'; and, while based in India in the 1880s, al-Afghani supported linguistic and territorial nationalism (*jinsiyya*) in the subcontinent even to the point of encouraging Muslim–Hindu unity, as opposed to unity with the wider Muslim community.[107] Yet, when writing in his journal, *al-Urwa al-Wuthqa*, which advocated pan-Islamic nationalism as the best means to revive the Muslim community and was sold throughout the Muslim world in the mid-1880s, al-Afghani condemned territorial or *jinsiyya* nationalism as no better than tribalism.[108] His support for pan-Islamism was in itself a pragmatic adjustment to context. By supporting the ideology propagated by the new Ottoman sultan, Abdulhamid II, he could ally his own brand of Islamic Reformism to the sultan's campaign against the perceived Westernism of the early Tanzimat.[109]

It is on account of their identification with modern anti-colonial nationalism that Islamic reformists have been credited with establishing the 'defensive' school of jihad;[110] radical Islamists have condemned them for it.[111] However, different thinkers constituted defensive jihad in different ways. Probably the most quietist interpretation of the doctrine was that of Sayyid Ahmad Khan in India, who argued that jihad should only be regarded as an obligation when there was 'positive oppression or obstruction in the exercise of their faith ... impair[ing] the foundation of some of the pillars of Islam'.[112] Khan hoped that such declarations would facilitate his strategy of accommodation with British colonial rule and help reverse the British policy of favouring Hindus over Muslims for administrative positions.[113] It was precisely such statements that earned him the hostility of al-Afghani, who advocated a much more forceful response to the British presence in colonial India. As for al-Afghani, his far-reaching activism often blurred revivalist and reformist understandings of jihad. He effectively practised *takfir* when he declared that Sayyid Ahmad Khan 'took some steps to throw off his religion and adopt the religion of the English'.[114] Following in the footsteps of the Barelvi movement, he sought to use Afghanistan as a base from which to rally support against British Imperialism in India,[115] and publicly lauded the Sudanese Mahdi's jihad against the British-backed Turco-Egyptian regime in Sudan.[116] Nevertheless, the principal inspiration behind al-Afghani's activities was his anti-colonial politics, rather than any rigorous attachment to religious scripture.[117] Moreover, he was happy to work with Hindus in India, and Christians and Jews in Egypt, in his battle against British colonialism.[118]

A more scripturally rooted articulation of the doctrine of defensive jihad came from al-Afghani's mentee, Muhammad Abduh. The classic jurisprudential ruling was that jihad should be understood as *fard al-ayn* (an individual duty imposed on every adult male Muslim) only when Muslim lands were invaded. But this was not enough for Abduh. In *al-Urwa al-Wuthqa*, composed during his anti-colonialist phase, he maintained that the entire community should be mobilized to protect the Dar al-Islam even in time of peace.[119] Similar arguments were later advanced by Osama bin Laden,[120] although given Abduh's heterodox religious views and subsequent reconciliation with the British it is perhaps unsurprising that he has not been taken as a role model by contemporary jihadis.

Like that of his mentor, Rida's conception of national and religious struggle evolved throughout his career. Similar to Sayyid Ahmad Khan and (at times), Abduh, during the early phase of his career he embraced Egypt's British occupiers, refusing to denounce them as imperialists and going so far as to accept Western narratives that portrayed the 'Anglo-Saxons' as a superior race.[121] During the First World War, Rida was even willing to cooperate with British plans to establish an Arab caliphate under King Hussein to replace that of the Ottomans.[122] However, after the British and French decided to divide the Arab territories of the Ottoman Empire between themselves following the war, Rida became increasingly disillusioned with the British and began to condemn their 'plot to colonize nations'.[123]

Reformism as proto-Islamism?

While the reformists foreshadowed the growth of twentieth-century religio-political parties in a number of regards, there was no linear evolution from Reformism to Islamism. Reformism was an intellectually and politically diverse movement that affected a broad range of intellectual and religious trends. Just as al-Afghani and Abduh influenced late-nineteenth-century nationalist movements, Sayyid Ahmad Khan's establishment of Aligarh laid the framework for the emergence of generations of secular-nationalist elites in Pakistan. Meanwhile, the schools established by the Ottoman reform movement educated the individuals who would shape Kemal's secular nationalism in post-Ottoman Turkey.[124] Many twentieth-century intellectuals who saw themselves as 'Islamic modernists' or 'Islamic liberals' opposed to Islamism had Abduh as a reference point.[125] Later 'radical Islamists', such as Mawdudi and Qutb, would criticize the reformists' emphasis on reason, as well as their propagation of a doctrine of defensive jihad.[126]

Nevertheless, as the first Islamist party, the Muslim Brotherhood continued to revere al-Afghani ('the announcer'), Abduh and Rida ('the archivist') as its intellectual forefathers.[127] In many regards, these individuals laid the framework for later Islamist activism. Journals such as *al-Urwa al-Wuthqa* and *al-Manar* helped disseminate the reformists' belief that Islam could be reconciled with contemporary political ideals and thus created a natural constituency among the educated elites that later Islamists could develop. Meanwhile, Rida's reformulation of the reformist tradition to bring it closer to Sunni orthodoxy would certainly have helped make it more accessible for Islamists. His theorization of the Islamic state would later prove useful to Khomeini and Mawdudi.[128] The reformists sought to downplay doctrinal and sectarian differences so as to broaden their appeal, and Islamists would later pursue the same strategy.[129] Like the reformists, Islamists sought to criticize and mobilize the *ulama* and the Sufis simultaneously.

Suggested reading: Primary

Jamal al-Din's Response to Renan, *Journal Des Débats*, from N. R. Keddie, *An Islamic Response to Imperialism* (London: University of California Press, 1983).

Read alongside:
Keddie, Nikki R., *An Islamic Response to Imperialism: Political and Religious Writings of Sayyid Jamal al-Din 'al-Afghani'* (London: University of California, 1983), pp. 89–99.

Questions: What does this say about whether Jamal al-Din al-Afghani (as one of the 'forefathers' of Islamism) was a 'fundamentalist'? What is his view of the relationship between religion and science? How does al-Afghani challenge Renan's conflation of rational capacity with racial identity? To what extent do we have to consider the context and the audience when examining this source? Why did al-Afghani express very different ideas about religion in other contexts?

Debate: To what extent was the character of Islamic Reformism shaped by European colonialism?

Debate readings:
Youssef M. Choueiri, *Islamic Fundamentalism: The Story of Islamist Movements* (third edition, London: Continuum, 2010), 23–7, 35–50.
Elie, Kedourie, *Afghani and 'Abduh: An Essay on Religious Unbelief and Political Activism in Modern Islam* (London: Frank Cass, 1997).
Sedgwick, Mark, *Muhammad Abduh* (Oxford: Oneworld, 2009).
Scharbrodt, Oliver, 'The Salafiyya and Sufism: Muhammad Abduh and his Risala al-Waridat', *Bulletin of the School of Oriental and African Studies* 70 (2007), 89–115.

5

The first Islamists:

Hasan al-Banna and the Muslim Brotherhood, 1928–54

The status of the Muslim Brotherhood (*al-Ikhwan al-Muslimun*) as the first Islamist political party places it at the core of every academic and political debate on Islamism. When it took power in Egypt for the first time in 2012 via the Freedom and Justice Party of Muhammad Morsi, these questions were brought to the forefront of the international agenda. Was the Muslim Brotherhood genuinely willing to adapt to democracy, or was it just using democracy as a vehicle to bring about an autocratic and repressive Islamist state? Would a Brotherhood government reject modern values, discriminate against religious minorities and express general hostility towards the West? These were the same questions that scholars had sought to answer ever since the Brotherhood was first established by Hasan al-Banna in Ismailiyya in 1928.

For a generation, the leading text on the Muslim Brotherhood was Richard Mitchell's seminal *Society of Muslim Brothers*, originally published in 1968. Mitchell's approach reflected that of the American scholarship of his day, which was driven by the assumptions of 'modernization theory'.[1] This postulated that Westernization and modernization were inextricably linked processes, and that the path to development in non-Western, postcolonial countries must emulate that of Western countries.[2] It followed that any movement that rejected Western values must be rooted in xenophobia, ideological atavism and traditionalism. To discount the West was to reject both modernity and democracy. This school of thought is very much evident in Mitchell's analysis of the Brotherhood's origins, methods and activism. He frequently emphasizes the essentially violent and xenophobic character of its politics – although he is perhaps more careful to highlight the colonial roots of this violent outlook than his critics credit – and in particular stresses the authoritarian character of al-Banna's leadership.[3] This pattern of analysis also coloured interpretations of the Brotherhood's demographic origins, as scholars of Mitchell's era identified the typical young Ikhwani as a rural–urban migrant struggling to adapt his traditional values to the modern life of the city.[4]

Since the 1960s, a newer generation of scholars has sought to challenge Mitchell and emphasize the Brotherhood's 'modern' credentials. One line of thought argues that the Brotherhood was influenced far more by modern ideologies such as nationalism and socialism than either its supporters or its critics would acknowledge, and that its religious slogans were mere window-dressing.[5] Naturally, this does not challenge Modernization Theory's dichotomy between the 'modern/secular' and 'Islamic'. In 1998 Brynjar Lia's *The Society of Muslim Brothers in Egypt: The Rise of a Mass Movement* offered a more confident challenge to the assumptions of Modernization Theory. Lia, who strongly criticized Mitchell's account, characterized the Brotherhood as a meritocratic movement that appealed not just to the socially alienated peri-urban poor but also to a core constituency of educated lower-middle-class students and professionals who sought to challenge the patrimonial basis of the existing Egyptian political order.[6] While Lia's scholarship offered a forceful challenge to the assumptions of Modernization Theory, it only fleetingly addressed one of the central problematics in the study of the Brotherhood and other Islamist groups – whether its ideology was rooted in Islam itself, or was a mimicry of Western secular ideologies.

Central to the ambiguity concerning the Brotherhood's status as a 'modern' movement is the question of its relationship to the 'reformist' and 'radical' trends. As we have seen, Ayubi argues that while the reformist trend of Afghani and Abduh sought to 'modernize Islam', the Muslim Brothers sought to 'Islamize modernity'.[7] Mura perhaps hints at al-Banna's ambivalent relationship to each of these trends when he comments that he sought to 'Islamize modernity' while 'modernizing tradition'.[8] Choueiri, meanwhile, represents the Brotherhood as the last wave of the 'reformist' trend, contending that while al-Banna was the first reformist to establish a political party, he followed Abduh and Rida in seeking to 'reconcile Islam with the modern world'.[9] However, Soage perceives an essential continuity between the ideology of al-Banna and that of Qutb, the foremost Islamist radical.[10] It is only by focusing on such critical historiographical debates that we can answer one of the most pressing questions of today: Can there be a 'moderate' Islamism, or was the radicalization of Islamism in the 1960s inevitable?

Egypt and the Middle East, 1919–c.1950

The Muslim Brotherhood emerged at a time of considerable political tumult in Egypt and the wider Middle Eastern region. British promises to the Hashemite Sharif Hussein of Mecca during the First World War had raised hopes that an Arab Caliphate might replace that proclaimed by the Ottoman sultan in Istanbul. Rashid Rida, one of the late Islamic reformists, offered himself as a go-between in these negotiations.[11] By the middle of the 1920s, neither an Arab nor an Ottoman Caliphate remained a possibility. The Ottoman Empire had been dismantled by the Turkish secular nationalists who seized control of Anatolia and the British imperialists who had retreated on their promises of the war years and divided the Levant between themselves and the French. Hussein's caliphal aspirations ended when the founder of modern Saudi Arabia, Abd al-Aziz Ibn Sa'ud, reconquered Mecca in 1924. Although considerable prestige accrued to the Saudis from their seizure of the Holy Places, Rida's plans to install Ibn Sa'ud as the next caliph never came to fruition. It might be argued that it was no coincidence that the Muslim Brotherhood was established only four years after the collapse of the final (widely recognized) caliphate. Yet, it is worth remembering that the Islamic world had been deprived of an effective caliph for many centuries until the Ottoman sultan, Abdul Hamid II, attempted to revive the title in earnest in the 1870s. Moreover, while the Brotherhood probably exploited the general sense of civilizational malaise that accompanied the downfall of the Ottomans,[12] the notion of the caliphate actually played only a relatively minor role in its rhetoric and ideology.[13]

Another major feature of the Islamic world in the first half of twentieth century was its penetration by global ideologies which were assisted by rapid advances in mass communications in their quest to offer holistic societal visions to mass audiences. In 1919, the Marxist–Leninist revolutionaries who had overthrown the Russian aristocracy two years earlier established the Comintern so as to globalize their campaign for a classless society; the Egyptian Communist Party was established in 1921. Soon afterwards, fascist parties glorifying racial nationalism and state authoritarianism seized power in Italy and Germany. Although there was no fascist equivalent of the Comintern, it has been suggested that fascist ideologies influenced a number of regional parties, including the Lebanese Phalangists, Young Egypt[14] and the Muslim Brotherhood itself.[15] Although, as we shall see, Islamist ideology can be clearly differentiated from that of the far left and the far right, the emergence of communism and fascism certainly helped to shape the political environment in which the Muslim Brotherhood operated.

Although arguments about communism and fascism feature prominently in the more polemical analyses of Islamism's origins, the local context in which the Brotherhood emerged was defined by two other 'isms' – colonialism and nationalism. In 1928, Egypt was in its forty-sixth year of British occupation, although both the 'Veiled Protectorate' (1882–1914) and the actual Protectorate (1914–22) declared when Britain severed Egypt from the Ottoman Empire had already come to an end. The nationalist revolution of 1919, led by the Wafd Party of Sa'ad Zaghlul, had forced the British to consent to Egypt's nominal independence and the drafting of a constitution that guaranteed the holding of nationwide elections with full adult male suffrage. In practice, colonialism continued – whether in the more narrow political sense, as the British forced the Egyptian kings to prorogue parliaments, or culturally, as Western professors and ideas dominated institutions such as the University of Cairo and the American University of Cairo, and Western missionary societies exploited the protected status granted to foreigners under the 1922 Allenby Declaration to proselytize in the country.[16] A similar situation obtained elsewhere in the region – nationalist revolutions in Iraq in 1920 and Syria in 1925 were violently crushed by the British and French respectively, but led to gradual concessions. In Iraq, a superficial system of liberal democracy was frequently undermined by party infighting and a constitutional monarch supported by an expanded royal prerogative and British airbases.

With the disappearance of the Ottoman Empire as an Islamic, multicultural and transnational polity, local intellectuals reacted to the European imposition of boundaries between a variety of semi-colonial countries by embracing ideologies of territorial nationalism. Sometimes, these nationalists spoke of their peoples' blood ties to those who had inhabited their region in the pre-Islamic past – the Phoenicians in the case of Lebanon, or the Pharaohs in Egypt.[17] By the 1930s, forms of nationalism espousing Arabism as a linguistic and cultural bond began to prevail, and – although Arab unity was never achieved – the establishment of the Arab League in 1945 was evidence of the vitality of this ideology.[18] Each of these nationalist movements was supported by the 'effendiyya' – members of an up and coming political class educated in semi-colonial, semi-secular schools. In the inter-war period, therefore, the Islamism of the Muslim Brotherhood was forced to compete with a number of less religiously orientated ideologies.

Hasan Al-Banna's early life and the founding of the Brotherhood

Al-Banna's childhood and education exhibit a number of themes pertinent to understanding the later generations of Islamists in Egypt and further afield who would attempt to emulate his career: the transition from a religious rural background to a semi-secular urban environment; the influence of Sufism; and the opportunities offered by state education. While al-Banna was typical of the majority of modern Islamists in that he was not trained as a religious scholar, it is perhaps significant that his father, Ahmad, was so schooled, having been a student at al-Azhar of Muhammad Abduh.[19] Ahmad was a small-scale landowner and the local Imam in Mahmudiyya, the provincial town where Hasan was born in 1906.[20] Therefore, although al-Banna did not pursue the religious sciences himself, the domestic education in classical Islamic studies he received at the hands of his father inculcated in him values that shaped his attitude towards his later, more secular education. Another major influence was the local branch of the Hasafiyya Sufi order, which the young Hasan would join as a disciple after having first taken an interest at the age of twelve. Noting al-Banna's immersion in Sufi modes of piety from an early age might help us challenge the oft-assumed dichotomy between Islamism and Sufism; al-Banna was not just passionately Sufi, but as a member of the Hasafi order he also engaged in a number of the heterodox and customary practices condemned by representatives of the revivalist tradition, such as tomb visitation.[21] It might be that the emotionally charged relationship between Sufi shaykh and disciple in the Hasafiyya order inspired al-Banna's own manner of relating to members of the Brotherhood.[22]

Al-Banna's intensely religious early upbringing shaped his behaviour as a school pupil. At his local primary school, he became the leader of its Society for Moral Behaviour. He reports in his memoirs that at one point during his membership of this society he engaged in moral vigilantism by reporting a local shipbuilder to the police for constructing a figure out of wood.[23] Such actions might be construed as representing a desire to restructure the urban environment he encountered in accordance with his religious principles, rather than to reconcile those principles with that new environment. Having spent three years in a Primary Teachers' Training School in Damanhur, at the age of sixteen he travelled to Cairo to attend the prestigious Dar al-Ulum. Again, he took against many aspects of city life, particularly the literary salons, the partying and the secular nationalism of the urban intellectuals that was bringing about the downfall of the Ottoman Caliphate.[24] Dar al-Ulum had been established in 1872 to provide a more 'traditional' alternative to the Anglophone curriculum of Cairo University, and this provided al-Banna with the unique blend of Islamic and Western learning that would shape his Islamist outlook and that of later generations. He studied subjects such as geography, mathematics, science and foreign languages alongside Islamic jurisprudence and Quranic exegesis.[25] The fact that the language of instruction was Arabic would have enabled him to embrace modern knowledge within his own cultural and linguistic framework.

Although al-Banna was hostile to what he perceived as the more dissolute characteristics of the urban social order, his intense identification with Sufism and its customary modes of belief enabled him to connect to the ordinary Muslim public. Indeed, one crucial factor in the rise of the Ikhwan as a mass movement was that it was willing to embrace the existing social and political order in a manner that later radicals (notably Qutb) would not. When, in 1927, al-Banna took up his job as a primary teacher in Ismailiyya, the city where he would found the Muslim Brotherhood in the following year, he saw that to spread his message it would be necessary to cultivate the most prominent members of the local community, including the Sufi shaykhs, *ulama* and elders of the leading families.[26] When he moved to Cairo in 1932 and began to expand the Brotherhood as a nationwide political force, he stepped up this policy by targeting Egypt's political and religious leadership. In the late 1930s, his movement was in favour with the rector of al-Azhar, Shaykh Mustafa Maraghi, and the Egyptian prime minister Ali Mahir Pasha, who sought a political force that could be used against the populist Wafd party.[27] In 1936, al-Banna wrote to King Faruq with a missive entitled 'Towards the Light' (*Nahwa al-Nur*), providing a series of recommendations for reshaping the social, economic and political order along Islamic lines.[28]

Al-Banna and his early movement were just as adept at penetrating society at large as they were the upper echelons of the political order. The Brotherhood's charitable and educational endeavours were crucial to its establishment of a wider social base. Beginning in Ismailiyya, each local branch of the movement that emerged established a mosque, school or social club that might serve as a focal point for communal engagement.[29] From the mid-1930s, they had also begun to establish pharmacies and healthcare clinics.[30] By the 1940s the Brotherhood was conducting benevolent activities in the majority of Egypt's towns and villages.[31] This provided the movement with a social base not enjoyed by other contemporary radical groups, notably the communists.[32]

One reason for the Brotherhood's growing popularity was its ability to present itself as a force that fought against the two great evils that beset the Muslim community: British colonialism in Egypt and British-backed Zionism in Palestine. While the British had granted formal independence to Egypt in the Allenby Declaration of 1922, they retained the right to maintain military bases in Egypt; and there was a particularly strong concentration of British troops at Ismailiyya, located near the vital British asset that was the Suez Canal. It is telling that the first six members whom al-Banna recruited to the Brotherhood were labourers working in one of the military camps – along with al-Banna, they took an oath to be 'troops [jund] for the message of Islam'.[33] From the beginning, the militarism of the colonial occupation appeared to find its parallel in the movement that resisted it. Yet, the Brotherhood did not immediately declare war on the foreign occupation.

Meanwhile, Britain's support for Zionist settlement in her League of Nations-backed Mandate in Palestine infuriated Arab nationalists and Islamists alike. In 1917 Lord Balfour, the British foreign secretary, had issued his famous declaration, promising the establishment of a 'Jewish nationalist home' in Palestine; and Britain's subsequent facilitation of Jewish migration to Palestine sparked fears that the local Arab population would lose out. Tying itself to the struggle of the Palestinians against Zionism and colonialism in Palestine further enabled the Brotherhood to expand its profile on both the national and international stage. From 1936 to 1939, large sections of the Arab population of Palestine rose up in protest against British support for Jewish immigration to their land, as well as against a British-backed plan to partition the territory into separate Arab and Jewish states. Liaising closely with the Higher Arab Committee in Palestine, al-Banna established a Central Committee for aid to Palestine that mobilized the movement's various regional branches in order to supply funds to the rebels. The Brotherhood also used its network of local mosques and schools to disseminate propaganda supporting the Palestinian cause.[34] Its pro-Palestine activism contributed markedly to the rapid expansion of its membership. Between 1935 and 1940, the number of active branches increased fourfold and the movement increasingly began to appeal to the youth.[35] It was also able to exploit the Palestine issue to delegitimize the existing political forces in Egypt, notably the secular-nationalist Wafd party that in spite of leading the government appeared unable to challenge British Imperialism and support the Palestinians.[36]

Membership and structure

Socio-economic analyses of the Brotherhood's membership are at the core of the debate over its relationship with 'modernity'. One view sees it as a movement appealing to migrants from the rural areas struggling to reconcile their 'traditional' values with those of the city.[37] Nevertheless, as Ziad Munson has persuasively argued, careful observation of membership data relating to the Ikhwan challenges overly deterministic assumptions about the relationship between rapid urbanization and identification with Islamists' ideology.[38] First of all, the mass mobilization of the Brotherhood actually occurred across two decades – from the late 1920s to the late 1940s – in which the rate of urbanization in Egypt had declined.[39] Far from representing those who existed at the margins of urban modernity, the leading Brothers had access to the professional networks that were at the core of the major cites' social elite.[40] Most noticeably, the upper echelons of the Brotherhood consisted largely of middle-class members of the *effendiyya* elite, trained either in the modern universities or institutions such as Dar al-Ulum. For instance, of the thirty-two Brothers tried following the 1948 Jeep case, there were eight civil servants, five teachers, seven white collar workers, seven small business owners, two students, a preacher, a farmer and a medical practitioner.[41]

There are many different interpretations of the significance of the middle-class and professional roots of the Brotherhood. Lia contends that its lower-middle-class roots made it 'the first non-elite political force to challenge the ruling classes in Egypt', arguing that they consistently emphasized meritocracy over social prestige.[42] Soage, meanwhile, emphasizes the fact that the majority of the movement's members were 'craftsmen, traders and professionals' in order to reject the notion that it 'worked for the promotion of the working classes'.[43]

Was the organization and structure of the society meritocratic? It is true that there were sections established to mobilize workers, peasants, professionals and students.[44] Nevertheless, Brotherhood ideology – at least if taken at face value – aimed to transcend class differences in the name of religion, rather than promote the interests of particular classes. The society's General Law required that individuals progress through the various stages of membership not on the basis of social prestige but in accordance with their study and memorization of important ideological tracts and collections of hadiths, knowledge of which was deemed essential to the Brotherhood's mission.[45] According to one's familiarity with these key texts, a member could rise from being an 'assistant' (musa'id) to 'associate' (muntasib) to 'worker' ('amil) and 'activist' (mujahid).[46] In theory, the organization of the Brotherhood was also highly democratic. The twelve members of the executive leadership body, the General Guidance Council, were elected by members of the movement's 100–150 strong Consultative Assembly every two years.[47] However, the fact that nine of the twelve members were to be from Cairo reinforced the urban bias of the movement.[48] That said, the Brotherhood's federated structure allowed for the establishment of branches in every district, which operated with a considerable degree of autonomy.[49]

For Lia, the Brotherhood's bureaucratic framework, as well as its systems of individual promotion and election to office, provide evidence that it was not driven purely by al-Banna's charisma, but that it possessed many of the 'legal-rational' characteristics identified by Weber as a more modern source of authority.[50] His revisionist account breaks here with that of Mitchell, who insists that the theoretically democratic regulations 'were in practice superseded by authoritarian direction'.[51] A key area of contention is the role of al-Banna as the General Guide. While Mitchell argues that he was 'the final and unqualified authority in the Society',[52] and cites numerous examples of hero worship by his followers as evidence of the centrality of his charisma, Lia seeks to qualify these points, noting for instance that the General Law required members to pledge themselves to 'the principles of the society' and not to al-Banna himself; and that by preaching the slogan 'the Prophet is our leader' the Ikhwan downplayed al-Banna's own personality.[53]

In the 1940s, the international dimension of Ikhwan membership expanded, as the movement established branches in most of the emerging nations of the Arab world. However, branches were often established as a result of local initiatives, and adapted their own policies to meet the specific political circumstances of their own countries. In Jordan, the local branch was established by a businessman, al-Atif Abu Qura, and achieved a more harmonious relationship with the local monarchy than al-Banna had managed.[54] The Syrian Brotherhood, established by Mustafa al-Sibai in the late 1930s, dabbled with socialist ideas more explicitly than the parent organization in Egypt.[55] In spite of its pan-Islamist rhetoric, the Muslim Brotherhood has largely remained a movement of the Arab Middle East, with the Jama'at-i-Islami, for instance, emerging as the predominant Islamist party in South Asia (see next chapter).

World War, the emergence of the Special Apparatus, and dissolution

When the Second World War broke out in 1939, the British moved troops back into Egypt en masse, and the country went on to act as the fulcrum of Churchill's war effort in the Middle East. Although the Anglo-Egyptian Treaty of 1936 had sanctioned a greater troop deployment by the British at time of war, these events predictably caused great consternation across the Egyptian political spectrum. The outbreak of the war provided another opportunity for the Muslim Brotherhood to expand. Although the Egyptian regime, under pressure from the British, restricted the activities of political parties, the Brotherhood's somewhat ambiguous status as a charitable organization enabled it to continue mobilizing support and growing.[56] In the first two years of the war, al-Banna called for members to avoid confronting the British occupiers and the Egyptian government, hoping that by avoiding repression he would be able to increase the movement's support base.[57] Meanwhile, he entered into secret contacts with dissident army officers – including future president Anwar Sadat – in the hope of arranging a joint movement against the British, although it seems that Sadat did not trust the Brotherhood sufficiently for these plans to reach fruition.[58] In October 1941, al-Banna moved towards public condemnation of the British, delivering a fiery speech calling upon the Egyptian public to 'rise up' against their 'imperialist policies'. As a result, he was arrested by the Egyptian government, along with other leading members of the Ikhwan.[59] After the Wafdist prime minister, Nahhas, pushed al-Banna to withdraw from the 1942 elections, the Brotherhood largely remained on the margins of the political scene for the rest of the war.

Nevertheless, the events of the war years had a significant impact on the future direction of the society. First of all, by reluctantly acquiescing in the British occupation, the Wafd party had delegitimized itself in the eyes of the public, so enabling the Ikhwan to challenge its status as the premier political party in Egypt.[60] The Brotherhood was now a serious competitor with the Wafd in previous strongholds; these included university campuses, the civil service and the rural areas.[61] Moreover, the repression it faced during the war had convinced the senior echelons of the Brotherhood that it must form a covert military wing. Established at some point between 1942 and 1943, the Special Apparatus was at the centre of the subsequent conflicts between the government and the Society that ultimately led to al-Banna's assassination in 1949. It benefited from both the military training given by the government to Egyptian civilians during the war and the proliferation of arms caches resulting from it.[62] It did not enter directly into conflict with the British or the government, but established its own intelligence service to spy on the occupiers.[63]

The activities of the Special Apparatus in the post-war years are at the core of debates as to whether the Brotherhood was (and is) a 'moderate' organization, or a violent group committed to more 'radical' strategies for political change.[64] In March 1948, a sequence of events suggestive of the latter began when two members of the Special Apparatus assassinated a judge, Ahmad al-Khazindar, who had just passed a death sentence on a young Ikhwani for throwing a bomb at a club frequented by British soldiers in Alexandria.[65] Later in the same year, the existence of the Special Apparatus became public knowledge for the first time when a jeep ferrying arms, explosives and secret files relating to the covert military wing was halted and searched in Cairo. Its leaders were arrested and on 8 December, Prime Minister Nuqrashi issued a decree announcing the dissolution of the Society of Muslim Brothers. Nuqrashi himself was dead twenty days later, assassinated in retaliation by a young member of the Special Apparatus. In February 1949, the government secret police took their own revenge, shooting al-Banna dead as he stood waiting for a taxi to take him to a meeting with government officials.[66]

Were the violent acts of the Special Apparatus evidence of the uncompromising character of Ikhwani ideology, or merely a by-product of government oppression? The verdict of the trial into the murder of Nuqrashi conducted by the Egyptian government in 1951 was that al-Banna had no advance knowledge of the political killings conducted by the Special Apparatus. There is evidence that he made a number of attempts to de-escalate the crisis that would ultimately claim his life. He proposed a mediation committee to resolve the 'dangerous situation' that had emerged after Nuqrashi's killing, and angered radicals within the Ikhwan by condemning an attempt to bomb the courthouse that stored the records taken from the Jeep intercepted in Cairo.[67] A common argument made in al-Banna's defence is that, by dissolving the Society in December 1948, the government weakened its command structure and therefore made it easier for hotheads in the Special Apparatus to commit solo acts of terrorism.[68]

Nevertheless, it is clear from his tracts on jihad that al-Banna was no pacifist. His *Risalat al-Jihad*, which was required reading for the Special Apparatus, declared: 'God gives the umma that is skilled in the practice of death and that knows how to die a noble death an exalted life in this world and eternal felicity in the next'.[69] The *Risalat* explicitly criticized those Muslims who used the distinction between the 'Greater Jihad' (the struggle within one's soul) and 'Lesser Jihad' (military jihad) to divert people from 'the importance of fighting'.[70] He glorified the early conquests and cited traditions requiring jihad against the 'people of the book',[71] although he also made reference to traditions that encouraged reconciliation with those who wished to avoid fighting the umma.[72] On the other hand, al-Banna did not at any stage pursue the interpretation of jihad later associated with radicals such as Qutb, Faraj and Bin Laden which approved the branding of other Muslims as *kafirs* and the use of violence against them, and neither did he permit rebellion against regimes deemed insufficiently Islamic.[73] He called for militant action against the British and the Zionists, but never against the Egyptian government. Indeed, he explicitly rejected *takfir*.[74] The Brotherhood frequently cited a tradition of al-Khidri, which declared 'The greatest struggle [jihad] is to utter a word of truth in the presence of a tyrannical ruler,' and used it to justify its policy of attempting to reform the government through petitions and public campaigning.[75] In short, while al-Banna encouraged militancy, he intended it to be directed only against those he perceived to be the external oppressors of Egyptian and wider Muslim society; he had not sought the domestic bloodbath that occurred in the late 1940s.

Sufis, scholars and Salafis: The Brotherhood's relationship with established Islamic trends

Al-Banna's relationship with the established religious trends in Muslim society was to some extent defined by his relationship with the original activist trend of reformers such as al-Afghani, Abduh and Rida. His own supporters identified him closely with al-Afghani, whom they perceived to be the spiritual father of their movement, and he was himself an avid reader of Rida's journal *al-Manar*.[76] Mitchell argues that al-Banna sought to continue Abduh's policy of preaching a simplified message of Islam that would enable the movement to transcend the doctrinal differences of the variety of religious groups he sought to mobilize, but also contends that in practice his own model of Islam increasingly began to resemble less the universalist tradition of Abduh than the conservative Hanbali vision with which the later 'Salafis' in the reform movement, such as Rida, had begun to identify.[77]

The expertise of al-Banna's father in Hanbali jurisprudence enabled the movement to forge connections with the Salafis of Saudi Arabia. Ahmad al-Banna had recently edited a new version of the traditions of Ahmad Ibn Hanbal, the *Musnad al-Fath al-Rabbani*, and the Ikhwan found a lucrative source of income selling copies of it in the Hijaz to prominent Saudis including Ibn Sa'ud himself.[78] However, Ahmad was by no means any more attached to Hanbalism than any of the other schools.[79] Al-Banna's declaration that the Saudi king was 'one of the hopes of the Islamic world for a restoration of its unity'[80] was probably prompted more by political and financial than strictly religious motives, as was the case with his courting of the Egyptian king. Towards the end of the 1930s, the Brotherhood's relationship with the Wahhabis began to wane as it outgrew its need for Hijazi patronage, and articles hostile to the Saudi monarchy were published in its newspaper.[81]

With a view to expanding the membership of the Brotherhood, al-Banna frequently attempted to court Salafi groups in Egypt, among them the Society for Religious Legality. However, the extent to which he genuinely embraced Salafism is open to question.[82] According to Lia, in spite of his friendly relations with Salafi groups, al-Banna feared that following them in their hostility to popular religious belief would undermine the mass appeal of the movement.[83] Indeed, he highlighted his religious flexibility in suggesting that

> We, the Brotherhood, are like an immense hall that can be entered by any Muslim from any door to partake of whatsoever he wishes. Should he seek Sufism, he shall find it. Should he seek comprehension of Islamic jurisprudence, he shall find it.[84]

Al-Banna's flexible attitude towards the membership and expansion of the Society may have led him to support forms of religious practice that amounted to a compromise between the competing outlooks of the various groups to which he sought to appeal. Kramer suggests that al-Banna 'felt that, like Islam as a whole, Sufism was in need of a process of cleansing and renewal on the lines advocated by the Salafi reformers'.[85] Nevertheless, he was only willing to travel so far in embracing Salafi hostility to the various customary practices associated with Sufism. For instance, he sanctioned the tomb visitations condemned by Salafis as a form of *shirk*, so long as they did not lead to attempts at intercession (*tawassul*) with the tombs' inhabitants.[86]

Although al-Banna himself maintained no formal affiliations to any Sufi order after the establishment of the Brotherhood, in its early years his new Society closely resembled a *tariqa*. Apart from adopting the same title as that of the guide (*murshid*) of a Sufi order, he encouraged Sufi practices such as intense self-discipline and devotional reflexes such as *dhikr* (constant and rapid repetition of words venerating God).[87] Brotherhood meetings were modelled on Sufi congregations (*hadrat*), and witnessed the chanting of hymns (*anashid*) and prayers common in Sufism.[88] Later on in the 1930s, the Ikhwan began to develop its own specific institutional identity; for instance, it adopted an official hymn to replace the earlier Sufi-inspired version, and some of its most prominent individuals began to maintain that it had made a complete break with Sufism.[89] Al-Banna himself, while denouncing Sufism where it encouraged factionalism or promoted social and religious libertinism, would never condemn it outright.[90]

Al-Banna's relationship with the existing scholarly elite was just as ambivalent as his relationship with the Sufis and the Salafis. Although he set out to challenge the docility of established scholarly institutions such as al-Azhar, he also sought to win the favour of leading *ulama* and recruit others to the movement. A number of scholars were brought into the first General Guidance Office that he established in 1933,[91] and the Brotherhood successfully set up a base among the Azharite student body in the 1930s.[92] Al-Banna was also a close friend of Mustafa al-Margahi, the rector of al-Azhar in the late 1930s, with whom he shared a mutual interest in combatting Christian missionary proselytization.[93] Al-Banna would later recall that he always showed deference to scholars whom he met in person, and yet he protested against the elitism of the established scholarly order. For example, in *Towards the Light*, he rejected the idea that the *ulama* should be considered akin to the clergy in Europe, declaring that 'all Muslims from the least to the most outstanding of them are "religious authorities"'.[94] Here we see the challenge to the existing scholarly elite posed by Islamists from more secular professional backgrounds. Nevertheless, al-Banna himself was not a jurisprudent and made no real attempt to revise the existing system of jurisprudence so as to break the *ulama*'s monopoly over religious knowledge. Wading into potentially divisive doctrinal and legal debates, he feared, might cause friction among his followers.

Fascism, communism, nationalism and evangelism: The impact of Western ideologies

Al-Banna was frequently compelled to articulate the relationship between his own particular vision and that of the mass ideologies of the day, such as communism, fascism and nationalism. Examining how he relates his Islamism to other contemporary ideologies helps to answer the question as to whether he is a 'reformer' or a 'radical'; in other words, whether he seeks to 'modernize Islam' by reconceptualizing it in accordance with, say, nationalist or Marxist principles, or seeks instead to 'Islamize modernity', thus only borrowing the language of these ideologies for the purpose of articulating his own vision of Islam. As we shall see, however, this particular dichotomy can be overstated. Soage, for example, claims that it was by importing a fascist model of totalitarianism into Islam that al-Banna inaugurated the radical trend that would later be fully fleshed out by Qutb.[95]

Soage describes al-Banna as a man 'fascinated by fascism',[96] and cites a number of features of his ideology and praxis as evidence of fascist influence: awareness of the utility of mass rallies and propaganda in an era of mass politics; the reconceptualization of Islam as a 'total' system; the 'portrayal of history as a process of decline from a mythical past' and aspiration to reclaim a 'lost utopia'; the establishment of the Rover Scouts as a paramilitary organization similar to the Nazi Brown Shirts and Mussolini's Black Shirts; and backing for the aristocracy and private property. She maintains that the Ikhwan enjoyed 'generous support' from the pro-Axis powers.[97] At the same time, a literature on the relationship between Islamism and anti-Semitism has emerged that seeks to identify the Nazi inspiration behind the Judeophobia of al-Banna and the Brotherhood.[98]

It is difficult to escape the parallels between fascist ideology and praxis and that of the Ikhwan. Ikhwani ideology resembled fascism with its emphasis on discipline, paramilitarism, anti-factionalism and obedience to a single leader.[99] The Brotherhood frequently used anti-Semitic language and al-Banna himself declared that 'upcoming nations require strength, and need to implant the military spirit into their people'.[100] But was there sufficient convergence between the ideologies of the Brotherhood and European fascism to class them together, or was Ikhwani Islamism a distinct ideology analogous to fascism in some regards but not others? Gershoni and Jankowski observe that to see Ikhwani ideology as a by-product of European fascism is to overlook its origins as chiefly an Islamic and anti-colonial movement.[101] In this context it is worth noting that al-Banna was always careful to represent his Islamism (or his Islam, as he would see it himself) as being conceptually distinct from fascism and other European ideologies. For instance, in *Towards the Light* he wrote that the 'pure militarism' of Mussolini and Hitler was distinct from 'the militarism of Islam', since Islam 'has sanctified force but has also preferred peace'.[102] While he was cautiously sympathetic to some forms of nationalism, he and his followers viewed the race-based nationalism of the European fascists as akin to the tribalism of the pre-Islamic *jahiliyya*.[103] He and his fellow Muslim Brothers also frequently denounced Italian fascist colonialism in Libya.[104] In his later writing, al-Banna used relatively detached language when dealing with fascism, characterizing it as a symptom of the broader malaise brought on by the excessive individualism of Western culture. This, he said, had 'led to the fragmentation of the social structure and family systems, and the eventual re-emergence of totalitarianism'.[105] Although the fascist regimes in Germany and Italy 'led the two countries to stability', they also forced their views on people and ultimately proved to be a 'real disaster', collapsing in the wake of the Second World War.[106]

Unlike fascist thinkers, who sought to impose homogeneity, al-Banna was eager to stress that Islam would safeguard the rights of minorities. He cited numerous Quranic passages to deny that his Islamic model would be 'incompatible with the existence of non-Muslims minorities in the Islamic nation',[107] although many of his critics maintain that the Brotherhood's anti-Semitic rhetoric and activities exposed the disingenuous character of such claims. During the Palestine Revolt of 1936–1939, Muslim Brotherhood press organs described Jews as 'a societal cancer',[108] while during the 1948 war between Israel and the Arab states bomb attacks on Jewish communities in Cairo and Alexandria were closely linked to the Muslim Brotherhood.[109] Nevertheless, Ikhwani anti-Semitism very much had its own context and origins, and can easily be distinguished from the biological racism of the Nazis.[110] Anti-Semitic language was usually justified with reference not to Hitler but through the (context-free) usage of religious texts, such as the Quranic passage which declared that 'strongest among men in enmity to the Believers will thou find the Jews and Pagans'.[111] Furthermore, the rise of anti-Semitism within the Brotherhood coincided with outbreaks of Jewish–Arab conflict in Palestine during the 1936–1939 Revolt; before the intensification of the conflict in Palestine Ikhwani periodicals were free of such language.[112]

With the decline of fascism and the rise in the prestige of the communist states that followed the Second World War, the Brotherhood developed a similar relationship with socialist and Marxist–Leninist discourse to that which the reformist thinkers of the nineteenth century had developed with the theorists of the European enlightenment. Leading figures within the Brotherhood asserted that all the values of socialism already existed in Islam.[113] As such, there was no need to import an atheistic set of values, and the Egyptian Communist Party soon became one of the Brotherhood's bitterest rivals. Al-Banna himself promoted 'reasonable socialism' as a means of providing an Islamically valid alternative to the Marxist corpus.[114] While he would denounce the upper class as 'the arch enemies of the Islamic call', he perceived their failure to be principally a moral failure, rooted in their inability to live out the example of the first generation of Muslims.[115] In 1936, the 'fifty point manifesto' attached to his letter to King Faruq had proposed, among other things, 'raising [the] standard of living' of Egyptian workers, nationalization of foreign-owned projects, and 'protect[ing] the masses from the oppression of multinational companies', by 'keeping these within strict limits'. One of the principal methods of wealth redistribution would be the Islamic Alms tax, or *zakat*.[116]

It could be claimed that al-Banna's use of quasi-socialist language was a pragmatic adaptation to the growing global power of Marxist–Leninist ideology before, and particularly after, the Second World War.[117] However, Lia argues that the Brotherhood's concern with social justice sprang from more homegrown moral economics.[118] This could explain why the Brotherhood itself was able to secure more popularity within Egypt than any of the local communist parties that emerged from the 1920s onwards. It is true that the Muslim Brotherhood relied to some extent on Marxist–Leninist 'Front' tactics, establishing separate workers', professional and student wings.[119] Nevertheless, it was the networks that grew out of its webs of charitable associations, and its ability to use these bodies to present itself as an immediate source of social justice in Egypt, that gave it real presence in society. It was from the local mosques or educational projects established by the Brotherhood that the local branches of the movement grew, and the central leadership granted each of them a considerable degree of autonomy.[120] Thus the Brotherhood prospered precisely because its organizational methods were functionally distinct from those of the local communist parties, which were undermined when their vanguardist approach and ideological elitism left them unable to plant roots within Egyptian society and consequently vulnerable to state repression in the 1920s and 1930s.[121]

Simms argues that al-Banna's ideas 'inform' and 'expand', another branch of Marxism, Gramscian theory. The Italian Marxist had contended that the bourgeois superstructure promotes a set of cultural values that justify and enforce its hegemony, and it is only when 'organic intellectuals' rise up from the oppressed populace that this ruling ideology can be challenged. By demanding that the Egyptian education system be transformed by making

Arabic the language of instruction and the Quran one of the cornerstones of the curriculum, Simms argues, al-Banna is fulfilling the role of the 'organic intellectual', attacking the hegemony of Western ideas and languages at the heart of the system of oppression in Egypt. This said, he acknowledges that al-Banna makes a fundamental break with classical Gramscianism, which perceives religion as a tool of cultural hegemony and not an ideology of liberation.[122] Since there is little evidence that al-Banna read or was directly influenced by Gramsci, it might be best to read his challenge to colonial hegemony as a parallel development rather than actual branch of Gramscian theory. At the same time, the idea that the Muslim Brotherhood embraced a form of 'liberation theology' has been seriously challenged by Soage, who observes that the majority of its membership hailed from the middle or lower middle class – tradesmen, craftsmen and urban professionals.[123]

While it was easy for al-Banna to dismiss Marxist–Leninist and fascist ideology as 'alien' to Islam, he had to negotiate his relationship with the core precepts of modern nationalism far more carefully. While Egypt was never a fascist or a Marxist–Leninist state, in the aftermath of the collapse of the Ottoman Empire both elites and the broader public had come to embrace a model of nationalism close to that of post-Westphalian Europe; that is, one in which sovereignty resided with a population inhabiting a demarcated stretch of territory. This form of nationalism was particularly popular at the time, as it seemed to offer the easiest route to emancipation from British colonialism. Throughout his career, al-Banna attempted to reconcile his pan-Islamic identification with the wider Islamic community, or umma, with the much more narrowly defined territorial nationalism of the Egyptian political environment in which he sought prominence.[124]

In his early writings, before the Brotherhood became fully 'political', al-Banna's hostility to nationalism was explicit and unqualified. In a 1933 pamphlet, he wrote that the 'notion of nationalism' was 'in contrast with the Islamic concept of Brotherhood'. Once this Brotherhood prevailed under the guidance of the Prophet, it 'melts away and disappears just as snow disappears after bright, strong sunlight falls upon it'.[125] However, as the Brotherhood began to expand as a mass movement from the mid-1930s, al-Banna found it necessary to establish a discourse of nationalism that enabled him to relate to the broader Egyptian public. At times, he would attempt to by-pass the ideological gap between pan-Islamism and nationalism by using terms such as umma (Islamic community), *watan* (territorial homeland) and *qawm* (people) in an interchangeable and ambiguous manner.[126] He also tried to clarify his earlier hostility to nationalist ideology by distinguishing between a meritorious religious nationalism and an unwelcome secular nationalism imported from Europe. While he accepted the principle of *qawmiyya*, or attachment to a particular group of people, he was hostile to *qawmiyyat al-jahiliyya*, which he believed sought to revisit the ethnic particularism of the pre-Islamic era and replace Islam and Arabism with the customs and languages of those times.[127] He also accepted the principle of *wataniyya*, or attachment to a particular country and the desire to strive for its independence (*wataniyya al-hurriyya wa'l-'izza*).[128] However, in the late 1930s he believed seeking independence for one's own country was not important in and of itself but as part of a struggle to recreate the wider umma. For instance, in *Towards the Light*, he argued that the 'Islamic homeland' should be constituted of

1. The country itself. 2 The other Islamic countries, for all of them are seen as a home and an abode for the Muslim. 3 This extends to the first Islamic Empire ... the Muslim will be asked before Allah why he did not work to restore its lands. 4 Then the homeland expands to encompass the entire world.[129]

In line with this strategy, al-Banna found it necessary to engage with the existing sociopolitical order in his country (Egypt) in the initial phase of his strategy for the unification of the umma. By addressing his fifty-point manifesto to the Egyptian king in 1936, he signified his willingness to work within the confines of the modern nation state. Notably, rather than urging the direct reinstatement of sharia, his manifesto more ambiguously recommended 'amending the law, such that it conforms to all branches of Islamic legislation'.[130] In other words, he was prepared to adjust the existing *national* laws to make them more sharia-friendly, rather than starting from scratch.

If in the 1930s al-Banna's approach appeared to be to Islamize the modern nation state, in the 1940s he showed himself even more willing to compromise with the principles of secular nationalism. It is significant here that in the 1940s the Brotherhood was seeking to challenge the Wafd party, which had lost its reputation as the premier nationalist movement in Egypt as a result of its acquiescence towards the British occupation during the Second World War. Al-Banna's *Message of the Teachings*, published in the early 1940s, proposed 'reforming the government so that it may become truly an Islamic government, performing as a servant to the nation in the interests of the people'.[131] As Mura suggests, this shows his increasing acceptance of the modern nationalist principle that sovereignty is vested in the people.[132] Islamic sharia is not an end in and of itself, so much as a means by which nationalist objectives are to be achieved. In this regard, al-Banna appears to continue the reformist logic of modernizing Islam, and fails to prioritize divine sovereignty over human sovereignty in the manner of later radicals.

A final stimulus only recently given due attention is the impact of missionary evangelism. The Muslim Brotherhood, especially in its early years, made considerable efforts to highlight the threat posed to the Islamic faith by Christian missionary societies operating in British-occupied Egypt. It particularly exploited the furore caused by scandals such as the 1933 Turkiyya Hasan affair, when a Christian missionary at the Swedish Salaam mission school was accused of beating a young Muslim girl to induce her to convert to Christianity. Although the missionary societies frequently acted as the religious and ideological nemeses of the Muslims Brothers, they also contributed a great deal to the formation of the worldview and tactical agenda of the Ikhwan. The Brotherhood developed its strategy of combining proselytization with the provision of social welfare precisely to thwart the Christian missionaries' strategy of using their domination of the charitable arena in Egypt to convert Muslims. Meanwhile, the activities of lay Protestant missionaries made the Ikhwanis aware that the modern print media could be used to empower those who wished to challenge the existing religious establishment – in their case, the *ulama*.[133] Missionary activities and Ikhwani responses highlight the importance of acknowledging the specifically *colonial* character of the Western influences on Islamism.

Suggested readings: Secondary

Mitchell, Richard P., *The Society of Muslim Brothers* (Oxford: Oxford University Press, 1969), Conclusion (pp. 295–331).

Was al-Banna's leadership of the Brotherhood authoritarian? What did its engagement in the Egyptian political arena say about the movement's attitude towards democracy? What did its attitude towards political violence say about its ideological character? How did transitions in the Egyptian political arena shape the politics of the movement? What was its relationship with earlier Islamic movements? Is this quite 'old fashioned' scholarship? Or should its perspective remain valid? On those last points and if you are keen and are thinking of doing this for the essay, it would be helpful to read the conclusion to Lia's *The Society of Muslim Brothers in Egypt: The Rise of a Mass Movement* as there is a really good criticism of Mitchell within it.

Munson, Ziad, 'Islamic Mobilization: Social Movement Theory and the Rise of the Egyptian Muslim Brotherhood', *Sociological Quarterly* 42 (2001), pp. 487–510.

What does Munson say about the idea that urbanization and social dislocation helped facilitate the emergence of the Brotherhood? What other factors contributed to its growth? Why was the Brotherhood able to establish itself in society and survive repression more effectively than the communists? What kinds of social backgrounds did members of the Brotherhood have? What does Munson say about the nature of the Brotherhood's ideology?

Suggested readings: Primary

Towards the Light/The Fifty Point Manifesto of Hasan al-Banna (1936**), http://www.ikhwanweb.com/article.php?id=802. (**– NOT 1947 as it says on the website and in Euben&Zaman, *Princeton Readings* where it is reproduced – see Mitchell, *Society,* p. 15).

How important is it to consider the audience and context of this source? What is al-Banna's attitude towards Western Civilization? What important events is he reacting to? What is his attitude towards Western Modernity? How does he see the relationship between Islam and nationalism? And the relationship between Islam and modern state legislation?

Hasan al-Banna, & 'Goals and Strategies of the Muslim Brotherhood', in John Calvert, *Islamism: A Documentary and Reference Guide* (Westport: Greenwood Press, 2008), pp. 20–5.

How important is it to consider the audience and context of this source? Is the influence of contemporary nationalist ideology visible here? How does the source emphasize social justice? Who does al-Banna believe should bring about the necessary change – state or society? How does he characterize the relationship between Islam and politics?

6

Islamism's chief theoretician:

Mawdudi, South Asia and the Jama'at-i-Islami

Whereas the Muslim Brotherhood emerged in 1928 as the first recognizably Islamist party in the Arab world, the first equivalent organization in South Asia did not arrive until 1941 with the founding of the Jama'at-i-Islami by Mawlana Abu'l-'Ala al-Mawdudi in British India. If Hasan al-Banna was the activist who began the Islamist journey in 1928, Mawdudi was the theoretician who helped to imagine its destination with his conceptualizations of the Islamic state. It is on account of Mawdudi's vision of an all-encompassing Islamic order that Choueiri sees him making a break with the 'reformist' past and inaugurating 'Islamic Radicalism', which he defines as:

> a politico-cultural movement that postulates a qualitative contradiction between western civilization and the religion of Islam. Its emphasis on Islam as a comprehensive and transcendental worldview excludes the validity of all other systems and values, and dictates an apparent restitution of a normative set of beliefs untainted by historical change.[1]

As implied by Choueiri, the extent to which Mawdudi's Islamism marks a genuine break with Western systems of thought is contentious. Roy Jackson, the author of a critical biography of Mawdudi, suggests that his writings are 'very much a product of the whole of his diverse upbringing and his own sense of confused identity', going on to observe that he never acknowledged the extent of his indebtedness to Western European intellectuals.[2] Others have contended that he merely rehashed Western totalitarianism with a veneer of Islam.[3] Vali Nasr, meanwhile, has described Mawdudi's thought as constituting a 'coherent Islamic ideology' and contends that apparent inconsistencies should be understood as a result of him 'working through a process' which had been completed by the time he achieved the peak of his influence in the 1940s.[4] The debate over Mawdudi's intellectual consistency is thus thoroughly interwoven with that concerning his authenticity as an 'Islamic' intellectual – as well as the conceptual integrity of his various understandings of jihad, revolution, democracy and the Islamic state.

Mawdudi's upbringing and the British Raj

Mawdudi was born in Hyderabad three years into the twentieth century, yet through his family and upbringing he had ties to all of the major political and religious institutions that had shaped Muslim history in India in the past century and before: the Mughal dynasty, the Chistiyya Sufi order, the Aligarh College established by the reformist Sayyid Ahmad Khan, and the Deobandi movement.[5] His grandfather had been a Chisti Sufi *pir* with strong ties to the court of the last Mughal emperor, who was dethroned by the British following the rebellion of 1857. On account of the family's close relationship with Sayyid Ahmad Khan, he sent his son to Aligarh College, only to withdraw him for fear that being taught to play cricket and wear English clothes was leading him to lose his Islamic values. It is perhaps to this experience of his father that Mawdudi's distrust of both the Islamic reformist tradition and the secular elites of India/Pakistan can be traced. Wary of the colonial education system, his father home-schooled his son, isolating him from other children and making him converse only in Urdu and study Islamic subjects to the exclusion of modern and secular ones. Nevertheless, as Mawdudi grew into an independent young teenager he began a journalistic career which led him to learn English and read the works of a variety of Western thinkers, from Plato to Nietzsche.

Mawdudi's induction into politics came with his participation in the Khilafat movement of 1919–1924. The Khilafat grew out of the campaign of pan-Islamic support for the Ottoman Caliphate first announced in 1878 by Sultan Abdul Hamid II, which had accelerated during the First World War as the Ottomans and their local allies attempted to mobilize South Asian Muslims to join the jihad declared by the sultan-caliph against the British Empire. Its formal aim was to defend the Ottoman Caliphate, then under threat from secular nationalism in Turkey as well as from British and French imperialism; it also allied itself to the campaign of Mahatma Gandhi's Indian National Congress to bring an end to the British Raj. What was notable about the Khilafat was that in spite of its evidently religio-political agenda, it incorporated both religious scholars such as the Deobandi-sponsored Jamiat Ulama-i-Hind (JUI) and graduates of secular institutions, including Aligarh.

While the mainstream of the Khilafat movement followed Gandhian tactics of peaceful civil disobedience, a faction known as the Tahrik i-Hijrat drew on the earlier mode of anti-British resistance practised by the revivalist Shah Abd al-Aziz, which declared India to be outside the Land of Islam and encouraged migration to Afghanistan. Mawdudi himself was involved in both of these movements, although in the second only briefly. In light of his upbringing and later hostility to the secular nationalists, it is perhaps surprising that it was through his contacts with an Aligarh graduate, the movement's founder Muhammad Ali Jouhar, that he first became involved in the Khilafat. In this period, Mawdudi also wrote for one pro-Congress newspaper, *al-Taj*, as well as two backed by the JUI, *Muslim* and *Jami'at*. Thus participation in the Khilafat taught Mawdudi that the methods of secular nationalists could be used to realize divine objectives. Although the movement disintegrated when the Turkish nationalists finally abolished the caliphate in 1924, it inspired Mawdudi's ongoing concern with the formation of an Islamic polity. He would no longer campaign for the restoration of the Ottoman Caliphate, but would pursue the quest to establish a divinely sanctioned leadership for the rest of his life. Meanwhile, his belief that the Arab and Turkish nationalists had betrayed the movement by conspiring with Britain to dismantle the Ottoman state led him to conclude that secular nationalists were not to be trusted.

The institution that shaped Mawdudi's intellectual development more than any other was the Dar al-Ulum Deoband, which gave its name to the Deobandi school. The Dar al-Ulum Deoband was first established in 1867 and sought to provide spiritual solace to Indian Muslims in the wake of the collapse of the Mughal Empire. Deobandism does not fit easily into either the 'revivalist' or 'reformist' brackets. Today it is often read as being synonymous with both Wahhabism and the Taliban, but its roots are in the South Asian, not the Arabian, revivalist tradition. It drew on the earlier efforts of Ahmad Sirhindi and Shah Wali Allah to reconcile Sufi teachings with the Quran and the Hadith.[6] Although Deobandism did not take the form of a Sufi *tariqa*, the views of Deobandis on Sufism were many and diverse, and most Deobandis preserved the *bay'ah* (oath of loyalty given by a pupil to a master) that was a feature of most Sufi orders.[7] However, in general the Deobandis' emphasis on the *hadith* led them to eschew the more syncretic and popular forms of Sufism that had flourished in India and facilitated the religious syntheses of the Emperor Akbar.[8]

Like the Islamic reformists, the Deobandis took Western institutions as a model, using British-style forms of bureaucratic organization, employing full-time teaching staff and holding examinations.[9] Unlike 'reformist' institutions such as Aligarh, however, the content of the curriculum was not focused on the academic disciplines of the post-Enlightenment West.[10] This is not to say that the content was purely 'religious': subjects such as logic, science and philosophy were all taught.[11] Mawdudi studied under two Deobandi scholars in Delhi between 1925 and 1926, receiving the *ijazahs* (certificates) that would qualify him as a Deobandi *alim*. In this regard he is somewhat atypical among twentieth-century Islamists, most of whom did not acquire formal scholarly credentials. This perhaps explains why Mawdudi opted not just to refrain from joining the scholarly establishment, but to keep his qualifications secret so that he could position himself as an external critic of the *ulama*. Thus we might regard his ideology as a form of continuity manifesting itself as a break. Yet, since he continued to work as a journalist, as well as a translator at Hyderabad's Uthmaniyyah University, Mawdudi remained open to a diverse range of philosophical and religious influences. In 1931 he began translating the Shia Persian philosopher Mulla Sidra, who had helped to inspire so much of Abduh and Afghani's activism.

It is perhaps surprising that it was *after* Mawdudi's study with the Deobandis that he experienced what Jackson refers to as his 'spiritual crisis'.[12] During this period he experimented with some of the more heterodox forms of Sufism disliked by the Deobandis to the extent of incorporating metaphorical references to the drinking of alcohol into his poetry. Meanwhile, in the 1920s and 1930s he upset religious scholars by donning Western attire and refusing to grow a beard. Jackson goes so far as to maintain that Mawdudi's return to a more orthodox form of Islam constituted a 'reconversion',[13] although, as we have seen, Nasr regards this as more of a 'working through' that led to the emergence of a full-fledged Islamic worldview.[14] It is worth noting, nevertheless, that two of Mawdudi's most significant texts, *Towards Understanding Islam* and *Jihad in Islam*, were published during his period of 'spiritual crisis'.

Communal politics and the foundation of the Jama'at

Unlike other founders of twentieth-century Islamist parties, such as al-Banna and al-Turabi, Mawdudi had enjoyed a lengthy journalistic and intellectual career before launching the Jama'at-i-Islami in 1941.[15] As a result, his views had already been shaped by the major intellectual and political trends in South Asia in the 1920s and 1930s, particularly the shift from pan-Islamism to communalism in the Indian Muslim political landscape subsequent to the failure of the Khilafat. The intensification of communalism in India has variously been attributed either to the British divide-and-rule policy (especially the decision of the colonial government to establish separate Hindu and Muslim electorates through the Indian Councils Act of 1909), or the rise of Hindu and Muslim Revivalism in the form of the Deobandi or Brahma Samaj and Arya Samaj movements. However, it was not the Deobandis or the Hindu nationalists who began the campaign for separate electoral constituencies, but rather the secular nationalists of the All-India Muslim League, founded by Abu'l-Kalam Azad in 1906.[16] It was not until 1930 that India's philosopher-poet, Muhammad Iqbal, proposed the formation of Pakistan as a separate Muslim state composed of four provinces in the north and west of India, and it was not until 1940 that the Muslim League under Muhammad Ali Jinnah – a lawyer trained in Britain – decided to commit itself to the movement for Pakistan.[17]

That Mawdudi himself opposed the drive for a Muslim homeland, whereas the secular nationalists supported it, is perhaps counter-intuitive. Mawdudi had certainly lost interest in cooperation with the Indian National Congress, whose leader Mahatma Gandhi had recently referred to Islam as a 'religion of the sword'.[18] Yet, he distrusted the secular Muslim nationalists even more, arguing that they were more interested in constructing the mundane as opposed to the religious foundations of their projected new state. Even though he had left the JUI, his position was initially somewhat similar to theirs. The Deobandi scholars believed that it was better to form a single Islamic community within a federal India, under the guidance of religious scholars and maintaining adherence to sharia, than to concede a form of Muslim separatism that would leave the umma subject to the whims of secular politicians.[19] Mawdudi did not believe that Muslims should submit to a Hindu government, but neither did he accept that the Muslim League's vision for Pakistan had sufficiently strong foundations and for a while he invested in the possibility that Islam might become the dominant religion within India. Later on, Mawdudi recognized that this attitude was over-optimistic, and reluctantly embraced Muslim separatism, but he remained hostile to the secularism and pro-British orientation of the League.

It was because of the Muslim League's secularism that Mawdudi felt the need to establish the Jama'at-i-Islami in 1941. The Muslim League mobilized Muslims politically, but not for Islamic ends; meanwhile, although Mawdudi admired the Islamic fervour of the Tabligh-i-Jamaat of Muhammad Iliyas, he thought it focused too narrowly on inspiring religious as opposed to sociopolitical change. This is why the Jama'at-i-Islami would emerge as the first *Islamist* party in the Asian subcontinent – it pursued a modern political agenda that was, at least nominally, inspired by Islam.

There were some parallels between Mawdudi's creation of the Jama'at-i-Islami and al-Banna's establishment of the Muslim Brotherhood thirteen years earlier; for instance, the Jama'at also derived its organizational structures from Sufi orders. Nevertheless, there were also differences in its approach. Jackson argues that Mawdudi's decision to move the Jamaat from the secularized metropolis of Lahore to the city of Pathankot in Punjab reflected his desire to re-enact the original *hijra* of the Prophet from Mecca to Medina. In this regard, his approach mirrored that of those earlier revivalist movements that had sought separation from, rather than reform of, societies believed to be corrupt and un-Islamic more than that of mainstream Islamists who sought to reform the system from within. However, the withdrawal was only ever partial, and the Jama'at would engage more in the politics of Pakistan in future years than the

Muslim Brotherhood was allowed to in Egypt. Nevertheless, at the beginning the strategy of the Jama'at was more focused on the creation of a pious elite than popular mobilization. In 1944, it expelled over half its members – three hundred individuals – because they did not meet its religious standards. Even Mawdudi, who established himself as the Amir of the Jama'at, had to ward off a serious challenge to his leadership from individuals who claimed that his short beard showed that his behaviour was not sufficiently pious. Although he sought to make a break with the existing scholarly establishment, many of the Jama'at's early recruits were religious scholars, including Deobandis. There is a notable contrast here with the Brotherhood, which was led by the professional elites educated in more secular institutions.[20] Indeed, whereas the Brotherhood used its presence among local communities to bring in members, Mawdudi focused on recruiting through his own journals such as *Tarjuman al-Quran*.

The sources of Mawdudi's thought

Like the majority of Islamists, Mawdudi took the Quran as his principal reference point and only tended to show awareness of Western (and to a lesser extent Muslim) ideologies when challenging them.[21] Nevertheless, his worldview represented a synthesis of a variety of the philosophies and political as well as religious ideas he had encountered during his complex upbringing. These might be broken down into four significant sources of influence: (i) Sunni methodologies promoting *ijtihad* and condemning *taqlid,* (ii) Iranian philosophy, (iii) Western political thought, from Plato through to Marx, and (iv) Western colonial ideology.

Mawdudi often expressed admiration for the Sunni revivers of *ijtihad,* dating back to Ibn Taymiyya whom he praised for having 'made *ijtihads* by deriving inspiration directly from the holy book, from the Sunnat, and from the way of living of the Prophet's Companions'.[22] He had already been strongly influenced by the earlier revivalist tradition of Wali Allah through his Deobandi education, and his work shows many parallels with that of the reformists. He resembled al-Afghani in his tendency to offer different discourses to different audiences, Abduh in his belief that education should precede mass democracy, and Rida in his conception of the Islamic state as a series of polities overseen by a caliph. Nevertheless, Jackson suggests that Mawdudi's commitment to the revolutionary overhaul of Islamic jurisprudence was limited, and that he remained a 'schizophrenic ijtihad-taqlid figure'.[23]

Perhaps one of the most striking commonalities between Mawdudi and the earlier reformists was their mutual indebtedness to the philosophical schools flourishing in Shia Iran, and particularly to the thought of the seventeenth-century thinker, Mulla Sidra, whose work 'The Four Journeys' Mawdudi translated in 1931. Like Mawdudi, Sidra attempted to fuse religion and philosophy, believing that man's worldly experience was a constant process of falling away from divinely inspired principles and that only adherence to sharia could prevent this regression. This probably inspired Mawdudi's belief that introducing sharia was essential to bringing about positive sociopolitical change.

Mawdudi explicitly discussed a number of Western thinkers in his works, from Greek philosophers such as Aristotle and Plato, to Enlightenment thinkers like Kant and Saint Simon, existentialists such as Nietzsche and revolutionaries like Marx. At times, he even used the writings of Bertrand Russell, an atheist, to back up his arguments. Yet, for the most part Mawdudi engaged polemically with texts by Western writers, to the point that he did not acknowledge the extent of their influence upon him. It should, of course, be recognized that Greek philosophy had been integrated into the Islamic corpus of thought nearly a millennium before the onset of British colonialism in India and featured heavily in the Iranian tradition referred to above. Two Platonic concepts had particular significance in Mawdudi's worldview – the utopia and the philosopher king. His vision of Muhammad establishing the paradigm of the ideal ruler as an intellectual, lawmaker and ruler in equal measure encapsulated Plato's 'Philosopher King'. It also bore parallels with the idea of the 'Perfect Human', or 'Insan Kamil', that had been fleshed out in Ibn Arabi and the Iranian philosophers. Iqbal's concept of *khudi* as a perfection of selfhood brought on by proximity to the divine, which itself drew on the Nietzschean ideal of the *Ubermensch*, was another major inspiration. Mawdudi's vision of the Islamic state might also be compared to a Platonic utopia, although Jackson suggests that his understanding of utopianism was far more literal than Plato's since he claimed both that it had existed in pristine form in the seventh-century Arabian Peninsula and that something akin to it could also be established in the modern world.

Mawdudi's exploration of Marxist–Leninist thought showed his ability to engage with more contemporary forms of Western political ideology. Following the Russian Revolution of 1917 and the subsequent efforts of the early Soviet regime to promote anti-colonial revolution in European colonies, Marxist–Leninist dogma became popular among India's nationalist elites.[24] Like many Islamists, Mawdudi expressed a great deal of concern about the possible impact of this atheistic ideology on the Islamic faithful, while recruiting into service some of the more tactically useful elements of Marxist rhetoric and praxis. Ostensibly, he condemned communism and capitalism with equal vigour, describing the former as an 'evil social condition'[25] and the latter as a godless and materialistic ideology.[26] In the 1950s, he opposed the Pakistani government's socialist measures of land reform, maintaining that Islam guaranteed rights to private property. Yet, at the same time, Mawdudi identified with the Marxist–Leninist drive to transform human society through revolution. In *Islam Today*, he explicitly compared Islam with communism, arguing that 'great movements that aim to revolutionize society can only succeed if they have a powerful and dynamic personality to drive it'.[27] Indeed, he argued that the 'party of God' (Hizbullah) should be conceived of as an 'international revolutionary party'.[28] As emphasized by a number of his detractors, he explicitly endorsed totalitarian outlooks by acknowledging that his Islamic order resembled the fascist and communist regimes:

> 'Its sphere of activity', he wrote, 'is coextensive with the whole of human life. It seeks to mould every aspect of life and activity in consonance with its moral norm and programmes of social reform. In such a state, no-one can regard any field of his affairs as personal and private.'[29]

Nevertheless, for Mawdudi the *purpose* of this kind of totalitarian revolutionary change was fundamentally different. The transformation intended was only to be cultural: socio-economic agendas were very much subordinate to this.[30] While the Jama'at might be compared to the Bolsheviks as a form of revolutionary vanguard with a top–down organizational structure, its aim was to empower a scholarly 'Islamic leadership' rather than an oppressed social class.[31] As Mawdudi observed, 'If power and leadership are invested in the right people, then society moves along the right lines ... . Good flourishes.'[32]

Mawdudi's emphasis on the transformative impact of the Islamic state arguably owed as much to British colonialism as to the Marxist–Leninist canon. The British colonial state in India was one of the most 'governmentalist' in all of Africa and Asia.[33] It had intervened in Indian society to promote widespread use of English in education, introduce new forms of taxation, and codify both Islamic and Brahminic legislation.[34] Mawdudi himself acknowledged the transformative impact of the colonial state when he observed that 'the conceptualization of the state by the nineteenth century scholars of politics is now utterly outdated ... now the state's arena has become almost as all-encompassing as that of religion. Now it also decides what you are to wear or what not to wear; whom you are to marry and at what age; what you are to teach your kids and what mode of life you are to choose.'[35] What was particularly significant from Mawdudi's perspective was that communal politics and the British agenda of divide and rule had turned control over the state into a zero-sum game – whoever controlled the state could implement an educational model that empowered either Muslims or Hindus.[36]

Mawdudi's concepts

The various, interlocking influences upon Mawdudi shaped the formulation of his trademark concepts, *jahiliyya* (the age of ignorance) and *hakimiyya* (divine sovereignty). It was Mawdudi's popularization of these two concepts that defined his legacy as the intellectual grandfather of Radical Islamism.

The idea of *jahiliyya* helped particularly to guide the radical Islamists' binary division of the world into the realms of 'true Islam' and of 'ignorance'. However, the term itself was not coined by Mawdudi – it appeared in the Quran, and was used by the early Arabs to describe the historical era before the dawn of Islam, in which paganism flourished in the Arabian Peninsula. Islamic thinkers such as Ibn Taymiyya, Ibn Abd al-Wahhab and Rida all saw *jahiliyya* as what Hartung terms a 'moral state' existing among Muslims who had lapsed back into practices that were a feature of the era before Islam.[37] In India, Muslim writers of Mawdudi's era also used the term to characterize the religious beliefs of the Hindu majority.[38] The fact that he lived in a state in which Muslims were outnumbered by those whose religious beliefs were, in his eyes, pagan and polytheistic, would certainly have informed Mawdudi's view that *jahiliyya* was pervasive. What was novel about his reworking of the concept was that he extended its scope to apply to the full period of Islamic history after the age of the Rightly Guided Caliphs.[39] He also expanded its meanings in order to establish a rhetorical foil for his ambition to introduce a powerful, interventionist state. For Mawdudi, *jahiliyya* constituted 'every course of action which runs counter to the Islamic culture, Islamic morals and conduct, or Islamic mentality'.[40]

One criticism of Mawdudi's concept is that it makes too stark a division between pre-Islamic Arabian society and the early Islamic community, when the latter almost certainly derived a number of its values and sociopolitical beliefs from the former.[41] Mawdudi's expansion of the concept has led his critics to blame him for inspiring the rigidly Manichaean understanding of *jahiliyya* propounded by the later radical, Sayyid Qutb.[42] Nevertheless, his defenders have argued that his reading of the concept was far more 'intellectual' and less 'political' than that of Qutb, and that he never intended it to be used to justify military action against established Muslim regimes.[43]

Mawdudi's second influential concept was the idea of *hakimiyya*, or divine sovereignty. Because ultimate sovereignty belonged to God, human beings were only entitled to exercise it as a form of vice-regency (*khilafa*) which constituted an act of servitude (*ubudiyya*) to God. In practice, this form of sovereignty had not existed since the death of Ali; after this, what Mawdudi regarded as unacceptable forms of human sovereignty, such as monarchy and Western-style democracy, had taken its place. For Mawdudi even nationalism was a form of human, as opposed to divine, sovereignty, as it assumed the innate as opposed to God-given right of a specific ethnic or cultural group to rule within a particular territory.[44] Mawdudi's reading of *hakimiyya* was not universally accepted, even among those sympathetic to Islamism. For Abu'l Hasan Nadawi, the problem with *ubudiyya* as complete obedience to the divine will was that it undermined the ability of believers to adopt religion out of free will.[45]

As to what kind of political and religious struggle was necessary to overcome *jahiliyya* and institute *hakimiyya* in practice, Mawdudi was more ambivalent.[46] What is clear is that his views contrasted markedly with those of the Islamic reformists, who thought the principal purpose of the doctrine was the defence of Islamic nations against foreign aggression. Indeed, he penned his seminal text *Jihad in Islam*, published in 1930, as a response to the claims of Ahmadi Muslims concerning the defensive nature of the doctrine.[47] For Mawdudi, the terms 'offensive' and 'defensive' were problematic because they assumed that jihad involved conventional warfare between competing nation states.[48] In his own view, jihad was a 'revolutionary struggle' which sought to 'alter the social order of the whole world and rebuild it in conformity with its own tenets and ideals'.[49] It could be understood as 'offensive' only insofar as it 'assaults the rule of an opposing ideology'.[50] There is a parallel here with the global jihad advocated by later radical Islamists, notably Sayyid Qutb. The influence of Marxist–Leninist models of global revolution is also evident. Nevertheless, Mawdudi was extremely ambiguous when it came to determining precisely what form the 'revolutionary struggle' would take and who should carry it out.

It has been observed that in general Mawdudi believed that the revolutionary struggle should be 'gradualist' and that it should mainly take the form of a campaign to cultivate a new model of leadership through education.[51] In many regards his outlook on jihad as *warfare* was closer to the reformist reading than that of the later radicals. He told a court in 1954 that (military) jihad could only be invoked in defence of the Dar al-Islam.[52] Moreover, unlike later militants, he focused on the performance of jihad as a prerogative of the Islamic state – although he denied that the jihad of the postcolonial Pakistani state in the disputed region of Kashmir was valid on the grounds that the Pakistani regime did not represent a genuine Islamic order.[53] Nevertheless, unlike the later pseudo-Taymiyyans such as Abd al-Salam Faraj, he did not provide any explicit justification for the declaration of 'bottom up' jihad by non-state actors against 'un-Islamic' regimes.[54] This said, Mawdudi was never explicit as to what strategy the 'international revolutionary party' should pursue against un-Islamic regimes if they did not respond to educationalist methods, and, given the obvious resonances with Marxist–Leninist militant vanguardism, it is perhaps unsurprising that later militants sought to appropriate Mawdudi's views on jihad.

Since Mawdudi's intention was to transform state elites rather than effect grassroots change, his commitment to the principle of mass democracy was only superficial. Nevertheless, he often spoke of his model as a form of 'theo-democracy', and – like the Islamic reformists – attempted to equate classical Islamic concepts with those underpinning post-Enlightenment democracy. He spoke of the *ahl al-hall wa'l-aqd* (those who loose and bind) as representing a form of parliament, and *shura* as a form of democratic consultation.[55] He even formulated the concept of *khilafa*, or human vice-regency, to argue that the Muslim community as a whole acted as successor to the Prophet in representing God on earth, and thus could democratically choose a leader or *Amir*.[56] Nevertheless, Mawdudi's views on democracy were essentially as elite-orientated as his views on revolution. He wrote that 'if the law of God needs interpretation no special group or race but all those Muslims would be entitled to interpret (*ijtihad*) who have achieved the capability of interpretation'.[57] By definition, this limited participation in law-making to a privileged scholarly elite.[58] In many regards, it foreshadowed Khomeini's model of the 'State of the Jurist'.

Mawdudi's Islamism in practice: The Jama'at and the politics of postcolonial Pakistan

When Pakistan gained independence in 1947, Mawdudi's career as a theorist had largely been completed.[59] Its existence as a predominantly Muslim yet secular state presented him with an opportunity to put his ideas concerning the Islamic order into practice. Yet, the transition from theorist to activist was by no means straightforward. His political models presupposed an idealized Islamic state that had yet to materialize, and – as observed previously – his notion of the form of struggle required to achieve it was very ambiguous. To begin the journey towards a pristine Islamic order, Mawdudi and the Jama'at had to compromise with many of the principles they had deemed un-Islamic – first of all, by conceding the existence of Pakistan as a nationalist entity created principally by the Muslim League and agreeing to participate in a secular political environment.

Mawdudi was ambivalent as to whether the Jama'at should pursue authoritarian or democratic means to effect political change, and indeed, as to whether it should participate directly in the un-Islamic political order at all or instead merely try to reform and educate its leaders from without. In the event, the Jama'at experimented with a mix of each of these approaches. In the early 1950s, it did not put forward candidates for the elections in Pakistan, instead offering its public support to candidates deemed particularly pious. In the late 1950s Mawdudi directed the Jama'at to participate in elections as a party in its own right, although ultimately this garnered it little success. The 1958 elections were cancelled due to the military coup of Ayub Khan, and in the 1970 and 1977 elections the Jama'at obtained only four and nine seats, respectively. These poor showings – the movement had fielded 151 candidates in 1970 – highlighted its difficulties in transforming itself from a scholarly elite into a mass political movement, although Nasr also blames its failings on the fact that the elections were 'controlled by a small elite – landlords and their patronage systems'.[60]

The decision of the Jama'at to ally itself with a military regime following the coup of Zia ul-Haq in 1977 might be interpreted as a response to its failures with mass democracy. Alternatively, Mawdudi had perhaps concluded that, just as the British Raj had demonstrated that domination of the state was essential to effect sociocultural change, Ayub Khan's military regime between 1958 and 1969 had showed that in a postcolonial environment ideologically driven groups could only succeed if they had the military autocrats on their side. Mawdudi himself had felt the force of military domination, having been imprisoned twice by Khan's regime. The military-Islamist alliance in Pakistan in 1977 was not as tight as that which brought about the 1989 coup in Sudan (see Chapter 10), but Zia was highly sympathetic to Mawdudi and appointed a member of the Jama'at to his cabinet. The Jama'at thus succeeded in effecting a degree of 'Islamization' from top down, as the general issued laws criminalizing alcohol consumption and reintroducing the *hudud* or amputation penalties for theft. However, the aspirations of the Jama'at that they would be able to validate this process 'bottom up' were not realized, as Zia cancelled elections that he had promised in 1979. The Jama'at slowly distanced itself from his regime as a consequence.

South Asian Islamism outside Pakistan: India, Bangladesh, Indonesia and Malaysia

When the partition of India was completed in 1947, the Jama'at-i-Islami was partitioned with it, and, following Mawdudi's departure to Pakistan, Abullais Nadwi emerged as the *Amir* of the movement in postcolonial India.[61] Nadwi faced a challenge similar to that which confronted Mawdudi in the days of the Raj: he led a movement aspiring to create an Islamic state in a predominantly non-Muslim country. Indeed, with the secession of Pakistan, Muslims were even more of a minority in India than before and initially Nadwi had to make greater efforts than those made by Mawdudi in Pakistan to prevent his movement from engaging with the *jahili* political system. Thus the Indian Jama'at boycotted the country's elections in 1951–52, as well as those of 1957.[62] However, since the Muslim population of India had not followed the Jama'at in abstaining from electoral politics in the 1950s, it shifted course in 1962: it participated in the elections of that year and those subsequent to it as part of a broader alliance of Islamic parties, justifying the decision on the grounds that entering the political arena was essential to preserving the interests of the Muslim population of India.[63] However, the Jama'at continued to ban its members from attending the Aligarh University, establishing separate 'Green Schools' which would educate Indian Muslims in line with its own ideological vision.[64]

One prominent Indian Islamist intellectual briefly associated with the Jama'at-i-Islami was Abu'l-Hasan Nadawi, the rector of a Deobandi-orientated institution of Islamic scholarship in Lucknow, the Nadwat al-Ulama. The Nadwat al-Ulama had particularly strong ties to the Middle East, and Nadwi was thus able to form links with Middle Eastern Islamists, notably Sayyid Qutb. It was through the Arabic language edition of Nadwi's *What Has the World Lost through the Decline of Muslims?*, to which the

Egyptian Islamist provided the foreword, that Qutb was introduced to the Mawdudist conceptualization of *jahiliyya* that would play such an import role in his own writing.[65] Nadawi himself further expanded the notion in this text by fleshing out a historical narrative in which the Umayyad and Abbasid Caliphs, as well as the religious scholars of the era, were responsible for the division between religion and state in post-Rashidi society and the resurgence of the values of the *jahiliyya*, notably monarchy, paganism and immorality.[66] However, he would later disassociate himself from what he perceived to be the overly 'political' approach of both Qutb and Mawdudi, arguing that focusing too narrowly on the acquisition of political power would lead to neglect of the religious dimensions of Islam.[67] He remained closer to the more preaching-orientated Tabligh-i-Jamaat movement than to the Jama'at-i-Islami, and reconciled himself with secular democracy in India, believing it to be the best means of preserving the interests of the Muslim minority.[68]

Since Bangladesh was part of colonial India until 1947 and then Pakistan until 1971, the Jama'at-i-Islami has strong roots in the country. The *Amir* of East Pakistan – as it then was – and then the Bangladeshi Jama'at after 1969, was Ghulam Azam, who had joined the movement in 1964 after falling under the influence of Mawdudi's writings.[69] The Jama'at's hostility to nationalism led both its eastern and western branches to support the efforts of the Pakistani military to prevent the secession of Bangladesh, ultimately in vain. After Bangladeshi independence, Azam was accused of war crimes by the country's liberation fighters and exiled, although he eventually returned, accepting the de facto reality of Bangladesh as Mawdudi had accepted the de facto reality of Pakistan in 1947. He continued to draw heavily on Mawdudist principles and strategies, treating the Bangladeshi Jama'at as a vanguardist elite rather than a mass movement, and constantly emphasizing the holistic character of Islam's presence in the social, economic, political and legal realms.[70]

Islamic politics in South East Asia was influenced by trends elsewhere in the Muslim world. In the 1900s, the global diffusion of the Islamic reformist ideas of Muhammad Abduh and Rashid Rida led to the establishment of the Kaum Muda ('young faction') movement in British-dominated Malaya, which dedicated itself to battling both un-Islamic customs and British colonialism.[71] In Indonesia, the Partai Sarekat Islam (PSII) was influenced by the pan-Islamic Khilafat movement in British colonial India, and expressed deep concern regarding the consequences of the collapse of the Ottoman Caliphate for the unity of the Muslim community.[72] However, in spite of adopting the slogan of Islamic unity, like Islamist groups elsewhere they also supported a specifically nationalist agenda in the context of the battle against Dutch colonialism.[73] In 1947, the PSII member Sekarmaji Kartosuwiryo founded a new party known as the Darul Islam, which developed ties with al-Banna's Muslim Brotherhood through Indonesians resident in Cairo.[74] Kartosuwiryo began to propose – rather in line with al-Banna's own strategy

– that forming an Islamic state within Indonesia would enable the Darul Islam to reach out to Islamists elsewhere and establish a global caliphate organized on a federal basis.[75]

From the middle decades of the twentieth century, South East Asian Islamists increasingly came to be incorporated into wider Islamist networks. One leader of Malaysia's Pan Malaysian Islamic Party (PAS) received personal tuition from al-Banna, and in 1968 the group established formal ties with Pakistan's Jama'at-i-Islami.[76] In Indonesia, the Indonesian Islamic Predication Council of Muhammad Natsir sought funding from Salafi institutions in Saudi Arabia and sent its young members to universities in the Middle East and Pakistan in which Islamist organizations such as the Muslim Brotherhood and Jama'at-i-Islami were firmly entrenched.[77] South East Asian students also forged networks with Islamist organizations while attending universities in the United States, and the participation of Malaysians and Indonesians in the Saudi-based World Association of Muslim Youth (WAMY) had a similar effect.[78] Anwar Ibrahim, the regional representative of WAMY, became the leader of the Assembly of Malaysian Muslim Youth (ABIM), which in contrast to PAS was committed to a more 'bottom up', educationalist strategy of establishing an Islamic state.[79] But Islamism in South East Asia also had distinctive characteristics and dynamics. A peculiar element of Anwar Ibrahim's activism in Malaysia was the use of Islamic pan-ethnic rhetoric to campaign for social justice on the behalf of marginalized Malays.[80] Ibrahim also diverged from Islamists elsewhere in that he chose to enter politics as a representative of a mainstream nationalist party, in this case UNMO – thus choosing to Islamize secular politics from within.[81] In 1993 he became the country's deputy prime minister.[82]

Suggested primary readings

Maudoodi, Syed Abul 'Ala, *The Islamic Movement: Dynamics of Values, Power and Change* (Leicester: Islamic Foundation, 1984) – Chapter 2 entitled 'Power and Society'.

Compared with Hasan al-Banna, does Mawdudi see change coming from bottom up or top down? What historical developments is Mawdudi reacting to? Is the worldview that Mawdudi expresses here 'totalitarian'?

Mawdudi, *Nationalism and Islam* (Lahore: Maktaba Jama'at-i-Islami, from J. J. Donohue and J. L. Esposito (eds), *Islam in Transition: Muslim Perspectives* (Oxford: Oxford University Press, 2007).

How does Mawdudi view the relationship between Islam and nationalism? What is the problem (for Mawdudi) with nationalism as a form of human sovereignty? What is the significance of Mawdudi's reference to traditions and the 'age of ignorance'?

Debate

'Mawdudi's writing lacked consistency, and derived more from Western intellectuals than he acknowledged.'

Questions: How reliant was Mawdudi on the Marxist tradition? What was his relationship with Western-style ethnic, linguistic and territorial nationalism? What was the legacy of the Greek and neo-Platonic Muslim philosophers to him and why was this significant? Was his relationship with Western intellectuals built upon synthesis, dependency or something else?

Debate readings:

Jackson, Roy, *Mawlana Mawdudi and Political Islam: Authority and the Islamic State* (London: Routledge, 2011).
Nasr, Seyyed Vali Reza, *Mawdudi and the Making of Islamic Revivalism* (Oxford University Press, 2012).

7

Marxist borrowings:

Islamism and the left

Mu'ammar Gaddafi's regime in Libya was described by critics as being akin to a 'watermelon', green on the surface but red within.[1] Although the Libyan leader's embrace of Islamic socialism was in many regards idiosyncratic, many Islamists – and not just self-professed 'Islamic Socialists' – have been criticized for their ideological dependence on Marxist thought. For some, Islamist mimicry of Marxism–Leninism was restricted to appropriation of regional communist parties' superior organizational and mobilizational techniques; for others, the circulation of left-wing political philosophies in university campuses in the Islamic world diluted the ideology itself, to the extent that its principal intellectual and political messages are now shaped by Marxist conceptual frameworks.[2] Prophets of Islamism's imminent demise tend to observe the latter position, contending that its intellectual interrelatedness with Marxism and the other totalistic ideologies of the twentieth century will ensure that it will enter the same 'oblivion' that they did.[3]

The representation of Islamism as a repackaging of Marxist philosophy for the benefit of a religious audience is far from uncontested. Those who trace Islamism's genealogy to pre-modern scholars such as Ibn Taymiyya or Muhammad Ibn Abd al-Wahhab,[4] or who think that Islamism represents a broader revival of the values and cultures submerged by European colonialism,[5] would be unlikely to accept such a thesis. Many have expressed fears that it is the desire of Eurocentric commentators to reinvent an old enemy that has led to the characterization of Islamism as a crypto-communist ideology.[6] Others might emphasize synthesis, not mimicry. Rather than simply parroting Marxist ideas, it has been suggested that the Islamic socialist Ali Shariati 'engaged with, appropriated, and contested' each and every prominent idea of that day.[7] Even the notion of tactical borrowing of techniques and forms of organization has been implicitly questioned; for example, Ziad Munson's research on the Muslim Brotherhood in Egypt argues that the first Islamist party achieved a far wider popular base than the Egyptian Communist Party precisely because its federated structure differed substantially from the more hierarchical system adopted by its communist rival.[8]

This chapter will explore these contrasting views on the relationship between Islamism and socialism through a number of case studies. Apart from assessing socialism's impact on mainstream Islamism, it will explore parties in Sudan and Syria that have actively described their orientation as 'Islamic socialist', as well as politicians like Mu'ammar Gaddafi and Ali Shariati who have been labelled as such.

Left-wing ideology: Some brief background

It is important to distinguish between socialism, communism, Marxism, Marxism–Leninism and Maoism.[9] The terms 'socialist' and 'socialism' themselves predate the emergence of Marx's texts by around thirty or forty years, having been coined by English and French economic reformers early in the nineteenth century. 'Socialist' conveyed the idea that 'ownership and control of the means of production should be held by the community as a whole and administered in the interests of all'.[10] In 1844 the German economic theorist, Karl Marx, established the concept of 'communism' to connote an advanced form of socialism in which capitalism and the state would be abolished altogether and replaced by a classless society with a decentralized system of authority.[11]

The nature of the sociopolitical vision in Marx's texts is debated by Marxists just as intensely as Islamists debate that of Islam's founding texts. What is not disputed, however, is that Marx believed human history to be defined by a continuous struggle (dialectic) between an economically exploitative class and the class of those they exploited in different modes of production: a process summed up in the term 'dialectical materialism'. Furthermore, his view of history was teleological, in that he believed that the dialectic propelled it through fixed stages – the modes of production of pastoralism or 'primitive communism', agricultural feudalism and industrial capitalism – to a classless society in which the absence of conflict brought history to an end: communism.[12] However, one of Marx's central ambiguities is that, given his emphasis on the inevitability of the successive socio-economic revolutions – that is, his historical determinism – he left unclear the role human agency should play – if any – in bringing about this change.[13] This left Marxists divided between 'structuralists' and 'intentionalists', the latter group believing that direct political action by revolutionary groups was essential to bring about the communist society.[14]

The foremost 'intentionalist' of the twentieth century was Vladimir Lenin, the architect of the Russian Revolution of 1917. Lenin broke with Marx's historical determinism by insisting that revolutionary action by a dedicated 'vanguard' was necessary to bring about the communist revolution.[15] He insisted that such a revolution would not bring about a classless, stateless society immediately, but that first of all it would be necessary for these revolutionaries to establish a 'dictatorship of the proletariat' to oversee the transition to the communist order. However, it was Lenin's writings on the subject of imperialism that made him of particular interest to Muslim intellectuals, the majority of whom were writing in colonial or postcolonial countries. Lenin described imperialism as 'the highest stage of capitalism', a product of capitalist nations competing to establish rule over underdeveloped territories in order to avoid an otherwise declining rate of profit by exploiting their cheap labour and primary resources.[16] His argument that the revolutionary vanguard must strike capitalism at its 'weakest' link, in these economic peripheries,[17] was of particular interest to political thinkers in the Muslim world. For instance, it has been suggested that Hasan al-Turabi's ploy of launching an Islamist revolution in Sudan in 1989 was rooted in this Leninist strategy.[18]

Lenin was far more open to the principle of anti-colonial revolution than Marx himself had been. Marx believed that, for all its sins and abuses, one of the advantages of colonialism was that it had begun to break down what he described as the 'Oriental despotism' that had prevented countries in Asia and elsewhere entering the capitalist phase of production – which was, of course, a necessary precursor to the revolution of the proletariat.[19] However, Lenin's First World Congress of the Communist International, which convened in 1919, affirmed the principle that revolution in Europe should be accompanied by revolution in the colonies. Lenin was encouraged by Mir Sultan-Galiev, the most prominent Muslim official in the Soviet territories of Central Asia, who insisted that revolution in Asia was essential to the success of revolution in Europe.[20] Lenin himself maintained that it was important to accommodate Islamic cultural values, although he remained wary of pan-Islamism.[21] In 1920, the Soviets convened the First Congress of the Peoples of the East in Baku, which was attended by many representatives of socialist and nationalist movements from Muslim majority territories in Asia and called for a united revolutionary effort by the Asian and European proletariats.[22] However, after the death of Lenin the potential for an alliance between Soviet and Islamic anti-colonial forces diminished.

The two most important trends that emerged within Russian communism following the death of Lenin in 1924 were Trotskyism and Stalinism. Stalinism represented the governing ideology of the Soviet Union under the leadership of Joseph Stalin (1924–53). Unlike Marx, who believed that the state must inevitably disappear, and Lenin who believed that it was only necessary in the transitional phase, Stalin put the state at the heart of his ideology, maintaining that a strong state was essential to protect the communist revolution from its capitalist enemies. In practice, this emphasis led Stalinism to develop into a form of extreme authoritarianism, or even 'totalitarianism', characterized by show trials, mass purges and the development of a cult of personality.[23] Stalin did not believe in supporting anti-colonial movements in Asia, and crushed Sultan-Galiev's plans to establish a pan-Islamic entity in Central Asia.[24] Stalinism was opposed by Leon Trotsky, a member of the Soviet Politburo who went into exile in 1929. Trotsky condemned not just Stalin's excessive centralization of power but also his focus on 'socialism in one country', arguing that for the revolution to survive it had to export itself to the rest of the world. He broke with Marxian historical determinism by insisting that twentieth-century society needed a 'permanent revolution', in which societies that were still underdeveloped or at the 'feudal' stage need not undergo a capitalist phase but could join the communist revolution directly.[25]

Another significant contributor to the development of twentieth-century Marxism was Antonio Gramsci, one of the founders of the Italian Communist Party in 1921. His main achievement was to introduce the notion that revolutionary class struggle should not just be a narrow quest for political power, but also encompass the cultural and intellectual realms. He believed that capitalists maintained their 'hegemony' not only through the state but also by disseminating forms of culture that encouraged the masses to consent to their own exploitation, and that it was essential for revolutionary intellectuals to challenge this system.[26] Since Western colonialism sought to maintain belief in the supremacy of Western culture, Gramscian ideas remain pertinent to an understanding of the worldview of various Islamists. Their concern with establishing a more authentically 'Islamic' culture as an alternative to the *jahili* system created by the colonial and postcolonial regimes bore notable parallels with the Gramscian belief that the creation of an alternative culture was essential to any counter-hegemonic strategy.[27]

Another particularly consequential development for revolutionaries in the Muslim world was the rise of Maoism in China in 1949. This mattered because China was the first major non-European power to turn towards communism and also because Mao was far more interested than Stalin in exporting his revolutionary ideology to the non-Western world. Like Lenin, Mao believed that the revolution must be initiated on the economic periphery of the capitalist world, and his emphasis on peasants coming to the forefront of the struggle was of particular interest to intellectuals in the colonial and postcolonial world.[28]

A specifically postcolonial alternative to socialism was offered by the Martinican psychiatrist, Frantz Fanon. Fanon was significant because he wrote his revolutionary tracts as a member of the Front Libération Nationale, a nationalist movement seeking to emancipate the predominately Muslim territory of Algeria from French colonialism during the Algerian War of Independence (1954–62). Fanon was critical of Western Marxism, and his ideals would parallel those of Islamists and Islamic socialists in a number of regards. Whereas Marxists believed that the most significant divide was between social classes, Fanon thought that it was between the colonized and the colonizer.[29] He thus condemned mainstream European Marxists for their failure to realize the exploitative character of colonialism.[30] He condemned French workers for supporting the French government during the War of Independence, and Algerian workers for integrating themselves into urban colonial society.[31] Fanon followed the anarchists and Maoists in emphasizing the revolutionary potential of the peasants, who lived on the margins of colonial society.[32] He also maintained that the lumpenproletariat – migrants from the countryside who had not been integrated into the urban economy – could be mobilized for anti-colonial revolution.[33] In this he anticipated movements in Iran and Sudan that attempted to mobilize the urban poor against secular elites (see Chapters 9 and 10).

The rise of socialism in the post-war Middle East and its impact on Islamism

Previous chapters have assessed the impact of fascism on the nascent worldviews of thinkers such as Mawlana Mawdudi and Hasan al-Banna in the 1930s and during the Second World War. In this era, when the axis powers posed the most substantial threat to the British and French empires in the Islamic world, it was not unusual for anti-colonial intellectuals to turn to fascist ideology for succour. After the crushing defeat of the major fascist powers, the Soviet Union and – shortly afterwards – the People's Republic of China emerged as the greatest threat to the European empires, and then to the American capitalist hegemony that followed in their wake. Throughout the late colonial and postcolonial Islamic world, students turned to the foundational texts of Marxism, and local communist parties emerged in Egypt, Sudan, Indonesia, Iran, Iraq and Syria.[34] Since both Islamist and communist parties tended to emerge among university-educated elites, their leaderships were often intimately acquainted, sharing both academic backgrounds and membership of the same professional associations.

As Marxism's influence on Islamism post-dated the Russian Revolution, it is specifically its Leninist variant that has often been cited as an influence on Islamist politics. Words such as 'Front' (*jabha*), 'Movement' (*haraka*) and Revolution (*inqilab* or *thawra*) entered the Islamist lexicon,[35] probably via the Arab socialist and communist rhetoric of the day. Islamist parties have been variously named 'Islamic Socialist Front' (Syria), 'Islamic Salvation Front/Front Islamique de Salut' (Algeria), 'Islamic Charter Front' and 'National Islamic Front' (both Sudanese). The borrowing of 'front' tactics from its communist rivals greatly facilitated Islamism's expansion. Islamist groups established their own workers' movements, and slowly became more successful than the communists at penetrating the major student and professional unions as well as the women's organizations.[36]

The founding fathers of Islamic Radicalism, Qutb and Mawdudi, never explicitly identified themselves as socialists, but the imprint of leftist thought on their ideologies is evident. Mawdudi's argument that a Muslim state, once converted to genuine Islam, would diffuse revolutionary principles throughout the world bore remarkable parallels with Lenin's ideals and he openly acknowledged that his understanding of the state was as totalistic as that of Marxist–Leninism.[37] Meanwhile Qutb, following the trend towards 'reasonable socialism' among Islamist intellectuals in the late 1940s and 1950s, published *Social Justice in Islam* to demonstrate that many socialist principles already existed in the Muslim faith.[38] Both Mawdudi and Qutb paralleled Marxist praxis in their emphasis on Islam as a 'revolutionary ideology' capable of bringing about radical social change, and this was particularly the case with Qutb, who constantly spoke of 'dynamism' and 'movement'.[39] Like Gramsci, Qutb believed that state and civil society were both aspects of the ruling superstructure, or the *jahiliyya*, as he would call it.[40] Yet, both maintained that Marxism and communism were atheistic ideologies which sought to replace the rule of one restricted group of humans with that of another.[41]

'Islamic Socialist' parties in Syria and Egypt

The first Islamist to propagate explicitly the principle of 'Islamic Socialism' was the Syrian Muslim Brother, Mustafa al-Sibai. Although al-Sibai had come under al-Banna's influence while studying in Cairo in the 1930s and established the Syrian Ikhwan as a branch of the mother organization in Egypt, his decision to establish an 'Islamic Socialist Front' (ISF) as its political wing marked his agenda out. While he advocated strengthening Syria's ties with the Soviet Union and – like many other Islamist groups – the ISF condemned 'feudalism' and advocated social justice, it has been charged that its usage of the term 'Islamic Socialist' was simply opportunistic.[42] Although al-Sibai argued that private property should not be used for the purpose of 'exploitation', he also acknowledged it as an 'inalienable right' and insisted that his Islamic socialism 'opens up wide horizons' to holders of capital.[43]

Although al-Sibai's pragmatic approach may have appeared to dilute Islamist ideology, under his leadership the Syrian Brotherhood was able at the time to achieve a greater number of its political objectives than its regional competitors. It won a small number of seats in the Syrian elections of 1947 and 1949, and in 1950 its representatives in parliament were able to secure the support of mainstream party members for the prioritization of sharia as the 'main source' of law in the constitution and also the stipulation that the head of state must be a Muslim.[44] Part of the reason for the Syrian

Brotherhood's success in the 1950s was its willingness to compromise with Arab socialist regimes in both Egypt and Syria. While the Egyptian Muslim Brotherhood was driven underground by Gamal Abdel Nasser's Free Officers in 1954, the Islamic Socialist Front embraced Nasser when he formed the short-lived United Arab Republic with Syria between 1958 and 1961. In 1959, al-Sibai published *Islamic Socialism*, which was embraced by Nasser as 'a major statement of ideology for Egyptian socialism'.[45] It remains open to question to what extent this form of 'socialist' Islamism in Syria might have persisted had it not been for the waning of Arab socialism's popularity in the decades that followed the 1967 Six-Day War. As it was, the Qutbist trend opposed to Nasserism became far more prominent in Syria and elsewhere.

Another intellectual who endeavoured to preserve the principles of Islamic socialism after 1954 was Hassan Hanafi, an Egyptian university professor. Like Shariati (see below), Hanafi studied at the Sorbonne, where he was influenced by the quasi-Marxist 'liberation theology' of Roman Catholic modernists such as Guitton.[46] Hanafi continued to praise Nasser even after the latter's persecution of the Muslim Brotherhood after 1954, maintaining that Egypt's president had brought about a genuine socialist revolution and the professor's own concepts of Islamic socialism were the best means to prevent this revolution straying from the religious path.[47] However, Hanafi's ideas never attracted the same level of support in Egypt as those either of the mainstream Muslim Brotherhood or its militant offshoots.

Ali Shariati

One of the intellectuals who made the most strenuous efforts to reconcile Islamist with Marxist thought was the Shia Iranian thinker, Ali Shariati.[48] Shariati is significant because, although he died two years before the 1979 Iranian Revolution, he is widely recognized as a source of intellectual inspiration for a number of the Revolution's participants, and Ayatollah Khomeini himself was compelled to draw upon his ideas. Shariati was born in 1933 in a village in northern Iran, where socialist influences were particularly strong on account of the region's proximity to the Soviet-controlled republics of Central Asia. However, Shariati was not attracted to the pro-Soviet Tudeh Party and first entered the political fray in the heady years of early 1950s Iran as a member of the Movement of God-Worshipping Socialists, a group which opposed the Western-aligned regime of Shah Reza Pahlavi, and maintained that Islam constituted a movement of international socialist revolution in its own right.

Shariati was, along with Hasan al-Turabi (see Chapter 10), among the first of the prominent Islamists who undertook their postgraduate education in the West. In 1959 he travelled to the Sorbonne in Paris, where he wrote a doctoral dissertation in medieval Islamic literature but devoted the bulk of his time to studying philosophy and sociology. The importance of Shariati's time at the Sorbonne was that he encountered a number of ideas about socialism that went beyond the conventional Marxist–Leninist dogma. For instance, he furthered his relationship with Proudhon, whose more moralistic take on socialism seemed compatible with his own Islamic orientation. He learnt a considerable amount from left-wing intellectuals who taught him at the Sorbonne, such as Berque, Gurvitch and Massignon. Shariati was also attracted by the revolutionary environment at the Sorbonne created by the support of left-wing intellectuals for Algeria's War of Independence; he would later translate a number of Fanon's works into Farsi. After his return to Iran, he began to deliver lectures at an Islamic Educational Institute known as the *Hosseiniyeh-i-Irshad*, combining left-wing social science with classical Islamic ideas.

A number of trademark Marxist concepts appeared in Shariati's lectures. For instance, he regularly emphasized the existence of a timeless struggle between an exploitative class and a class known as the 'oppressed' or *mostafzin*. He became a master at mapping the various historical struggles of the Islamic past onto a quasi-Marxist model of historical determinism, whereby each stage of economic development was marked by a struggle between the oppressive 'class of Cain' and the suffering 'class of Abel'. He explained that in the classic Quranic tale 'Abel ... represents the age of a pasture based economy, of the primitive economy that preceded ownership' while Cain 'represents the system of agriculture, and individual or monopoly ownership'.[49] Like Marx, Shariati believed that this dialectical struggle would end only when the oppressed class overthrew its oppressors, arguing that this would lead to 'the system of Abel' being 'established anew'.[50]

Shariati also reformulated the concepts of *shirk* and *tawhid*, used in a largely theological context by many of the thinkers we have studied previously, to load them with new political and socio-economic meanings. He explained that *tawhid* signified 'awareness, activism and revolution', whereas *shirk* constituted 'social and racial discrimination'.[51] He reconciled his new concept of *shirk* with the conventional theological understanding of it as a form of polytheism by arguing that it occurred as a result of man worshipping money more than he worshipped God.[52] His idealistic reading of Marxism also appears to have been informed by Gramscian concepts such as hegemony and the manufacturing of consent. He lamented that 'although we are not in a physical slavery ... our hearts and will powers are enslaved. In the name of sociology, education, art, sexual freedom, financial freedom, love of exploitation, and love of individuals, faith in goals, faith in humanitarian responsibilities and belief in one's own school of thought are entirely taken away from within our hearts!'[53]

Was Shariati genuinely committed to reconciling Islam and socialism, or was he simply a pragmatist using religion as a means to communicate revolutionary ideals to the broader public? It is likely that, as with al-Afghani, his upbringing in Iran would have left him well versed in the Indo-Iranian philosophical tradition and particularly the notion of separate discourses for elites and masses. He drew heavily on Marxist critiques of religion in order to label 'the clergymen' a part of the oppressive superstructure.[54] At the same time, it needs to be recognized that Shariati's notions of dialectical struggle drew considerably on his own Iranian and Sufi heritage. The notion of Manichaeism – one of Fanon's trademark concepts – as a dualistic battle between good and evil can be traced back to Zoroastrianism, the pre-Islamic faith of Ancient Persia. Shariati was also drawn towards Sufism, and his notions of *tawhid* and *shirk* were rooted in Sufi ethical principles that emphasized unity with the divine essence and escape from the materialism of worldly life.

Shariati's overall relationship with Marxism was ambivalent. At times he would accept that he was a Marxist; at other times he would refuse the designation. Unlike many Islamists, he did not brand Marxist thought atheistic, even arguing that Marx himself was more of an idealist than the many materialists who followed him. He tended to criticize contemporary Marxist organizations more than he did Marx himself. In particular – and following Fanon – he lambasted their failure to recognize that the main source of oppression in late-twentieth-century society was colonialism, and that the various peoples of the third world as a whole now constituted a more significant oppressed class than the urban workers. Indeed, Shariati first helped to popularize the term *mostafzin* in the context of translating Fanon's *The Wretched of the Earth* into Farsi as *Mostafezin-e Zamin*.[55] Here, Shariati made a break with the conventional Marxist argument that religion and nationalism were simply tools of the bourgeoisie, arguing that in an Iranian context they played a vital role in enabling the *mostafzin* to assert their independence from colonialism. Since Iran was, in Marx's sense, still rooted in the static 'Asiatic mode of production', it would be a mistake to assume that the population could be mobilized in the same fashion as in capitalist Europe.

Another line of thought contends that the philosopher who provided the core of Shariati's philosophy was not Marx, but Martin Heidegger, the German philosopher whose counter-enlightenment ideals and quest for authenticity had led him to support the Nazis. Heidegger believed that the Industrial Revolution had led man's true nature and history to be submerged, and that it was only by reconnecting to the past that man could rebel against the vices of the current order. Heidegger saw a battle between materialism and spiritualism, which his Iranian readers, such as the philosophy professor Fardid and former Marxist Jalal Al-e-Ahmad mapped on to the struggle between the soulless West and the religious East. Shariati would have lived with many of these intellectual trends and his understanding of history can easily be characterized as Heideggerean, in that it sought to mobilize the revolutionary potential of a mythical past. Mirsepassi suggests that Shariati's use of Marx is thus secondary to his use of Heidegger insofar as he deploys Marxist rhetoric only in the context of trying to highlight the revolutionary potential of the past. Although certain radical left wingers have embraced Heidegger, he is better known for his influence on the far right, and his apparent influence thus leaves Shariati's status on the 'Islamic left' open to question.[56]

The reactions to Shariati in Iran and elsewhere were many and diverse. Unsurprisingly, doctrinaire Marxists objected vehemently to his religious idealism, and particularly his claim that the division between 'belief classes' was as significant as the division between 'economic classes'. They argued that his emphasis on religion was reactionary, as was his failure to recognize the fact that for Iran to progress towards a classless society it first needed to undergo a capitalist phase. Even Fanon, who had helped to inspire his break with conventional Marxism, warned Shariati that his emphasis on religion risked introducing a retrogressive element into the anti-colonial struggle.[57] At the same time, Shariati's lectures were greatly admired by members of the Mojahedin-i-Khalq, a guerrilla organization founded in 1965 which embraced Islam as an ideology of quasi-Marxist revolution against the oppressive regime of the Shah. Many of Shariati's own students would go on to join the Mojahedin-i-Khalq after attending his lectures at the *Hosseiniyeh-i-Irshad*.

Shariati was neither the founder nor the leader of the Mojahedin-i-Khalq, but the close attachment to his own ideology of a militant Islamic socialist organization created a serious dilemma for him. Until the early 1970s, he had pursued a gradualist approach that stressed disseminating theoretical perspectives that would facilitate revolution in the long term. However, as the Mojahedin-i-Khalq began to confront the Shah's regime head on, and its leaders were arrested and executed, Shariati's students at the *Hosseiniyeh-i-Irshad* began to criticize him for not giving more vocal support to the militant struggle against the regime. As a result, Shariati began to praise the Mojahedin-i-Khalq openly and emphasize their capacity to bring about revolutionary change in the here and now. As a result, SAVAK – the Shah's security agency – arrested him in 1972 and closed down the *Hosseiniyeh-i-Irshad*. Three years of imprisonment made Shariati more cautious, and when he was released he returned once more to emphasizing the merits of gradualism and careful theoretical development. However, after his death in England in 1977 Shariati's students remembered the revolutionary Shariati more than the gradualist Shariati, and it was the legacy of the former that was evoked during the Iranian Revolution of 1979.

The ties between Islamic socialists in Libya and Sudan

The ties between Islamic socialists in Libya and Sudan were perhaps even more significant than those between their counterparts in Egypt and Syria.

Many have claimed that the ghost author of Gaddafi's *Green Book*, the guiding text of Libyan Islamic Socialism, was a Sudanese, Babikir Karrar.[58] Karrar himself was the founder of Sudan's first leftist Islamist party, the Islamic Liberation Movement (ILM), which he established with fellow students at Gordon Memorial College (later the University of Khartoum) in Sudan in 1948. What was remarkable about the ILM was that a number of its founding members, including Karrar himself, had previously been involved in Marxist student bodies.[59] Karrar broke away from the campus communists when he began to perceive their ideology to be too atheistic for his tastes, but still made *Das Capital* one of the ILM's core texts.[60] He would exercise a substantial influence on Sudan's Islamists, but broke away from the mainstream movement in 1954 when it grew closer to the Egyptian Muslim Brotherhood, forming his own separate faction which would compete in the 1965–9 democratic period as the Islamic Socialist Party (ISP). The ISP had little electoral success in Sudan, but its members went on to play crucial roles in the establishment of Libyan Islamic Socialism when Nimeiri's coup of 1969 drove them to Libya as refugees.

In 1969, Colonel Mu'ammar Gaddafi's 'Free Officers' overthrew the Sannussi monarchy of King Idris in Libya and inaugurated a revolutionary regime. This development bore evident parallels with the Free Officer coups of Colonel Nasser and General Neguib in Egypt in 1952, and that of Colonel Nimeiri in Sudan. However, while the Libyan regime – like those of Egypt and Sudan – was capable of speaking the language of Arabism and socialism, it also paid more heed to religious sentiments. Gaddafi ordered the closure of nightclubs and the wearing of Islamic dress.[61] Nevertheless, beyond this the regime began with little ideological coherence – the leading members of the Revolutionary Command Council all had military rather than university educations, and were initially short on ideas when it came to the practicalities of constructing socialism.[62] It was in 1972 that Babikir Karrar's Islamic Socialists arrived in Libya, having fled Nimeiri's coup in 1969 and then been abandoned by their former Saudi patrons.[63] Karrar became involved in the production of the new regime's leading newspaper, *al-Fajr al-Jadid*,[64] in which the first chapters of the *Green Book* – to become the regime's most treasured ideological tome following its publication in 1975 – would appear.[65] A couple of sources have gone so far to maintain that Karrar was the 'ghost' author of the whole of the *Green Book*,[66] although this has been denied by one leading Islamic socialist.[67]

The *Green Book* outlined a programme of socialist anarchism. It envisaged the complete disappearance of the central state and its bureaucracy, and their replacement by a series of committees run locally by ordinary citizens. In contrast to the inferior Western models of representative democracy in which both parliamentary delegates and the parties they represented became a part of the ruling capitalist system, it proposed a model of direct democracy.[68] The *Green Book* also drew heavily on Marxist concepts of economic development, and demanded the abolition of wage labour. However, unlike

Marxist theorists, its author(s) did not maintain the need for revolutionary class struggle, insisting instead that there should be equilibrium between various groups at all levels of the economy.[69] For Gaddafi, the *Green Book* presented a 'Third Universal Theory'. Like many Islamists, Arab nationalists, and Arab/Islamic socialists, therefore, he was willing both to challenge and appropriate leftist ideas in the name of producing a more culturally valid alternative to socialism.

Unlike Islamist texts, the *Green Book* failed to make any reference to Islam and the Quran – although it is of course worth remembering that green is the colour of Islam. In spite of its failure to include any overt Islamic references, it did declare that 'the natural law of any society is grounded in either tradition (custom) or religion ... Constitutions', it continued, 'cannot be considered the law of society. A constitution is fundamentally a (man-made) positive law, and lacks the natural source from which it must derive its justification.'[70] There are evident parallels here with the Islamist concept of *hakimiyya*, which similarly considers man-made forms of legislation invalid. Gaddafi also drew on trademark Islamist concepts to further his assault on the existing scholarly establishment, describing his revolutionary ideals as a form of *ijtihad* attacking *taqlid* as he called on members of the public to 'seize the mosques'.[71] At the same time, it is worth noting that there was no call for the abolition of wage labour in the Quran or hadith,[72] and few Islamists elsewhere adopted such slogans. These calls may reflect Gaddafi's beliefs (and those of other contributors to the *Green Book*), which paralleled Shariati's, in that they maintained that society needed to return to 'primitive communism'. In the case of Libya this meant a revival of the (to some extent imagined) Bedouin ideals that were part of Gaddafi's own heritage.[73]

In order to realize the anarchic order envisaged by the *Green Book*, Gaddafi established a system of 'Popular Congresses' and 'Popular Committees'. The Popular Congresses, members of which were ordinary citizens, would draw up the legislation and make the policies that would then be executed by the Popular Committees. At the national level these bodies constituted General People's Congresses and General People's Committees, which in theory would not act except on prompting from the lowest rung of the system.[74] However, in practice the system became far more hierarchical. The central state bureaucracy never disappeared and technocrats appointed by Gaddafi retained a considerable degree of administrative power.[75] Furthermore, the colonel established in 1977 a series of 'Revolutionary Committees' to oversee the Popular Congresses and Popular Committees. These were vested with a variety of powers to enable them to ensure adherence to revolutionary ideology, which included the right to replace leaders of the Popular Committees.[76] Unsurprisingly, the Popular Committees and Congresses had no role in shaping Libya's foreign policy,[77] and could do little to prevent the various human rights abuses that characterized Gaddafi's reign until he was overthrown by a popular uprising in 2011.

In spite of its failings, the Libyan Islamic socialist experiment acted as an important reference point for Sudan's own Islamic project. Following the failure of a coup attempt he had backed in Sudan in 1976, Gaddafi made the former ISP member Abdullah Zakariyya responsible for transferring the Libyan system of Revolutionary Committees to Sudan. Zakariyya first attempted to establish these committees after returning to Sudan during the Intifada that overthrew Nimeiri in 1985,[78] but he made little progress until Umar al-Bashir's pro-Islamist coup of 1989. At this stage, together with other Sudanese with experience in Libya, Zakariyya helped establish a system of 'Popular Committees' that would act as the Salvation Regime's basic unit of administration. These were eventually incorporated into a 'National Congress', which in theory adopted principles of direct democracy similar to those ostensibly practised in Libya.[79] Unfortunately, the Sudanese experiment also descended into de facto authoritarianism (see Chapter 10).

The waning of Islamic socialism

The Islamist left experienced a relative decline in the last quarter of the twentieth century because the political left as a whole within the Muslim world had experienced a decline. Communist parties, in spite of their popularity among students, professionals and trade union elites, struggled to plant roots among the population at large and thus left themselves vulnerable to oppression by regimes that were becoming increasingly authoritarian.[80] In Iran, the Tudeh Party was infiltrated and undermined by SAVAK.[81] By the time of the Iranian Revolution in 1979 it had abandoned the hope of indoctrinating a religious orientated public and thus judged that the Islamist regime of Ayatollah Khomeini, on account of its anti-imperialist ideology, was best suited to advance Iran through the particular historical phase it was in. It therefore publicly supported Khomeini's regime, before that same regime turned on it and crushed it even more ruthlessly than had the Shah.[82]

In Sudan, the association of the Sudan Communist Party with a failed coup against Nimeiri in 1971 led to the execution of its leaders and the emasculation of its various networks by the May Regime's security agencies. In Egypt, the local communist party merged itself into Nasser's Arab Socialist Union in 1965, and left-wing activists were subsequently targeted by the regime of Anwar Sadat when in the 1970s he reopened his country's economy to the Western market.[83] The turn away from Maoist ideology in China and the collapse of the Soviet Union in 1991 dealt them further blows.

With the local communist parties experiencing what appeared to be a terminal decline, it was less imperative for the Islamists to demonstrate that they could be just as socialist as the socialists. Also, since the time of Nasser's persecution of the Muslim Brotherhood the mainstream of the Ikhwan had begun to distance itself from Islamic socialism, an ideology that resembled that of its oppressors. Nasserist oppression led many Islamists to seek shelter and support from Saudi Arabia, whose booming oil economy was enabling it to disseminate its ultraconservative brand of Salafism – largely devoid of any socialist content – throughout the Muslim world. Beholden to a regime that aligned itself with the United States – most notably during the 1990 Gulf War – and was fiercely opposed to revolutionary Iran, the majority of Sunni Islamists lost their interest into promoting a quasi-leftist agenda. Olivier Roy coined the term 'neo-fundamentalism' to describe the resultant shift in Islamist ideology in the last two decades of the twentieth century towards an agenda more concerned with moral and theological reform rather than social revolution.[84] The position of the 'neofundamentalists' was at once both radically conservative and accommodationist, in the sense that they refused to recognize modern governments as valid, but at the same time abandoned any strategy of transforming them or establishing new regimes. Many were happy to live in the West, albeit in a state of spiritual isolation. Whereas many Islamists rejected multipartyism in favour of a single revolutionary 'party of god', for the neo-fundamentalists even a single 'Islamic' political party was an innovation derived from Western models.[85]

The imprint of leftist ideology on Islamism did not disappear immediately – for instance, the quasi-Leninist tactics of Hasan al-Turabi did help bring about the 1989 Islamist coup in Sudan and, as we have seen, Abdullah Zakariyya helped to bring the Libyan system of 'Popular Committees' to Sudan in its wake. However, it was Salafi charities that funded and helped to administer these Popular Committees, and they began to reflect the moralistic outlook of these organizations. While Islamists continued to derive important strategic, tactical and organizational lessons from leftist movements, the actual ideological content was becoming far less comparable.

Secondary source reading

Chatterjee, *Shariati and the Shaping of Political Islam in Iran* Chapter 3, 'The World as Tawheed'.

> How does Shariati's upbringing compare to that of other Islamist thinkers we have studied? What social and political transformations in Iran enabled the emergence of Ali Shariati's revolutionary ideology? How did Shariati's notion of Tawheed compare with that advanced by previous Islamic thinkers? How was Shariati influenced by Sufism and the Iranian philosophical tradition?

Debate – 'Was Islamism simply Marxism–Leninism in Islamic window-dressing'?

> Sub-questions: What significant differences are there between Islamist and Marxist ideology? Are there similarities in the Marxist–Leninist and Islamist understandings of historical change? How do Islamism and Marxism–Leninism

understand the role of class, and methods of political organization/revolutionary mobilization? Can Islamism be compared more with some forms of Marxism than others? What specific features of socialism/communism did Islamists also perceive to exist in Islam?

Extra readings for debate: Roy, Olivier, *The Failure of Political Islam* (transl. Carol Volk, Cambridge, MA: Harvard University Press, 1994). See also readings for Chapters 6 and 8 (on Mawdudi and Qutb).

Suggested primary source readings

Ali Shariati, *On the Sociology of Islam: Lectures* (Berkeley: Mizan Press, 1979), read Chapter 2 entitled 'On the Philosophy of History: Cain and Abel'.

The text is taken from lectures Shariati originally delivered in Iran around 1966 or 1967 (see Chatterjee). Think about the following questions:

How does Shariati's model of historical change mirror Marxism? Is it purely dependent on Marxism? How is class and the idea of class struggle significant to Shariati's analysis? How does he integrate religion into his analysis? Does Shariati alter revivalist/reformist conceptualizations of *tawhid* and *shirk*? What does his narrative say about Islamism's relationship with the seventh-century past? How does Shariati see the relationship between human morality and the sociopolitical order?

8

Hate-filled extremist or brutalized intellectual? Sayyid Qutb

For many, the Egyptian intellectual Sayyid Qutb was the radical Islamist par excellence, on account of the succour which his notorious and widely banned *Milestones* has given to a youthful generation of Muslim militants seeking to challenge 'secular' regimes both at home and abroad. Since identifying him in the aftermath of the 2001 terrorist attacks on the World Trade Center as an inspiration for al-Qa'eda, Western analysts have come to locate Qutb as a pivotal figure in a wider genealogy of Islamic thinkers; this links pre-modern 'fundamentalists' such as Ibn Taymiyya and Muhammad Ibn Abd al-Wahhab to modern militants such as Osama bin Laden in a chain of ideas predestined to generate the atrocities of the present day. It is uncontroversial that Qutb, at least in the later and most significant phase of his career, promoted a violent, exclusivist and universalist form of *jihad*. But was Qutb's violent activism an inevitable development of the modern Islamist activism first begun by al-Banna and Mawdudi? Was the Qutbist interpretation of *jihad* bound to inspire the atrocities committed by militant organizations such as al-Qa'eda, and now ISIS? Was Qutb's ideology rooted in Islam, or a by-product of European totalitarianism?

Qutb's relationship with al-Banna is central to these debates, since al-Banna is widely regarded as the founder of mainstream Middle Eastern Islamism. Was Qutb's extreme ideology symptomatic of a wider malaise in Islamist thought, or simply an aberration brought about by specific circumstances? For Soage, the answer is clear. Qutb's thinking is a 'logical extension' of al-Banna's – they both rejected reason, advocated the use of violence to bring about the Islamic state, and understood Islam as a totalitarian system.[1] Others contend that Qutb's violent activism was brought about by the specific political context of the 1950s, in which members of the Muslim Brotherhood, including Qutb himself, were imprisoned, tortured and executed by the Egyptian regime of Gamal Abdel Nasser. This is the period in which Qutb produced his most radical and most frequently cited texts, but it was also a time when he was physically infirm and under severe psychological strain. It is, therefore, open to debate whether these works should be understood as representative of the core of his own ideas, let alone Islamism broadly. As Adnan Musallam argues, were it not for his execution by the Egyptian regime in 1966, 'the possibility was fair that Qutb would have clarified many of the controversial terms he had posited in his prison writings', and that they would not have been open to reinterpretation by extremist groups such as al-Qa'eda.[2] Meanwhile, Calvert – in contrast to Qutb's Arabic language biographer, Abd al-Fattah al-Khalidi – argues that while the Egyptian Islamist may have inspired the binary worldview of al-Qa'eda, there is nothing in even his most radical writings that might justify the terrorist organizations' targeting of civilians.[3]

Furthermore, we need to ask: Is Qutb's ideology even Islamic, or at least *purely* Islamic? For Roxanne Euben, his radicalism is not rooted in hostility towards the West per se so much as a contempt for rational, post-Enlightenment modernity that was shared by radical intellectuals in both the Islamic world and the West.[4] Many attribute Qutb's totalitarian and exclusivist worldview to the influence of Nazi ideals on al-Banna in the 1930s, or the Brotherhood's defensive mimicry of Marxism.[5] As to whether the Western totalitarian ideologies impacted directly on Qutb's *Weltanschaung*, or whether his response to modernity was analogous to, but not derived from, that of fascist and Marxist thinkers, there is still debate.[6] All of this highlights the significance of examining the whole of Qutb's political and intellectual career, not just the later and more studied period in which he rejected Western culture in its totality but also the early years in which – as a secular intellectual – he embraced and explored a wide range of Western ideas.

Before Radicalization

Sayyid Qutb was only a 'radical Islamist' for at most the last twelve years of his life.[7] Prior to this stage, his biographers have identified a number of distinct phases of ideological maturation: the rural traditionalism of his village upbringing in Musha, the liberal secular nationalism of his early Cairo years, religious nationalism, moderate Islamism and finally the radical interpretation of this ideology that defined his prison years. These ideological shifts were not peculiar to Qutb, but related to wider ideological developments within Egyptian intellectual and political milieus.

Qutb's upbringing and early career were remarkably similar to those of Hasan al-Banna. Like al-Banna, he was a son of rural Egypt who migrated to the big city to pursue a career in education, enrolling at Cairo's Dar al-Ulum seven years after the founder of the Ikhwan. Perhaps in contrast to the experience of other Islamists, Qutb's rural upbringing in Musha, the village in Upper Egypt where he was born in 1906, shaped his worldview throughout his career. This is surprising, since the heterodox religious and cultural practices of Musha were of the sort rejected by the more urbane Islamists of the era. He grew up among villagers who worshipped the tomb of their local saint, Abd al-Fattah, and was even visited by local women as a specialist in the occult after purchasing and studying books on astrology and magic. Qutb would go on to admit that his beliefs in occult phenomena 'were more deeply embedded in his soul than education and that the *'afarit* of his childhood and youth continued to inhabit his adult imagination'.[8] His rejection of rationalism might be traced to this childhood belief in forces beyond human interpretation, just as much as his later adherence to the principles of *hakimiyya*.

In other respects, the impact of Qutb's upbringing in Musha was more conventional. He grew up in a family of notables, albeit one of declining status, and his seniors implanted him with orthodox religious and national beliefs. His father was a medium landowner and active member of Mustafa Kamil's National Party, and the young Sayyid came to identify strongly with these beliefs during the years of the Egyptian nationalist uprising of 1919. Two of his uncles attended al-Azhar, and brought back copies of religious texts that Qutb eagerly digested. His conservative attitudes towards women, whose state of relative emancipation in the cities unsettled him, also had much to do with beliefs about female submissiveness and domesticity that came with his rural upbringing. At the same time, it was not merely 'tradition' that defined his distrust of the city. Qutb grew up in an era in which the Egyptian state was adopting an increasingly interventionist approach towards rural society, disenfranchising medium landowners like his father and centralizing power in ministries in Cairo. It was the declining fortunes of his family that pushed Qutb to travel to Cairo in the hope of joining the ranks of the *effendiyya*, and earning a professional salary.

In 1929 Qutb enrolled at Dar al-Ulum, Egypt's principal teacher training college, seven years after Hasan al-Banna had entered the same institution. Given the institution's emphasis on blending a modern Western curriculum taught in Arabic with study of the religious sciences, it is perhaps unsurprising that it gave birth to two of the twentieth century's foremost protagonists in the campaign to Islamize modernity. Nevertheless, unlike al-Banna, who founded the Muslim Brotherhood in 1928 soon after graduating from Dar al-Ulum, Qutb did not immediately turn towards Islamism or even Arabism. He was frustrated that its curriculum did not offer him the opportunity to broaden his intellectual horizons by learning English, and in the late 1930s encouraged his brother Muhammad to enrol at the more Europhile Egyptian University so that he might expand his worldview. Qutb was at this point very much a product of Egypt's 'Liberal Age',[9] an age in which in spite of the growing success of nationalist ideology many of Egypt's elite still gravitated intellectually towards Europe. It was in this era that Egypt's most prominent literary intellectual, Taha Husayn, courted controversy by arguing that the Quran should be understood as a product of its historic context, and the prominent al-Azhar-educated sharia judge Ali Abd al-Raziq maintained that there was no need for a caliphate in the modern Islamic world.[10] The Muslim Brotherhood was still in its formative years and Qutb was a member of the relatively secular Wafd party, which was comfortably the most popular party in an era of Western-style parliamentary democracy and universal male suffrage.

At Dar al-Ulum, Qutb developed a close intellectual relationship with the prestigious nationalist poet, Abbas al-Aqqad. It was as part of al-Aqqad's literary circle, al-Diwan, that Qutb would emerge as an intellectual in the years following his graduation from Dar al-Ulum and entry into the Ministry of Education. The members of al-Diwan were Anglophile, secular nationalists as well as advocates of philosophical and literary individualism, and Qutb's writings of the time corresponded more with their worldview than with the religious values of his childhood. He even accused one of his literary opponents, al-Rafi'i, of resorting too readily to religion, declaring 'Religion, religion ... this is the battle cry (saiha) of the feeble and the weak person who defends himself with it whenever the current threatens to sweep him away.'[11] In another of his articles of the 1930s, he outraged his future comrades in the Muslim Brotherhood by apparently advocating nudism. Much like Mawdudi and al-Afghani before him, he appeared to be having a 'crisis of faith'.

It was traumatic events in Qutb's life, and the broader Egyptian political arena, that appeared to push him slowly back to religion. The death of his father in 1933, that of his mother in 1940, and a failed love affair in the early 1940s, left him feeling isolated and in need of spiritual solace. His physical health also deteriorated throughout the 1940s; he was ill for months on end. These personal ruptures were matched by those of the wider Egyptian political arena. First of all, Egyptian intellectuals and the public at large grew increasingly disenchanted with the secular-nationalist Wafd party, which Qutb himself abandoned. The Wafd party was prevented by the British and their ally, King Fu'ad (1917–36) – who repeatedly used his constitutional prerogatives to prorogue parliament – from exercising the democratic mandate obtained from its repeated election victories. When it settled a negotiation with the British by signing the Anglo-Egyptian Treaty of 1936, and consented to form a pro-British government during the revived British occupation of the Second World War, it lost popular respect. A widely publicized corruption scandal in 1943 further damaged its image. At the same time, intellectuals began to disavow the liberal secular nationalism associated with the Wafd, and to emphasize Egypt's Arab, Islamic and 'Eastern' identity.

Qutb's increasing interest in Arabism and Islam was not initially the result of an outright identification with Islamism. Indeed, even at this stage he was subject to negative scrutiny by the Brotherhood; for example, al-Banna criticized the commentaries he published on the Quran in 1945 and 1947 for focusing on its artistic style as opposed to its religious message. Qutb did not immediately place the same comprehensive emphasis on Islam as the Brotherhood. His concern was to find a form of national identification that would not borrow excessively from Europe as did the view of Egypt put forward by Taha Husayn's *The Future of Culture in Egypt*. Indeed, before turning to Islamism he even dabbled with Pharaohonicism (ironic given his denunciation of Nasser as a pharaoh during his Islamist phase), Easternism and Arabism – particularly at the time when the Arab Revolt in Palestine was fostering the spread of 'Arab' consciousness in the region. Soon, he began to argue that Islam could provide the spiritual basis for a national revival. At this stage, his position was closer to that of reformists such as Jamal al-Din al-Afghani in the nineteenth century – he sought to instrumentalize Islam as a source of national consciousness, rather than maintain that it should transcend nationalism, as was later the case.

Radicalization when?

Towards the late 1940s, Qutb adopted a far more political style of writing, and – although he did not join the Muslim Brotherhood until 1953 – his *Social Justice in Islam* of 1949 is usually regarded as his first 'Islamist' tract.[12] However, much about his shift towards Islamism remains contested. Was Qutb ever a 'moderate' Islamist, and, if so, at what stage was he 'radicalized'? Various 'turning points' have been proposed that might have led him to adopt a more exclusivist interpretation of Islam and unremittingly hostile view of the West – his anger at the support of US president Harry Truman for Jewish migration to Palestine, his unhappy visit to America in 1948–50, the blossoming of his relationship with the Indian radicals Mawdudi and Nadawi from 1951, and his conflict with Nasser's Free Officer regime and subsequent imprisonment and torture. The debates over the causes of Qutb's 'radicalization' are implicitly linked to the wider controversies over whether a 'moderate Islamism' actually exists and whether 'Islamic Radicalism' displays Islamism's inherent violence, or is merely a defensive adaptation to the violent authoritarianism of the secular military and one-party regimes that have persecuted it.

Qutb's negative reaction to the sexual liberalism of American society during his 1948 visit is often cited in less specialist accounts as the experience that brought about his radical hostility to the West,[13] yet many of the radical views attributed to the influence of his time in America had already begun to take form. Many of them can be traced back to Qutb's anger at the tenacity of British colonialism in Egypt as well as American support for Zionism in Palestine. Like many Egyptians, he was alienated from the mainstream Wafd party by its decision to support Britain's redeployment of troops in Egypt during the Second World War, although he initially turned not towards the Muslim Brothers but to the more elitist Sa'adist party. However, following the war, Qutb's ideological orientation increasingly began to mirror that of the Ikhwan, even as he turned down invitations from al-Banna to join the organization.[14] Infuriated by the continuing British presence in Egypt, he lambasted the Cairo political establishment in his writings for its subservience to the whims of the occupying power. Seeking to compete with the growing number of increasingly vocal radical leftist and anti-colonial movements in the country, Qutb established a journal entitled *al-Fikr al-Jadid* (New Thought) in which he articulated his anti-Westernism through the prism of Islam, arguing that a return to the Muslim religion would offer a viable alternative to the atheism of the communist world as well as to the sexual depravity of the West. Having – like many Middle Eastern nationalists inspired by Woodrow Wilson's fourteen points – initially seen America as a paragon of the ideal of national self-determination, Qutb now raged against Truman's support for the migration of another 100,000 Jewish refugees to Palestine. Such policies convinced him that all Western nations were alike in their pursuit of colonial domination – the 'organized extermination of the Red Indian race' by the Americans became a subject of his writing.[15]

Qutb's visit to America from 1948 until 1950 to study pedagogical methods thus appears to have confirmed an established contempt for Western society. His antipathy to American attitudes was probably as much political as cultural – he witnessed sympathy towards the newly created state of Israel, and was mortified by the gleeful reactions to the assassination of Hasan al-Banna in 1949. In the 1940s, America was still a racially segregated society and Qutb experienced this himself when a ticket seller at a cinema in Colorado – assuming he was an African American – refused him entrance. In *The America I Have Seen*, published in 1951 after his return to Egypt, Qutb railed against what he perceived as the racism, the materialism, the cultural superficiality and the sexual immorality of American society. Yet, his condemnation allowed of exceptions. For instance, he noted that some American films, such as *Gone with the Wind*, *Wuthering Heights* and *Song of Bernadette* were 'brilliant' and 'elevated', although qualifying this judgement with the observation that they were 'exceptional' classics in what was otherwise a shallow genre.[16]

It was at the beginning of the 1950s that Qutb began to establish more formal relationships with Islamists abroad, as well as in Egypt. On the pilgrimage to Mecca, he met Abu'l-Hasan Nadawi, the Indian Islamist whose translations brought a number of Mawdudi's ideas into the Arabic-speaking world. Having already written an introduction to Nadawi's own *What Has the World Lost by the Decline of Muslims?*, Qutb began to integrate Mawdudi's trademark concepts into his own works. In 1951, he began more and more to identify himself with the Egyptian Brotherhood, writing in two Ikhwani media outlets, *al-Da'wa* (The Call) and *al-Muslimun*. Although he did not at this stage become a formal member of the Brotherhood, he still exerted a radical influence upon it, vocally supporting the young militants in the society who disregarded the instructions of the leadership and began to attack British forces stationed in the Suez Canal Zone.

Although Qutb never witnessed an Islamist revolution, it was through his contacts with the Muslim Brotherhood that he became intimately involved with the Free Officer coup of 1952 that overthrew the Egyptian monarchy and a few years later brought an end to the British occupation. The Free Officers had emerged in the late 1940s, and had strong ties with both the Muslim Brothers and the communists.[17] In 1952, military revolutionaries as well as civilian leftists and Islamists all shared a common class-based hostility towards the established social order in Egypt – they were, for the most part, effendis from Egyptian families who had risen to social prominence as a result of the country's expanding public education sector but were frustrated by the stranglehold that the landholding elites maintained over the upper echelons of the state.[18] Qutb and Nasser, the leader of the Free Officer cell that conducted the coup, were – in spite of later becoming implacable enemies – both a part of this revolutionary milieu. It was in Qutb's house that the Free Officers met with members of the Ikhwan to ensure their support for the planned coup. The Ikhwan subsequently gave its public support to the Free Officers' seizure of power, and General Muhammad Najib, a high-ranking military commander who became president with the support of the Free Officers in 1953, was also sympathetic to their movement. In 1953, Qutb was employed as an educational advisor by his regime.

However, in spite of admiring Qutb's radical sentiments, the Free Officers were not Islamists and it soon became clear to him that they would be unwilling to implement an Islamist programme. Frustrated with the Free Officers, Qutb finally joined the Brotherhood in February 1953. In this period, he remained close to the mainstream of the movement, supporting the moderate leadership of al-Hudaybi. Yet, in January 1954, together with Hudaybi, he fell foul of the Free Officers when skirmishes between Ikhwanis and regime supporters led to the dissolution of the Brotherhood. The Muslim Brothers pinned their hopes on Najib, who was more open to political pluralism but was slowly losing control of the revolutionary movement to the more authoritarian Nasser. In 1954 Nasser replaced Najib as president and came to dominate the Egyptian political scene for the next sixteen years, emerging as the most implacable opponent of the Islamists. In October, he only narrowly survived when a member of the Brotherhood's Special Apparatus allegedly attempted to shoot him as he delivered a speech in Alexandria. As was the case with the assassination of al-Nuqrashi in 1949, there is no firm evidence that the leadership of the Brotherhood had directed the activities of the Special Apparatus. Indeed, there is considerable speculation as to whether the assassination attempt was real, or whether it was staged by Nasser and his supporters.[19] Subsequently, Qutb and leaders of the Brotherhood – recently released from prison by Nasser – were interned a second time around, on this occasion with more serious consequences.

The treatment to which Qutb, along with the other Muslims Brothers, was subjected by the military authorities after 1954 led to the final phase of his radicalization. By the time he was sentenced in July 1955, the Egyptian courts had already executed six leading Ikhwanis. Qutb himself experienced a severe deterioration in his physical health and was tortured while awaiting trial. At his first hearing he revealed the marks that this abuse had left on his body. Nevertheless, the court determined that he would serve fifteen years of hard labour at the notorious Tura prison. Although his physical infirmity excused him from the labour regime, Qutb was to witness even worse horrors in 1957: twenty-one of his fellow Ikhwani prisoners were shot dead by the prison guards for refusing to go out to work.

Again, Qutb's brutalization highlights the role of the colonial and postcolonial states in forming the totalitarian agenda of Islamist ideology. It was in these same years, elsewhere in North Africa, that the psychiatrist and postcolonial theorist Frantz Fanon was using the Algerian independence struggle to elaborate his thesis that modern revolutionary violence was a cathartic response to the violence inflicted on the colonial subject by the colonial state. Nasser was an Arab nationalist and champion of the global anti-colonial cause, but Qutb saw him as a CIA proxy, just as Fanon considered many of the urban nationalists in Algeria and elsewhere to be veiled successors of the European colonial state.[20] In was in the years of his incarceration by Nasser's regime that Qutb would produce his four most politically radical texts, notably his revision of his earlier Quranic commentary *In the Shade of the Quran* and his famous manifesto for revolutionary violence, *Milestones* (sometimes also translated as *Signposts along the Road*). Under pressure from Egyptian publishing houses, the government in Cairo allowed him to continue writing from his cell. While these works were couched in religious rhetoric and supported by frequent references to medieval theologians, Calvert argues that their overall outlook shows remarkable parallels with Fanon's notion of 'cleansing violence'.[21] Just like Fanon, Qutb began to see the world divided into two inseparably opposed Manichaean realms that divided the oppressor from the oppressed. Making use of Mawdudi's notions, he was by then denouncing the contemporary states and societies of the Muslim world for existing in a state of *jahiliyya* that was submerging true Islam.

Following his release from prison in 1964, it was Qutb's efforts to pursue the strategy of militant vanguardism laid out in *Milestones* that ultimately led to his demise, although he actually achieved far less than his later imitators before his rearrest in 1965. In January of that year he had joined around two hundred militant Ikhwanis who, having been inspired by his teachings, had established a group known as 'Organization 1965'.[22] Like the earlier Special Apparatus, this organization was very much independent from the Ikhwan leadership – they had approached Hudaybi as General Guide, but ultimately ignored his advice to remain focused on an educationalist approach.[23] Qutb warned the group not to attack the regime before they had acquired sufficient support to be in a position to overthrow it, but sanctioned the establishment of a paramilitary programme and helped to draft plans for Nasser's assassination.[24] However, the government quickly cracked down on the organization and Qutb was arrested in August 1965 – and put on trial again, this time for his life. Government agents relayed to Qutb via his sister a message that they would allow him to avoid the noose if he confessed to conspiring with other anti-regime forces in Egypt, but he rejected this offer and was hanged on 29 August 1966.[25]

Qutb's *jihad* against Nasser: Kharijism, classicism or Leninism?

Before Qutb's trial in 1965, he was subjected to a rigorous interrogation by the government's intelligence chief, Salah Nasr, in the course of which he was accused of following the doctrine of the most radical of the Kharijis, Nafi Ibn Azraq.[26] The Egyptian government regularly attempted to stigmatize members of the Ikhwan by characterizing their beliefs as Khariji, knowing well the contempt for Kharijism in mainstream Sunnism.[27] As we have seen, the Sunni theologians of the classical era sought to counter Khariji radicalism by maintaining that only God could judge whether a self-professed Muslim was genuine in his commitment to the faith, and maintained that for a human to denounce another Muslim as a non-believer (*takfir*) was a grave sin. It was not just the government that used this conventional Sunni outlook to challenge Qutb, but also his fellow Ikhwani prisoners in the 1950s and 1960s, who believed that Qutb's constant denunciation of contemporary Muslim society as *jahili* was tantamount to *takfir*.[28] In 1969, a text entitled *Du'at la Qudat* (preachers not judges) was published under the name of Hasan al-Hudaybi. There has since been considerable speculation as to whether this was published by Hudaybi himself, or whether the Egyptian intelligence services chose to publish it in his name in an attempt to de-radicalize Egypt's Islamists.[29] Without mentioning Qutb personally, the text condemned those who sought to label entire Muslim societies as *jahili* and warned that those who took it upon themselves to denounce the entire Muslim community had put themselves on a level with God in a manner similar to the Kharijis.[30] The depiction of Qutb's beliefs as Khariji is now so common that they are described as such in some scholarly works on the Egyptian radical.[31]

Qutb was evidently aware that he might struggle to differentiate his position from that of the Kharijis. Like most Islamists, therefore, he took pains to avoid identification with the Kharijis in his writings. It is noticeable, for example, that in his Quranic commentary he included no references to the Kharijis, and steered clear of the conventional Sunni practice of warning of the dangers of their views.[32] However, on the occasions when he was pressed on the subject by Salah Nasr and by members of the Brotherhood he responded that he was not guilty of practising *takfir* since he had only sought to highlight the manner in which the condition of *jahiliyya* made it impossible for Islam to flourish. He maintained that he was not denouncing individuals Muslims, since in a *jahili* society it was impossible for them to be aware of the true requirements of their faith.[33] Indeed, he wrote in *Milestones* that it was on account of the *jahili* system that 'the Islamic worldview remains obscured in our minds'.[34]

In seeking to articulate a more moderate position than that of Qutb, the authors of *Du'at la Qudat* gave particular attention to the widespread recent usage of the term *jahiliyya* in Islamist circles: the prevailing argument that Muslim society had returned to a condition akin to that prevalent in the age of ignorance, they maintained, had justified the adoption of *takfiri* positions. They explicitly blamed Mawdudi for the prevalence of the *jahiliyya* concept, knowing that it would be difficult to target the recently martyred Qutb.[35] Yet, Mawdudi's defenders have maintained that it was Qutb who distorted his concept and gave to it an extremist character. Osman maintains that whereas Mawdudi focused on the realm of 'conceptual' struggle, it was Qutb who identified the *jahiliyya* as a system that had to be physically opposed.[36] Whereas Mawdudi showed some willingness to reform the existing states and societies of the Islamic world from within, Qutb urged that the vanguard of true believers should cut itself off entirely from the *jahili* system.[37] It is also worth observing that Qutb and Mawdudi wrote in very different contexts. Mawdudi popularized the term in India in the 1930s and 1940s, at a time when Muslims were subject to the rule of a non-Muslim colonizer and also outnumbered by adherents of other faiths. By contrast, Qutb was using the term at a time when Egyptian society had been predominantly Muslim for centuries and the Egyptian state had recently gained popular respect by bringing an end to a foreign, non-Muslim occupation. This is why, although both men used the concept of *jahiliyya* to characterize Muslim societies in general, the context in which he was writing made Qutb's usage more controversial.

Although Qutb's opponents criticized him by making reference to the classical Sunni positions, he sought support for his own arguments from the classical theologians who wrote on the subject of *jihad*: his own efforts, he maintained, were an attempt to rescue the classical position from its distortion by 'Orientalists'.[38] Like Mawdudi, he condemned the reformist understanding of *jihad* as a defensive doctrine linked to modern nationalism. In this regard, his approach was less than radical, representing a return to the attitude of the original jurisprudents, whose views on the subject had been revised by reformers such as Abduh. These jurisprudents, who wrote during a period of continuous Umayyad and Abbasid expansion, had articulated the *jihad* doctrine in a narrow military sense in order to justify their continuing conquests.[39] In particular, Qutb relied on the classical jurisprudential principle of *naskh*, which sanctioned the abrogation of certain Quranic passages by other passages which came later in the order of revelation. In practice, this meant that Qutb was able to follow the classical jurists in legitimizing *jihad* as a form of military expansion on the basis of a number of passages from the later 'Medinese' verses of the Quran. In these verses, the Prophet and the early believers resorted to armed conflict following their expulsion from Mecca, where they had originally adopted what would now be called an 'educationalist' approach.[40]

Qutb has often been understood as part of a genealogy of militant radicalism linking Ibn Taymiyya and Ibn Abd al-Wahhab to bin Laden.[41] While it is true that he referred to Ibn Taymiyya in *In the Shade of the Quran* as a scholar who had called for *jihad* against non-Muslim regimes,[42] he did little more than this to engage with the Damascene scholar other than cite the works of his pupil Ibn Qayyim al-Jawziyya; and he did not mention him at all in his most famous text, *Milestones*.[43] Although his brother Muhammad Qutb would later integrate his ideas into the Salafi–Wahhabi tradition, Qutb himself was not greatly indebted to this tradition. He did, apparently, circulate Ibn Abd al-Wahhab's writings, along with those of Ibn Taymiyya and the twentieth-century Islamists, to the fellow prisoners he radicalized in al-Tura jail.[44] Nevertheless, his denunciation of both Muslim and non-Muslim societies alike as *jahili* effectively rendered Ibn Taymiyya's distinction between the Dar al-Islam and Dar al-Harb irrelevant.[45] In *Milestones* he only discussed the concepts of *shirk* and *tawhid* in passing,[46] and, although in recommending that his vanguard perform *hijra* to escape the *jahili* society Qutb mirrored a number of the eighteenth and nineteenth-century revivalist movements, other reference points probably came from an earlier period. Qutb was far more immersed in the Sufi outlook than the Salafi–Jihadis of today. He enthusiastically identified with the tradition of *jihad* as an emotional and spiritual experience pursued by those such as the eleventh century Moroccan Sufi Ibn Yasin.[47]

Although Qutb's *jihad* spoke to a historical Sufi and scholarly tradition, as a 'lay' intellectual he followed other Islamists in creating a new interpretation of the faith that superimposed twentieth-century political language and agendas on the seventh-century past. Qutb himself explicitly disavowed Marxism, declaring that while it 'bore the imprint of faith' it was 'antithetical to the nature of human instincts'.[48] Nevertheless, its imprint upon Qutb was greater than he acknowledged, and went beyond the mere use of the term 'vanguard' to describe his revolutionary group. His entire revolutionary model mirrored Marxism in its teleological thrust. Islam, for Qutb, was 'a practical movement that progresses from one stage to the next, utilizing for each stage practically effective and competent means, while preparing the ground for the next stage'.[49] Furthermore, he was almost certainly influenced by Mawdudi's own quasi-Leninist model of the 'party of God' as a 'revolutionary party', but, unlike Mawdudi, was explicit concerning the 'inevitability of *Jihad* ... taking a military form in addition to its advocacy form'.[50] His indebtedness to the general European revolutionary tradition – particularly Rousseau's notion of being 'forced to be free' – has been much commented on. A similar argument enabled Qutb to overcome the Quranic admonition that there must be 'no coercion in religion' by insisting that the purpose of his *jihad* against the world's existing sociopolitical order was to bring an end to oppressive systems that prevented individuals from choosing Islam freely.[51]

Some commentators have sought to characterize Qutb as a crypto-fascist for following other Islamists in their admiration for far-right ideologies in Europe.[52] Berman suggests that he was probably influenced by a number of Nazis who fled to Egypt following the Second World War, although there is little in the way of direct evidence for this.[53] What we do know is that Qutb expressed a great deal of admiration for the French pro-Vichy surgeon, Alexis Carrell, whom he described as a 'dissenting rebel against industrial civilization'.[54] Carrell's writings frequently evoked fascist themes, advocating natural selection and eugenics and calling for a small elite to separate itself from urban modernity and its corrupting influences.[55] It is to this last notion in particular that Qutb's vanguardist model might be traced.[56] Apart from his reference to Carrell – a relatively obscure figure within far-right thought – Qutb gave little reason to be identified with fascism. However, it is evident that he was a virulent anti-Semite, and his 1951 text *Our Battle with the Jews* (*Ma'arakatuna ma' al-Yahud*) sought to depict Jews as the agents of a malign conspiracy against Arabs and Muslims throughout the world. The extent to which his anti-Semitism had fascist roots has been much debated. As with most of his arguments, he supported his claims of Jewish plotting by reference to the Quran.[57] Yet, Qutb's 'paranoid style' might also be regarded as a specific product of a colonial and postcolonial environment in which populations saw their governments as being subject to alien political control, thereby making it easy for political radicals to label certain groups as 'foreign' in order to blame them for the country's exploitation.[58] However, even in this context his views did have echoes of the anti-Semitism found in various Western ideologies: it was the control of global financial institutions by the Jews, he argued, that made possible their 'conspiracies'.[59]

Was Qutb's extremism shaped less by his engagement with Western and Muslim radicals and more by the abuses he suffered at the hands of the Egyptian state? Should we treat the writings which he produced in conditions of extreme psychological duress as being representative of the overall corpus of his thought, just because it was those writings which earned him his later notoriety? Arguably we should not, although it needs to be acknowledged that a number of the radical agendas of *Milestones* were foreshadowed in the texts Qutb published prior to his incarceration. For instance, it was in his *Islam and Universal Peace,* published in 1951 that Qutb made the argument that it was justifiable to overthrow non-Muslim regimes in non-Muslim countries on the grounds that such regimes would prevent the spreading of Islam.[60] Qutb's universalism, anti-Semitism and anti-Westernism all emerged out of his fury at Western colonialism and Zionism, as well as his engagement with the major global ideologies of the day. Yet, it was his brutalization within Nasser's prisons that led his condemnation of the existing Muslim sociopolitical order to take an absolute form, and led him to conceive such a stark contrast between Islamic and non-Islamic forms of governance.[61] He was *not* predestined to take these positions – as we have seen, he willingly participated in Nasser's government for a period and had been an official in the education ministry in the parliamentary era. We do not know whether, if Qutb had lived to witness Anwar Sadat's reconciliation with the Ikhwan in the 1970s, he would have revised these views.

Qutb's Islamic order

Whereas Mawdudi was a theorist of the Islamic state who made little effort to consider the journey towards it, the opposite was the case with Qutb. It is precisely because his model presented only an antithesis to Western values that it proved so attractive to the next generation of young militants, who were more concerned with battling neocolonialism and secular regimes than contemplating the shape of the political order that would replace them.[62] Qutb frequently fell back on the argument that the precise forms of the Islamic state would have to be decided when the *jahili* system had been removed, and be adapted to whatever circumstances the Muslim community then faced.[63] While he did – often following Mawdudi – flesh out a number of basic characteristics of his Islamic system, the purpose of his discussions of this ideal order was more often to delegitimize the existing order than to establish a new one. Since, unlike al-Banna, he sought no accommodation with the established sociopolitical order, Qutb did not have to propose any compromises with contemporary nationalism, secular legislation or Western-style parliamentary democracy. He certainly saw his Islamic state as representing some form of democracy, but he did not use Western terminology to describe it.[64] In short, it is necessary to distinguish between Qutb's journey, in which his small vanguard rejected every aspect of the existing sociopolitical system, and the order that his vanguard sought to achieve, in which some form of Islamic democracy might flourish.

Qutb followed Mawdudi's understanding of *khilafa* as a form of human vice-regency in arguing that the entire Islamic community should choose the caliph.[65] Toth contends that this takes Qutb away from standard Sunni and Shia positions in the direction of the Khariji model.[66] Qutb himself was vague as to how precisely the Islamic community would express their wishes.[67] Nevertheless, like Mawdudi, he believed that granting the Islamic community the right to legislate would be tantamount to putting human sovereignty on the same level as divine sovereignty.[68] Like the reformists, he advocated *shura* (consultation) but, unlike later reformists, did not equate it to parliamentary democracy. He recommended the formation of *shura* councils but suggested that they only need be convened at the time of crisis, and moreover that their precise form would be decided once the Islamic state had emerged.[69]

The exact form that the caliphate would take was of relatively minor interest to Qutb; his real concern was the comprehensive implementation of sharia. As a result, it was more important that his Islamic state should be a nomocracy – a form of governance by a particular set of laws or principles – than for it to be either an autocracy or democracy.[70] For Qutb, *hakimiyya* or divine sovereignty, was instituted principally through divine legislation, which implied that, were genuine sharia to prevail, the need for the state would disappear – an echo of Marx.[71] Nevertheless, Qutb's sharia differed from classical sharia in that its scope was far more comprehensive. It 'covers every possible human contingency', he wrote, 'social and individual, from birth to death'.[72] Anyone who accepted 'secular' forms of law was thus defying God's authority.[73] Yet, classical Islamic law had always distinguished between 'crimes against God' and 'crimes against man',[74] and the Umayyad and Abbasid Caliphates had always operated a number of other legal systems of pre-Islamic origin in parallel with divine sharia (see Chapter 2).

Qutb did not even recognize the legitimacy of the Umayyad and Abbasid Caliphates. This is why his project to sweep aside un-Islamic regimes and reintroduce a pristine Islamic order was far more ambitious than that of his supposed ideological progenitor, Ibn Taymiyya. Whereas Ibn Taymiyya's fatwas were targeted at one specific group (the Mongols), Qutb's *jahiliyya* doctrine delegitimized every single self-professed Islamic regime that had followed the age of the Rightly Guided Caliphs. As we have seen, Ibn Taymiyya recognized compromises between the ideal of the 'kingly Caliphate' and 'Prophetic Caliphates',[75] but Qutb's writings renounced all the post-661 caliphates on the grounds that they had lost their Islamic identity when they embraced the monarchical systems of the pre-Islamic *jahiliyya*.[76] It was one of the paradoxes of Qutb's thought that even though he legitimized his global jihad with reference to the jurisprudence underpinning Umayyad and Abbasid expansion, he did not see these caliphates as genuinely Islamic in their own right. Qutb identified with the religio-political ideals that facilitated this expansion, but not the political adaptability that sustained it. His was essentially a pathological political-historical outlook borne out of his torture in Nasser's jails and his rage at contemporary Western colonialism, which jaundiced his view of the Islamic past so much that he saw the introduction of Greek philosophy into Islam as an aspect of the historic *jahiliyya*.[77]

Qutbism: The legacy

As we have seen, a number of scholars identify Qutb as a historical intermediary between the pre-modern 'Salafis', such as Ibn Taymiyya and Ibn Abd al-Wahhab, and the militant Salafis of the present day. Although his influence on bin Laden is unquestionable, his status as a Salafi is not. Qutb might well be regarded as a 'Salafi' because of his focus on decline after the era of the first Muslims. Nevertheless, his 'Salafism' owed more to the *jahiliyya* concept and his identity as a postcolonial intellectual than it did to the theology of Muhammad Ibn Abd al-Wahhab. However, like a number of Salafis, Qutb sought to make a break with the four established schools of Islamic law and introduce an entirely new one.[78]

It was not until after his death that Qutb's writings were integrated into the Salafi canon, after the Saudi regime welcomed his brother Muhammad Qutb.[79] Muhammad Qutb, along with other Muslim Brothers who had fled secular authoritarianism in the Arab world to take shelter in the more religiously conservative environment of Saudi Arabia, helped to facilitate the intellectual convergence between revolutionary Islamism and Salafi–Wahhabism that had been foreshadowed by Rashid Rida. For instance, he matched the Mawdudist–Qutbist doctrine of *hakimiyya* with Wahhabi teachings on *tawhid*.[80] Muhammad Qutb personally taught Safar al-Hawali, one of the leading intellectuals of the Sahwa movement of the 1990s who opposed the royal family as the Qutbists had opposed Nasser.[81] Sayyid Qutb's influence on Saudi politics highlights his ambiguous status in Salafism – the Saudi religious establishment, keen to delegitimize the Qutbist Sahwis, denounced him for what they regarded as his poor knowledge of Islamic jurisprudence and identification with Sufi doctrines.[82]

While bin Laden explicitly identified with Qutb's struggle against the world of *jahiliyya*, there is little justification to be found in his texts for methods such as suicide bombing and the hijacking of civilian aircraft. The *jihad* Qutb imagined was targeted at government institutions, and grounded in the classical *jihadi* tradition, which eschewed the targeting of civilians.[83] What was groundbreaking in the long run was the global scope of Qutb's vision and the manner in which he legitimized grass-roots militant action against Muslim regimes.

In Egypt, the mainstream Muslim Brotherhood under Hudyabi did its best to distance itself from Qutb's ideas. Although Hudaybi was careful not to condemn Qutb personally, once Umar al-Tilmisani became general guide he explicitly distanced the movement from the radical intellectual's views.[84] In 1971, Anwar Sadat amnestied the majority of the Muslim Brotherhood leadership, and from this point the mainstream of the movement under Hudaybi and subsequent general guides remained committed to civil action in the formal Egyptian political arena. Nevertheless, Qutb's thought influenced a number of separate organizations that emerged in the 1970s with the aim of establishing themselves as the vanguard he had envisaged. The Takfir wa Hijra (denounce and flee) group established by Shukri Mustafa in 1971 was one such group, although it embraced the principle of *takfir* far more explicitly than did Qutb.[85]

Suggested reading: Secondary

Calvert, John, *Sayyid Qutb and the Origins of Radical Islamism* (Oxford University Press, 2013), Chapter 6 on 'Radicalization'.

Questions: How did the prison experience affect Qutb's worldview? Can we compare Qutb with contemporary European ideologues? To what extent did his thought mark a break previous thinkers, for example, Mawdudi, Abduh, al-Banna – how novel was his concept of *jahiliyya*? How novel was his understanding of *jihad*?

Soage, A. B., 'Hasan al-Banna and Sayyid Qutb: Continuity or Rupture?', *Muslim World* 99 (2009), pp. 294–311.

Questions: To what extent did the approach of Sayyid Qutb mark a radical break with that of previous Islamist thinkers, such as al-Banna and Mawdudi? How similar were their concepts of the Islamic state? Did they have a similar understanding of totalitarianism? And of *jihad*/revolution? How did they both look at the reformist/modernist tradition?

Suggested reading: Primary

Bergesen, Albert J. (ed.), *The Sayyid Qutb Reader: Selected Writings on Politics, Religion and Society* (London: Routledge, 2008) – pp. 43–80 on Qutb's Prologue to *al-Anfal* in *In the Shade of the Quran*. Also, to get the context on Qutb's writing of *In the Shade of the Quran*, look up index references to this book in Calvert's text as it will give you some idea of how his writing was shaped by his own personal and political experiences.

Questions: To what extent is Qutb's interpretation of the Islamic past reliant on twentieth-century contemporary political beliefs? How has Western colonialism shaped Qutb's worldview? How important is it to consider the context in which he was writing? Does Qutb transform/distort Mawdudi's concept of *jahiliyya*, and *jihad*? Or is this simply Mawdudi writ large? Is this programme more radical of Hasan al-Banna?

9

The rule of the jurist:

Khomeini and the 1979 Iranian Revolution

So far, most of the movements studied in this text have identified with the Sunni expression of Islam adhered to by the majority of Muslims. The first two, the Muslim Brotherhood and the Jama'at-i-Islami, were founded by Sunni Muslims and run by Sunni Muslims. The Islamist organization that features so prominently in Western media coverage today, ISIS, is a rigidly Sunni movement that since it first emerged has violently persecuted Muslims adhering to the minority Shia faith. Yet, the first Islamist Revolution of the twentieth century, which overthrew a secular pro-Western monarchy and installed a regime modelled on Islamist understandings of sharia and the state, occurred not in the Sunni Muslim world but in Shia Iran. This anomaly within Islamism's historical trajectory raises a serious question – how is it that the classic 'others' of the Sunni Islamists, the Shia, were able to achieve the feat that they would all seek to emulate in later years? Perhaps Shia Islamism is a unique phenomenon that deserves to be analysed independently of its Sunni equivalents. Yet we have already seen that Jamal al-Din al-Afghani, the intellectual forefather of Sunni Islamism, derived a number of his activist concepts from his Shia education in Iran. And, as will be considered more fully below, Ayatollah Khomeini's view of the Islamic state was inspired by his engagement with a number of Sunni thinkers. Furthermore, Hasan al-Turabi, the ideologue who inspired the next successful Islamist takeover – in Sudan in 1989 – openly sought dialogue with the Shia and invited the Iranian Revolutionary Guards to Khartoum.

While Shia Islamism cannot be discussed in isolation, therefore, an examination of the historical background of Shi'ism in Iran is indispensable.

The country now known as Iran was first Islamized following the defeat of the Persian Empire at the Battle of Ctesiphon in 637 CE, which occurred during the initial wave of Arab Conquests in the Age of the Four Rightly Guided Caliphs; it subsequently became an integral territory of the Umayyad and Abbasid Caliphates.[1] Although the inhabitants did not become predominantly Shia until the emergence of the Safavids in the fifteenth century, they retained other distinct characteristics. As one of the great empires of the ancient world, Persia acted as an intellectual, cultural and scientific repository upon which subsequent Islamic civilization greatly relied. Persian would overtake Arabic as the language of literature and indeed the language of court in many of the states of the Muslim world.[2] As we have seen, many Islamists blame the introduction of Persian culture for the disappearance of the religiously inspired political systems that flourished during the era of the Prophet and the Rightly Guided Caliphs (or just the Prophet and Ali, in the case of the Shia), and the re-emergence of the monarchical system under the Abbasids and Umayyads. Indeed, throughout its history up to the Islamic Revolution of 1979 Iran was ruled not by Ayatollahs such as Khomeini but by dynasties of Shahs – whether it be the Buwayhids or the Ghaznavids during the Abbasid period, or the Safavids between the fifteenth and eighteenth centuries, or the Qajars and the Pahlavis of the modern era.

It was 'Twelver', or *Ithna' Ashari*, Shi'ism that rose to prominence in Iran in the fifteenth century and has prevailed until the present day. Twelver Shi'is profess allegiance to the eleventh Imam after Ali, whom they believe secluded himself (or went into 'occultation') in the ninth century AD. As a result of this belief in a 'hidden Imam', Twelver Shi'ism has had both quietist and messianic strains throughout history. The *ghulat* or 'extremist' form represents the Imam as a messiah whose return will establish heavenly rule on earth, whereas a more apolitical and mainstream variant suggests that the 'hidden Imam' will return only at the end of days.[3] The doctrine of awaiting the return of the Hidden Imam (*intizar*) has tended to encourage Shia scholars, much like Sunni ones, to accept the political status quo. The only exceptions to this rule have come when a prominent statesman or religious leader has declared himself the reincarnation of the Twelfth Imam, as was the case with Shah Ismail, who founded Safavid Iran in 1487.[4] During their tenure, the Safavids Shahs slowly enforced adherence to Twelver Shi'ism throughout Iran, and established a scholarly apparatus that outlasted their own downfall in the eighteenth century. Following the decline of the Safavids, the Shia *ulama* resolved to return to the doctrine of awaiting the return of the Imam at the end of time and thus largely abstained from engagement in political affairs.[5] Yet, the disappearance of the Safavids also enabled them to reclaim the historic position of Shia scholars as the intermediaries between the faithful and the hidden Imam, and to exercise an increasingly significant role in Iranian civic and religious (as opposed to political) life. The emerging power of this scholarly elite in the eighteenth century coincided with the increasing hegemony of the Usuli school of jurisprudence, which advocated a rationalist form of *ijtihad*, within Iranian Shi'ism.[6] This paralleled the revivalists' reintroduction of *ijtihad* in the Sunni Muslim world, and quite possibly inspired Afghani and Abduh's rationalist application of the principle.[7] With the predominance of the Usuli school came a new clerical hierarchy, or *marji'iyya*, led by the *mujtahids* (i.e. those who practised *ijtihad*).[8] By the early twentieth century the most prestigious of these scholars came to style themselves Ayatollahs – literally, 'signs of God'.

The autocratic tendencies of a new Iranian royal dynasty, the Qajars, encouraged a number of the *mujtahids* to reconsider their role in political life. In particular, the *mujtahids* played an increasingly visible public role in response to the combined threat posed to both religion and the economy by the Qajars' increasingly close relationship with the British and the Russians. The introduction of secular education by the Qajars in the second half of the nineteenth century undermined the prestige of their own seminaries, whereas their granting of tobacco monopolies to British merchants threatened to undercut local commerce.[9] The result was an alliance between the *mujtahids* and local commercial elites against the Qajars. It was during the Constitutional Revolution of 1905–11, which sought to restrict the powers of the Qajar dynasty, that a group of *mujtahids* first proposed that they might act as the 'overseers' of a parliamentary and constitutional system of government; this anticipated Khomeini's post-1979 'Council of Guardians'.[10] As was the case in India, the *ulama* were seeking to exercise a more political role precisely because the onset of colonialism – in this case a more informal colonialism – had led to a situation where they felt that control over the state and control of the values and outlook of society could not be separated.

As the twentieth century unfolded, the stakes were raised. Modernizing autocrats, secular nationalists, liberal democrats, Soviet Russians and their local communist allies, *mujtahids* and oil-hunting British and American imperialists all competed to capture the Iranian state. In 1921, the British – seeking to protect their recently acquired oil concessions in Iran – backed the rise to power of a minor army officer, Reza Khan.[11] Reza Khan, although no Western lackey, pursued a policy of aggressive Westernization and secularization, as well as cultural Persianism. He adopted the dynastic title 'Pahlavi' – the name of a Persian language of the Sassanid era – and glorified Iran's pre-Islamic heritage while demonizing Arab culture. Pahlavi nationalism was inspired by the racist ideologies prevalent in Europe, championing the 'Aryan' Iranians against the 'Semitic' Arabs.[12] The Shah thus stood for everything that Islamists were coming to see as *jahili*, harking back to ethnic antagonisms similar to those prevailing in the 'age of ignorance'. Yet, it was the British who in 1941, fearing the consequences of his close relations with Nazi Germany, replaced their erstwhile cat's paw with his more pliable son, Muhammad Reza.

In cultivating more open relationships with the Western powers while maintaining the autocratic tendencies of his father, Muhammad Reza managed to provoke the simultaneous opposition of liberal democrats, *mujtahids* and communists. As a result, with the backing of both the pro-Soviet Tudeh Party (established in 1941) and the more politically active contingent of the *marja'iyya* under Ayatollah Kashani, in 1951 Muhammad Mossadeq of the National Front succeeded in becoming prime minister and laid out plans to nationalize Iran's oil industry. Fearing Mossadeq's links to the Tudeh, American intelligence officers collaborated with pro-Shah army officers in an effort to force his resignation. Although Mossadeq's downfall is widely attributed to this plot, his demise seems in fact to have been chiefly brought about by his simultaneous alienation of the *mujtahids* and the communists. He distanced himself from the Tudeh for fear that it was becoming too powerful, and was then fatally weakened by demonstrations engineered by clerics angry at his increasing secularism. Whatever the degree of US responsibility for Mosaddeq's ouster, the Americans became the Shah's principal backers over the next three decades, as they slowly took over more and more of Britain's informal empire in the Middle East. The CIA helped the Shah to establish his brutal security apparatus, SAVAK. Meanwhile, Iran became a highly attractive location for American expatriates – there were over fifty thousand resident in Iran by 1979.[13]

One significant player in the 1951–1953 crisis was the Fidayiin-i Islam movement of Navvab Safavi. Safavi was inspired by Hasan al-Banna and in many regards his organization acted as the Iranian equivalent of the Muslim Brotherhood and Jama'at-i-Islami. Like Mawdudi and Hasan al-Banna, Safavi came from a scholarly family but undertook his education in a modern, secular institution; like them, he also conceived of the relationship between Islam, government and society in comprehensive terms.[14] However, unlike the Jama'at and the Brotherhood the Fidayiin-i Islam did not remain a major force after the death of its founder. One reason for this was the greater role played by the clerics in the politics of Iranian Islamism, and the fact that Khomeini and the other radicals in the *marja'iyya*, who had close ties to Safavi in the 1940s and 1950s, were willing to take on his mantle after his execution in 1956. Another was the fact that Safavi was not willing to adopt the gradualist approach of al-Banna and Mawdudi, and the Fida'iyyin resorted to political violence right from the outset. They assassinated Ahmad Kasravi, a prominent secularist intellectual, in 1946, and General Razmara, a noted opponent of Mossadeq's plans to nationalize the oil industry, in 1951. A shared interest in economic nationalism and anti-imperialism briefly led the Fida'iyyin to support Mossadeq's premiership, but after he rejected their demands for an Islamization of the legal system they adopted terrorist methods against his regime as well. Three years after the downfall of Mossadeq, Safavi was sentenced to death by the Shah after a failed attempt on the life of his prime minister.[15]

Although it survived the crisis of 1951–1953, the Iranian regime's close relationship with the CIA and the American government prevented it from gaining any real legitimacy. Because it promoted secularization and Westernization in equal measure, opposition to it frequently took a cultural and a religious form.[16] It was this context that the anti-Western and anti-Enlightenment philosophies of intellectuals such as Heidegger gained ground within Iran's intellectual elite.[17] The Tudeh Party slowly lost popularity as a result of its outspoken support for the atheistic Soviet Union, and thinkers such as Jalal Al-e-Ahmad and Ali Shariati, who blended Islam with socialism, came to be the most effective critics of the regime's support for capitalist imperialism. Jalal Al-e-Ahmad criticized the 'civilization of the machine',[18] condemning industrial soullessness in a manner similar to thinkers such as Qutb and Carrell. He coined the term *Gharbzadegi* to denounce excessive attachment to Western culture. It was precisely because the Shah had secularized the educational environment in Iran that a number of student-based movements emerged that followed these Islamic socialist figures rather than the *mujtahids*.[19] Yet, the figure who accrued most power during the revolution was an Ayatollah, Ruhollah Khomeini.

Khomeini and Khomeinism

Khomeini was the most prominent of the twentieth-century Islamists who identified with the formal scholarly establishment, as opposed to those who were graduates of secular schools and challenged the *ulama's* monopolization of the religious agenda. This was possible for Khomeini because, as we have seen, the Usuli *mujtahids* of Iran were well ahead of their Sunni counterparts in their use of a rationalist form of *ijtihad*, independence from the state and willingness to adapt their understanding of Islam to new political contexts. Nevertheless, Khomeini was not representative of the Shia *marja'iyya* as a whole. His origins were comparatively marginal. Born in the minor provincial town of Khomein in 1902, he came from a line of relatively inconspicuous religious scholars.[20] He grew up in conditions of extreme poverty, in a mud brick house that he shared with around thirty others, and his father was murdered when he was still young.[21] His maternal relatives sent him to the Fayzieh seminary in Qum to study with the prominent Shia theologian, Abdul Karim Ha'iri, and it was there that subsequently he taught Sufi philosophy and *fiqh*.[22] It seems that, like Qutb and Mawdudi, Khomeini went through a phase when he moved away from orthodox Islam, writing Sufi poems and experimenting with mysticism.[23] Nevertheless, his intellectual precociousness earned him promotion in 1936 to the rank of *mujtahid* at a surprisingly early age.[24] Many of the clerics who went on to play prominent roles in the Iranian Revolution were students of Khomeini, rather than products and then representatives of the orthodox religious establishment as a whole. Notable among these were the Ayatollahs Hussein Montazeri, Morteza Mottaheri and Muhammad Behesti, as well as Hojjat al-Islam Akbar Hashemi Rafsanjani.[25]

Khomeini became a prominent oppositionist because he was more willing than other clerics to adapt his political language to chime with the oppositional discourse articulated by left-leaning Islamic thinkers such as Shariati.[26] Although he had been criticizing the regime in his writings since the 1940s, it was not until the 1960s that he mobilized his students into a political organization, the Nahzat-i-Islami, and became one of the most vocal opponents of the Shah.[27] His platform was the movement of mass opposition to the Shah's 'White Revolution' reform measures of 1963, which had angered the clerical establishment by introducing female suffrage and a number of land reform measures.[28] The clerics objected to the enfranchisement of women on religious grounds, and feared an attack on the landholding classes who contributed substantially to their own finances.[29] In spite of being a member of the *marja'iyya*, Khomeini was versatile enough to focus less on these issues and more on the concerns of the broader public, particularly the revolutionary generation of students who were leading the anti-regime mobilization. He denounced the regime for its corruption, autocracy, and electoral malpractice, as well as for its attacks on peasants, students and workers alike.[30]

In 1964, following another confrontation with the regime, Khomeini went into exile, in 1965 eventually settling in the Shia holy city of Najaf in Iraq.[31] Here he encountered a group of radical Shi'i scholars led by Baqir al-Sadr, who promoted an activist form of Shi'ism that sought to compete with socialism in its revolutionary intent.[32] It was in Najaf that Khomeini's theory of Islamic government underwent its most radical shift. In his 1943 work on the public role of the Shia clerical establishment, *Kashf-i-Asrar*, he had condemned the Shah for his neglect of Islam but nevertheless maintained the position that was then conventional among Shia *mujtahids*; namely, that the cleric might advise the government but never replace it outright.[33] He wrote that 'the mujtahids have never rejected the system of government nor the independence of Islamic governments ... even when the governments are oppressive and against the people, they will not try to destroy the rulers'.[34] Yet, by the late 1960s, Khomeini had shifted his position radically: by then, he was advocating the principle of *Velayat-i-Faqih*, or 'the State of the Jurist'.[35] Khomeini's theory maintained that

> the contemporary jurist is the heir to the prophet's authority. Whatever was entrusted to the prophet has been entrusted by the Imams to the jurists. The jurists have authority on all matters. They have been entrusted with the power to govern, rule and run the affairs of the people.[36]

This radical transformation of Khomeini's political ideology owes a great deal to his confrontation with the regime in 1963, following which he began to advocate its outright removal. But another contributing factor was his increasing intellectual indebtedness to the Sunni Islamist tradition, and particularly to thinkers such as Mawdudi and Rida, both of whom had explored the role that the *ulama* should play in the Islamic state. Khomeini, who met Mawdudi in Mecca in 1963, translated a number of his writings and found his concept of theo-democracy particularly appealing.[37] The Ayatollah's notion of the jurist acting as a Platonic 'philosopher-king' practising *ijtihad* bore remarkable parallels with the style of Islamic leadership advocated by these two thinkers.[38] Meanwhile, al-Banna's Muslim Brotherhood may well have influenced the organization of Khomeini's Nahzat-i-Islami, possibly via Safavi's Fidayiin.[39] What united the Iranian Islamists with their Sunni counterparts across the sectarian divide was an identification with activist Sufism as well as a perception of Islam as an holistic, all-embracing system.[40] At the same time, Khomeini made an explicit break with the quietist tradition in Twelver Shi'ism that maintained it was acceptable for true Muslims to hide their real beliefs in the face of oppression while they awaited the return of the Twelfth Imam. In 1963 Khomeini issued a *fatwa* abolishing this practice of *taqiyya* (dissimulation) outright.[41]

Like many Islamists, Khomeini used the perception that Western colonialism posed an existential threat to Islam to justify an equally totalistic assertion of that Islamic identity in response. Islam, he wrote, was 'the school of those who struggle against imperialism'.[42] Like Qutb and Mawdudi, Khomeini asserted that it was the 'imperialists' who had spread the notion that Islam was an apolitical faith confined to the private sphere.[43] Indeed, he argued that it was only colonialism that stood in the way of the materialization of the *velayet-i-faqih*, noting that 'this slogan of the separation of religion and politics and the demand that Islamic scholars not intervene in social and political affairs have been formulated and propagated by the imperialists; it is only the irreligious who repeat them'.[44] Anti-colonialism was at the heart of his rhetoric – it was his opposition to a law introduced by the Shah granting American soldiers immunity from criminal prosecution by the Iranian legal system that had been the direct cause of his exile in 1964.[45] The apparently paranoid elements of his rhetoric, which frequently referred to the 'agents' and 'devoted servants' of 'imperialism',[46] must be understood in the context of the common knowledge of CIA intervention in the 1953 crisis and training of the Shah's security services.[47] The Shah was certainly more culpable of complicity with Western neocolonialism than Nasser. Yet, Khomeini's rhetoric equated secularism, and even opposition to his 'rule of the jurist', with imperialism, thereby making all of his opponents traitors to Islam.

Even though Khomeini positioned himself as the defender of an authentic Islam that had been swept away by colonialism, his own views were – at least in the opinion of many of his peers in the religious establishment – somewhat unorthodox. Like al-Afghani and Mawdudi, he had supped deeply from the Indo-Iranian philosophical tradition and was influenced by Plato, Ibn Arabi and Mulla Sidra. His earliest works in the 1930s were on the subject of *Irfan*, a form of Sufi-orientated philosophy which posited that an individual could obtain new knowledge of the divine will through integration of his soul with that of God.[48] Khomeini taught on *Irfan* at Qum in the 1940s and the majority of the students who went on to join him in the Nahzat-i-Islami were individuals who shared his outlook.[49] This is why it is important to stress that it was the Khomeinists, not the *marja'iyya* as a whole, who eventually dominated the Iranian Revolution. At the same time, Khomeini knew the importance of presenting himself as a more orthodox scholar to the wider Muslim public, and – from the 1940s onwards – also became an expert in conventional jurisprudence.[50] Like al-Afghani, he probably understood the utility of operating at more than one level of discourse.[51] Yet, the imprint of *Irfan* on his praxis is visible. It is possible that his concept of the Nahzat-i-Islami as a form of vanguardist organization bore the imprint of Marxism–Leninism, possibly mediated by Qutb or Mawdudi. Yet, it may well have been more directly influenced by Mulla Sidra's focus on a pious elite, the members of which each came close to the ideal of the 'perfect man' through proximity to the divine essence and were thus in a position to restore a more genuine form of Islam.[52] In particular, his belief (similar to that of Mawdudi) that the leading *mujtahid* should act as a 'philosopher-king' was rooted in the concept that special knowledge could be acquired through *Irfan*.[53]

Come the revolution: The downfall of the Shah and the advent of the Islamic Republic

It would be a mistake to understand the revolution that overthrew the Shah in 1979 as a solely Islamist phenomenon, or as a straightforward battle between religion and secularism. Those who campaigned against the Shah from 1977 to 1979 came from a diverse range of social and ideological backgrounds, and their protests did not begin as the result of the regime's refusal to introduce sharia law. The two most significant factors in the outbreak of the revolution were an economic downturn brought on by hyperinflation, and the international pressure brought on the Shah to liberalize his regime.[54] Human rights organizations, including Amnesty International, raised awareness of the brutal practices of SAVAK and, as a result, the American government compelled the Shah to release a number of political prisoners.[55] The domestic opposition was not fully appeased, however, and seized the opportunity to demand further measures of liberal reform. The initial campaign was spearheaded by the National Front, the body that had galvanized support for Mosaddeq in 1951. Protests initially grew out of liberal, secular, middle-class and urban institutions, notably university campuses and intellectual groups such as the Writer's Guild. In the first year of the revolution, these groups would call not for an Islamic state but for a return to the system of liberal constitutional monarchy that had been one of the founding achievements of the earlier Constitutional Revolution.[56]

The problem with the National Front was that it could not compete with the militant clerics when it came to mobilizing support beyond its middle-class base. The networks that Iran's clerics had created in the bazaars and mosques gave them the capacity to generate a real mass movement that transcended class divisions. Not all of the militant clerics were themselves Khomeinists. One of the first Islamic groups to join the revolution from within Iran was the Freedom Movement, composed of left-leaning clerics such as Ayatollah Mahmud Taleqani as well as Islamic modernist professionals such as Mehdi Bazarghan.[57] Like the National Front, the Freedom Movement campaigned for a revival of the 1906 constitution, but nevertheless represented an important point of contact for Khomeini, still in exile in Iraq at that time. The Khomeinists themselves began to mobilize in the Ayatollah's powerhouse in Qum towards the end of 1977, following the mysterious death of Khomeini's son, Mostafa, who was widely believed to have been assassinated by SAVAK.[58] Their protests intensified in January 1978 when the regime's leading newspaper published a lengthy character assassination of Khomeini. Over four thousand student theologians marched in protest, resulting in clashes with the regime's security forces and the making of new martyrs.[59]

Although the various Ayatollahs who participated in the protests – both Khomeinist and non-Khomeinist – did not initially demand an Islamic Republic, they drew heavily on the language of revolutionary Shi'ism. In December 1978, Taleqani, a number of Khomeini's students, and other oppositionists used the Ashura festival – which commemorated the martyrdom of the third Shia imam, Hussein, at Karbala in 680 – to mobilize a two million-strong demonstration against the Shah.[60] Khomeini himself labelled the Shah 'Yazid', after the Umayyad Caliph who had slaughtered Hussein and his followers at Karbala.[61] In spite of the fact that his text proposing a 'State of the Jurist' had already been published, Khomeini deliberately played down his desire for an Islamic Republic, focusing instead on forming a broad front with the rest of the opposition to drive out the Shah.[62]

The revolution was not initially a revolution of the political left. In fact, the one economic class that had been most alienated by the Shah's policies in the 1970s were the bazaari merchants, blamed by the regime for spiralling inflation and subjected to a variety of draconian measures to ensure price control and prevent hoarding.[63] The alliance between the bazaaris and clerics was a significant one throughout the revolution. Meanwhile, urban labourers, who had initially benefited from the Shah's focus on economic development, did not join the revolution until half way through 1978, when the economic downturn finally began to take its toll on them.[64] The Tudeh Party, worn down by SAVAK repression, did not break with its anti-revolutionary strategy until the revolutionary struggle had nearly reached its denouement, finally coming out in favour of armed revolution in January 1979.[65] At that point, the two leftist militia organizations, the Mojahedin-i-Khalq and Fida'iyyin-i-Khalq, after arming and mobilizing thousands of members of the public, led a number of successful assaults on the garrisons of the regime's security forces.[66]

By February 1979, the Shah was gone, a brief attempt to form a compromise government under Shahpur Bakhtiar of the National Front having been undermined by public anger at the repeated killings by the Shah's security services.[67] As the Shah departed, Khomeini arrived, returning from his exile in Paris to considerable popular adulation. He continued his strategy of developing a broad front among the Islamically orientated political forces, publicly cooperating with members of the Freedom Movement and other radical clerics in a body known as the Revolutionary Council.[68] The Revolutionary Council established local revolutionary *Komitehs* as well as local revolutionary courts which acted as judge, jury and executioner in disposing of various old-regime politicians and SAVAK officers. It was a member of the Freedom Movement, Mehdi Bazarghan, and not a Khomeinist, who formed the transitional cabinet. Meanwhile, Khomeini sought to consolidate his political and military strength. His movement established its own political party, the Islamic Republican Party (IRP), under Ayatollah Beheshti, along with a newspaper.[69] The Khomeinists also established a number of militia organizations, including a Mujahidin i-Inqilab i-Islami movement to rival the leftist Mojahidin-i-Khalq and Fida'iyyin i-Khalq, as well as the more elite Revolutionary Guard.[70] They also created the *Hizbullahis*, a more street-based movement largely drawn from the urban poor, which would play the foremost role in enforcing Khomeini's various morality codes in future years.[71]

In spite of the failure of the National Front to compete with the radical clerics, it was by no means guaranteed that a regime based on Khomeini's principle of the *Velayet-i-Faqih* would emerge out of the revolution. Even after the downfall of the Shah and a referendum result declaring that 98.2 per cent of the Iranian population favoured an Islamic Republic, Khomeini did not immediately campaign for a state ruled by jurists. In June, Bazarghan's cabinet of middle-class technocrats unveiled a constitution that replaced the monarchy with a president rather than an Ayatollah, and paid lip service to Islam without mentioning either sharia or the clerics.[72] However, the cabinet decided to submit the constitution for revision by an Assembly of Experts, and when popular elections were held for this body, over two-thirds of the seats were won by clerics, most of whom had ties to Khomeini's IRP.[73] Exploiting the growing political strength of the IRP and its various affiliated militias, the genuine popular support for the idea of clerical rule, and the downfall of Bazarghan as prime minister, the clerics in the Assembly of Experts amended the constitution to give supreme executive power to Khomeini as the Imam and ruling jurist.[74]

The *Velayat-i-Faqih* in practice

The Iranian Revolution provided Khomeini with an opportunity to realize his vision of the Islamic state never afforded to the likes of al-Banna, Qutb and Mawdudi. Although he made some inevitable concessions to pragmatism, most of the basic principles of his *Velayet-i-Faqih* model – insofar as they had been given any real substance in his writings – were put into practice. The constitution of the Islamic Republic declared that 'in the time of the occultation of the 12th Imam in the Islamic Republic of Iran the mandate to rule [*wilayat-i amr*] and leadership of the people [*imamat-i ummat*] are the responsibility of a just, pious jurist aware of the times'.[75] The first supreme jurist was, of course, Khomeini himself. Khomeini also adopted the title of Imam – a controversial choice and one which was received with distaste by many established clerics, since in Shia Islam this term was historically only used with reference to Ali and his eleven successors. While Khomeini did not officially pronounce himself to be the Twelfth Imam, many of Khomeini's followers revered him as al-Mahdi returned to the earth.[76]

Nevertheless, Khomeini did find it necessary to make more concessions to the principle of human sovereignty than he did in the idealistic blueprints he provided in *Islamic Government*, giving the Assembly the prerogative of drafting legislation while making its passage subject to the approval of a 'Council of Guardians' composed of six religious scholars and six lawyers.[77] The constitution winked at Mawdudi's notion of 'theo-democracy' in basing sovereignty on the popular as well as the divine will.[78] However, Abol Hasan Bani Sadr would later claim that Khomeini had informed him 'You are always talking about the 11 million people who voted for you, but there is no such thing as public opinion, neither in Iran nor anywhere else.'[79]

Bani Sadr attributed Khomeini's contempt for public opinion to his attachment to Aristotelian and Platonic philosophy.[80] While Khomeini's campaign for sharia was central to his legitimacy, it was indeed his interest in *Irfan* and the ideal of the philosopher king that informed his style of governance. He even went so far in 1983 as to observe that 'I may have said something yesterday, changed it today, and will change it again tomorrow. This does not mean that simply because I have made a statement yesterday, I should adhere to it.' Khomeini justified this capriciousness on pragmatic grounds, observing that such turnarounds were justifiable as 'we intend to implement Islam'.[81] This approach enabled Khomeini to overcome the obstacles posed by both sharia and the Council of Guardians while maintaining the principle of divine sovereignty by conferring his own powers on the Majlis when the Council of Guardians blocked its legislation.[82] In 1987, in a missive to his later successor, Ali Khamenei, he went as far as to declare that

> the government, which is part of the total vice-regency of the Prophet ... is one of the foremost injunctions of Islam and has priority over all other secondary injunctions, even prayers, fasting and the hajj ... [and] is

empowered to unilaterally revoke any lawful agreement ... if the agreement contravenes the interests of Islam and the country. It can prevent any matter, whether religious or secular, if it is against the *interests* of Islam.[83]

One commentator observes that this doctrine, which came to be known as *Velayet-i-Motlaq* (absolute guardianship), was unprecedented in Islamic jurisprudence and resembled the outlook of such radical authoritarians as Stalin and Robespierre.[84] However, it is worth repeating that Khomeini's ideology represented the worldview of only a portion of the Shi'i clerical elite. Only one fellow Ayatollah, Montazeri, was willing to support the concept of *Velayet-i-Faqih* when Khomeini put it into practice, whereas many of the most prominent among them, including Shariatmadari and Abu'l-Qasim al-Khu'i, actively opposed it.[85] Khomeini's support therefore came principally from his own students, most of whom had only achieved the lesser rank of *hojjateslam*.[86] Ali Khamenei, who replaced Khomeini as *Rahbar* (Supreme Leader) following his death in 1989, was one such figure.[87]

Exploiting the somewhat flexible character of Khomeini's revolutionary authority, his followers made a number of compromises with nationalist and leftist ideology, despite maintaining that they had made a revolutionary break with the nationalist and Marxist ethos of the day. The regime clamped down on the Mojahedin-i-Khalq, the organization that had attached itself to the Islamic socialist principles of Ali Shariati, yet continued to adopt much of Shariati's rhetoric in practice. Khomeini's repeated declarations that 'the country belongs to the slum dwellers'[88] appear to evoke a Fanonian concern with the lumpenproletariat. Khomeini and the IRP had successfully mobilized the urban poor by integrating them into the *hezbollahi* militias and using them against the more affluent opponents of Islamist rule.[89] Like many of its Arab socialist neighbours, the Islamic Republic introduced measures of land reform and privatization. In 1980, for example, the government established a Centre for the Transfer and Revitalization of Land that transferred 185,000 hectares to the most impoverished among the peasantry, and by 1982, 80 per cent of private industry had been nationalized.[90] However, the Khomeinists were never just the defenders of the *mostafezin*, or oppressed. As we have seen, they received a great deal of support during the revolution from the *bazaaris*, or urban merchants. This sector merged with the rural landowners to prevent any further leftist measures after the heady early years of the revolution. Land redistribution went no further after 1980, a bill to put foreign trade under public ownership was defeated by the *bazaaris* and their allies in parliament, and a number of measures were taken against organized labour, including a ban on strikes.[91]

In the early days of the revolution, the leaders of the new regime claimed to be abandoning nationalism in the name of pan-Islamism. In practice, however, Iran's international agenda often came closer to representing a form of pan-Shi'ism, as the regime armed only Shi'i groups in Iraq and Lebanon. In most regards, its foreign and domestic policies came to resemble those of a conventional nation state. Khomeini claimed that his war against Saddam's Iraq (1980–8) represented a battle between Islam and unbelief,[92] but it began as a result of a territorial dispute in the Persian Gulf that reflected a more prosaic nationalist concern with the delineation of boundaries.[93] Iran only had modest success in mobilizing Iraq's substantial Shia population against Saddam, and did little to intervene in the Iraqi dictator's massacres of Shi'is in 1991.[94] Meanwhile, Iran's revolutionary clerics, having committed themselves to moving away from linguistic nationalism in the immediate aftermath of the revolutionary moment of 1979, had by the end of the 1980s begun to praise the Persian language again as being superior to Arabic.[95] Khomeini himself often spoke of the 'Iranian fatherland' and 'honourable people of Iran', and barred a close supporter from putting himself forward as a presidential candidate on the grounds of his Afghan parentage.[96]

Suggested readings

Vanessa Martin, *Khomeini and the Making of a New Iran,* chapter entitled 'Visions of the Islamic State: I' (London: I.B. Tauris, 2003).

What were the precedents for Khomeini's model of the 'state of the jurist' (*velayet i-faqih*)? What historic developments shaped Khomeini's viewpoints from the 1940s through to the 1970s? What practical matters did Khomeini's theory of the state address? How did his position compare with that of other Shia *mujtahids*?

Kingshuk Chatterjee, *Ali Shariati and the Shaping of Political Islam in Sudan,* Chapter 7 (New York: Palgrave Macmillan, 2011).

What was the specific legacy of Ali Shariati to later Iranian Islamists? How coherent was Islamic Revolutionary Ideology during and after the Revolution? How contested was the notion of *velayet i-faqih*?

Suggested primary source reading

Ayatollah Ruhollah Khomeini, *Islam and Revolution: Writings and Declarations of Imam Khomeini* (ed. Hamid Algar) (Berkeley: Mizan Press, 1980), pp. 25–54 (The original version dates from 1970.)

How does Khomeini present his theory as a response to colonialism? Why does Khomeini dislike human forms of government (including monarchy and parliamentary democracy)? Can you see the traces of other thinkers here? Should this be understood as the blueprint for a distinctively Shia form of Islamism? How does Khomeini define the role of the jurist? How does he justify the role he gives the jurist with reference to Islamic history? Can we see more of a practical blueprint here than we do in, for example, Mawdudi, Qutb? How does Khomeini characterize sharia? How does he understand *tawhid* and *shirk*?

10

Reformer, radical or maverick? Hasan al-Turabi and Islamism in Sudan

Following the establishment of Khomeini's Islamic Republic in Shia Iran in 1979, the 'Salvation Revolution' in Sudan ten years later marked the first takeover of an established state by an Islamist movement in the Sunni Muslim world. The character of the two movements was quite distinct. While Khomeini's movement seized power during a genuine popular revolution, the National Islamic Front (NIF) could hardly claim convincingly that it was riding a wave of popular resentment against an 'imperialist' regime when it took over in Khartoum in 1989. The NIF, which had emerged out of the Sudanese wing of the Muslim Brotherhood but had by this point detached itself from the Egypt-based movement, stood only at third place in democratic polls in 1986 and therefore resorted to a military coup to capture the state. There are similarities with the electorally unsuccessful Jama'at-i-Islami's backing of the Zia Regime in Pakistan, although the role of the Sudanese Islamists in Umar al-Bashir's coup of 1989 was far greater than that of their Pakistani counterparts in 1977. Al-Bashir and the majority of his fellow putschists were hand-picked by the NIF from an Islamist cell cultivated in the military by the Sudanese Islamic Movement, and, although they initially sought to mask the ideological character of their coup by appointing a cabinet full of technocrats, real power lay in a set of institutions run in parallel by civilian and military Islamists. Between 1991 and 1995 Hasan al-Turabi, the charismatic intellectual who had led the Sudanese Islamic Movement since the 1960s, convened the Popular Arab and Islamic Conference, inviting Islamists from all over the globe to Khartoum to unite in opposition to Western imperialism. The Sudanese regime offered citizenship to numerous militant Islamists fleeing the various authoritarian and monarchical regimes within the region, most notoriously playing host to Osama bin Laden and his nascent al-Qa'eda organization between 1991 and 1996.

This chapter is largely devoted to the 'Civilizational Project' of al-Turabi and the Sudanese Islamists. On account of its 'multiple marginality'[1] – situated at the periphery of the 'Middle East and North Africa' and sub-Saharan African regions alike – Sudan's Islamist experiment has not been studied as much as its Iranian equivalent. It is true that the Sudanese Islamists were less successful in constructing a state system defined by Islamist ideology than their counterparts in Iran, largely due to their over-reliance on a military alliance and their efforts to impose a narrowly defined form of subjecthood on a country that was both culturally and religiously diverse. Yet, it is important to study Sudan nevertheless, for the 'Civilizational Project' in spite of its failings represented the most serious effort by a Sunni Islamist regime hitherto to use the machinery of the modern state to restructure society in line with its ideological vision. It is important to understand why al-Turabi was able to achieve what he did, and yet why he was never able to engineer a form of Islamist order as enduring as the 'Council of the Guardians' in Sudan. It has been argued that the particular authority given to the clerical elite as representatives of the hidden Imam in Twelver Shi'ism was what enabled Khomeini to go further that Sunni Islamists ever have[2] – and it is true that al-Turabi was never able to establish himself as an Imam like Khomeini. Yet, it might also be argued that it was Sudan's religious diversity that made it particularly unsuited to an Islamist regime.[3] Compared with other countries in which Islamist groups have taken power, Sudan offers an important case study because it had a particularly sizeable non-Muslim population before the secession of the south in 2011.

An important debate in this book so far has turned on the question of whether Islamist ideology is inherently violent and exclusivist, or whether such of these characteristics as it has exhibited are the product of specific historical circumstances. That the NIF seizure of power led to an intensification of political violence in Sudan is unquestionable – the new regime established infamous 'ghost houses' in which the country's citizens were held incommunicado and tortured; it also set up 'Popular Defence Force' militias which were indoctrinated with Islamist ideology and which committed widespread human rights abuses against marginalized populations in the battle against the Sudan People's Liberation Army rebels. Once Hasan al-Turabi was removed from the government by the officer who had led the 1989 coup on his behalf, Umar al-Bashir, he admitted that the 'Civilizational Project' of the 1990s had been a debacle; and a number of his fellow Islamists agreed. Yet, even until his death in 2016, a number of al-Turabi's champions maintained that his ideas were not 'radical' or 'extremist' at all, but that rather, he had successfully brought Islam, modernity and democracy into harmony.[4] Was the brutality and authoritarianism of the Salvation Regime not, therefore, traceable to Hasan al-Turabi's ideology – was it a product of a specific set of historical circumstances? Some have maintained that the principle of Islamist democracy should not be judged by the failure of an experiment with it in a country not homogeneously Muslim and in which military authoritarianism was entrenched.[5] Al-Turabi himself was eager to show regret over the decision to rely on a military coup to bring about an Islamist Revolution, attributing the failings of the Salvation Regime to his erstwhile allies in the army and fellow Islamists whom he believed had betrayed him.[6]

Al-Turabi's numerous critics have maintained that his ideology is very much responsible for the downfall of the Salvation Regime, and that his protestations of its liberal and democratic character were a mere tactical feint by a ruthless and uncompromising thinker.[7] The debate about the 'radical' and 'reformist' trends in Islamist and proto-Islamist ideology discussed earlier in this text is crucial here. For al-Turabi's defenders, his ideas can be traced back to Abduh,[8] whereas others maintain that his beliefs concerning the character of the Islamic state and the role of jihad do not differ in essence from 'radicals' such as Mawdudi and Qutb.[9] Some have – as with Mawdudi and Qutb – sought to identify parallels with the totalitarian ideologies of the Western world, one going as far as to characterize al-Turabi as an 'Islamist Lenin'.[10] Abdullahi Gallab has argued quite stridently that al-Turabi's project 'failed because of its relationship to totalitarianism' and not 'because of its relation to Islam'.[11] Yet, we need to focus not just on parallels with Nazi and Soviet regimes but also on colonial government in Sudan and elsewhere, since the colonization of al-Turabi's intellect during the era of British rule in Sudan helped to form some of his more totalistic intellectual and political visions.[12] Another approach maintains that by focusing too much on the Islamists influenced by their Western education, we risk overlooking the role of Sufi and Salafi groups, with little interest in Western political ideals, as the engineers of the Islamic project in Sudan.[13]

Colonialism in Sudan: Background

Islam was spread to Sudanic Africa by merchants and itinerant Sufi preachers, rather than conquering armies. The territory that constitutes modern Sudan first began to embrace Islam in the thirteenth century, and by the sixteenth century the great ruling dynasties of the day, Dar Fur and Dar Funj, had begun to adopt Islamic laws and institutions while leaving largely intact the customary practices of the populations over which they ruled. The vast majority of Sudanese Muslims embraced Islam through identification with a variety of Sufi orders, such as the Qadiriyya. The earlier Sufi orders in Sudan developed a largely syncretic relationship with local cultures, and their members often treated the leaders of these orders as saints, or *walis*. Throughout the eighteenth and nineteenth centuries, relatively more orthodox forms of Islam began to appear. When the Ottoman vassal and ruler of Egypt, Muhammad Ali, conquered Sudan in 1820, sharia courts practising the Hanafi school of law prevalent throughout the Empire followed in his wake. At the same time, a number of Sufi *tariqas* influenced by the Revivalist trend – such as the Sammaniyya, Tijaniyya and Khatmiyya (explored in Chapter 3) – arrived in the country during the eighteenth and nineteenth centuries. It was an adherent of the Sammaniyya *tariqa*, Muhammad Ahmad, who declared himself the awaited Mahdi and overthrew the British-backed Turco-Egyptian government, establishing the Mahdist State (1885–98).

The Mahdist uprising is often celebrated by Sudanese nationalists as the country's first revolution against a colonial power. Yet, it was the subsequent Anglo-Egyptian Reconquest, which brought about the Anglo-Egyptian Condominium of Sudan (1899–1956), that established the sociopolitical order that the Sudanese Islamists would both react against and exploit. The half-century of Britain's rule over the Sudan – nominally as the equal partner of Egypt – created a number of grievances that would feature frequently in the rhetoric of Islamist intellectuals such as Hasan al-Turabi. First, the British made strenuous efforts to separate the largely non-Muslim and 'African' southern region of Sudan from the 'Arab' north, giving responsibility for educational provision for the former to Christian missionaries. Second, they introduced legal codes modelled largely on those of Britain's existing colony in India, relegating sharia to the realm of family law and thus effectively turning qadis into 'women's judges'.[14] Finally, they nurtured a semi-Anglicized, secularized elite at Gordon Memorial College – named after the general famously defeated by the Mahdi in 1885 – that would dominate political life in the country after official independence in 1956.

In spite of their pursuit of a form of authenticity politics, the majority of the pioneering generation of Sudanese Islamists were educated in the very same colonial institutions they later condemned, including Gordon Memorial College. Just as in Egypt, the early Sudanese Islamists largely hailed from the *effendiyya* elite that had experienced modern education – although in the Sudanese case, the leading educational institutions were still firmly under the control of the British. The Islamic Liberation Movement – the forerunner to the later NIF – was founded at Gordon Memorial College by alumni of Hantoub Secondary School, a Sudanese variant of Eton established by the British at the end of the colonial era to produce an Anglophone elite fit to govern the country after independence. They and their fellow students studied Shakespeare and played polo and football. Hasan al-Turabi himself – in spite of the fact that he later condemned the *effendiyya* as an 'alien ruling caste'[15] – was a graduate of both Hantoub and Gordon College, where he was a keen footballer and chess player. He never got the opportunity to play football as much as he would have wished, since his father – one of the sharia judges marginalized by the colonial administration – was, like Mawdudi's, convinced that a domestic education in Islamic jurisprudence was the best way of preventing the colonization of his intellect.[16] Al-Turabi thus absorbed Western colonial knowledge and classical Islamic knowledge in equal measure during his time in Sudan, and – as with Mawdudi – his Islamist worldview derived from a synthesis of this twin inheritance.

Hasan al-Turabi and his colleagues began their Islamist careers during a boom in higher and postgraduate education in the late colonial and early postcolonial world. Al-Turabi himself acquired a doctorate in law from the Sorbonne, and his fellow Islamists had doctorates in subjects such as genetics, clinical biochemistry and philosophy.[17] Indeed, al-Turabi was at the Sorbonne (1959–64) at around the same time as Ali Shariati, and, like him, mixed in circles supportive of the Algerian War of Independence.[18] Like earlier reformists such as al-Afghani and Abduh, al-Turabi would have seen travelling to Paris as a means of fleshing out a relationship between Islam and modernity not controlled by the colonial power in his own country.[19] Before and after his doctoral studies, he served as a law lecturer at the University of Khartoum (as Gordon College became), but retained his concern that British colonialism had created an artificial divide between the realm of sharia and the 'modern' world of the *effendiyya*.[20]

The rise of the Sudanese Islamic Movement

The Sudanese Islamic Movement emerged out of a loose coalition of Ikhwan-inspired groupings in the 1940s and 1950s, some of which identified as members of the 'mother' organization in Egypt while others sought to maintain their independent, 'Sudanese' character. In 1954, largely as a result of sympathy with the Muslim Brothers being persecuted by Nasser, members of the 'Sudanese' organization, the Islamic Liberation Movement, agreed to merge with the more pro-Egyptian groups in order to form the 'Muslim Brotherhood' of Sudan.[21] In 1964, Hasan al-Turabi became the secretary general of the movement and from the 1970s increasingly began to distance the organization from the leadership of the Brotherhood in Cairo. With al-Turabi at the helm, it slowly came to be known as the 'Islamic Movement', whereas a separate 'Muslim Brotherhood' faction broke away in the 1980s and maintained its allegiance to the Egypt-based leadership. In the periods in which political pluralism was sanctioned in Sudan, the Muslim Brotherhood/Islamic Movement formed political parties – the Islamic Charter Front between 1964 and 1969, then the NIF from 1986 until 1989.

The Sudanese Islamic Movement has often been identified with its charismatic leader, Hasan al-Turabi. Already enjoying respect as a law lecturer recently returned from the Sorbonne, he rose to prominence as one of the foremost protagonists of the October Revolution of 1964, an event that brought an end to the first military regime of Ibrahim Abboud and ultimately ushered in the country's second parliamentary regime. The movement against Abboud was largely led by students and university-educated professionals, and al-Turabi acquired his position of secretary general of the Muslim Brotherhood and Islamic Charter Front on account the prestige he acquired among campus Islamists for speeches he made against Abboud during this period. After 1964, he consistently advocated a 'political' approach, encouraging the Sudanese Islamists to pursue their objectives within the established sociopolitical order, and thus accept and work with whatever form – parliamentary or military – it happened to assume at any one time.

Nevertheless, it is noteworthy that al-Turabi was not able to exercise the same level of authority in constructing the Sudanese Islamic Movement as al-Banna had in shaping the Muslim Brotherhood in Egypt and Mawdudi the Jama'at-i-Islami. The movement emerged as a collective organization of like-minded individuals who all drew their inspiration from such established Islamists as Qutb, al-Banna, Mawdudi and al-Ghazali. There was also considerable sympathy with Salafism of the 'purist' kind in the Sudanese Islamic Movement, which forged close links with the Ansar al-Sunna, a Saudi-backed organization which has been growing in popularity in Sudan up to the present. One of al-Turabi's most prominent challengers for the leadership of the movement was Jafa'ar Shaikh Idris, who had an academic interest in Ibn Taymiyya and had maintained ties to the Ansar al-Sunna since his teenage years. A number of Sudanese Islamists believed that Mawdudi's 'educationalist' strategy offered a more viable approach than the narrowly 'political' strategy of al-Turabi, which they feared would force the Islamists to abandon their principles in the name of achieving power. Yet, the charismatic al-Turabi fought off all of these challenges, and maintained his leadership of the movement for over thirty-five years.

The method of al-Turabi that the 'educationalists' objected to most was his tendency to form alliances with non-Islamist politicians, including both democrats and authoritarians. The reason for this was that, like the Jama'at-i-Islami in Pakistan, the Sudanese Islamic Movement and its various political offshoots only had relatively limited success in democratic elections. Hasan al-Turabi's charisma was at its strongest among the educated elites, and had little impact outside the central urban areas. He only succeeded in winning a seat in the Sudanese parliament once, in 1965, in a 'graduate seat' in which the voting register was restricted to members of the educated class – when he competed in 'geographic' seats, where the principle of 'one man, one vote' applied, he lost out on both occasions. As a result, he attempted to pursue his campaign for an 'Islamic' constitution by forging alliances with his brother-in-law, Sadiq al-Mahdi, the great-grandson of Muhammad Ahmad al-Mahdi. However, the descendant of the nineteenth-century Revivalist was never able to fully reconcile himself with the twentieth-century Islamist. In both the second and third parliamentary periods (1965–9 and 1986–9), Sadiq al-Mahdi's Umma Party, in spite of its electoral alliances with the ICF and then the NIF, failed to support the programme for the Islamization of the constitution and the law that was advocated by al-Turabi. It was for this reason that he resorted to two alliances with military dictators – Jafa'ar Nimeiri between 1977 and 1985, and Umar al-Bashir between 1989 and 1999.

What made al-Turabi's alliance with Nimeiri's 'May Regime' (1969–85) all the more unconventional was that this government had initially been anti-Islamist. Nimeiri was the leader of a 'Free Officer' movement modelling itself on its Egyptian namesake led by the Muslim Brotherhood's persecutor-in-chief, Gamal Nasser. Hasan al-Turabi was the first politician to be imprisoned by the left-leaning coup plotters, and the Islamic Movement joined the armed opposition to Nimeiri's secular regime, helping to stage an invasion from Libya in 1976 in a bid to overthrow it. However, al-Turabi's imprisonment was never as brutalizing as that of Qutb, and in 1977 he willingly participated in the reconciliation of the 'National Front', including party leaders such as Sadiq al-Mahdi, with the Nimeiri Regime. Nimeiri's government had lacked a strong ideological basis since his bloody rupture from the Sudan Communist Party in 1971, and allying with the Islamists offered him an opportunity to bolster his own legitimacy by calling attention to his pious credentials.

Following the reconciliation, some members of the Islamic Movement entered Nimeiri's Sudan Socialist Union, and al-Turabi himself was appointed to oversee a committee charged with revising Sudan's laws to ensure conformity with sharia. In 1979 Nimeiri made al-Turabi attorney general, and it has often been assumed that he was the principal architect of the 'Islamizaton' of the Sudanese legal system in 1983. However, the introduction of the 'September Laws' in 1983 showed the precise extent to which al-Turabi's willingness to ally with dictators such as Nimeiri had forced him to compromise with his principles to secure the rule of sharia. Nimeiri himself, like a number of military presidents in his era, saw the introduction of sharia not as a means of bringing about an Islamist Revolution but of outbidding the Islamists in their appeal to the religious consciences of the public. While al-Turabi played a considerable role in laying out the legal framework for the September Laws, in 1983 Nimeiri removed him from the post of attorney general and had lawyers from relatively obscure Sufi backgrounds draft the final version without any contribution from the Islamist *shaikh*. The penal and criminal codes reflected Nimeiri's own authoritarian agenda more than classical sharia. He established 'Instantaneous Justice Courts' which, within a year, imposed around hundred sentences of hand amputation for theft, a glut of *hudud* penalties that would have been impossible had the strict evidential requirements for such divine punishments demanded in classical sharia been applied. Al-Turabi himself had also maintained that such penalties should only be imposed in a perfect Islamic society – one in which people would never have to steal to survive. Yet, when Nimeiri introduced the new laws, al-Turabi vigorously supported them, declaring in Fanonesque language that they had brought about 'our cultural and psychological independence'.[22]

Al-Turabi's frequent political U-turns demonstrated just how adaptable Islamist ideology could be when the political environment allowed it. This was particularly the case in Sudan, where politics was far more changeable than in Egypt, with three parliamentary periods and three authoritarian regimes in the last half of the twentieth century. As already hinted, al-Turabi was willing to ally with both military autocrats and parliamentarians because – like most Islamists – he saw the Islamic state principally as a nomocracy; that is, government by a particular set of laws or principles, in this case sharia. Whether this were to be achieved by a democracy or a dictatorship was a secondary consideration. Although he was no doubt aware that Nimeiri's law codes included deviations from classical sharia, al-Turabi probably rationalized continuing support for the dictator on the grounds that his laws remained closer to 'true' sharia than the secular ones prevailing before. This was a costly error. By supporting Nimeiri's 'September Laws', al-Turabi associated himself with a set of arbitrary codes condemned by the vast majority of other political forces in Sudan, forces that joined together to overthrow Nimeiri in the Intifada of 1985. Although Nimeiri had turned against the Islamic Movement two weeks before this, al-Turabi was denounced as a stooge of his former schoolmate by the other political groupings in the country, who banded together in an organization known as the National Alliance which excluded al-Turabi's NIF. The widespread opposition to the NIF, which was the only prominent party not to sign the National Alliance's 'Charter to Protect Democracy', made it very hard for al-Turabi to achieve his political goals in the subsequent parliamentary democracy. Forever associated with his support for a law code he had not written, he went on to campaign for a very similar penal code when he became attorney general as part of a coalition with Sadiq al-Mahdi's Umma Party. Soon after the non-NIF parliamentarians combined to block al-Turabi's sharia proposals, on the grounds that they would hamper peace negotiations with the non-Muslim rebels of southern Sudan, he resorted to another alliance with the military, arranging for a secret NIF cell in the Sudanese army to overthrow the parliamentary regime.

Al-Turabi's political influences

As we have seen, partly as a result of his adaptation to multiple, shifting political contexts, Hasan al-Turabi was one of the most ideologically mutable Islamists so far discussed.[23] He has variously been labelled a Leninist, a fascist, a reformist and a Qutbist. Yet, identifying him as essentially either a 'leftist' or a 'Qutbist' is difficult, for he adjusted his ideology to each new situation he faced. Nowhere is this more visible than in his fluid relationship with Marxism–Leninism. Al-Turabi rose to political prominence during the heyday of Islamic socialism. He was first recruited into an Islamist organization by Babikir Karrar, who had formed the Islamic Liberation Movement after abandoning communism on the grounds of its perceived godlessness. Although he left the Muslim Brotherhood to form his own party in 1954, he greatly influenced al-Turabi's praxis. In particular, his notion of five 'keys to power' – the economic, organizational, military, popular and foreign keys – prefigured al-Turabi's own strategy for turning the NIF into a party that could seize the state.[24] It is al-Turabi's usage of Karrar's legacy that has earned him the reputation of an 'Islamist Lenin'. His defeat of the 'educationalist' faction within his own movement might even be seen as akin to Lenin's victory over the Mensheviks,[25] and thus the victory over a more long-term 'structuralist' approach of an 'intentionalist' strategy emphasizing instead the capacity of a revolutionary vanguard to bring about social revolution.[26]

In the 1960s, the Sudan Communist Party (SCP) of Abd al-Khaliq Mahjub represented the Sudanese Islamists' principal competitor in the battle for the hearts and minds of the urban public. As a result, al-Turabi borrowed much from SCP praxis, while also attempting to outbid the communists by offering an Islamist form of socialism. He learnt a great deal from the SCP's 'front' tactics – hence the 'Islamic Charter Front' and 'National Islamic Front' – and established satellites of the Islamic Movement within the workers', students', professionals' and women's movements. Following Islamic socialists like Shariati, he offered a dialectical reading of history in which there was a battle between *tawhid* and *shirk*, the latter occurring when 'the link between God and money is cut'.[27] In the 1960s, he was a vocal supporter of workers' rights to strike. Yet, once the SCP had been crushed by Nimeiri in 1971 and the Sudanese president had orientated his now only nominally 'socialist' regime towards the Western bloc, al-Turabi was happy to abandon his Islamic socialism. He developed his movement into a 'corporation'[28] using capital from Saudi-financed Islamic banks, and was content to support the regime's measures against organized labour in his position as attorney general. Yet, in the midst of his conflict in 1999 with the Islamic Movement's second military ally, Umar al-Bashir, he reconsidered his relationship with socialism, concluding that it would be desirable 'to bring the whole Communist experience into Islam, because it is the experience of humanity'.[29] As a result, he established close relations with the SCP on entering the opposition once more.

In spite of al-Turabi's rapprochement with the SCP in the later years of his life, Sudanese leftists have tended to brand him a 'fascist' throughout his political career, which is perhaps unsurprising, as much Marxist thought tends to perceive a dialectical struggle between communism and fascism. A more persuasive argument suggests that al-Turabi followed fascist thinkers in advancing a form of 'palingenesis',[30] that is, the creation of a revolutionary order based on an imagined past. There are, for instance, notable parallels between al-Turabi's desire to reinvent the seventh-century Islamic past and the Italian fascists' evocation of Roman imperial glory.[31] Yet, there are also notable differences. While fascist thinkers harked back to a glorious past in order to make a break with the ideals of the Western enlightenment, it was the more recent history of colonial and postcolonial authoritarianism that Hasan al-Turabi railed against. The values he associated with his imagined seventh-century past – whether disingenuously or not – were often akin to those of the post-Enlightenment West, such as democracy and multiculturalism.

Al-Turabi's radical politics need to be understood not simply as a product of interaction with Western far-right and far-left ideologies. They also reflected the colonial and postcolonial environment of which he was a part. A great deal of his rhetoric bears the imprint of Frantz Fanon, the Martinican postcolonial theorist and champion of the Algerian struggle against the French, with whose works he probably came into contact while moving in radical, pro-Algerian circles in Paris. Al-Turabi often spoke of the 'cleansing' potential of his Islamist resurgence in a manner evoking Fanon's exploration of the purgative and psychologically emancipatory effects of anti-colonial violence. This is most visible in the claim he made after Nimeiri's introduction of *hudud* (amputation) penalties in his 1983 penal code; namely, that 'affirmation of the principle of cutting the hand of the thief is cutting off all the doubts and cultural defeatism we were suffering from'.[32] Yet, al-Turabi's own relationship with his colonial upbringing was ambivalent,[33] and he never entirely abandoned the worldview that accompanied his education at Hantoub and Gordon College. His 'Civilizational Project' of the 1990s bore many of the hallmarks of the British colonial 'civilizing mission', and he spoke of African societies being 'united by backwardness and fragmentation and crises'.[34]

As noted above, al-Turabi found that studying in France was a means of reflecting on the relationship between Islam and post-Enlightenment modernity outside a British colonial context. He often sought to justify his own decision to seize power by force with reference to the French Revolution, arguing that European history showed that such acts were the only way of bringing about genuine social and political change. Indeed, he found much to admire in the French revolutionaries, whom he praised for rebelling against an established clerical elite – much as he saw himself leading a rebellion against the established scholarly elite. It is often claimed that his 'fundamentalism' broke faith with the values of the philosophers whom he had studied during his time at the Sorbonne, yet many of his more authoritarian tendencies emerged as a result of his identification with European philosophers. In particular, his works often identified sharia with the 'general will', a concept fleshed out by the Swiss philosopher, Jean-Jacques Rousseau. Rousseau's belief that the people could be 'forced to be free' in the name of this 'general will' was a significant influence on the French Revolutionaries, and possibly, as we have seen, on Qutb.

Al-Turabi's relationship with various politico-religious trends within Islamism, as well as Muslim society at large, was just as nuanced and pragmatic as his relationship with Western political thinkers. He drew heavily on the earlier reformist tradition, and particularly the outlook of Muhammad Abduh. Like a number of Islamic reformists, al-Turabi sought to identify classical Islamic concepts such as *shura* and *ijtihad* with Western post-Enlightenment values like democracy and free thought.[35] Like Abduh, he held that a rationalist approach to the principle of *ijtihad* was necessary so that Muslims could renew Islamic jurisprudence and make it relevant to contemporary society. Al-Turabi's rationalist outlook led him, like Abduh, to be condemned as a 'Mu'tazilite' by 'purist' Salafis. At the same time, like al-Afghani, Abduh and al-Banna, he believed that it was important to transcend religious and doctrinal differences so as to unite the Muslim community in a common front against Western colonialism. This led him to reach out to Shi'is, neo-Mahdists, Sufis and even his Salafi critics.

Just as al-Afghani sought to champion the Sudanese Mahdi as an opponent of British imperialism, so al-Turabi sought out alliances with the neo-Mahdist Umma Party of the Mahdi's great-grandson, Sadiq al-Mahdi. Just as al-Afghani encouraged Shia-Sunni unity, al-Turabi reached out to the revolutionaries of Khomeini's Iran, inviting them to attend his Popular Arab and Islamic Conferences between 1991 and 1995. He even went so far as to maintain that the terms 'Sunni' and 'Shia' should be abandoned altogether.[36] Members of prominent Sufi *tariqas* were also brought into the Islamic Movement. Al-Turabi's approach towards Sufism was comparable to that of the 'neo-Sufis' of eighteenth and nineteenth-century Revivalism: he was wary of excessive loyalty being given to particular Sufi shaikhs, but realized that the *tariqas* themselves could act as important vehicles for the transformation of the Islamic community. His relationship with the Salafis was even more complex. He courted the support of the Saudi-backed Sudanese Ansar al-Sunna during his leadership of the Islamic Movement, and was apparently on good terms with the Saudi Grand Mufti, Abd al-Aziz Ibn Baz. He advocated a form of 'Salafism' that was more comparable to the 'modernist Salafism' of the first half of the twentieth century than the prevalent 'purist' trend of the latter half, because he used rationalism to discern the values of the *salaf*, or pious ancestors. As a result, he was frequently branded an apostate by a number of latter-day Salafis, and his execution was openly called for by many of the Jihadist-Salafi preachers whom the Sudanese regime invited to Khartoum during the militant era of the 1990s.

While al-Turabi's outlook was in many regards similar to that of the 'Islamic reformists', he was politically active in an era in which the rise of 'Islamic Radicalism' shaped the politics of Islamic resurgence. Mawdudi and Qutb's texts were widely read in the Islamic Movement, and al-Turabi's Islamist career began as Nasser's persecution of the Egyptian Brotherhood sharpened Qutbism into an ideology that rejected any form of compromise with the existing sociopolitical order. Nevertheless, al-Turabi was usually quite explicit about the distinction between his own approach and that of the radicals. His text on the *Islamic Movement in Sudan* made it very clear that he sought to reject the radicals' position of making an absolute break with the *jahili* (ignorant) society.[37] He lambasted Mawdudi's Jama'at for its overly elitist approach, and offered a model of Islamic revolution that ostensibly, at least, prioritized the role of a resurgent Muslim society over that of the state. Unlike Mawdudi, he clearly differentiated between his Islamist vision and that offered by the various totalitarian regimes of the day.[38] Yet, at the same time, the various concepts that featured so prominently in the radical Islamist lexicon, such as *jahiliyya, hakimiyya* and *khilafa,* were all used by al-Turabi. He would have understood the popularity of such concepts well, but was careful to use them in a less rigid manner than the radical Islamists. For instance, he would use the term *jahili* to castigate specific opponents (such as the communists), rather than society as a whole, and evoked a dialectical struggle between *jahiliyya* and true Islam throughout Muslim history, rather than seeing *jahiliyya* as all-encompassing.

Islamic democracy and the Islamic state: Theory

Al-Turabi's writings represented an ambitious effort to marry Islamic values with post-Enlightenment political theory.[39] Yet, he struggled to overcome two fundamental flaws in his theory. First, he equated the creation of liberal and democratic institutions with the rebirth of institutions and practices from an idealized seventh-century past – and yet failed to give concrete substance to the 'original' Islamic democracy. Second, the successful functioning of his democratic Islamic state required the reconciliation of human with divine sovereignty, which he maintained could be achieved by equating sharia to Rousseau's 'general will'. The difficulty was that he also insisted on the supremacy of divine sovereignty over the 'rule of men'. As to how exactly the Muslim public would produce sharia rule democratically, al-Turabi was often quite vague. He maintained that popular 'consensus' should play a role in shaping sharia, expanding the classical notion of *ijma* (consensus) so that it was no longer the prerogative of religious scholars, but included the public at large.[40] Yet, at the same time, he also stated that consensus should be subjected to sharia itself.[41] This left it unclear as to who exactly was responsible for interpreting the classical sources (the Quran and the Sunna) so as to produce the sharia rulings that would enable modern Islamist governance. Al-Turabi's enemies argued that he wanted to empower himself as a ruling *mujtahid* akin to Khomeini, yet he never adopted any theory that was the equivalent of Khomeini's 'rule of the jurist'; nor did he advocate any institution similar to Iran's Council of Guardians, overseeing legislation to ensure its conformity with sharia. There was a fundamental gap at the core of al-Turabi's theory of sovereignty, into which the military would later step.

One means by which al-Turabi sought to enable a popular movement for an Islamic state was through encouraging his followers to emulate the 'direct democracy' which, he maintained, had existed in the seventh century. This form of democracy, al-Turabi argued, was superior to Western democracy in that it did not establish political parties as mediators between the people and the public. Al-Turabi maintained – somewhat spuriously – that the third of the Rightly Guided Caliphs was directly chosen through a process akin to a modern general election, with both women and men voting en masse.[42] It is noteworthy that al-Turabi maintained that it was the Kharijis who had preserved this original model of Islamic democracy after the seventh century more than any other religio-political faction, demonstrating just how unconventional an approach he was willing to take.[43] Yet, al-Turabi was also faced with the same problem that faced the Kharijis in the Umayyad and Abbasid world – how to make a political model that supposedly worked well in the egalitarian, largely nomadic society of the seventh-century Arabian Peninsula function equally well in a larger, more complex and more urban society.

Islamic democracy and the Islamic state: Practice before 1989

It is important to distinguish between al-Turabi's ideal, democratic Islamic state and his transitional journey towards it. In the name of reaching his goal, as we have seen, he was willing to forge numerous alliances with non-Islamists and authoritarians. However, his alliance with Nimeiri and his arbitrary 'Islamization' programme of 1983 led him to be viewed by many of his opponents as an outright opportunist, and, as we have also seen, he was willing to go so far as to support measures – Nimeiri's extensive use of the *hudud* penalties – that starkly contradicted the vision of the Islamic state he had hitherto preached.

The downfall of Nimeiri and the re-emergence of parliamentary democracy in 1986 offered al-Turabi another opportunity to engineer his Islamic resurgence using democratic means. The NIF had by this point developed into a mass movement, using the funds obtained from its relationship with the Islamic banks to finance a series of charities, health clinics and schools that enabled the organization to expand its membership. It thus performed far better at the polls than did the Islamic Charter Front in the 1960s, although it was still heavily reliant on the graduates' constituencies. Although al-Turabi failed to obtain a seat himself, in 1988 and 1989 he served as attorney general and then foreign minister in coalition governments with his brother-in-law, Sadiq al-Mahdi. Explaining his participation in a multiparty system was a challenge for al-Turabi, who had argued against the existence of political parties in his *al-Shura wa'l-Dimuratiyya* and refused to sign the National Alliance's Charter to Protect Democracy. Nevertheless, he continued to distinguish between the Islamic ideal and the transition towards it, maintaining that a party-free *tawhidi* system had to be achieved democratically, rather than through force, and that it was the aim of the NIF to achieve this. In 1989, of course, he resorted to using force to impose his *tawhidi* order.

Another feature of the NIF's participation in the democracy of the later 1980s was al-Turabi's adjustment to a political context shaped by nationalism, civil war and the question of non-Muslim rights. The Second Sudanese Civil War, which had broken out in 1983, intensified throughout this period and the rebels of the Sudan People's Liberation Army (SPLA) bitterly opposed al-Turabi's campaign for a return of Nimeiri's 'September Laws'. Previous rebel movements in the largely non-Muslim southern Sudan had campaigned either for self-determination or autonomy, but the SPLA leader, John Garang, declared that he was fighting for a 'New Sudan' in which secularism and social justice would prevail. With the civil war as the central issue of Sudanese politics at the time, al-Turabi and his new party tied their campaign for sharia to the rhetoric of the northern Sudanese nationalists, who opposed the SPLA as they had previously opposed southern rebel movements – hence the 'National' Islamic Front. In an effort to resolve the question of non-Muslim rights under sharia and confront Garang's secularism, the NIF's 'Sudan Charter' of 1987 declared that the predominantly Muslim population of northern Sudan should be subject to the new Islamic law codes, while the southern region should be exempt. Al-Turabi would later maintain that an Islamic state would guarantee non-Muslim rights, as in the seventh century the Constitution of Medina had recognized their 'religious, cultural and administrative privileges'.[44] Yet, in proposing to introduce sharia law in the north and refrain from applying it in the south, al-Turabi was compromising with the nationalist logic of the late-twentieth-century world, which advocated the application of laws on a territorial as opposed to a communal basis.

The Islamic state and Islamic democracy in practice after 1989

Al-Turabi was nominally more committed to engineering an Islamist Revolution democratically than, for instance, Mawdudi. Why, therefore, did he resort to a military coup in 1989?[45] Together with his fellow Islamists, he often maintained that they were forced into the coup because the Sudanese military, like their counterparts in Egypt and Algeria, had succumbed to Western pressure and would not allow them to bring about sharia governance by democratic means. Specifically, they argued that when in early 1989 the army commander-in-chief, Fathi Ahmad Ali, pressured

Sadiq al-Mahdi to remove the NIF from his coalition government to enable a peaceful resolution of the southern conflict, they realized that it would be impossible to reach the goal of the Islamic state using purely civil measures. These claims have always been somewhat disingenuous – the NIF had united all other political forces in the country against them in 1989, and al-Turabi's proposed sharia code had already been rejected by the majority of Sudanese parliamentarians. The force that the Islamists and their allies in the military used in 1989 clearly amounted to something more than defensive violence. As part of their strategy of *tamkin* (enabling), they ruthlessly purged many from the army, police forces and judiciary, empowering in their place either committed Islamists or those willing to embrace the new ideological order. They also targeted the political parties, as well as the labour and professional unions that had backed the 1985 Intifada against Nimeiri. Many of those who were arrested by the regime were held incommunicado and tortured in secret 'ghost houses'. After he went into opposition ten years later, al-Turabi blamed the abuses on the military, although it seems likely that civilian Islamists who had entered the security services or established separate militias also bore considerable responsibility.

Because the gap between liberal theory and authoritarian practice was glaring, al-Turabi was careful to maintain public distance between himself and the regime he had secretly engineered. As the coup was planned, he arranged with al-Bashir that he would be sent to prison with the leaders of the other political parties, so that the largely secular regimes of the region would not recognize the ideological character of the coup. Accordingly, al-Bashir installed a non-partisan cabinet, but the government was in practice run by a secret 'leadership bureau' in which power was shared between military and civilian Islamists. Al-Turabi's dissimulation cost him a great deal of his public credibility when the full details were exposed ten years later, and limited his power in the short term as well. Al-Bashir and his fellow coup plotters hailed from a carefully cultivated Islamist cell inside the Sudanese military. As a result, al-Turabi's relationship with the new military president was much closer than his previous one with Nimeiri or Mawdudi's with Zia. Nevertheless, the steps he took to conceal his role in the coup prevented him from exercising a form of control as direct as that of Khomeini in Iran.

In spite of the authoritarian character of their seizure of power, the military-backed Islamists attempted to use their control of the state to manufacture a functioning 'direct democracy'. In line with al-Turabi's strategy of merging the Islamic Movement into society, the institutions of the old Islamic Movement were replaced with a 'National Congress'. In theory this served as a multilayered democratic institution which enabled citizens to exercise power through councils located at 'basic', 'local', 'province' and 'state' levels. In practice, however, the lower rungs of the system often lacked the resources to challenge the upper echelons. When the military-Islamist vanguard theoretically handed over power to the public in the regional and national elections of 1995 and 1996, therefore, the National Congress was incomplete. Instead of acting as a parliamentary institution in its own right, it sent 125 representatives to a National Assembly, the remaining seats in which were filled via conventional geographic elections.[46] The regime made a number of compromises with the principle of representative as opposed to direct democracy. It banned the participation of political parties in the elections, which led to a high rate of popular abstention despite the claims of the official media. Nevertheless, seeking to provide his regime with more democratic legitimacy, al-Turabi attempted to partially restore political pluralism under the guise of the somewhat ambiguous slogan of *tawali* ('allegiance'). Fearing that this would lead to loss of power by the army and the National Congress, both military and civilian Islamists blocked al-Turabi's cautious efforts at democratization, and eventually a power struggle led to his removal from government in 1999. Ultimately, his reliance on a vanguardist approach and inability to develop a consistent model of Islamist democracy cost him power.

The popular Arab and Islamic Congress and al-Turabi's jihad

One of the reasons why al-Turabi did not take any formal position in the Salvation Regime was that he wished to focus his energies on exporting Islamist revolution abroad.[47] To achieve this, he established a transnational institution known as the Popular Arab and Islamic Conference (PAIC), which he hoped would act as a more radical version of the Saudi-based Organization of the Islamic Conference (OIC). In establishing the PAIC, al-Turabi temporarily abandoned his less ambitious Sudan-focused Islamism in favour of a pan-Islamic agenda that sought to challenge the nationalist ideologies he believed to be a legacy of Western colonialism. Sudan's borders were opened to migrants from all over the Arab world, many of them militants fleeing secular regimes.

With al-Turabi as its secretary general, the PAIC convened three sessions between 1991 and 1995. These were attended by a variety of Islamist organizations from all over the globe, including Hamas, Hizbullah, Palestinian Islamic Jihad, Egyptian Islamic Jihad, Tunisia's Ennahda party and the Jama'at-i-Islami. His most controversial guest was the al-Qa'eda leader, Osama bin Laden. Bin Laden had no formal role in the PAIC and al-Turabi maintained that he had only ever been invited to Sudan to do business, but it seems that al-Qa'eda made use of its sanctuary in Sudan to mobilize and conduct operations abroad. At the same time, al-Turabi invited delegates from the Islamic Republic of Iran to attend the PAIC, and the Sudanese intelligence services established a close relationship with Iran's

Revolutionary Guards, although this was officially denied by the government in Khartoum. Although the Iranian–Sudanese cooperation only went so far – the Iranians objected to use of the term 'Arab' in the PAIC's name – to bring Sunni and Shia radicals together in one institution was a marked achievement for al-Turabi, particularly in light of the later intensification of sectarian tension in the Muslim world brought on by the Syrian conflict and the rise of ISIS.

With the role of convenor of what some commentators have described as a 'terrorist internationale',[48] it is not surprising that al-Turabi has often been accused of promoting a militant or Qutbist form of jihad. However, in his many writings, interviews and public statements, al-Turabi usually maintained that he only advocated a 'defensive form' of jihad akin to that urged by the reformists whom Mawdudi and Qutb had criticized for being overly apologetic. The fact of the matter is that al-Turabi often defined 'defence' quite loosely. At times, therefore, he approached the Qutbist argument that force could be used to overthrow political systems standing in the way of Islam's peaceful expansion. And in describing the NIF's campaign against the Sudanese regime it overthrew in 1989 as a jihad, and providing support to various militant groups fighting the Arab regimes, al-Turabi was giving sanction to the principle that non-state actors could legitimately wage jihad against established Muslim regimes. At other times, 'defensive' jihad appeared to mean something more modest, and the militant groups he hosted at the PAIC considered him to be too moderate or even pro-Western. They resented his support for the 1993 Oslo Accords signed by his close friend Yasir Arafat, and his role in the surrendering of the pro-Palestinian Venezuelan revolutionary, Carlos the Jackal, to the French. Al-Turabi's understanding of jihad remained, like most of his other concepts, highly fluid.

Islamism elsewhere in sub-Saharan Africa

Since the expansion of the Muslim Brotherhood in the 1940s was restricted principally to the Arabic-speaking world, Sudan was the only country of sub-Saharan Africa where the Ikhwan played a substantial role in establishing an Islamist movement. When Islamism spread throughout the rest of the region on the latter half of the twentieth century, its emergence was more directly connected to the impact of the Islamic Revolution in Iran and the internationalization of the Salafi–Wahhabi variant of the ideology. Some of the most popular texts of Salafi–Wahhabism, including Ibn Taymiyya's writings and Muhammad Ibn Abd al-Wahhab's *Kitab al-Tawhid*, became widespread, particularly in West Africa. In East Africa Salafism and Islamism spread, though more slowly on account of the hostility to the Arabic language that was tied to the legacy of the slave trade.[49] Groups such as Nigeria's Izala movement that were inspired by Salafi–Wahhabism tended to focus their energies more on education and doctrinal reform than political revolution. Indeed, Tanzanian Salafis have cultivated friendly relations with Britain.[50] Following the 1979 revolution in Iran, however, a number of groups and individual thinkers emerged that identified the Khomeinist state as a model to aspire to. These included Said Musa in Kenya, Ahmad Khalifa Niass who attempted to establish a 'Hizbullahi' organization in Senegal, and South Africa's Qibla organization.[51]

Since Islamist and Salafi rhetoric offered a variety of actors a means to challenge the social and political status quo, it needs to be understood that local dynamics and grievances shaped the manner in which groups adhering to these ideologies emerged. Just as a variety of African statesmen and rebels embraced Marxist–Leninist ideology during the Cold War to seek Soviet and Chinese support against their domestic enemies, it is possible that a number of groups in sub-Saharan Africa have embraced Islamist ideology for pragmatic as much as ideological reasons. In the 1990s, it was the regime in Khartoum – the ideology of which was to some extent derived from Marxism–Leninism – that attempted to export its own brand of revolutionary politics to East and Central Africa, but most the militant groups that drew on its support did so for their own reasons.[52] For instance, it has been suggested that the Rwenzori-based Allied Democrat Forces' motive for embracing Islamist ideology was to obtain support from the regime in Khartoum for its campaign against the Ugandan government.[53] The Oromo National Liberation Front and Ogaden Liberation Front, both fighting for freedom from Ethiopian rule, presented themselves to the Islamists in Khartoum as Muslims oppressed by a Christian regime to gain its support, but never really diverged from conventional national liberation politics in practice.[54] Often Muslim groups in sub-Saharan Africa embraced radical politics more because they felt marginalized by non-Muslim majorities in their own countries than because they wanted to revolutionize Muslim society as a whole.[55] Elsewhere, sociopolitical upheaval – such as that brought about by Julius Nyerere's project of compulsory villagization in Tanzania – led uprooted individuals to embrace new ideologies in a quest for belonging.[56]

Nigeria's Boko Haram, which has waged a violent insurgency against the Nigerian State since 2009, presents the classic example of a movement that uses the language of transnational Salafism to articulate a form of radicalism more rooted in local history and local grievances. It first was first formed in 2009 by members of the *Yusufiyya* religious movement who sought revenge for the execution of their spiritual leader Muhammad Yusuf and the massacre of over 1,000 of the movement's followers by government forces. Muhammad Yusuf had preached in a mosque named after the contemporary Salafi icon Ibn Taymiyya, and had been a member of the Salafist Izala organization earlier in his life. Yet the *takfiri* discourse he used to denounce Nigeria's corrupt ruling establishment was just as driven by the desire to re-establish a rural moral economy violated by a kleptocratic government as it was by a desire to rule in accordance with Salafi precepts. Marginalized groups in northern Nigeria have a long history of incorporating global Islamic trends into movements against ruling elites they deem oppressive – whether that be the Fulani pastoralists who supported the Revivalist elements of Uthman Dan Fodio's jihad against the Hausa aristocracy of the eighteenth century, or the slaves and economically marginalized peasantry that joined Mahdist movements against the nineteenth-century Fulani leadership and twentieth-century colonial state.[57]

Like the Sudanese Islamists in the 1980s, Muhammad Yusuf and his followers initially received considerable support from the more secular ruling establishment before their violent rupture with it. The very same governor of Borno State, Ali Modu Sheriff, who launched the violent crackdown of 2009 had earlier facilitated the rise of the Yusufiyya as he sought to used sharia as a political tool during his election campaign of 2003.[58] A similar trend emerged in Somalia after the collapse of the Siad Barre regime in 1991 led to anarchy and civil war. The embattled regime of Ali Mahdi Muhammad, who came into power with limited popular support after Barre's fall, saw sharia as a means of mobilizing popular support and guaranteeing social and political stability. From 1994 onwards the fragile Somali government established Islamic Courts in Mogadishu, which implemented the *hudud* penalties and helped to stem the upsurge in organized crime that had followed the collapse of the old regime, but also fostered a space within which various Islamic political groups could empower themselves. Of these the most powerful – and most comparable to Islamist groups elsewhere – was al-Ittihad al-Islami, formed in 1992. Al-Ittihad's cadres included members of both the pre-1991 army, and educated urban types, and like the Muslim Brotherhood it entrenched itself in Somali society by using a tiered membership structure. It was backed by the Islamist regime in Khartoum, and may well have possessed ties to al-Qa'ida as well as providing logistical support for the attacks on the American embassies in Kenya and Tanzania in 1998. Yet al-Ittihad was as much a product of its local Somali political context as it was a manifestation of transnational Islamism.[59]

One significant difference between sub-Saharan Africa and the Middle East and North African region in which Islamism first emerged was that, with the exception of Algeria, colonial rule in in the latter area had been more informal in character. In countries such as Nigeria and Zanzibar, Islamist and Salafi legal activists – like al-Turabi in Sudan – proposed sharia as a more explicitly postcolonial phenomenon, an alternative to the foreign legal codes introduced under colonial rule.[60] Like the Muslim Brotherhood in Egypt, Salafi and Islamist organizations in sub-Saharan Africa learnt a great deal from the Christian missionary groups, which constituted another legacy of the colonial era they sought to confront.[61] They also adopted the techniques of homegrown Christian groups, notably the use of open-air conferences to disseminate their message.[62]

Suggested readings

Gallab, Abdullahi Ali, *The First Islamist Republic: The Development and Disintegration of Islamism in Sudan* (Aldershot: Ashgate, 2008).

In what ways does Gallab describe the ideology of Hasan al-Turabi and the Sudanese Islamists as being 'totalitarian'? Where did they derive this totalitarian ideology from? What were the consequences of this totalitarian outlook for the practice of the Islamist regime in Sudan in between 1989 and 1999? What was the relevance of the concept of *hakimiyya* to the Sudanese Islamists?

Ibrahim, Abdullahi Ali, 'A Theology of Modernity: Hasan al-Turabi and Islamic Renewal in Sudan', *Africa Today* 46 (1999), pp. 195–222.

How does al-Turabi view the ulama, the Sufis, the effendis and Mahdism? (One branch of Choueiri's 'Revivalism', discussed in topic 2) How does Ibrahim challenge al-Turabi's critics? Is his ideology a 'modern' ideology? How does he view the relationship between the Islamists and the existing secular state? (And how would this compare with the approach of either Qutb or Mawdudi)

Suggested primary source reading

Hasan al-Turabi, 'The Islamic State', in John L. Esposito (ed.), *Voices of Resurgent Islam* (New York: Oxford University Press, 1983).

How does al-Turabi characterize the journey towards the Islamic state – is it a 'top down' or 'bottom up' process? Does his vision here correspond more with that of the 'Reformists' (e.g. Afghani, Abduh) or the 'Radicals' (e.g. Qutb, Mawdudi)? How does he view the relationship between Islam and nationalism? Does he see the Islamic state as a democracy?

Debate (after discussion of primary source): Which of these two authors' arguments do you find the most convincing? Does the primary source lend weight to Gallab's view of al-Turabi as a totalitarian or Ibrahim's view of him as a modernist?

11

Between sharia, custom and patriarchy:

Islamist views of women, women as Islamists

The form of governance that Islamism most frequently advocates, as observed previously, is a nomocracy; that is, the rule of a certain set of legal (sharia) principles. Since sharia law contains numerous prescriptions regulating the economic, marital and sexual lives of the female population, women's issues have featured just as centrally in debates between Islamists and their opponents as debates about democracy, Western imperialism and human rights.[1] Women frequently appear in the Western media as victims of Islamist sharia's harsh penalizations of non-marital sex and 'immodest' dress. Yet, an excessive focus on women as the passive subjects of sharia governance risks promoting a narrative that denies their own agency and leaves a neo-Orientalist West as the only possible saviour.[2] In fact, the realm of Islamist politics has never been an exclusively masculine affair – women have been important agents as champions as well as opponents of Islamist ideology. One of the three lawyers who helped to compose the first sharia code in Sudan, Badriyya Suleiman, was a woman.[3] Zaynab al-Ghazali, the leader of the women's branch of the Muslim Brotherhood, was among the most active protagonists of its struggle against the Nasser Regime in the 1950s and 1960s. And throughout the Iranian Revolution women took to the streets en masse to campaign for as well as against Khomeini and his regulations on the mandatory wearing of the headscarf.

Nevertheless, the vast majority of prominent Islamist intellectuals have been men, and they have often used their influential positions to make a number of normative claims about the role and position of women. Most of the thinkers we have studied so far, including Shariati, Khomeini, Mawdudi, Qutb and al-Turabi, have sought to comment on women's issues. Some male Islamists have expressed extremely conservative views on women's rights, whereas others have adopted positions that either accept or at least compromise with the global rise of feminism. However, even the socially conservative Islamists should not be understood as straightforward 'traditionalists'. As Hisham Sharabi has observed, 'neo-patriarchy' in the Arab world is often more a masculinist reaction to the psychologically emasculating impact of colonialism than a re-emergence of a historic 'traditionalism'.[4] At the same time, should it be automatically assumed that the Islamist response to the onset of modernity was entirely retrogressive? Since feminism (as understood in the West) is itself a product of the modern, post-Enlightenment world, its relationship with Islamism can be analysed along much the same lines as the relationship between Islamism and modernity. Is it possible for there to be an 'Islamic feminism', whether it is a synthesis of Islam and feminism or a consequence of feminism being absorbed by Islam – 'Islamized'?[5]

Women in the Muslim World before Islamism

Was the seventh-century Islamic community idealized by the Islamists a patriarchal one? Partly because of the paucity of historical evidence, scholarly interpretations differ. One narrative maintains that the harsh environment and frequency of warfare in the seventh-century Arabian Peninsula encouraged its patrilineal and nomadic societies to value women principally for their reproductive purposes, and that this consequently shaped the Islamic outlook.[6] However, the Prophet's first wife, Khadija, was a successful businesswoman.[7] Another narrative – popular among Islamists, but also repeated in a number of academic accounts – maintains that the advent of Islam in the seventh century inspired a break with the inherent patriarchy of Middle Eastern and Arabian custom, and that the resumption of patriarchy in subsequent Islamic society was a result of the Quranic ideals being forgotten and the patriarchal customs of the various societies conquered by Muslims reasserting themselves.[8] The Quran, for instance, gave them the right to possess property and have support through pregnancy in case of divorce. However, many subsequent Islamic societies have tended to disempower women – for instance, granting men considerably greater rights than them in divorce and child custody.[9] There were relatively few female rulers – Shajarat al-Durr in Egypt being a notable exception – and no woman ever acquired the rank of caliph.

Some of the foremost protagonists of the revivalist trend have been mooted as Islamic feminists, although these claims remain contentious.

DeLong-Bas, for instance, maintains that Muhammad Ibn Abd al-Wahhab was one of them, arguing that in reviving the women's rights established in the Quran and challenging misogynistic customs he helped to further the status of women. For example, she contends that by enforcing Quranic standards Ibn Abd al-Wahhab gave women greater powers in the realms of marriage and divorce, and ensured that they were granted the Islamic inheritance rights that were often denied them in rural areas.[10] There have been critical responses to DeLong-Bas's argument, and Khaled Abu El-Fadl and Eleanor Doumato, among others, have continued to insist that Wahhabi doctrine in both its historic and contemporary forms is responsible for the oppression of women in contemporary Saudi Arabia.[11]

More controversially, DeLong-Bas goes so far as to defend Ibn Abd al-Wahhab's decision, during his early years as a preacher in Uyayna, to stone a woman to death for illicit sexual intercourse. For her, the case demonstrated Ibn Abd al-Wahhab's 'concern for justice for women',[12] because he devoted time to considering whether her activities might be a result of mental illness or physical coercion, and gave her multiple opportunities to repent and abandon her sexually transgressive behaviour before ultimately deciding to execute her. DeLong-Bas adds that 'the final outcome of the case was due to the woman's deliberate choice to continue her immoral sexual behaviour'.[13] An alternative reading by al-Rasheed uses the account of the stoning to highlight the woman's agency, arguing that it was her confrontation with Ibn Abd al-Wahhab that led to the latter's expulsion from Uyayna. Al-Rasheed also suggests that it was on account of women's agency that Ibn Abd al-Wahhab was subsequently accepted in Diri'yya, as the more pious women of the town appreciated the Shaykh's efforts to combat adultery and pressured Ibn Sa'ud, through his wife, to accept him.[14]

The Islamic reformers followed a similar methodology to that attributed by DeLong-Bas to Ibn Abd al-Wahhab, maintaining that a revival of genuine Quranic values would lead women to be emancipated from their customary restraints. Qasim Amin, a follower of Muhammad Abduh, lamented that although 'originally women in Islam were granted an equal place in human society ... unacceptable customs, traditions, and superstitions inherited from the countries in which Islam spread have been allowed to permeate this beautiful religion'.[15] Amin, who openly advocated women's primary education, has often been described as the 'father of Egyptian feminism', but has also been bitterly criticized by subsequent generations of feminists.[16] Like Abduh, he was influenced by the colonial ideology of Cromer, and his advocacy of women's education served somewhat androcentric purposes, as he constantly emphasized that the purpose of schooling women was to enable them to raise a generation of modern nationalist males.[17]

Throughout the twentieth century, both colonialist and nationalist regimes in the Muslim World pursued a vision similar to that of Amin, treating women's advancement as an instrument of nation-building while paying little attention to feminist concerns regarding the social status of women. For instance, the Nasserist regime in Egypt educated women en masse and encouraged women to enter the modern economy but did little to challenge the family law codes, based on sharia, that condemned women to domestic oppression by male relatives.[18] Some regimes – such as French colonial Syria and Algeria, and nationalist Iran – decreed the unveiling of women, although this was often tied to a discourse of 'modernity', 'progress' or even 'assimilation' as much to women's rights, and this has set the scene for much of the culturalist and nativist backlash against unveiling.[19]

Qutb and Mawdudi: Radical Chauvinism

The writings of Mawdudi and Qutb, the most prominent 'Islamic radical' intellectuals, were among the most stridently anti-feminist of the whole Islamist trend. Often, this anti-feminism stemmed from a perception of feminism as Western and thus 'other'. Mawdudi, for instance, saw Western sexual libertinism and Western feminism as one and the same, and responsible for unprecedented 'nudeness and sex perversion'.[20] As one of his translators explained, 'the "nudist" trends in the West, manifesting themselves in the "bikini" and the "birthday suit", should surprise no-one, as they are the outcome of the so-called movements launched for the rights and emancipation of women.'[21] Mawdudi also blamed the 'Western' campaign for women's independence for undermining the importance of women's domestic roles.[22] For his part, Qutb thought that the diffusion of Western ideals of womanhood to Egypt in the 1940s had led to 'discord' (*fitna*).[23] At the same time, the social conservatism of both of these thinkers often leaned on the pseudo-scientific views of gender that had emerged in the colonial and semi-colonial medical institutions of the day.[24] Qutb, for instance, claimed that recent research at the Egyptian University had established that women were by their nature suited only to work in the home.

Neither Qutb nor Mawdudi was brazenly misogynistic, both claiming that their Islam respected the female sex. Mawdudi insisted that Islam had 'honoured the woman and elevated her status in society',[25] while Qutb maintained that 'woman has been guaranteed complete equality with man'.[26] Both cited the Quran's granting of inheritance rights to women as evidence of this equal treatment, and Mawdudi argued that Islam gave women considerable scope to choose their husbands, divorce and remarry.[27] Both proposed that women should be granted a degree of education,[28] Mawdudi going so far as to suggest that a woman of 'extraordinary abilities of the intellect' would never be prevented by Islam from going to university.[29] Yet, both maintained that there were substantial physical and mental differences between men and women, and that their social responsibilities should be arranged accordingly. Qutb went on to observe that the recognition of men's testimony as worth twice that of women under sharia did not imply any overriding gender inequality because the man happened on account of his social role to be better equipped as a judge – 'by the nature of the tasks of motherhood, woman develops her emotional and passionate side, whereas the man develops his reflective and deliberative side'.[30]

What is remarkable about Mawdudi's attitude towards women is that there was a distinction between his perception of the role of women in his ideal Islamic state and his behaviour towards women in his private and political lives. In the elections of 1965, his Jama'at-i-Islami backed Fatima Jinnah against Ayub Khan, which he justified on the grounds that his priority was to defeat the secularist agenda of the latter candidate.[31] Such an approach can easily be understood as a form of pragmatism that distinguished between the exigencies of the journey towards the Islamic utopia and the social order that would exist upon arrival, an outlook similar to that of Zaynab al-Ghazali (see below). Yet, in his personal life, Mawdudi allowed his wife, Mahmudah Begum, to ride a bicycle and break purdah, even though his texts would demand that Muslim women adhere to it.[32] It is possible that, like al-Afghani, he believed the outlook of the elite must inevitably differ from that of the masses.

The Iranian Revolutionaries: Mobilizing women

Ali Shariati's perspective on the role of women in Islamic struggle offers an interesting contrast with that of Mawdudi and Qutb. Unlike them, he saw Eastern traditionalism as being just as oppressive to women as Western libertinism. Like them, he condemned the over-sexualization of women in the West but also gave his arguments a sociological and Marxist slant. 'In the same way that Western worldwide colonization stupefies the mind of its own youth through narcotics', Shariati averred, 'Western colonialism designs and promotes Freudianism and sexual liberty into the Eastern countries in exchange for their raw materials.'[33] It is possible that Shariati was influenced by Fanon, whose essay *Algeria Unveiled* had argued that French colonialism sought deliberately to unveil Muslim women as a means of assimilating them to the colonial order.[34] At the same time, he also attacked social conservatives who attempted to 'hold [women] inside [the house] by creating bonds, obligations and restrictions and depriving [them] of all [their] human and religious rights'.[35]

Shariati's efforts to construct a new role model for Muslim women employed a methodology similar to that used by Sunni reformists such as Muhammad Abduh and Qasim Amin. Like them, he suggests that the original Muslim community of the seventh century had held socially progressive attitudes towards women, but that these historic values were lost because subsequent generations had made too many compromises with pre-Islamic tradition.[36] In particular, he sought to rehabilitate Fatima, the daughter of the Prophet and wife of the first Shia imam, Ali Ibn Abi Talib, as an exemplar for young women caught between traditionalism and 'Freudianism'. Fatima, in Shariati's view, was a politically active woman concerned with social justice, 'a woman who throughout the whole of her life ... felt herself to be a responsible, committed person, a part of the destiny of the community, defending what was right, supporting justice in thought, idea and deed and confronting the usurpation, oppression and deviation which existed in her society'.[37] Perhaps even more significant was Shariati's evocation of the prominent Shia figure, Zaynab, who became a pivotal leader of the Shia community after her brother, the Imam Hussein, died following the Battle of Karbala in 680. Speaking of her struggle against the Umayyad forces, Shariati observed that 'when Zaynab saw that the revolution had begun, she left her family, her husband and her children, and joined the revolution ... when she saw that a struggle and a revolution had begun against an oppressive system, she joined the revolution and was beside her brother Husayn in all stages'.[38] The evocation of Zaynab by Shariati and other intellectuals during the 1970s encouraged women to take on militant roles in the struggle against the Shah's regime.[39]

Khomeini's various pronouncements on, and policies towards, women represent a form of conservative adaptation to the upheaval of traditional gender roles brought about by the Revolution. Prior to 1979, he had little sympathy with any form of female political activism – the movement of protest he led against the Shah in 1963 had been partly motivated by his opposition to the electoral enfranchisement of women.[40] But he was quick to recognize that women had mobilized en masse during the protests that brought about the end of the Shah's regime, and that they had to be acknowledged – if not actively empowered – as a political force. 'Beloved and Courageous Sisters', he told a group of women in Qum soon after the downfall of the Shah, 'you fought shoulder to shoulder with the men and ensured the victory of Islam'.[41] After the Revolution, he quickly accepted the principle of full female enfranchisement.

Immediately after the downfall of the Shah, Khomeini's regime introduced laws requiring women to wear the hijab in public at all times. However, this was probably designed to limit any damaging consequences of their entry into the public sphere – which he seemed to have accepted as inevitable – rather than restrict them to the domestic sphere. Drawing on the rhetoric of Shariati and other Islamists, who had lamented the sexualization of women through exposure to the Western market, these laws were also a defensive measure against Western consumerism and the globalization of Western culture. Even more women marched in support of the laws as against them.[42] However, Iranian feminists have blamed Khomeini for legislation encouraging the sexualization of women and girls by Iranian men.[43] This includes Khomeini's support for temporary (*sigheh*) marriage, a circumstance in which women had few rights, as well as his lowering of the age of marriage to the beginning of puberty.[44]

Hasan al-Turabi

Hasan al-Turabi's various positions and claims regarding the status of women in Islam mark him out from the majority of other Islamists, although he was not a straightforward feminist. To some extent, his cultivation of an apparently feminist position was a product of his trademark pragmatism and tendency to adopt the methods pursued by the Sudan Communist Party, which had already established a 'front' among the educated women of the major towns.[45] Nevertheless, his first writings on the position of women in Muslim society, which appeared in the 1970s, were extremely controversial. As in a number of his other works, he followed a methodology similar to the Islamic reformists, although – in keeping with the more rigid Salafism of his time – he focused heavily on the status of women in the era of the Prophet and the Rightly Guided Caliphs. Like the earlier reformists, he argued that Islam had originally granted women numerous rights but that the initial social progress of the seventh century had not continued because the post-Rashidi societies had reverted to the misogynistic custom of previous eras. Al-Turabi explicitly condemned men for their treatment of women throughout the ages. He even maintained that Quranic injunctions 'were sent down as restrictions on men with a view to preventing them from transgressing against women, as is their natural disposition and their actual practice in many societies'.[46]

Al-Turabi went further than most Islamists in encouraging female participation in public life, supporting the entry of women into the judiciary,[47] backing female candidates from his own parties to stand for parliament, and bringing female singers to perform at the meetings of his Popular Arab and Islamic Conference.[48] As his political career progressed, he continued to break taboos concerning the role of women in Muslim society. He proposed that women should be allowed to become president,[49] lead the Muslim community in prayer and marry non-Muslims should they choose; such statements produced considerable criticism from mainstream scholars as well hard-line Salafis.[50] Yet, there are a number of reasons why it remains difficult to view al-Turabi as a 'feminist' in the Western sense. He justified his statement that a woman should have the right to marry a non-Muslim not because this was an inherent right but because this would create the opportunity for her to guide her husband to Islam.[51] Like most Islamists, al-Turabi also considered that the spreading of Western sartorial and sexual freedoms constituted a form of oppression of women because it commoditized their bodies.[52] Yet, by maintaining that when women dressed themselves 'simply to attract, charm and excite'[53] they were capitulating to

Western ideals, he denied them any agency, power or right to make decisions about their own bodies.

Women under Islamist regimes

If there is one constant in the experience of women under Islamist regimes, it is that they have been subject to some form of state coercion to make them conform to the Islamist ideal of the 'moral' woman. For example, the post-1979 Iranian regime, aside from mandating the compulsory wearing of the headscarf, also established revolutionary courts that often used their arbitrary powers to execute women for adultery.[54] The application of the classical legal principle that a woman's testimony should only be considered half that of a man worsened the situation of women charged with this offence, as well as other offences against their husbands.[55] Male-dominated Hizbullahi militias were granted considerable autonomy and terrorized women whom they regarded as improperly dressed on the streets.[56] The legal powers of men over women in realms such as marriage, divorce and child custody all increased – for instance, on the presumption of their consent, fathers were entitled to marry off daughters while they were still children.[57]

As for Sudan, after the Islamist coup in 1989, the state became intensely concerned with female morality, and particularly the clothes worn by women in public. The regime decreed mandatory wearing of *hijab* for women, and empowered a variety of male-dominated para-police bodies, including the Public Order Police and Popular Police, to punish women who failed to adhere to vaguely defined standards of 'appropriate' dress.[58] An aspect of the regulation of women's lives specific to Sudan was that the Public Order Laws became a part of the country's existing culture wars. The Public Order Police, backed by the Islamist government in Khartoum, had a tendency to target women who had migrated from the 'African' peripheries of Sudan to the major cities, blaming them in particular for the distribution of alcohol and spreading of sexual licentiousness. Al-Turabi never gave a great deal of support to the Public Order Laws when he was involved with the regime, and after he went into opposition after 1999 he openly criticized them.[59] Given that the Public Order Police's campaigns to regulate women's clothing only intensified after 1999, it is open to question whether these were as much a result of the regime's increasingly 'neofundamentalist' direction as of al-Turabi's own revolutionary Islamism.

It significant that it is not in Iran and Sudan that women have been subject to the most wide-ranging restrictions, but rather the kingdom of Saudi Arabia. The kingdom has not witnessed an Islamist takeover or 'revolution' – although the Wahhabi revivalist movement that first emerged in the eighteenth century still dominates the religious establishment in the country – and has maintained good relations with the capitalist West. Yet, it has enforced fatwas issued by its senior religious scholars that have variously banned women from driving, undressing in boutiques, attending mosques while menstruating or during childbirth, and dressing in anything other than a black *abaya* while in public.[60] Patriarchy in Saudi Arabia does not simply derive from Wahhabi ideology, but from the country's political and economic structure. The most restrictive fatwas began to be issued in the 1980s, when the regime was concerned with bolstering its image as a pious government following the assault by militant Islamists on the Grand Mosque of Mecca in 1979. The domination of Saudi Arabia's economy by the oil industry also facilitates patriarchy, since its workforce is predominately male and women thus have few means of economic advancement.[61]

The other 'neo-fundamentalist' regime that oppressed women in a manner similar to the Saudis was the state of the Taliban in Afghanistan (1996–2001). Unlike the Sudanese Islamists, the Taliban government manifested its harsh character and outlook towards women from the outset. While it is true that a number of women fought in the jihad against the Soviet-backed government of Najibullah,[62] the Taliban movement that overthrew the initial *mujahidin*-backed regime of Burhannudin Rabbani was rigidly patriarchal in its outlook. The Taliban were dominated by young men who had grown up in refugee camps in the Pakistani city of Peshawar, where they were isolated from women and exposed to the Salafi–Wahhabi ideology promoted by a variety of Saudi-backed NGOs – although Pashtun custom would also shape their conservative outlook.[63] The reason that the policies of the Taliban provoked so much international outrage was that unlike Saudi Arabia, where the Wahhabi religious establishment had always put severe restrictions on the political and economic empowerment of women, Afghanistan had previously been governed by a modernizing socialist regime that had sought to educate women and bring them into the professions. Rather than simply preventing women from entering the economy and the education system, the Taliban government forcibly removed them from schools and colleges and barred them from taking up any profession outside of health work.[64] Women were only allowed into health work because male doctors were barred from treating them (and vice versa). They were required to wear burkas outside the home, and the principle of hijab was taken so literally that homeowners were required to cover up glass windows to prevent women being observed from the outside.[65] It is one of the great ironies of recent history that the Taliban emerged from a mujahidin movement originally backed by the United States. Western regimes that defended subsequent interventions in the name of the rights of women were seeking to rescue them from a 'Frankenstein'[66] to which they had helped give birth.

Islamist women

The activism of female Islamists has often appeared paradoxical – by campaigning for sharia within the male-dominated public space, they have contravened the very ideal of female domesticity that many of them have championed.[67] No one encapsulates this apparent inconsistency more than

Zaynab al-Ghazali, the founder of the Muslim Women's Association in Egypt. She founded this organization in 1936, having previously been a member of Huda Sharawi's Egyptian Feminist Union but having left it to commit herself to a more exclusively 'Islamic' struggle. There is perhaps a parallel here with male Islamists who abandoned nationalist and left-wing parties they came to regard as too secular, but took to their new groups ideas and techniques learnt from them. Like the Brotherhood itself, the Muslim Women's Association did not act as a political party but focused instead on proselytization and charitable work. In this context, al-Ghazali was able to restrict her activism to stereotypically 'feminine', maternal realms such as education and healthcare. However, as the battle between the regime and the Egyptian Islamists became more intense, in 1949 she agreed – following an earlier refusal – to formally affiliate her organization to the Muslim Brotherhood.

After 1949, al-Ghazali's activism was explicitly political, and she quickly became involved in the destructive conflict between the Brotherhood and the regime of Nasser. In the period between 1954 and 1965, she played an instrumental role in reconstructing the Ikhwan following Nasser's assault on the movement, and helped to distribute drafts of *Milestones* – Qutb's call to arms – to militant cells that were forming outside of prison. In 1965, she was among those arrested following Organization 1965's plot to assassinate Nasser. The six years of imprisonment and torture she subsequently endured formed the basis of her later memoir, *Days of My Life (Ayyam min Hayati)*. Through this bestselling book, al-Ghazali managed – at times seemingly in spite of herself – to popularize the notion that women were just as capable as men of undertaking militant political activity, and just as capable of standing up to the regime's brutal security agencies. Like Qutb, she was offered lucrative incentives to renounce her opposition to the regime, and like Qutb she refused them – and suffered the consequences.

Al-Ghazali's activism manipulated and subverted the claims of Islamists like Qutb that men and women had discrete and complementary responsibilities. It was precisely because men were busy working in the urban economy, al-Ghazali would later argue, that women had a special responsibility to engage in political activity. This was particularly the case for women willing to forego parenthood in the name of the Islamic struggle – a choice that al-Ghazali through her own example maintained was perfectly acceptable (although she would later contradict this view). This is another instance in which the distinction between the ideal Islamic state and the revolutionary journey towards it was significant – women were to become militant activists precisely so that they could return to a life of domestic servitude in the utopia to which they aspired.[68] The women who participated in the Afghan jihad in the 1980s and 1990s adopted a similar logic, maintaining that adherence to conventional Islamic norms was not required in a period of civil strife.[69] Like male nationalists, reformists and radicals before her, al-Ghazali would also – in spite of her other claims – emphasize the maternal role of women as one that essentially facilitated (and was thus secondary to) the tasks of the men involved in the Islamic struggle: they had to 'build the kind of men that we need to fill the ranks of the Islamic Call'.[70]

Islamist women in Sudan lived out a paradox similar to that of Zaynab al-Ghazali. While the regime promoted early marriage for the population at large, female activists eschewed it so that they could enter a variety of professions and indoctrinate women throughout the country. For instance, a new generation of female Islamist teachers arose in Sudan's expanding education system, moving away from their families to co-habit with their fellow professionals based at a variety of schools throughout the country.[71] Even though there had been an Islamist takeover in Sudan, Islamists like al-Turabi still considered the country to be in a phase of transition towards an Islamic order[72] – and thus the distinction between the journey and the final destination that helps us understand the inconsistencies of al-Ghazali's activism is also relevant in the case of Sudanese Islamists.

Although many women adhered to Islamist norms in Sudan as a result of state coercion, there was also a great deal of support for al-Turabi's vision of women's roles, especially among university-educated females. Seventy per cent of women at the University of Khartoum had been wearing 'some form of hijab' in 1988, the year before the Salvation Regime made it mandatory,[73] and even before 1989 the only two female MPs in the Sudanese parliament were members of al-Turabi's National Islamic Front.[74] Although women hardly achieved a significant degree of political power vis-à-vis men under the Salvation Regime, there was some sectoral representation for women in the National Congress.[75] Many Islamist women produced rhetoric similar to that found in al-Turabi's various writings, maintaining that they were pursuing an agenda that sought to liberate women from the patriarchal traditions of *jahili* pre-Islamic society.[76]

In spite of the Iranian state's multiple oppressive practices against women, those who have been willing to embrace Islamist ideology have been able to participate in the Islamic Republic's political system, albeit in a highly circumscribed manner. They have been allowed to stand as candidates for the Iranian *majlis* and even the presidency, although the male-dominated Council of Guardians has the power to veto candidates and has frequently used this power to prevent women from standing.[77] In 1997, nine women put themselves forward as presidential candidates, and all nine were barred from standing.[78] Meanwhile, in all the elections in the first ten years after 1979 only six women were able to acquire seats in parliament.[79] Nevertheless, women have also been able to make use of their suffrage to support more liberal male candidates.[80] Islamist women also scored a number of victories elsewhere. For instance, they have pressured the regime to allow their participation in communal prayer recitation and in 1986 the first women began to enter theological colleges in Iran, which holds out the prospect that they may be in a position to contest male domination of the clerical establishment in the future.[81]

Is it possible to describe Islamist women as 'Islamic feminists'? It is true that, in spite of their ideological opposition to Western feminism, many have shared the outlook of its 'second wave': they see women as the victims of a timeless oppression, first by traditional and then by capitalist society, dominated by sexually exploitative men.[82] The willingness of Islamist women to put themselves forward as presidential candidates demonstrates that Iranian Islamism is not ideologically monolithic, and separate 'patriarchal' and 'feminist' strands may exist within it.[83]

Suggested reading: Primary source

Zaynab al-Ghazali interview with Hagga Zaynab, 1981, and Excerpt from *Days of my Life* (1972), in Roxanne Euben and Qasim Zaman (eds), *Princeton Readings in Islamist Thought* (Princeton: Princeton University Press, 2009).

What role does Zaynab al-Ghazali see women playing in the Muslim Brotherhood, and society at large? Did the nature of her political activism confirm or confront established gender roles? Are there contradictions in al-Ghazali's worldview? How independent is her outlook from that of the male-led Muslim Brotherhood?

Debate

'Have Islamist thinkers sought to empower or oppress women?'

Are there parallels with left-wing movements that have sought to empower women? Have Islamist thinkers sought to confine women to domestic roles? How diverse have the positions of various Islamist thinkers on the matter of women's social status been? Would it be appropriate to characterize Islamist positions on the status of women as 'reactionary'?

12

From Hizbullah to the Taliban:

The militant wave

For the majority of individuals and movements we have studied so far, grass-roots militancy was not the most effective way to influence politics. In the eighteenth century Ibn Abd al-Wahhab allied with the Al Sa'ud dynasty, just as al-Mawdudi and Hasan al-Turabi rose to influence by allying with military dictators in the twentieth century. Al-Afghani and Abduh sought to influence established rulers or nationalist elites, while the Muslim Brotherhood and Hasan al-Banna alternated between cooperating with rulers and falling back on their military arm, the Special Apparatus. Yet, in the last two and a half decades of the twentieth century, militant Islamist groups emerged that sought to mobilize ordinary Muslims in order to make a more radical break with the existing sociopolitical order. These included organizations such as Egyptian Islamic Jihad, the Algeria-based Group Islamique Armée and the Taliban in Afghanistan.

Most of these militants drew heavily on the ideology of Sayyid Qutb, and – as with Sayyid Qutb – there has been debate about the respective significance of their classical and contemporary influences. Were they 'fundamentalists' following Ibn Taymiyya and Muhammad Ibn Abd al-Wahhab, or was it the nationalist and socialist ideologies of the day that shaped their worldview? The emergence of militancy in the late 1970s was arguably a result of the failure of the original nationalist revolutionary groups, which had seized power but – in the face of growing economic difficulties – were struggling to make a success of their populist and welfarist programmes. Fawaz Gerges, however, has suggested that the Islamist militants who waged war on these regimes should be understood as 'religious nationalists', as they sought to liberate their own particular nation from the rule of secular tyrants.[1] The extent to which the militants still needed to pay attention to the ideological content of Arab (as well as African, Afghan and Pakistani) nationalism, particularly in terms of its socialist content, is still very much open to debate. As we have seen, Olivier Roy argues that in the late twentieth century both militant and moderate Islamist groups began to abandon their quasi-socialist agendas and turn to a more socially conservative 'neo-fundamentalism'.[2]

Islamists battling the 'near enemy' – that is, the 'apostate' regimes that had supposedly abandoned sharia and entered into alliance with non-Muslim powers – were not the only militants in the last quarter of the twentieth century.[3] Muslims also took up arms to defend their territory against non-Muslim encroachment, the most notable cases being in Palestine, Chechnya, Bosnia and Afghanistan; other Muslims embraced militancy in the name of the Islamic Revolution promoted by Shia Iran. The militants who in the 1990s began to attack the 'far enemy'[4] – that is, Western countries – will be discussed in the following chapter.

The rise of Islamist militancy: 1979 and all that

Coinciding as it did with the 1400th year of the Islamic *hijra* calendar, the year 1979 already had the potential to inspire revolutionary sentiments among young Muslims influenced by millenarianism.[5] Indeed, 1979 was marked by the occurrence of four significant historical events, all of which helped to catalyse tensions brought about by a more structural series of political and socio-economic crises into a widespread movement of militancy directed against both foreign occupiers of Muslim territories and Muslim regimes deemed 'unIslamic'.[6] These events were:

1 the signing of a peace treaty between Egypt and Israel
2 the Soviet occupation of Afghanistan
3 the Iranian Revolution
4 the seizure of the Great Mosque of Mecca by a group of Saudi militants led by Juhaynam al-Utaybi.

The signing of a peace treaty by the Egyptian president, Anwar Sadat, and the Israeli president, Menachem Begin, seemed to mark the final capitulation of Arab nationalism, which had previously represented the most successful ideology of resistance to both Zionism and Western neocolonialism. In the eyes of an increasingly rebellious younger generation, the Arab nationalist regimes had already been discredited by the crushing defeat of the Syrian and Egyptian armies at the hands of the Israeli military during the Six-Day War of 1967.[7] Before this, Qutbist militants in Egypt had struggled to mobilize the mainstream Muslim Brotherhood against Nasser's regime because the battle against Zionist oppression in Palestine took priority, and Nasser was essential to that effort.[8] After the war, Islamists began to blame the 1967 defeat on the country's failure to adhere to sharia law and thus maintained that the battle against Nasser was a necessary phase of the wider struggle against Israel.[9]

As for the Soviet invasion of Afghanistan, this encouraged Muslim regimes to attempt to divert attention from their failures in Palestine and at home by rallying the Muslim community to defend their soil in Central Asia from the atheistic communists. Various Arab states, together with Pakistan, gave financial support to both Afghan and non-Afghan *mujahidin* fighters striving to remove the invading Soviet forces and the local leftist regime they had come to support. It is perhaps surprising that, in spite of the Islamist insurgencies they later faced, non-Islamist Muslim regimes empowered a wide variety of non-state militant groups in the country to fight in the Afghan jihad. The reason for this was that it would have seemed safe to back militant groups which were fighting to reclaim Muslim soil, and the majority of both Afghan and non-Afghan fighters in the conflict would not have embraced militancy against 'apostate' Muslim regimes. Yet, the Afghanistan conflict facilitated the growth of Islamist militancy against the Muslim regimes themselves. The occupation of Muslim territory by the world's most powerful communist regime in alliance with a local socialist government had so discredited left-wing opposition movements that the field of revolt against the corrupt sociopolitical order was left clear for the Islamists. Afghanistan also delegitimized those Muslim regimes that had close ties with the Soviet Union.[10] Moreover, the gathering of Islamist combatants in Afghanistan and north-west Pakistan provided an opportunity for groups on which the secular regimes had effectively clamped down to reorganize in a new base abroad. Ayman al-Zawahiri's Egyptian Islamic Jihad, which (re-)established itself in Peshawar in 1986, is an example.[11]

In an era of intensifying sectarianism in the Middle East, it may seem counter-intuitive that the revolutionary regime in Shia Iran should attempt to foster militancy in the Sunni Muslim world; yet, this is exactly what it did. What was significant about the Revolution was its revelation that a grass-roots uprising could unseat an autocratic regime that had strayed from Islamic principles, and the Khomeinists were careful to downplay Shi'ism in their efforts to export their revolutionary rhetoric. In the Arab world, Khomeini's regime struggled against the anti-Iranian sentiment brought about by the 1980–1988 Iran–Iraq War. Nevertheless, it managed to inspire the creation of Fatih al-Shiqaqi's Palestinian Islamic Jihad as well as Hizbullah, a party representing the Shia community of Lebanon.[12] Tehran's efforts also bore fruit in Asia and sub-Saharan Africa, as it forged strong links with movements in countries like Senegal, Sudan and Malaysia.[13] However, given the overwhelmingly Sunni character of these regions, pro-Iranian thinkers usually attempted either to articulate Iranian revolutionary slogans while professing a Sunni identity, or encourage unity between Shi'ism and Sunnism – in both cases, rather in the manner of Jamal al-Din al-Afghani in the nineteenth century.[14]

It was the effort of Shia Iran to promote revolution in the Sunni Muslim world that led Saudi Arabia – the most unabashedly anti-Shia of all the Muslim regimes in the late 1970s – to promote its own form of pan-Islamism. Like the Egyptian regime, it increasingly publicized its own religious credentials and used proselytizing agencies such as the Muslim World League and World Assembly of Muslim Youth to broadcast its form of Salafism-Wahhabism all over the world.[15] For Riyadh, this policy also had the advantage of diverting potentially militant religious activism away from the kingdom itself, where the regime had recently been rocked by the seizure of the Great Mosque of Mecca by a group of young militants under Juhaynam al-Utaybi. Exploiting the millenarian expectations that accompanied the dawn of the new Islamic century in 1979 and hoping to declare an individual named Muhammad al-Qahtani the Mahdi, Juhaynam's group held the mosque for two weeks before the Saudi government – with the assistance of a French security team – managed to clear them out.[16] Al-Utaybi was part of a group called Jama'a al-Salafiyya al-Muhtasiba, which differed from Islamist militants elsewhere in that its ideology was essentially 'rejectionist' and anti-modern, idolizing the original Wahhabi Ikhwan movement that had helped to create the Saudi state in the 1920s.[17] Yet, the movement was also significant because it highlighted the increasing frustration of less affluent Saudis at the apparent decadence and pro-Westernism of the royal elite, and demonstrated that even in the most officially pious regime of the Muslim world militant groups were willing to challenge the Islamic legitimacy of the established government.[18]

In the shade of Sayyid Qutb: The battle against the 'Near Enemy' in Algeria, Egypt and Syria

As we have seen in Chapter 7, the first Islamist to issue an uncompromising call for jihad against the existing sociopolitical systems of the Muslim world was the Egyptian Muslim Brother, Sayyid Qutb. Following Qutb's exhortation to battle *jahili* (ignorant) regimes in his seminal tract *Milestones*, and his execution by the Egyptian state in 1966, a variety of militant Islamist groups emerged which targeted the 'secular' or 'apostate' regimes in countries like Syria, Egypt and Algeria. A number of common patterns underlying the shift to militant activism can be identified in these cases. First, each of these regimes espoused an Arab nationalist ideology that Islamists regarded as secular and rooted in a 'human' form of sovereignty. While they were careful to pay lip service to Islam and sharia in their rhetoric, their criminal and civil law codes were largely inspired by those of the post-Enlightenment West. Each of these regimes had risen on a tide of anti-colonial sentiment, but eventually they came to be seen by many of their citizens as client states of either the West or the Soviet Union. Second, in each of these countries, a more militant offshoot of the established Islamist movement was strengthened by government oppression of mainstream groups committed to civil politics. Third, socio-economic changes in each of these countries – population growth, increased rural migration to urban areas, and the expansion of the higher education sector – gave rise to new social groups that were increasingly marginalized by states less committed to the populist slogans of the 1960s.

The first wave of militancy in Egypt was led by those who were imprisoned during Nasser's crackdown on the Muslim Brothers following the establishment of Qutb's Organization 1965, and subsequently released during Sadat's amnesty of 1971. These militants are often referred to as 'Qutbist' because of their adherence to the programme outlined in *Milestones*. However, since Qutb had been executed soon after publishing this book and was thus unable either to provide leadership or clarify debatable points within it,[19] the 'Qutbist' phenomenon turned out to be somewhat diffuse. Among the youthful generation of those who were held in Nasser's prison camps and were most influenced by Qutb's ideology, two groups emerged. Both followed Qutb's principle that it was necessary to establish distance between themselves and the corrupt, *jahili* society, but they differed over how exactly to interpret his principle of *'uzla*, or isolation. One group thought it sufficient either for true believers at once to isolate themselves spiritually as opposed to physically from the current society or confront it after their movement had grown in strength. Another insisted that *'uzla* must be interpreted as a form of total separation, whereby true Muslims would denounce the unbelieving society and perform *hijra* (flight) so as to recreate a genuine Islamic society on its margins.[20] It was from the latter faction that Shukri Mustafa's 'Society of Muslims' emerged.

Shukri Mustafa was a young agronomy student who hailed from a village near Asyut in Upper Egypt.[21] He rejuvenated the 'Society of Muslims' after his release from prison in 1971 – its previous iteration having disintegrated after its leader renounced his principles – and acquired a number of followers in both Upper Egypt and Cairo. Although, like the original Muslim Brothers in the 1930s and 1940s, he came from the educated class, the generation of lower-middle-class graduates he represented did not have the same level of access to the country's urban power centres. His rejection of the sociopolitical order was a result of more than just Nasserist persecution. All that his generation of rural migrants could anticipate following their poor quality university educations was a guaranteed but inadequately paid job in the country's overstaffed public sector, which forced them to wait many years longer than their fellows in the village until they could marry. When members of the Society of Muslims 'denounced' and 'fled' from the urban centre to live in the impoverished outskirts of Cairo where the state had little presence, they were doing more than just emulating the Prophetic model – they were abandoning a society that could do little to meet their socio-economic needs. Young women absconded with members of the 'Society of Muslims', thus enabling its members to avoid the conventional rules of marriage that had kept them single for so long. Until 1976, Shukri Mustafa was principally concerned with expanding his new group and sought to avoid the state rather than confront it. This strategy fell apart when his group was forced to compete with other groups that advocated direct confrontation with the state. In attacking defectors from their own movement to these other groups, members of the Society ran into the security services, and a number were arrested and put on trial. In an effort to force the regime to release its members, the Society of Muslims kidnapped a senior scholar and former minister, Muhammad al-Dhahabi, executing him when their demands were not met. As a result, Shukri Mustafa and other leaders of the group were arrested, tried and themselves executed, dozens of others were imprisoned, and the movement disappeared. The attempt to raise a pious vanguard in isolation had failed.

Part of the reason that the 'Society of Muslims' was sucked into a battle with the Egyptian government was because other militant factions compromised with Qutbist principles and chose to denounce the state, rather than state and society at large. This attitude lent itself to a more plausible and immediate strategy for revolutionary Islamic change – removing the *jahili* state, rather than cultivating the Islamic society in isolation. Many separate militant organizations following this approach formed themselves spontaneously, and eventually came to be little more than a loosely organized network variously known as al-Jihad, Jama'at al-Jihad, Tanzim al-Jihad or more recently Islamic Jihad and Egyptian Islamic Jihad. As was the case with the Society of Muslims, the majority of its members were rural migrants from Upper Egypt, and they exploited other networks of independent mosques in the peripheral urban areas over which the state exercised little formal control.

Ayman al-Zawahiri, a man who would later acquire fame for his part in the battle against the 'far enemy', entered this movement after feeling outrage at Qutb's killing. Yet its leader, Abd al-Salam Faraj, would become a pioneer of the strategy of targeting the 'near enemy' when he published a pamphlet called *The Neglected Duty* (or *al-Farida al-Gha'iba*, sometimes translated as the *Hidden Imperative*). Like al-Banna, al-Faraj was willing to begin the broader Islamic struggle by taking over the existing nation state and 'Islamizing' it: 'We have to establish the rule of God's religion in our own country first,' he urged.[22] Unlike al-Banna, he was willing to advocate openly the forceful removal of the existing system to achieve this end. Al-Faraj declared that 'there is no doubt that the first battlefield for jihad is the extermination of these infidel leaders and to replace them by a complete Islamic order'.[23] However, there were many disagreements in the Jama'at al-Jihad as to how exactly the 'infidel regimes' should be overthrown. One faction, including Ayman al-Zawahiri, decided to play the long game, planning to wait until they had infiltrated the military so effectively that they could rule through it after overthrowing the current leaders.[24] However, as was the case with the Special Apparatus of the original Muslim Brotherhood, hotheads in the organization overtook the long-term strategists by pre-empting their confrontation with the state.

In 1981, a young army officer and Jama'at al-Jihad member called Khalid Islambuli assassinated Anwar Sadat at a military parade. Although his plan had received the assent of the organization's leadership, the more cautious elements argued that without a mass Islamist uprising in Cairo the act would be vainglorious, as ultimately proved to be the case.[25] Following the assassination, the regime decimated the group's networks: several leading members were arrested and al-Faraj and Islambuli were both tried and executed. In 1986, the Jama'at al-Jihad was relaunched by al-Zawahiri in Peshawar as 'Egyptian Islamic Jihad', and again it became sucked into an intense conflict with the Egyptian regime, now under Sadat's successor Hosni Mubarak. Eventually, al-Zawahiri became frustrated at the Egyptian jihadis' short-termist approach, and abandoned the tactic of prioritizing the 'near enemy' altogether by aligning Egyptian Islamic Jihad with bin Laden's al-Qa'eda.[26]

One organization closely affiliated with the Jama'at al-Jihad was al-Jama'a al-Islamiyya, another group that recruited heavily among upper Egyptians who were not as well integrated into middle-class urban Egypt as members of the Muslim Brotherhood.[27] Like the Jama'at al-Jihad, al-Jama'a al-Islamiyya committed itself to militant activity against the regime, but it also followed an educationalist strategy akin to that of the Brotherhood mainstream. Ironically, it was the Egyptian regime itself that had cultivated and given support to al-Jama'a in the early 1970s, when Anwar Sadat had reconciled with the non-Qutbist Ikhwanis in an effort to cultivate the image of a 'pious President'.[28] Al-Jama'a emerged as a largely campus-based organization at a time when Egypt's higher education sector was expanding rapidly, and quickly transformed itself into a mass movement by using similar tactics to the Brotherhood: organizing public gatherings, summer camps and sports groups.[29]

The Egyptian regime had originally regarded the Islamist student movement as an anti-leftist proxy on campus, but turned against it after realizing that it was growing too powerful; this drove it into the company of the militants.[30] By the mid-1990s, both al-Jama'a al-Islamiyya and Egyptian Islamic Jihad were waging a sustained insurgency against the government in Upper Egypt. In 1997, al-Jama'a al-Islamiyya perpetrated a serious terrorist atrocity at Luxor, killing sixty-eight civilians, mainly Western tourists.[31] However, it has been argued that al-Jama'a al-Islamiyya was as much a movement of marginalized Sa'idis (Upper Egyptians) as a radical Islamist organization; that, in other words, its various assaults on the tourism industry were provoked by the financial support it gave to an exploitative regime rather than by hostility to Westerners and pre-Islamic culture.[32] It showed little interest in Egyptian Islamic Jihad's shift towards a 'global jihad', and began to seek an accommodation with the regime after moderates in the movement reacted with horror to the Luxor massacre.[33]

Whereas the Egyptian government successfully factionalized the Islamist opposition by offering an olive branch to 'moderates' after 1970, the Ba'athist regime that seized power in Syria in 1963 was unrelenting in its persecution of the Muslim Brotherhood; as a result, the militant opposition to it developed a broader base. The Islamists in Syria resented the regime of Hafez al-Assad because it was dominated by Alawi Shias, it was radically secular in character, and it promoted land reform measures that undermined the urban Sunni bourgeoisie with links to the Ikhwan.[34] In 1964, Marwan Hadid, a Syrian Ikhwani influenced by the publication of *Milestones*, formed an organization called the 'Combatant Vanguard' which eventually led the mainstream Muslim Brotherhood into armed opposition to the regime during the insurgency of 1976–82.[35] Egypt and Jordan, which constituted the 'Near Enemy' for their own militant Islamist opposition, were willing to back the Muslim Brotherhood's opposition to a regime that grew close to Shia Iran after 1979.[36] The Syrian conflict had increasingly taken on a sectarian character, with members of al-Hadid's Combatant Vanguard massacring Shia Alawis in the military.[37] In 1982, the regime put an end to the Brotherhood's rebellion by bombarding its stronghold in Hama, razing one-quarter of the city to the ground and killing over twenty thousand people.[38]

The situation in Algeria in the 1990s was similar to that of Syria in the 1970s. In 1992, the Algerian military banned the mainstream Islamist party, the Front Islamique de Salut, following its victories in the first round of national elections in the previous year, and prevented further polls from taking place, thus driving all of the country's Islamists into armed opposition to the regime.[39] However, it should be noted that before the military regime had cancelled elections and clamped down on the 'moderate' Islamists, the militant faction dominating the campaign against the junta, the Group Islamique Armée (GIA), was comprised of Salafi–jihadist factions already wedded to the view that militant jihad was the only means to establish an Islamic state in the country.[40] The GIA's brutal campaign against the Algerian government and people, therefore, was a result not of the regime 'radicalizing' the mainstream Islamists but allowing a separate 'radical' faction to seize the initiative. The Front Islamique de Salut did form its own armed wing, the Armée Islamique de Salut (AIS), but these militants distanced themselves from the ideology and the brutal acts of the GIA, and continued to negotiate with the regime, laying emphasis on the elections that were cancelled rather than the 'infidel' character of their opponents.[41]

Many of the GIA fighters had participated in the Afghan jihad in the 1980s, and were deeply influenced by Qutb's *Milestones* as well as by the Egyptian jihadis they encountered abroad.[42] The battle against the 'near enemy' had particular resonance in Algeria because the history of Western colonialism in that country stretched back further than in most parts of the Muslim world. The French had ruled Algeria as a settler colony from 1830 until 1962, and, although they had been forced out by the Front Libération Nationale

(FLN), Algerian Islamists believed that the initial wave of liberation had failed to emancipate the country's population and postcolonial government from the French language, culture and secular ideals.[43] The GIA's outlook has (like Qutb's) been described as 'Manichaean',[44] a term which the famous postcolonial philosopher and FLN activist, Frantz Fanon, helped to popularize. Fanon argued that only a comprehensive break with the colonial system could lead to genuine decolonization, and in attempting to ban French language newspapers and shut down schools where the French language was taught the GIA appeared to be attempting such a break.[45] Of course, Fanon himself would have criticized the use of religion.[46] Yet, the legacy of French cultural colonization made Algeria an even more fertile ground than Egypt for the growth of a Qutbist ideology that denounced state and society at large.[47] Having excommunicated the Algerian population en masse, the GIA went on to perpetrate a number of brutal massacres against unarmed Algerian villagers throughout the period of the Algerian Civil War, which were condemned by the AIS and provoked the wrath of the population as a whole.[48] The GIA became increasingly factionalized, and the insurgency fell apart.[49]

Irredentist Jihadism

A number of militant movements target neither the 'near' nor the 'far enemy'. Rather, they are *irredentist* movements: they seek to reclaim Muslim territory encroached on by non-Muslim invaders. These movements can be distinguished from irredentist movements elsewhere in that many of them do not follow an ethnic or secular-nationalist logic but seek instead to maintain the territorial integrity of the Muslim community as a whole, as it is conceived of by pan-Islamists.[50] Having said this, a number of them recruited within, and were principally concerned with the liberation of, their own country. It is necessary, therefore, if rather confusing, to make a further distinction; namely, between 'pan-Islamist' and 'nation-based' forms of Islamist irredentism.[51]

'Pan-Islamist' irredentism emerged as a major global phenomenon during the Afghanistan conflict of the 1980s, when governments and businessmen all over the Muslim world funded co-religionists to travel to Afghanistan and defend Muslim territory from Soviet encroachment. Many ordinary citizens with little sympathy for attacking either 'apostate' regimes or the 'far enemy' joined this jihad.[52] Unlike other forms of militancy, these campaigns received considerable support from representatives of the official religious establishment in various Muslim countries: since, they declared, Muslim territory had been encroached upon, it was an 'individual duty' (*fard kifaya*) incumbent upon every capable member of the community to fight in its defence.[53] The leader of the force that came to be known as the 'Arab Afghans', Abdullah Azzam, began to conceive of it as a mobile institution that could respond to any invasion of the Dar al-Islam.[54] Azzam was killed in a car bomb in 1989, but others followed his lead. In 1992, Abu Abd al-Aziz 'Barbaros', a Saudi national and veteran of the Afghanistan conflict, led a squadron of international jihadis to resist the ethnic cleansing of Bosnian Muslims by Serb militias in a campaign which also received the blessing of mainstream Muslim clerics.[55] Three years later, Ibn Abd al-Khattab, another Saudi national, led a multinational battalion of jihadis in an effort to free the predominantly Muslim region of Chechnya from rule by the Kremlin.[56]

What is noticeable about the Chechen conflict is that jihadis from various countries hijacked an existing separatist movement that was originally secular in character.[57] Elsewhere, jihadis have boasted of involvement in irredentist struggles – such as in Somalia and Kashmir – where their presence and physical impact was minimal.[58] However, in a number of territories irredentism has acquired a specifically Islamist character. One of these is Palestine, which is discussed below. Another is Somalia, where the rise of Islamism has been attributed both to state failure and the perception that African Union peacekeeping forces – as well as the Ethiopian troops they replaced – represent alien forces annexing Muslim territories; hence the rise of al-Ittihad, the Union of Islamic Courts and al-Shabab.[59] In the Indian-controlled territory of Kashmir, a movement known as the Jihad Council played the foremost role in the insurgency that broke out against rule by Delhi in 1990. Of the 844 insurgents killed in the fighting in 1991, less than a handful came from outside of Kashmir,[60] although many were trained by Pakistan's Inter-Services Intelligence (ISI) in the same camps that had housed the mujahidin fighters in Afghanistan.[61] Nevertheless, by the turn of the century Lashkar-i-Taiba, a Pakistan-based pan-Islamist group following the ideology of Abdullah Azzam, had become a significant player in the Kashmir conflict.[62]

Though their rationale was primarily irredentist, both the nation-based and pan-Islamist movements sought to impose Islamist ideology in the areas that came under their influence. In Somalia, the Union of Islamic Courts sought with a considerable degree of success to impose sharia law where customary or secular legislation had previously held sway.[63] The jihadi commander, Abu Abd al-Aziz 'Barbaros', maintained that before he arrived in Bosnia 'one could not distinguish the Muslim from the Christian' whereas Muslim women 'were dressed, but were really exposed'.[64] They attempted to coerce women into veiling and men into growing their beards, but – given the external character of their movement – had little success.[65]

A number of 'irredentist' movements were willing to take the fight beyond the Dar al-Islam and attack occupiers, or perceived occupiers, of Muslim territory on their own turf. Al-Shabab has attacked civilian targets in Kenya and Uganda, claiming that this was retaliation for the contribution of these nations to the African Union force stationed in Somalia.[66] Lashkar-i-Taiba has launched major attacks in India, including the killing of 174 people in Mumbai in 2008 which Pakistan's ISI was also accused of assisting.[67]

In spite of the extreme methods they have used, these groups had more restricted agendas than the global jihadi movements that will be discussed in the next chapter. Nevertheless, the geopolitical impact of the 9/11 attacks and the rise of the 'War on Terror' has encouraged major powers to try to delegitimize Islamist irredentist groups by labelling them as 'terrorist' in a manner that associates them with the global jihadis and underplays the political background to their militancy. Vladimir Putin's rhetoric towards the Chechen jihadis is one example of this strategy.[68]

Shia militancy and sectarianism in Iraq and Lebanon

After 1979, the Iranian regime made strenuous efforts to export Islamic Revolution to the rest of the Muslim world. Although it downplayed its Shi'i rhetoric, it was most successful in countries with large Shia populations, notably Iraq and Lebanon. The militants in these territories differed from those in the Sunni countries: they were not purely 'non-state' agents but trained and organized by the Iranian government's Revolutionary Guards.

Tehran dedicated its most strenuous efforts to mobilizing the predominantly Shia population of Iraq, where for most of the 1980s it waged war against the Sunni and Ba'athist regime of Saddam Hussein. Iraq did already have its own movement of grass-roots opposition to Hussein, in the al-Da'wa Party. This was backed by the Iraqi Shia cleric, Muhammad al-Baqir al-Sadr, a man whose ideas mirrored those of Khomeini but who was also very much independent of him.[69] After the Iranian Revolution broke out in 1979, the al-Da'wa party had organized a campaign of militant opposition to the Ba'ath regime, openly attacking government buildings.[70] With the outbreak of the Iran–Iraq war in 1980, al-Da'wa relocated to the Islamic Republic, but refused to endorse Khomeini's *Velayet-i-Faqih* ideology; as a consequence, it was under another Shi'i cleric, Muhammad Baqir al-Hakim, that Tehran helped to set up the Supreme Council of the Islamic Revolution in Iraq (SCIRI).[71] The Iranian Revolutionary Guards trained Iraqi prisoners of war, as well as Shia expelled from Iraq by the Ba'athists, into an organization known as the 'Badr Brigades', which officially became the military wing of SCIRI and in practice a proxy militia of the Tehran government in the war against Saddam.[72] While the Iranian regime backed SCIRI and al-Da'wa from outside, within Iraq support for grass-roots Shi'i militancy suffered – most still regarded the conflict as a war between nations rather than a sectarian or an Islamist–secularist conflict, and the Shia parties in Iran came to be seen as traitors even by many Shia Iraqis.[73]

Western intervention from 1991 to 2003 played a considerable role in the intensification of Shia militancy within Iraq itself, on account of the consequent destabilization and eventual collapse of the Ba'athist regime.

As Saddam's government was reeling from its defeat in the Gulf War of 1991, SCIRI and the Badr Brigades intervened in a popular revolt in Shia-dominated southern Iraq. SCIRI's association with Iran undermined the uprising but the mass killings of Shia Iraqis by the regime in the wake of the revolt further intensified sectarian tensions in Iraq.[74] After the American-led 'coalition of the willing' removed the Ba'athist regime in Baghdad in 2003, sectarian militancy began to dominate Iraqi politics. While a lingering identification with Arab nationalism had prevented Islamism and sectarianism from setting the agenda during the 1980–1988 conflict, the process of 'deba'athification' had eviscerated the Iraqi nation state and left neighbouring Iran far greater scope to intervene.[75] With the Iraqi army, police and healthcare system dismantled, sectarian militias such as the Badr Brigades and Mahdi Army of Muqtadar al-Sadr were among those best positioned to provide physical security and other services to the suffering population.[76] Internecine Sunni–Shia violence continued, and parties with barely concealed sectarian biases dominated the post-Saddam elections.[77] Al-Da'wa and SCIRI both distanced themselves from their former patrons in Iran, and together entered into a party known as the United Iraqi Alliance, which would dominate the parliamentary regime after the 2005 elections. They remained committed to the principle of a united Iraq, but their thinly disguised pro-Shia bias alienated the Sunni population and thus played into the hands of ISIS as a sectarian organization that sought to bring an end to the Iraqi nation state (see next chapter).

The emergence of Iranian-backed Shia militancy in Lebanon followed a similar pattern to that in Iraq: it developed and to some extent subverted an existing pattern of nation-based Shia militancy against the local regime. As the Lebanese Civil War (1975–90) broke out, many of the marginalized Shia community in South Lebanon flocked to join Amal, a militia movement that opposed the dominant position of the Sunni and Maronite communities within the national government. Following the mysterious death of Amal's leader in Libya, the charismatic Shia cleric Musa Sadr, in 1978, and the seismic impact of the Iranian Revolution in the following year, in 1982 Hizbullah emerged as the premier force of militant Shi'ism in Lebanon. The 'Party of God' was established under the direct supervision of the Iranian ambassador and Iranian Revolutionary Guard forces stationed in Lebanon, and endorsed Khomeini's *Velayet-i-Faqih* model.[78] However, in practice Hizbullah pursued a modus operandi similar to 'irredentist' movements elsewhere, rather than the 'near enemy' jihadists of various Sunni countries in the region. In 1982, Israel had invaded Lebanon on the pretext of expelling Palestinian refugees it believed to be using the country to stage attacks against her, and US peacekeeping forces soon followed. Hizbullah prioritized the battle against the invading forces over that against the Lebanese state, launching numerous attacks – including suicide attacks – against US and Israeli troops in Lebanon.[79] After the US and Israeli militaries withdrew from Lebanon, Hizbullah continued to identify itself as a shield against Zionist aggression, and was at the forefront of efforts to repel another Israeli invasion in 2006. However, within the domestic Lebanese political arena, it pursued an accommodationist rather than a militant approach, maintaining that while it aspired to establish an Islamic state in Lebanon it would use civil means to do so.[80] US and Israeli forces aside, its bloodiest confrontations were with its Shi'i competitor, al-Amal, rather than the Lebanese regime.[81]

Hamas and the Israel/Palestine conflict

On account of the unique dynamics of the conflict in Israel and Palestine, Hamas – as the territory's principal militant Islamist organization – possesses its own specific strategic and ideological agendas. It might be considered a 'religious nationalist' group battling the 'near enemy' in its own territory, like al-Jama'a al-Islamiyya or the Front Islamique du Salut.[82] However, since the 'near enemy' is a non-Muslim regime which it perceives to be occupying one of the heartlands of the umma, rather than a secular or semi-secular and authoritarian Muslim regime, its approach is markedly different from that of other militant groups. Hamas was founded in 1987 as the military wing of the Muslim Brotherhood's Palestinian branch, which was set up in 1946 and had until then pursued an 'educationalist' strategy, eschewing violent confrontation with the Israeli regime.[83] Since it first mobilized during a mass civilian uprising against the Israeli government in 1987, Hamas quickly attempted to establish itself as a mass movement rather than a secretive Qutbist vanguard. The leaders of the Palestinian Muslim Brotherhood, including the charismatic Shaikh Ahmad Yasin, also became the leaders of Hamas, and, since their first enemy was Israel, they pursued the same open-ended approach towards Muslim society in Palestine adopted by the mainstream Brotherhood elsewhere. Like the Egyptian Muslim Brotherhood and al-Turabi's Islamic Movement, the Palestinian Ikhwan – and later Hamas – established numerous mosques, schools and medical centres to facilitate their development into a mass movement.[84]

The struggle that Hamas advocated was simultaneously nationalist and pan-Islamic. The 1988 Charter maintained that as Palestine was a land of such crucial historic significance, possessing the third most holy of Islam's sanctuaries, 'liberation of Palestine is then an individual duty for every Moslem wherever he may be'.[85] Such an appeal would have made sense at a time when the multinational campaign to support Afghanistan was at its peak but the Charter also made numerous efforts to compromise with conventional nationalist ideology and in particular that of the Palestinian nationalist groups. It praised the struggle of 'secular' organizations such as Yasir Arafat's Palestinian Liberation Organization (PLO) against Israel, maintaining that if it were not for their failure to recognize the necessity of sharia governance they would have exactly the same outlook. Hamas ideologues have frequently observed that Islamic and nationalist ideals might be mutually complementary,[86] although they have gone further in their search for Palestinian national idioms and national heroes than many Islamists. It is notable that Hamas's Charter puts considerable effort into casting as heroic the struggle of Salah al-Din al-Ayyubi against the Crusader armies of the medieval era, and laments 'ideological invasion' by 'orientalists and missionaries' subsequent to his defeat of Palestine's European invaders. Yet, according to their own logic, Islamists should consider Salah al-Din al-Ayyubi a secular tyrant who typified the monarchical ideals of the era that followed the decline of the Rightly Guided Caliphs.

Although Hamas was formed as a militant organization, it resembled the Muslim Brotherhood more than other militant organizations: it was willing to develop into a mass movement, adopt a conventional nationalist programme and avoid targeting Muslim regimes. Is it, therefore, more capable of ideological moderation than these other militant groups? This is a complex question. Different commentators have sought to identify sources of influence as contrasting as Qutb, modernists and the Salafi–jihadists.[87] Evidence of a 'modernist' outlook is the movement's willingness to embrace capitalism, democracy and Western science.[88] The disposition to embrace conventional nationalism and electoral politics clearly differentiates the ideology of Hamas from that of Sayyid Qutb, who in spite of his radical anti-semitism was far less willing than Hudaybi to put the struggle against Israel before the struggle against Nasser.[89] Since 'the Jews' or at least the Israeli government constitute the 'Party of Satan', the Muslims as a whole become the 'Party of God'.[90] This binary favoured by the radical Islamists, therefore, is not used to divide Muslim society itself.

Litvak argues that it is Hamas' readiness to embrace suicide bombing as a tactic and extol martyrdom that brings its ideology close to that of the Salafi–jihadists, although he recognizes that it is far less concerned with doctrine and far less inclined to denounce other Muslims as non-believers.[91] He contends that Hamas has transformed the Israel-Palestine conflict into a holistic inter-religious struggle and promoted a cult of martyrdom, making its adherents far more concerned with the virgins of Paradise than mundane grievances concerning land.[92] Hamas's defenders have argued that its resort to suicide bombing, which has led it to be labelled a 'terrorist' organization in the West, is a result of a process of radicalization brought on by the actions of the Israeli state. It was, in fact, just two years after the Israeli regime arrested Ahmad Yassin that Hamas founded the Izz al-Din Qassam Martyr's Brigades, which conducted the majority of its suicide attacks in the 1990s.[93] There is a possible parallel here with the Egyptian state's crackdowns on the Muslim Brotherhood leadership in 1948–9 and 1954, which respectively enabled the Special Apparatus and then later on the Qutbist organizations to adopt a more confrontational strategy without being reined in by the organization's headquarters. Hamas's defenders have also maintained that suicide bombing is not evidence of inherent extremism, so much as a tactic of last resort designed to safeguard Palestinian life by deterring the Israelis from themselves targeting

Palestinian civilians. Between 1987 and 2006, 998 Palestinian children died as a result of the conflict, in contrast to 137 Israeli children.[94]

One significant obstacle to Hamas's moderation is its problem with anti-Semitism, or Judeophobia. Some Arab authors have rejected the notion that Hamas or other Arab groups can be 'anti-Semitic' as Arabs are Semites themselves.[95] Indeed, the importation of European anti-Semitism to the Muslim world has led to much anti-Arab hostility; for instance, in Iran.[96] Terminological debates aside, it is clear that a number of the central tropes of European Jew-hatred have featured in Hamas's rhetoric. The original Hamas Charter of 1988 spoke of a Zionist conspiracy to control global governments by manipulating the economy and the education system, and made reference to the notorious European anti-Semitic forgery, the *Protocols of the Elders of Zion*, to support its claims. It also used the terms 'Zionist' and 'Jew' interchangeably.[97] However, Hamas's defenders have observed that it was written by a single party member and published without consultation, that it does not reflect the views of the membership as a whole and that in practice the Hamas leadership have rarely referred to it since.[98] Yet, as recently as 2000, Hamas described the Holocaust as 'an alleged and invented story with no basis', and its militants continue to draw on Sayyid Qutb's 1951 text, *Our Battle with the Jews (Ma'arakatuna ma' al-Yahud)*.[99]

The Taliban: A neofundamentalist state?

The capture of the Afghan state by the Taliban in 1996 appeared to confirm Olivier Roy's thesis that Islamic movements had turned to a 'neo-fundamentalism' that was more concerned with morality than political or socio-economic revolution.[100] Even though Afghanistan had been a hub of pan-Islamic activism in the 1980s, by the early 1990s it was the graveyard of revolutionary Islamism. The original mujahidin movement of the 1980s had included Afghan Islamist groups, notably the Jama'at-i-Islami of Burnahuddin Rabbani and the Hizb-i-Islami of Gulbuddin Hekmatyar. The first party was a branch of its Pakistani namesake, which also supported the Hizb-i-Islami. Yet, in spite of their ties to South Asia's first Islamist organization, in the midst of the anti-Soviet conflict and subsequent civil war both of these groups lost a great deal of their ideological commitment and were sucked into a world of ethnic politics and realpolitik.[101] The Jama'at-i-Islami's commander, Ahmed Shah Masood, captured Kabul in 1992, and – although he did not impose any particular Islamist programme – soon faced a backlash from those who perceived that he represented the interests of the ethnic Tajik minority. The Pashtun-dominated Hizb-i-Islami and Hekmatyar opposed Masood, but grew weaker after alienating the Saudis over their support for Saddam. Meanwhile, the wanton looting and sexual violence that accompanied the civil war discredited the competing Islamist groups even further.

Out of the moral bankruptcy of the conventional Islamist parties rose the Taliban's rigid moralism. Unlike individuals such as Rabbani and Hekmatyar, the leaders of the Taliban had experienced no form of Western education. Most had grown up in refugee camps in Pakistan's North-West Frontier Province, isolated from their culture and society and with few economic options. This made them peculiarly vulnerable to indoctrination by the Jama'at Ulama-i-Islam, a group of rigid Deobandi scholars which – with support from the Pakistani security services – ran a militant network of *madrasas* designed to prepare Pakistani youngsters for jihad in Afghanistan and Kashmir. Although elsewhere the turn to neofundamentalism was associated with an educationalist strategy and retreat from the formal political arena, like militant Islamists in Egypt and Algeria the Taliban were willing to confront the 'near enemy' – even though in their case the 'near enemy' was nominally Islamist. Although morality was at the centre of their discourse, the profound moral crisis of an Afghan society devastated and wracked with insecurity after decades of conflict enabled them to make this a political call to arms against the dysfunctional regime of Rabbani. With the crucial backing of Pakistan's ISI, they were able to sweep aside the mujahidin forces, occupying Kandahar in 1994, and then finally Kabul in 1996.

Taliban government was government by its own version of sharia more than it was government by any particular political or ideological programme. The most powerful ministry in the regime was the ministry for 'the Promotion of Virtue and Prevention of Vice'.[102] The Taliban banned music, football, beardless faces, chess and television, and closed down the majority of the country's schools. In this regard the Taliban seemed to correspond more than any other movement to the caricature of Islamism as a rejection of modernity, which was perhaps not surprising since the recent impact of Western modernity on Afghanistan had been so devastating. They were, of course, also a product of the very modernity they rejected so vehemently. The movement's knowledge of sharia law was in practice fairly rough and ready, and these extreme measures had as much to do with the desire of the Taliban to position themselves as the saviours of society suffering from a comprehensive moral breakdown as they did with rigorous adherence to classical jurisprudence. Evidence of this is the Taliban's repeated violations of the classical injunction against spying on neighbours and invading households in the name of their moral restructuring of Afghan society. The form of sharia they introduced was heavily influenced by customary Pashtun law, although at the same time they banned various customs which went against more formal sharia.[103]

At times, the brutal authoritarianism of the Taliban led them to deviate from sharia. The torturing, castration and extra-judicial murder of the Soviet-era president, Najibullah, following the seizure of Kabul in 1996, offended the religious sensibilities of many Afghans. The decision of the leader of the Taliban, Mullah Muhammad Omar, to adopt the title 'Amir al-Mu'minin' also jarred with the Islamic values of the majority of the population. The secretive Omar had no connections to the family of the Prophet that would have justified such self-styling. His government was in practice highly autocratic and centralized – there were no elections, no parties, and supreme authority was vested in Omar as Amir al-Mu'minin. The Taliban were careful to represent this as a return to the original Prophetic model of the Arabian Peninsula, maintaining that Islam did not sanction elections or political pluralism, although of course there was a noticeable continuity with the authoritarianism of the Soviet and post-Soviet regime. A shura council was established, but rarely consulted. In their ruthless quest to maintain power, the Taliban overlooked sharia injunctions against the use of narcotics so as to reap dividends from the booming opium trade.

In spite of their formal emphasis on sharia, a number of the Taliban's agendas were somewhat more particularist. Like so many movements before them, they were sucked into, and helped to perpetuate, the various ethnic conflicts that had intensified the civil war. The Taliban were a predominantly Pashtun movement, and were regarded as such by much of the Afghan population. This prevented them from entrenching themselves in the non-Pashtun areas. In 1998, in retaliation for the killing of Taliban troops in the northern city of Mazar-i-Sharif, the Taliban retook the city and proceeded summarily to execute thousands of ethnic Hazaras, Tajiks and Uzbeks in the region.[104] The killing of the Shia Hazaras nearly brought war with neighbouring Iran, as nine diplomats from the Islamic Republic were caught up in the fighting.

In the international arena, the Taliban was a somewhat insular movement, with few designs to export pan-Islamic revolution. Its rigid Sunnism dictated hostility towards Shia Iran, and it established few contacts with the other Islamist regime of the day – that in Sudan.[105] The US government, however, was initially happy with its emergence because of its anti-Iran stance,[106] and Omar wrote reassuringly to the Clinton administration: 'We are far from you', he said, 'and do not intend to harm you and cannot harm you either'.[107] Accordingly, the Taliban did not support Osama bin Laden's declaration of war against America in 1998, but their decision to continue playing host to the Saudi jihadist ultimately brought about the American invasion of 2001 and the downfall of their regime. Since their ouster from Kabul by the invading American forces, the Taliban have transformed themselves into a movement of resistance to non-Muslim occupation, much like the original mujahidin movement of the 1980s.[108] They have thus abandoned a number of their neofundamentalist concerns for a more political approach in an effort to establish a broad base of support in the country at large.[109] Out of power, the Taliban militias no long upbraid members of the public for watching television or shaving their beards. Like Islamist movements elsewhere, they have now learnt to use a discourse of human rights in condemning American neo-imperialism, and to use Western technology in their battle against American hegemony.[110]

The Kharijis, Ibn Taymiyya and the Wahhabis: Pre-modern inspirations?

In a heated battle for the 'hearts and minds' of the Muslim public, both militant Islamists and their critics have attempted to mobilize the legacies of pre-modern 'radicals' either to legitimize or delegitimize militant ideas.[111] Associations with Muhammad Ibn Abd al-Wahhab and the movement he founded, the Wahhabiyya (see Chapter 3), are cited in different contexts either to heroize or demonize a wide range of militant organizations; meanwhile, militant groups are usually eager to claim a precedent in the jurisprudence of Ibn Taymiyya (see Chapter 2), while their Muslim and non-Muslim opponents seek to refute such a link. However, the seventh-century Khariji movement responsible for the assassination of the Caliph Ali (see Chapter 2) almost universally forms a negative comparison, and militant groups invariably reject such an association. For instance, the 'Society of Muslims', which acquired the popular name 'Takfir wa Hijra' on account of its willingness to denounce the existing Muslim society in Egypt and its efforts to seek complete separation from the sinful mainstream, seemed to a number of Egyptians to be an obvious successor to the Kharijis.[112] Yet, the Society never claimed this label, and moderates in the movement even attempted to persuade their leader to downscale militant activities to avoid such negative comparisons.[113] A similar series of dynamics have guided the use of the label 'takfiri', since the denunciation of other Muslims as non-believers (*takfir*) was a key element of classical Khariji practice. While militants themselves do not use the term as a self-descriptor, many government officials and critics of militancy prefer this term to 'jihadist' as they do not want to legitimize their activities as a genuine form of Islamic struggle.[114]

In the wake of Sadat's assassination by Jama'at al-Jihad, both the perpetrators and their state prosecutors attempted to use against the other the label of Kharijism. In *The Neglected Duty*, published posthumously following his execution, Faraj declared: 'All Muslim Imams command to fight these [Kharijis]. The Mongols and their likes – the equivalent of our rulers today – are (even) more rebellious against the laws of Islam than those who refused the zakat tax, or [the Kharijis].'[115] Here Faraj followed Ibn Taymiyya in describing the Mongols as Kharijis, and then transferred the label onto Sadat's government. Umar Abd al-Rahman, the blind al-Azhar Shaykh who acted as an informal mentor to the Jama'at al-Jihad, maintained that it was always justified to rebel against a nominally Muslim ruler who 'institutes non-Islamic personal status laws, aids Zionists, constructs an ecumenical house of worship, establishes relations with the greatest enemy of believers [the Jews], signs the Camp David accords, and avows that there is no religion in politics and no politics in religion'.[116] The problem for the Jama'at al-Jihad was that they could not prove that, for all his apparent malfeasances, Anwar Sadat was the equivalent of the Mongol rulers who had actively overthrown the Abbasid Caliphate and introduced their own customary code, the *Yasa*. There has been much criticism of the ahistoric 'Mongolizing' of rulers who, unlike their thirteenth-century predecessors, descended from families that had been Muslim for generations.[117] Yet, the problem for the Egyptian government was that it could not prove Sadat was Ali Ibn Abi Talib – the original victim of the Kharijis – either. As Umar Abd al-Rahman observed at his trial, 'Did Ali borrow the basis of the law from the Persians and Romans? Was his rule based on socialism or democracy?'[118]

It might be argued that the increasing intellectual and religious influence of Saudi Arabia, as well as Saudi-backed institutions such as the World Assembly of Muslim Youth, was what led to Salafi texts such as those of Ibn Taymiyya and Muhammad Ibn Abd al-Wahhab becoming key readings for Islamist militants. This is partly true, although with exceptions such as Abu Abd al-Aziz Barbaros and Ibn Abd al-Khattab, the majority of the militants who evoked Ibn Taymiyya and Ibn Abd al-Wahhab were neither from Salafi–Wahhabi backgrounds nor trained in Salafi–Wahhabi religious institutions. Rather, key interpreters of Ibn Taymiyya were often individuals from relatively secular educational backgrounds who read independently the texts the Wahhabis had popularized. Abd al-Salam Faraj, the pioneer of pseudo-Taymiyyan militancy in the late twentieth century, was an electrical engineer not an *alim*, and his readings of the medieval thinker have been criticized for their scholarly ineptitude.[119] He cites Ibn Taymiyya's fatwas against the Mongol invaders of the Arab world, in which the medieval scholar declared that those who supported them 'in spite of their pretension to be Muslims – not only glorify Genghis Khan but also fight the Muslims', to support his belief that it was essential to wage jihad to overthrow the infidel regime of Anwar Sadat.[120]

The criticisms of Faraj's reading of Ibn Taymiyya have been numerous. First of all, his context-free comparison between Sadat's regime and that of the Mongols, which he used to justify his call for a political revolution to establish a more genuine Islamic state, failed to recognize that Ibn Taymiyya himself had advocated supporting the far from perfectly Islamic regime of the Mamluks against the invading Mongols so as to defend Islam.[121] Arguably, Sadat's regime was far more comparable to that of the Mamluks than the Mongols, who were invaders and recent converts.[122] In Michot's view, Faraj fails to understand that Ibn Taymiyya saw the territory controlled by the Mongols – including Mardin, the subject of his famous *fatwa* – as being neither fully a 'domain of war' nor a 'domain of peace', but rather as one possessing a composite status. Faraj therefore mistakenly interprets Ibn Taymiyya as placing requirements on Muslims living under nominally Muslim rulers similar to those inhabiting a 'domain of war', when in reality his argument is more complex.[123] Furthermore, Michot claims that Ibn Taymiyya's various pronouncements on the territory controlled by the Mongols were shaped more by his concern for the souls of the Muslims living there, rather than for the question of whether Mardin was a legitimate Islamic state or not.[124]

Abdullah Azzam, who had received theological training from al-Azhar, was on much safer ground with his analysis of Ibn Taymiyya since his concern was not so much to delegitimize established Muslim regimes but to rally resistance against invaders of Muslim lands. He cites Ibn Taymiyya's observation that 'when the enemy has entered an Islamic land, there is no doubt that it is obligatory on those closest to the land to defend it, and then on those around them, for the entire Islamic land is like a single country. Also (it is compulsory) to go forth to meet the enemy without permission from parents or people to whom one was in debt. The texts of (Imam) Ahmad are quite clear on this.'[125] It might be argued that the phenomenon of youthful, grass-roots irredentist militancy that emerged in the 1980s did have its roots in Ibn Taymiyya's thought – and indeed in the broader Hanbali jurisprudential tradition, since Ibn Taymiyya himself draws on Ahmad Ibn Hanbal to support these claims. Lashkar-i-Taiba, as an irredentist group following Azzam's teachings, have gone so far as to label their 'martyrdom operations' as 'Ibn Taymiyah Fida'i missions'.[126]

While militants such as Ibn Abd al-Khattab and Abu Abd al-Aziz 'Barbaros' were Wahhabis, they did not – as we have seen – have a great deal of success in indoctrinating the populations they militarized. Gulbuddin Hekmatyar had training in a Salafi–Wahhabi religious institution but later turned to the less Salafi-orientated Popular Arab and Islamic Conference of al-Turabi and made a political break with Saudi Arabia; this suggests that Wahhabism may not have been the principal determinant of his ideological worldview.[127] All of this leads us to question whether the 'Wahhabi' militants of the day were influenced as much by contemporary socio-revolutionary messages as religious doctrine.[128]

Suggested readings: Secondary

Fawaz Gerges, *The Far Enemy: Why Jihad Went Global* (Cambridge: Cambridge University Press, 2005), Chapter 1.

Questions: How significant was the distinction between militants targeting the 'near enemy' and those targeting the 'far enemy' and why did it emerge? Who were the 'near' and 'far' enemies exactly? To what extent were jihadis focused on 'national' agendas? Was identification with nationalism ideological or pragmatic? Was the shift to global jihad inevitable, or a consequence of a specific set of policies pursued by Western governments and regimes in the Muslim world?

Suggested readings: Primary

Look at both the following sources:

Hamas Covenant, 1988, http://avalon.law.yale.edu/20th_century/hamas. asp. Look at the Introduction AND articles 1–2, 5–6, 12–15, 22–23, 25–27.

(You may find it helpful to look at some of the texts from the reading list as background here.)

Questions: What is the significance of jihad in Palestine being an 'individual duty' (you might want to look up this concept in, for example, the Gerges text)? How does the position of Hamas contrast with that of religious nationalists in Algeria, Syria and Egypt, and that of global jihadis, for example, Al-Qa'eda? How do they view other nationalist groups in Palestine? Who is the 'enemy' exactly for Hamas?

13

The extremist fringe? Al-Qa'eda, ISIS and the dawn of global jihadism

Following the repeated terrorist atrocities perpetrated against civilians in America, Britain and Europe over the last decade and a half, it is perhaps unsurprising that many Westerners regard 'Islamism' as synonymous with Islamic State in Iraq and Syria (ISIS) and al-Qa'eda. As we have seen, Islamism itself is an ideologically broader phenomenon, and groups such as al-Qa'eda and ISIS constitute only an extremist fringe of the movement it inspires. Al-Qa'eda and ISIS are classed as 'extremists' because they are willing to take their revolution beyond the Muslim world and launch attacks on the West; because they wish to make a break with the existing system of nation states in the name of establishing a global caliphate; and, most of all, because they have few qualms about inflicting casualties on civilians. The extent to which their global jihadism marks a radical break with previous Islamist ideology is open to question. Al-Banna, Mawdudi and al-Turabi all envisaged a global Islamic state that would transcend national boundaries, although in practice they retreated into more pragmatic nation-based strategies. Qutb, with his virulent 'otherization' of American society and commitment to 'offensive' jihad, is often seen as a precursor of al-Qa'eda, yet in practice even he was more concerned with the battle against the local *jahili* regimes than with exporting revolution to the West. Furthermore, none of these thinkers explicitly condoned the targeting of non-combatants.

As we have seen, Fawaz Gerges makes an important distinction between Islamists whose principal agenda is to battle the 'near enemy' – that is, 'apostate' or only nominally Muslim governments – and those concerned with attacking the 'far enemy', specifically Western countries. It was only in the middle of the 1990s that a select group of militant Islamists decided to make extending the jihad onto Western soil a principle in its own right, leading to Osama bin Laden's declaration of war against America in 1998 and ultimately the terrorist attack on the World Trade Center on 9/11. When ISIS emerged as a breakaway faction of al-Qa'eda, they sought more strenuously than the original organization to bring about an immediate revolution within the Muslim world, but nevertheless retained an ideological and strategic commitment to attacking the West. Meanwhile, the majority of the militant groups studied in the last chapter have disavowed both of these groups. Given their 'extremist' character, the question of their status within Islamism and, indeed, Islam itself, remains particularly contentious. As the journalist Graeme Wood discovered, saying that ISIS is genuinely 'Islamic' is a lot more controversial than saying the same of the Muslim Brotherhood.[1]

The Afghan War and the emergence of transnational militancy

It was the campaign to liberate the Muslim territory of Afghanistan from the Soviet occupation of 1979 that drew jihadis out of their comfort zones, battling the 'near enemy' in countries such as Egypt and Syria. What facilitated the 'transnational' or 'pan-Islamic' character of the struggle was that numerous Muslim scholars – as well as international activists such as the Palestinian militant Abdullah Azzam – characterized the Soviet invasion as an assault on the Dar al-Islam (land of Islam) as a whole, which made participation in the conflict an individual duty (*fard al-'ayn*) incumbent on every healthy adult male in the Muslim community.[2] The bulk of the fighting in the conflict was conducted by a mujahidin movement comprised of Afghan nationals who were given considerable financial support by the Pakistani, Saudi and American governments.[3] However, there was a sizeable contingent of foreign combatants drawn largely from Arab countries with the support of militants like Azzam and a number of charitable organizations.[4] This body of 'Arab Afghan' fighters was relatively small in comparison with the homegrown mujahidin and made little direct impact on the overall war effort, although their contribution to the Battle of Jaja in 1987 lent these militants – including a young Saudi businessmen named Osama bin Laden – international repute.[5]

The precise role of the American and Saudi governments in creating a 'Frankenstein' that would later come back to haunt them has ever since been intensely disputed. While it is widely accepted that the Saudis and Americans helped to bankroll the Afghan mujahidin, some have denied that either government supported the 'Arab Afghans' who would contribute so significantly to international jihadism in later years.[6] However, Gerges maintains that the Saudis gave financial support to Azzam's Services Bureau, an organization that helped to train the international fighters.[7]

The 'Arab Afghans' were a mix of established militant Islamists from armed groups that fought secular regimes in Egypt, Syria and elsewhere, and ordinary members of the Muslim faithful with few grievances against their own regimes but a belief in the necessity of defending the Dar al-Islam from invasion. Neither group would at the time have conceived of Afghanistan as the launch pad for a global jihad against the West, but the shared experiences of this international fighting force would encourage many of the non-Islamists to join the militant Islamist groups and many of the militant Islamists to conceive of a struggle that transcended their parochial nation-based agendas.[8] One such individual was the leader of Egyptian Islamic Jihad, Ayman al-Zawahiri. In 1986 al-Zawahiri reorganized his Egypt-based Tanzim al-Jihad into Islamic Jihad (sometimes Egyptian Islamic Jihad) in Peshawar, a Pakistani town near the Afghan border used as a base by Afghan and Arab Afghan militants.[9] Two years later in the same town, bin Laden exploited the expertise and connections he had acquired by funding his mentor Abdullah Azzam's Services Bureau to found al-Qa'eda, the organization that would later earn him such notoriety.[10]

Zawahiri, bin Laden and al-Qa'eda: The shift to global jihad

It is unlikely that either Azzam or bin Laden conceived of al-Qa'eda as a weapon with which to strike either the 'far enemy' or the established Muslim regimes when they first established it. Both were essentially 'irredentist' or 'classical' jihadis, motivated by the belief that it was the duty of each individual Muslim to defend Islamic territories when they were occupied by a non-Muslim invader.[11] They saw it as a form of international strike force to be used to defend Muslim lands whenever they came under threat, but never against a Muslim regime – however corrupt. Things changed when Ayman al-Zawahiri – who had relocated his Tanzim al-Jihad (now Islamic Jihad) to Peshawar in an effort to regroup and continue his battle against the Egyptian regime – began to drive a wedge between bin Laden and Azzam. After Azzam's death at the hands of unknown assassins in 1989, al-Zawahiri grew closer to bin Laden, and Islamic Jihad began to merge with al-Qa'eda.[12] Al-Zawahiri, with his years of experience in the Egyptian underground, was a vital asset to the new organization as the two groups both relocated to Sudan in 1991 following bin Laden's condemnation of the Saudi–American alliance in the Gulf War and subsequent expulsion from his home country.

For the first half of the 1990s, the operational priorities of al-Qa'eda and Islamic Jihad remained different. Al-Zawahiri's organization remained intent on toppling the Egyptian regime, although a more militant younger generation in Islamic Jihad pushed him to escalate the confrontation and abandon the gradualist strategy that he had employed in an attempt to bring down the government by infiltrating the military.[13] Meanwhile, bin Laden pursued the original al-Qa'eda strategy of attacking non-Muslim invaders of Muslim territories, staging a number of somewhat ineffectual interventions in countries such as Bosnia, Yemen and Somalia.[14] At this stage, he did not try to launch any attacks in the West itself – a rather ill-conceived effort by jihadis under Ramzi Yousef to attack the World Trade Center was not directly linked to al-Qa'eda.[15]

In the middle of the 1990s there were two major developments in al-Qa'eda's worldview and strategic approach. First, bin Laden – still bristling at the decision of Riyadh to exile him – eventually came around to al-Zawahiri's way of thinking concerning the pro-Western Muslim regimes.[16] Second, both al-Zawahiri and bin Laden, following a series of reverses for jihadis battling regimes in Egypt, Algeria and elsewhere, came to the conclusion that the only way to defeat the 'near enemy' was to bring down the 'far enemy' that backed it.[17] In some regards this was an act of desperation, particularly on the part of Islamic Jihad, which was financially and morally exhausted after a crackdown in 1995 by the Egyptian regime and in need of a new target to reinvigorate the jihad.[18] The pressure successfully exerted on the Sudanese government by the Americans in 1996 to expel bin Laden and al-Zawahiri, which forced their return to Afghanistan, is also likely to have convinced them that striking the American puppeteer directly was their only chance of victory. Although al-Qa'eda still recognized the 'near enemy' as an enemy, therefore, it resolved that the struggle to bring America to its knees must precede any efforts to overthrow 'infidel regimes' and create revolutionary states within the Muslim world.

In 1998, bin Laden and al-Qa'eda issued a *fatwa* from their new base in Afghanistan that was tantamount to a declaration of war not just on the American government, but also on the American people as a whole. It begged 'every Muslim who believes in Allah and wishes to be rewarded to comply with Allah's order to kill the Americans and plunder their money whenever and wherever they find it'.[19] Attacks on Western targets soon followed. Later in 1998, al-Qa'eda bombed American embassies in Nairobi and Dar as-Salaam, leaving 224 dead.[20] Similar efforts to target embassies in Rome and Paris in 2001 were foiled by Western intelligences agencies, before bin Laden's organization perpetrated its most infamous act of global terrorism – the destruction of the World Trade Center in New York on 11 September 2001.[21] The 'planes operation', as it was known, was jointly planned by bin Laden and Khalid Shaikh Muhammad, an independent jihadi who had joined the organization after bin Laden's move to Afghanistan. Together they trained a group of hijackers who seized planes travelling to the United States, and crashed them into two of the World Trade Center's towers, as well as the Pentagon, killing a total of 2,977 people.[22] In a 'letter to America' following the attacks, bin Laden declared that al-Qa'eda was attacking the Americans on account of their support of the invasion of Muslim territories in Lebanon, Somalia, Chechnya and Kashmir, and also because 'under your supervision, consent and orders, the governments of our countries, which act as your agents, attack us on a daily basis'.[23] Even the global jihad, therefore, was justified with reference to America's role in the 'irredentist' and 'nation-based' struggles. However, bin Laden also called on the Americans to enter Islam and follow sharia law, and warned them that they should 'prepare for fight with the Islamic nation' if they did not. Whatever its roots, the conflict he envisioned was now a global one.

The problem with bin Laden's strategy of worldwide mobilization of Muslims to attack America as an 'individual duty'[24] was that the vast majority of Muslims did not think that attacking the far enemy was either tactically or religiously viable; nor did the vast majority of jihadis. Bin Laden had only been able to persuade Saudi nationals to join his organization in Afghanistan between 1996 and 2001 by leading them to believe that they would be defending Russian-occupied Chechnya as opposed to attacking America.[25] His actions were rejected by 'classical jihadis' and militants focused on the near enemy, who believed that his struggle against America was unjustifiable and would provoke a vicious retaliation.[26] Many militants were particularly critical of al-Zawahiri for allowing Islamic Jihad to associate itself with bin Laden's agenda.[27] The plan to attack the World Trade Center had even been rejected by the Shura Council of al-Qa'eda itself, though bin Laden ignored it and carried on with the attack regardless.[28]

Invasion, sectarianism and the rise of Islamic State

In the aftermath of the attacks on the World Trade Center, all the fears of jihadis who had warned against targeting the 'far enemy' were realized. The American military occupied Afghanistan and overthrew the Taliban government, at the same time eliminating numerous high-ranking al-Qa'eda operatives in the country and depriving it and other jihadi groups of the 'strong base' (*qa'eda sulba*) envisaged by Abdullah Azzam in the 1980s.[29] Al-Qa'eda had lost the command centre from which it had trained, funded and directed its various operatives,[30] and its control over its various branches and affiliates became far more loose. It managed later to launch attacks against Western civilians in Spain, Bali and elsewhere,[31] but its various offshoots also began to return to the principle of attacking the 'near enemy' first. For instance, in 2004 al-Qa'eda in the Arabian Peninsula began a (largely unsuccessful) campaign against the Saudi regime.[32]

The al-Qa'eda offshoot that had the most success in returning to a strategy of targeting the 'near enemy' was al-Qa'eda in Iraq. This later morphed into the Islamic State in Iraq, and then into the organization variously known as ISIS, Islamic State in the Levant (ISIL), Islamic State (or so-called Islamic State) and Daesh. The circumstances that enabled its rise were the fallout from the removal of the Ba'athist regime of Saddam Hussein in 2003, and the intensification of Sunni–Shia sectarian tension in the region. The rise in Sunni–Shia conflict was certainly facilitated by the American invasion, for this led to the dismantling of the Iraqi army and ruling party and thus the demolition of the only non-sectarian institutions in the country, but the roots of Iraq's fragmentation also date back to its war with Iran in the 1980s.[33]

It was in this context of intense sectarianism that al-Qa'eda's independently minded chief operative in Iraq, the Jordanian militant Abu Musab al-Zarqawi, refocused his organization towards the 'near' enemy – although the near enemy was now not an authoritarian Muslim regime (dismantled by the Americans in any case) but an entire religious group, the Shia. Al-Zarqawi frequently maintained that the Shia of Iraq were traitors who had aided and abetted the American invasion, likening them to the thirteenth-century Shia Abbasid official, Ibn al-Alqemi, who had supposedly helped betray Baghdad and the Abbasid Caliphate to the Mongols.[34] He repeatedly asserted that the Shia were a more important target than the Americans, and between 2003 and 2006 launched numerous suicide attacks on Shia mosques and Shia holy places.[35] Al-Zarqawi's fondness for intra-Muslim violence marked a distinct contrast to the approach of al-Zawahiri and bin Laden, whose pragmatism had stretched to allying with al-Turabi at a time when his regime had forged close links with the Iranian Shia.[36] Al-Qa'eda, while condemning numerous 'near enemies', had feared that too many attacks on fellow Muslims would sow divisions that would undermine its efforts to mobilize support against the most important enemy, America.[37] Al-Zawahiri thus sent numerous missives to al-Zarqawi expressing his frustration at his rash course of action.[38]

Al-Zarqawi broke with long-term al-Qa'eda strategy in one further, and highly significant regard. In April 2006, he declared that he was about to establish an Islamic state in Iraq – an objective that bin Laden and al-Zawahiri had sought to defer until sufficient numbers of Muslims had been re-educated.[39] Although al-Zarqawi was killed by American forces only two months later, his replacement as leader, Abu Ayyub al-Masri, fulfilled his predecessor's wishes by transforming al-Qa'eda in Iraq into the Islamic state of Iraq.[40] Thinking it rash, the al-Qa'eda leadership was exasperated with this move, but nevertheless openly recognized the new state from its secret base in Pakistan.[41] Al-Masri's state, headed by one Abu Umar al-Baghdadi (not to be confused with Abu Bakr al-Baghdadi), was a flop from the start. Al-Masri's messianism undermined his strategic vision and his rigid hostility towards even the Sunni mainstream alienated the majority of the Iraqi population from the new state. During their post-2006 'surge', US forces in Iraq were able to mobilize Sunni leaders against this new organization and al-Masri and Abu Umar were eventually tracked down and killed by American and Iraqi troops in April 2010.[42] Abu Umar al-Baghdadi was then replaced by Abu Bakr al-Baghdadi, who renamed the group 'Islamic State in Iraq and Syria' (ISIS, sometimes also translated Islamic State in Iraq and the Levant/ISIL) as it attempted to expand westwards.[43]

In 2014, Abu Bakr al-Baghdadi decided that his organization represented not just the 'Islamic State in Iraq and Syria', but *the* 'Islamic State', for the entire world, and renamed it as such.[44] Whatever its grandiose ambitions, the new organization (labelled so-called Islamic State by some media organs) learnt from the mistakes of its predecessor. It avoided messianic rhetoric and, having studied previous American tactics, appreciated the importance of co-opting Sunni tribal leaders.[45] What really distinguished the new entity was that it described itself not just as an Islamic state but as a revival of the caliphate. Moreover, Abu Bakr al-Baghdadi (originally Ibrahim Awwad Ibrahim al-Badri) not only took the name of the first caliph but – following his group's capture of Iraq's second city, Mosul – copied word for word the language of the prophet's successor in declaring his ascension to this office.[46] Al-Baghdadi's announcement of a caliphate was greeted with ridicule by the majority of Muslim scholars – moderates and militants alike – but the wealth it acquired through its capture of Mosul's oil refineries enabled it to grow in support and attract recruits from all over the world. As of 2014 it was able to deploy thirty-one thousand combatants.[47]

In precipitately declaring a caliphate and ruthlessly targeting the country's Shia population, 'Islamic State' made a comprehensive break with the al-Qa'eda strategy of preparing gradually for a new Islamic order and limiting attacks to Western targets. Al-Qa'eda, by this time under the leadership of Ayman al-Zawahiri following bin Laden's death at the hands of American Special Forces in 2011, renounced the would-be caliphate. In many regards, the newly led organization represented a return to the strategy of targeting the 'near enemy' – whether it be the Shias, or the Iraqi regime. Yet, unlike the 'religious nationalists', it did not seek to capture an existing state and 'Islamize' it, but rather to establish a new order from scratch. This has allowed 'Islamic State' to articulate a comprehensive break with nationalist ideology and the regional boundaries established by the British and French following the collapse of the Ottoman Caliphate after the First World War – 'no more Sykes Picot' has been an important slogan.[48] Establishing a presence in Syria – in spite of the defection of its first affiliate group, Jabhat al-Nusra – has enabled 'Islamic State' to maintain that it transcends national boundaries, although in practice it has often adapted to local territorial realities.[49] Its ambitions in the Middle East remain paramount, although the group has not abandoned the strategy of targeting the 'far enemy'. The majority of the attacks in Western countries claimed by 'Islamic State' have been perpetrated by 'lone wolves' inspired, but not actively overseen by it. However, the recent attacks in Istanbul, Paris and Brussels were perpetrated by individuals directly recruited and trained by the movement's leadership.[50]

Ideological origins of global jihadism: Wahhabism, Qutbism or something else?

It is a commonplace of post-9/11 discourse on al-Qae'da, and its various franchises and offshoots (including ISIS) that these groups adhere to a 'Wahhabi' ideology. Such claims, although not far-fetched, often rest on insufficient examination of the exact doctrinal, theological and ideological links between Wahhabism and global jihadism other than the emphasis of both on *takfir* and *tawhid* – the meanings of which concepts have in any case been contested by Wahhabi scholars themselves. The precise extent to which Wahhabism has inspired the global jihadi brand remains contentious, particularly among those who are either critics or defenders of the Saudi state religion. Let us summarize five competing positions

1   Global jihadi ideology draws on the ideology propagated by the Saudi state and religious establishment, as well as the various charities they have sponsored.

2   Global jihadi ideology represents the return of the more militant Wahhabism – very different from the current variety promoted by the Saudi state – that emerged during the conflicts of the late eighteenth, nineteenth and early twentieth centuries.

3   Global jihadism has very little relationship with Wahhabi theology, being shaped more by the revolutionary Islamism of Sayyid Qutb and his adherents.

4   Global jihadism represents a fusion of Salafi–Wahhabi and Qutbist ideals.

5   Global jihadism uses Wahhabi and Qutbist terms and idioms but loads them with meanings emerging from concerns characteristic of the post-1989 world.

The first of these claims, which features prominently in anti-Saudi polemics,[51] blames Riyadh for promoting a militant brand of its state ideology via transnational institutions such as the World Association of Muslim Youth. Practices shared by the Saudi state and the 'Islamic State' established by ISIS have been identified – notably the employment of a Saudi-style 'religious police' and the demolition of shrines.[52] The Saudi regime helped publicly to fund and propagandize the transnational jihadis who battled against the Soviet-backed regime in Afghanistan in the 1980s and later gave birth to the al-Qa'eda franchise.[53] However, the Wahhabi religious establishment itself gave the campaign in Afghanistan only limited support – for the most part describing it as a 'collective' rather than 'individual' duty for Muslims – and the kingdom's efforts to promote the campaign probably had more to do with 'state populism' than religious ideology.[54]

While al-Qa'eda might have emerged from a Saudi-backed campaign in Afghanistan, its anger at the decision of the government in Riyadh to host American troops during the Gulf War (1990–1991) pushed it into radical opposition to the Saudi regime, and encouraged it to re-examine official Wahhabi propaganda. In the late 1990s and 2000s a new generation of independent scholars emerged which backed al-Qa'eda and promoted a more militant interpretation of Wahhabi ideology than that of the official religious establishment.[55] The new mujahidin, as well as the scholars who back them, have contested the Saudi regime's moderate readings of the Wahhabi doctrines of *al-wala wa-l-bara* (loyalty to God and the Muslims before all else) and *isti'ana bi'l-kuffar* (seeking the assistance of unbelievers). In 1990, the Saudi Grand Mufti, Abd al-Aziz bin Baz, had issued a *fatwa* declaring that Saddam Hussein's assault on Kuwait had made a temporary violation of the doctrine concerning *isti'ana bi'l-kuffar* necessary and the seeking of American support justified. This provoked furious debate inside and outside Saudi Arabia. Al-Zawahiri, bin Laden and the pro-al-Qa'eda Shu'aybi school in Saudi Arabia have all used the principle of *al-wala wa-l-bara* to denounce the Saudi regime's close relationship with the American government.[56] In the view of these radicals, the Saudi elite's failure to give loyalty to the Muslim community first and foremost justifies their resort to *takfir* – that is, denouncing the Saudi government as an 'unbeliever' regime – and declaring jihad against it.[57]

The willingness of transnational jihadis to contest the Saudi regime's moderate stance on *takfir* and *al-wala wa-l-bara* has led some to brand its most recent manifestation – ISIS – as a return to the 'original' or 'untamed' Wahhabism that preceded the establishment of the kingdom. As we have seen, nineteenth-century Wahhabi scholars such as Sulayman and Abd al-Latif articulated an uncompromising version of these doctrines to justify the original capture of Mecca from the Ottomans at the beginning of the nineteenth century, and later on the denunciation of Saudi amirs who had sought Ottoman and British aid. The same militant discourse of *takfir* was adopted by the al-Ikhwan warriors whom Abd al-Aziz deployed to conquer the territory that became contemporary Saudi Arabia, and subsequently demobilized as part of his efforts to transform the kingdom into a more 'modern' regime willing to enter into relationships with a variety of non-Wahhabi and non-Muslim states.[58] A number of the Ikhwan rejected the Saudi regime's new outlook, and rebellions had to be forcibly suppressed. It has been suggested that – as with Juhaynam al-Utaybi, the militant who seized the Grand Mosque of Mecca in 1979 – the emergence of ISIS represents a recrudescence of the militant 'Ikhwan' brand of Wahhabism.[59] Whether this is the 'original' or 'real' Wahhabism, or simply an alternative and less compromising form of the doctrine, is very much open to contention.

One narrative promoted by apologetic accounts such as that of Natana DeLong-Bas is that the transnational and global jihadism of today has little to do with the 'original' Wahhabism of the eighteenth century, which was educationalist in outlook, and more to do with the Qutbist militancy which in the 1960s the Egyptian Muslim Brothers began to export to the kingdom and the wider Muslim world. For DeLong-Bas, the Qutbist exhortation to 'offensive' jihad marked a distinct break from the 'defensive' doctrine of the movement's founder, Muhammad Ibn Abd al-Wahhab.[60] It was the very fact that Qutb had fought against a Westernized regime in Egypt that made his ideology more relevant than that of Ibn Abd al-Wahhab to militants who sought to battle similar regimes within and without the Muslim world.[61]

Whether or not Wahhabism can be entirely absolved, there is little doubt that Qutbism had a marked impact on the ideology of the global jihadis. Qutb's quasi-Marxist praxis may well have given the doctrine-obsessed Salafis the ideological ammunition they needed to transform their theological doctrines into a more action-orientated strategy in order to challenge regimes in Saudi Arabia and elsewhere, and his emphasis on God's sovereignty triumphing over human forms of rule may well have helped militants to delegitimize the regimes of their day.[62] Similarly, his doctrine of 'permanent revolution' and belief in a Manichaean duel between Islam and the Western world may have been what enabled jihadism to go 'global'.[63]

Another view is that transnational and global jihadism represents a fusion of Salafi–Wahhabi and Qutbist ideology. As we have seen, Qutb's own ideology was not fully 'Wahhabized' during his own life time, but his brother Muhammad and a number of other Muslim Brothers who fled to Saudi Arabia from Egypt as well as Syria played a considerable role in merging it with the Salafi–Wahhabi canon. Their teachings influenced intellectuals such as the leader of the Sahwa movement, Safar al-Hawali, who would go on like Qutb to warn of an all-encompassing and transhistorical conspiracy against Islam.[64] Al-Hawali's most prominent text was *Kissinger's Promise*, which denounced American neocolonialism as well as the Saudi regime's willingness to support it. While the Sahwa has been described as an 'Islamist' movement, in order to denounce the regime for prioritizing its allegiance to the Americans over the loyalty it owed the Muslim community it drew not just on the language of *hakimiyya* but also on the established Salafi concept of *al-wala wa-l-bara*.[65] Although Sahwa intellectuals did not go so far as to advocate open confrontation with the Saudi regime, the al-Shu'aybi school and jihadis such as bin Laden and al-Zawahiri would later advocate just that. It has been argued that this extension of the principle of *wala wa'l-bara* to justify attacking the regime that failed to adhere to it was novel,[66] although, as we have seen, Wahhabi intellectuals had used *takfiri* discourse to justify attacking Muslim regimes before this. It is probably the influence of Qutbism – in addition to other factors, such as the rise of electronic media and the delegitimization of the existing governments – that has allowed non-state actors such as al-Qa'eda to justify attacking regimes they have denounced as 'infidel', whereas nineteenth-century Wahhabis would have required such a campaign to be conducted by a legitimate state led by an amir.

The Global Jihadists' relationship with the classical 'forefather' of contemporary Salafism, Ibn Taymiyya, was almost certainly influenced by the cross-fertilization of Wahhabism and Islamism, particularly the Egyptian variant. For instance, both al-Qa'eda and ISIS drew heavily on Egyptian Islamic Jihad's Imam al-Sharif, who – following Faraj – interpreted Ibn Taymiyya's fatwas in such a manner as to claim that it was an 'individual duty' to attack secular rulers.[67] In declaring war on America in 1998, bin Laden cited Ibn Taymiyya's statement that 'fighting to repulse [an enemy] … is aimed at defending sanctity and religion'.[68] He never explained how this would extend to taking the fight abroad to sever 'the head of the snake'. Meanwhile, ISIS have drawn specifically on Ibn Taymiyya's anti-Shia fatwas,[69] which were genuinely virulent; although, as Michot has observed, they could not have inspired ISIS' sanctioning the pronouncement of individual Shia as non-believers.[70] Critics of Ibn Abd al-Wahhab blame him for introducing this *takfiri* element into the Salafi worldview.[71] It might be, however, that it was the extreme polarization of Sunni and Shia identity brought about by the Saddamist regime and post-2003 sectarian conflict that has facilitated the uncompromising rhetoric of ISIS towards the Shia.

In spite of its official commitment to an uncompromising form of Salafism – one that denied the validity of most post-Rashidi jurisprudence – ISIS often undermined its own supposedly rigid theology by deriving many of its precedents from the eighth and ninth centuries, or even later. For all their universalistic and pan-Islamic rhetoric, ISIS grew as a branch of al-Qa'eda that had broken away from the main leadership and was thoroughly shaped by its Iraqi environment. This is why Harun al-Rashid, the Abbasid caliph who ruled from Baghdad, was idealized by ISIS just as much as the rulers of seventh-century Medina – and in spite of al-Rashid's reputed fondness for wine![72] ISIS rhetoric frequently evoked the millenarian prophecies of the eighth and ninth-century Umayyad and Abbasid world,[73] and Al-Zarqawi took as a role model Nur al-Din Zengi, a medieval ruler with a reputation for using brutality and civilian slaughter as a means to an end that is reflected in much ISIS strategy.[74] This irony of the ISIS worldview was that while it uses classic Salafi language to denounce existing scholarly knowledge as innovative, at the same time it 'reintroduce[s] on the sly the right to innovate'.[75] It is arguably because its 'Salafi' ideology – posturing as orthodox yet innovative in practice – broke so comprehensively with the bulk of established jurisprudence that the incorporation of these more heterodox influences was possible.

There is much evidence that global jihadi agendas were shaped less by Salafism or any other form of religious doctrine and more by the outlook and practices of the various left-wing and anti-Western revolutionaries of the late-twentieth-century world. Given that the global jihadis expressed so much interest in the liberation of Palestine, it would be unsurprising if they were not influenced – in spite of its secular-nationalist outlook – by the methods of the Palestine Liberation Organization (PLO), which was in turn influenced by the agendas of militant leftist alliance such as the Western Red Army Faction and Japanese Red Army. The Western Red Army Faction, for instance, helped the PLO to invent plane hijacking as a terrorist technique.[76] When al-Qa'eda operatives sought haven in Sudan in the 1990s they would have rubbed shoulders both with members of these Palestinian factions and their non-Muslim allies such as the Venezualan revolutionary Carlos the Jackal, who had also been invited to the country by the Islamist regime in Khartoum. While bin Laden almost certainly did not reflect on Marx as carefully as Ali Shariati, his decision to target the Twin Towers – America's commercial and financial hub – reflected an anti-imperialist and anti-capitalist agenda as much as a religious one.[77] Bin Laden's 'Letter to America' was certainly replete with religious moralism, but also declared that 'your law is the law of the rich and wealthy people'. Using similar language to the environmentalist left, bin Laden fumed that 'you have destroyed nature with your industrial waste and gases more than any nation in history', and fulminated against the US government's 'refus[al] to sign the Kyoto agreement so that you can secure the profit of your greedy companies and industries'.[78]

Extremism versus Islam

In recent years, there have been fierce debates in the West as to whether 'Global Jihadism' or 'Islamic Extremism' can be accepted as in any way 'Islamic'. Reacting to Barack Obama's refusal to use the adjective 'Islamic' when describing ISIS, the American journalist and scholar, Graeme Wood, wrote in *The Atlantic* in 2015 that, in spite of the protestations of moderate Muslims, ISIS was indeed 'Islamic. *Very* Islamic'. Wood maintained that however extreme its religious views were, they owed their origin to 'coherent and even learned views of Islam', and that the majority of the Muslim critics of ISIS had not studied their religion's founding texts as earnestly as had its own scholars.[79] He also quoted the Princeton scholar, Bernard Haykel, as saying that those Muslims who labelled ISIS 'un-Islamic' were 'embarrassed and politically correct, with a cotton-candy view of their own religion'.[80] Citing Haykel's relativistic approach to religious truth, Wood proposed that multiple interpretations of Islam were possible and that it was therefore impossible to describe the views of ISIS as less 'Islamic' than those of the Muslim mainstream. He went so far as to argue that those who claimed that ISIS was not 'Islamic' had themselves fallen into the trap of acting in accordance with the extremist notion of *takfir*; that is, denouncing other Muslims as infidels.

Wood's article, which proved to be the most widely read online piece that year,[81] provoked a hostile reaction from Muslim and non-Muslim liberals. Were Haykel and Wood's relativistic approach to Islam and ISIS to be accepted, it was said, a polytheistic reading of the Quran would be no less valid than one that was monotheistic.[82] It was also pointed out that describing ISIS as 'un-Islamic' was not tantamount to *takfir* since the ideas and actions of individuals can be denounced as untrue to the faith without excommunicating the individuals themselves.[83] For Wood's critics, 'cherry picking' from the Quran by ISIS – taking 'what they like and ignoring what they do not' – is hardly as valid as the rigorous methods of exegesis (*tafsir*) developed by the classical jurisprudents.[84] A compromise position has been adopted by Fawaz Gerges, who maintains that ISIS 'is Islamic', but 'borrows heavily but selectively from the Islamic canon and imposes the past on the present wholesale'.[85] Against this, however, it can be argued that a selective reading of the core texts is un-Islamic because it ignores the core principle of *tawhid*. Hasan al-Turabi, for instance (a critic of ISIS in his later years), argued that what the correct *tawhidi* approach to the Quran requires is to resist the temptation to interpret any passage in isolation from the rest of the text, using this approach to criticize, for instance, context-free interpretations of the 'sword verse'.[86]

Denouncing global jihadi groups like ISIS as unbelievers drags Muslim scholars opposed to them into risky jurisprudential territory. In consequence, many choose instead to label them as Khariji (see also Chapters 2 and 12). The comparison with this group makes sense from the perspective of Muslim critics because its enables them to distance groups like al-Qa'eda and ISIS from Islam without resorting to *takfir*.[87] Even fellow Salafi–jihadist preachers such as Abu Qatada have been willing to denounce ISIS as Kharijis for abusing the principle of *takfir*.[88] ISIS scholars have rebutted such claims, maintaining that, unlike the Kharijis, they do not denounce fellow Muslims as unbelievers purely on the grounds of sinful behaviour.[89] It is an uncomfortable fact for them that their group's ideological father, al-Zarqawi, did as much.[90]

Another criticism of ISIS is that it is an authoritarian, rigidly Sunni movement that has incorporated former Ba'athist officers and built up a personality cult around its leader – and thus is in direct line of descent from the departed Ba'athist regime of Saddam Hussein. Online critics have mocked the ISIS slogan 'A Caliphate in Accordance with the Prophetic Method' by suggesting that it should instead be 'A State in Accordance with the Ba'athist Method'.[91] Wood's critics have noted that ISIS's close relations with a number of former Ba'athists give the lie to the notion that it is really 'Islamic'.[92] It is true that a number of high-ranking Ba'athist officers have joined ISIS, and that their experience as pillars of Saddam's authoritarian system helped their Salafi–jihadist allies construct their new state.[93] On the other hand, to see this as a resurgence of Ba'athism is probably to concede to a narrow form of anti-ISIS polemic, for there is no real evidence that either al-Baghdadi's state or any of the former Saddamists within it now espouse any form of 'Ba'athist' ideology. There is also no reason to assume that guardians of the old regime would maintain their ideological commitment to Ba'athism, if it was ever heartfelt in the first place.[94] On balance, it seems more reasonable to conclude that the Islamic State is run not in line with Ba'athist ideology but 'in accordance with the Ba'athist Method', insofar as it ruthlessly terrorizes its own population to maintain its rule in the name of that ideology.

It is not just the ideology of al-Qa'eda, ISIS and related movements that has led the Muslim, Islamist and even jihadi mainstream to denounce them, but the various methods and practices they pursue in the name of that ideology. Al-Qa'eda have frequently been condemned by moderate Muslims on the grounds that the killing of thousands of civilians in the 9/11 attacks violated all classical sharia regulations governing the conduct of warfare, not to mention Islam's respect for the sanctity of life. The principle of whether suicide bombing in general (if, for instance, directed at non-civilian targets) is religiously legitimate is more contentious. One Salafi–jihadist scholar, Abu Nasir al-Tartusi, declared in a 2005 *fatwa* that any form of such attack was *haram*, citing Quranic passages that forbid suicide.[95] The prominent Qatar-based scholar Yusuf al-Qaradawi, however, argued that suicide bombing might even be considered a religious duty for Muslims in occupied territories in Iraq and Palestine, while condemning the London bombers.[96] There have been many historic examples of Islamic warriors sacrificing themselves by plunging into situations in which they have little chance of physical escape,[97] although the act of destroying oneself and one's opponent using explosives is a distinctly twentieth-century phenomenon. The Kamikaze and Viet Cong resorted to the practice before any jihadists,[98] and the fact that Islamist organizations such as Hamas used the practice before the Salafi–jihadists suggests that the practice may derive from various other political movements that influenced Islamist ideology more than Wahhabi scripturalism.

Islamist terrorism in Europe and America: Global jihadism or Western Malaise?

While the 9/11 Twin Towers attacks represented the most famous of all the atrocities perpetrated by militant Islamists on Western soil, they were far from being the only ones. Some preceded 9/11, including the first attempt to bomb the same target in 1993 and the 1995 attacks by the GIA in mainland France. After the expulsion of al-Qa'eda from Afghanistan in 2001, attacks were carried out in its name in a number of European capitals, notably Madrid in 2004 and London in 2005. In many regards, the intensification of Islamist terrorism in Europe and America in the 2000s and 2010s appears as the next wave of global jihadism, the natural extension of a strategy that began with bin Laden's declaration of war on America in 1998. Yet, while al-Qa'eda and now ISIS have encouraged and celebrated the increasingly frequent terrorist atrocities on Western soil, it is open to question whether or not we should identify Islamist terrorism in the Western world as a Western phenomenon defined by its own contexts and circumstances, just as we often do with Islamism in Africa or South Asia.

While the majority of those who have perpetrated terrorist atrocities in Europe and America are citizens of their respective countries, analysts sometime downplay the domestic character of this form of terrorism by emphasizing the direction that these individuals received from terrorist organizations abroad, which in some cases does not become clear till many years after the attacks.[99] It is also argued that while Salafi and Islamist organizations in Europe do not directly incite individuals to terrorism, such organizations inculcate radical worldviews that make them far more vulnerable to the propaganda of groups such as ISIS and al-Qa'eda.[100]

The academic debate about the roots of Islamist extremism came to the fore in France after a series of attacks – nominally inspired by ISIS – at the Charlie Hebdo offices and then the Bataclan in 2015, and then again in Paris in 2016. The aftermath of these attacks saw – at time explosive – exchanges between French scholars of Islamism including Olivier Roy, Gilles Kepel and Francois Burgat. Olivier Roy proposed in 2016 that the recent terror attacks were simply the manifestation of a dissident and nihilistic youth culture within France itself, the 'Islamization of Radicalism', rather than vice versa.[101] To corroborate his thesis he analysed a sample of over hundred individuals who had either participated in terrorism in France or left France to wage jihad abroad, and which included all those who were protagonists in the most notorious attacks in France and Belgium. Roy observed that a great number of these individuals – 60 per cent of whom were second-generation immigrants – had led irreligious lives before their sudden conversion to 'Salafi' Islam, regularly drinking and visiting clubs and bars. Far from being a product of socially conservative religious families, they tended to choose their own spouses and reject their parents' authority.[102] For Roy, Western jihadis' vision of the caliphate lacked real foundation, and they were more concerned with violence, death and struggle per se than with real-world politics in Muslim countries.[103] Roy's thesis came under attacking from two important directions. Francois Burgat, speaking from a left-wing and postcolonial perspective, argued that Roy's emphasis on spontaneous and homegrown nihilism conveniently overlooks the role of Western colonialism – both historic and present – in feeding the resentment that drives contemporary jihadism.[104] Meanwhile, Gilles Kepel attacked the more liberal elements of Roy's argument, maintaining that his lack of expertise in Arabic was leading him to overlook the genuinely theological and particularly Salafi orientation of a number of jihadis in France.[105]

Suggested reading: Secondary

McCants, William Faizi, *The ISIS Apocalypse: The History, Strategy and Doomsday Vision of the Islamic State* (New York: St Martin's Press, 2015), Chapter 6 'A Caliphate Reborn'

Questions: How did ISIS break with the former logic of Sunni jihadism? How authentic is the ISIS model of the Caliphate? How and why was the legacy of the Abbasid Caliphate significant for ISIS' rhetoric? What approach has ISIS taken to ruling the territories under its control? Why have the leaders of ISIS toned down their emphasis on the arrival of the Mahdi?

Suggested reading: Primary

Osama bin Laden's 'letter to America', *The Observer*, 24 November 2002, http://www.theguardian.com/world/2002/nov/24/theobserver.

Questions: What historical events is bin Laden reacting to? How contemporary is the ideology that he expresses? Are there parallels with other Islamist ideologies here or should this be treated as a distinctive 'extremist' variant?

And finally, does a comparison of these two texts support Gerges's 'near enemy'/'far enemy' distinction?

Scott Lucas, 'Iraq and Syria Document: ISIS' Declaration of a 'Caliphate' for All Muslims', 30 June 2014, http://eaworldview.com/2014/06/iraq-text-isis-declaration-caliphate-muslims/.

What is this significance of ISIS' understanding of the Caliphate? Why did ISIS change its name to Islamic State? Is it fair to say from this document that ISIS/Islamic State is less influenced by Western ideologies than earlier militant organizations? What function does religious law serve in ISIS ideology?

14

Twenty-first-century Abduhs? Post-Islamism, democracy and the Arab Spring

Not every Islamist movement over the last forty or so years has dedicated itself to bringing about sharia-based governance through revolutionary militancy. Some participated in parliamentary democratic regimes before aligning themselves with military dictators (Hasan al-Turabi's National Islamic Front, Pakistan's Jama'at-i-Islami); in other situations, groups that had embraced democratic politics turned militant as a result of regime repression (the Front Islamique de Salut, FIS); elsewhere, militant movements moved towards embracing democratic politics (Hamas and Hizbullah); other groups have remained more consistently committed to politics even under monarchical and authoritarian regimes (the Jordanian and Egyptian Muslim Brotherhoods, Ennahda in Tunisia, Morocco's Justice and Development Party). Meanwhile, the scepticism of religious activists towards the authoritarian state brought about by the revolution in Iran has led to speculation that there has been a shift towards 'post-Islamism'. This term has been subject to multiple definitions. For Olivier Roy, it signified a move away from Islamism as a revolutionary ideology towards a 'neo-fundamentalism' restricted to the private sphere; it was influenced by Saudi Salafism and more concerned with private morality.[1] For Asef Bayat, on the other hand, 'post-Islamism' did not mean the outright disappearance of Islam from the political arena so much as the appearance of an ideology that 'strives to marry Islam with individual choice and freedom, with democracy and modernity'.[2]

The victory of Islamist parties in post-Arab Spring elections in Tunisia and Egypt in 2011 seemed to refute the notion that the region was 'post-Islamist' in Roy's sense. However, their subsequent adoption of 'moderate' political agendas suggested that an 'ideological evolution' had occurred, with Islamists adopting more flexible ideologies and showing a willingness to abandon calls for sharia and embrace political pluralism.[3] However, the extent to which this 'ideological evolution' was novel remains an open question. Islamists have been participating in multiparty democracies since Mustafa al-Sibai and the Syrian Muslim Brotherhood in the 1940s. In 1964, Hasan al-Turabi and the Sudanese Islamists joined leftists and Arab nationalists in a civilian uprising in Sudan that made little reference to sharia, and after the downfall of the military they allied with a number of other parties in a parliamentary regime. A quarter of a century later, al-Turabi backed a military coup that overthrew the country's third parliamentary regime and attempted to impose the Islamist brand of sharia by force. In today's world, many of the critics of 'democratic Islamists'[4] such as al-Ghannushi and Erdogan maintain that their openness to pluralistic democratic systems is a short-term tactic designed to facilitate the long-term goal of authoritarian sharia governance. But if Islamism is capable of being so disingenuous, why is it assumed that it is the pro-democratic West that is being deceived? Are the 'Muslim Democrats' of today the al-Afghanis of France or the al-Afghanis of India?

Islamism, elections and civil opposition in Algeria, Tunisia and Egypt

In Algeria, Tunisia and Egypt parties such as Ennahda, the FIS and the Muslim Brotherhood seized the opportunity provided by regimes moving in the direction of 'liberalized autocracy'[5] to pursue a form of restricted participation in the formal political arena and also to expand their presence outside it. In Egypt, the Muslim Brotherhood stood candidates in a number of elections after Sadat's amnesty of 1971. Although government manipulation of the electoral process prevented Brotherhood-backed candidates gaining more than a modest share of the vote, probably more important was the fact that it used the end of the restrictions against it to entrench itself within 'civil society', as well as among the public at large. Throughout the 1980s, bodies linked to the Brotherhood won victories in student elections across the country, and it also won over many of the most important professional unions in this decade, including those of the doctors, pharmacists and engineers.[6] Meanwhile, it expanded its networks of charities, healthcare institutions and schools so as to act as a 'state within a state' in urban and rural areas where the government could establish little presence. These networks enabled it to react far more effectively than the government to a major earthquake in 1992, further increasing its popularity among the Egyptian population at large.[7]

Was the approach of the Egyptian Brotherhood 'post-Islamist', or at least more moderate than that of the Qutbist militants in Egypt? Between 1971 and 2011 the mainstream of the Muslim Brotherhood committed itself to pursuing its political objectives in Egypt through non-violent and democratic means, in spite of the severe government repression from which it sometimes suffered, notably following the attempt on President Hosni Mubarak's life in Addis Ababa in 1995. Whether the anti-Qutbist pamphlet *Du'at la Qudat (Preachers not Judges)* was published by the Ikhwan's General Guide, Hasan al-Hudaybi or by the Egyptian intelligence services, the movement held to its principles, maintaining in a 'statement of democracy' during the wave of repression in 1995 that 'we the Muslim Brothers always say that we are advocates not judges'.[8] In forming an electoral alliance with the Wafd party in 1984, they displayed a de facto acceptance of political pluralism.[9] Partly as a result of reformist pressure applied by the younger generation of Ikhwanis, the Brotherhood has acknowledged the right of women to stand as MPs and declared that it will treat Coptic Christians as citizens rather than as *dhimmis* (protected religious minorities).[10] However, in 2007 Bayat still observed that the Brotherhood had not become fully 'post-Islamist', noting that its elderly leaders still insisted on rule by sharia and persisted with the established Islamist slogan 'Islam is the Solution'.[11]

In Tunisia, the mainstream Islamist party remained largely, though not exclusively, committed to civil opposition to military authoritarianism since it first emerged as the Islamic Tendency Movement (MTI) in 1981.[12] During the 1980s, never being officially recognized as a party by the government, the MTI did toy with the idea of overthrowing the regime of Habib Bourguiba by force. It established a 'Security Group' similar to al-Banna's Special Apparatus, which in 1987 appears to have been on the point of acting when it was pre-empted by an internal coup by Zine el-Abidine Ben Ali that removed Bourguiba. Ben Ali initially sought to open up the political arena, promising fresh elections. The MTI responded by rebranding itself as 'Ennahda' (Renaissance), a move which appeared to signify a change of ideological orientation. First, by opting to avoid reference to their faith in the party's name, Tunisia's Islamists appeared to have conceded to Ben Ali's argument that no one party should represent Islam. Second, the name Ennahda harked back to the Islamic reform movement of the nineteenth century with which intellectuals such as Muhammad Abduh and the Tunisian statesman, Khair al-Din al-Tunisi, were associated. Many others in the Tunisian elite identified Khair al-Din as a reference point, and this position seemed to mark a shift away from the ideological exclusivism of Islamist radicalism towards the liberal and rationalist approach of the nineteenth-century reformers.

In spite of the name change, Ben Ali refused to recognize Ennahda as a party, the result being that its members participated in the elections of 1989 as independents. According to the official result, candidates associated with Ennahda won 14.5 per cent of the vote, though their genuine vote share may have been double that figure. It seems that these results, along with the victories of the FIS in the elections that occurred in next door Algeria in 1990, convinced Ben Ali that integrating the Islamists into the political system would be too risky; as a consequence, his repression of them intensified and their leaders were driven into exile. The Ennahda leadership was split over how to respond to the repression. One prominent faction, led by Salah Karker and influenced by Qutbist ideology, advocated violence and pursued contacts with militants in Afghanistan and Algeria. However, Ennahda's Executive Bureau, led by Rashid Ghannushi, dismissed Karker and made an official statement in 1995 committing itself to a non-violent approach.

In his early career Ghannushi, who would later obtain a Nobel Peace Prize for his role in facilitating Tunisia's democratic transition, was a relatively conventional Islamist. He studied at Tunisia's principal school of Islamic theology, Zaytouna, but found its approach to Islam too static for his liking. He went on to read philosophy in Damascus and in 1968 proceeded to a Masters at the Sorbonne, a few years after Shariati and al-Turabi had attended the same institution. His early reference points were Iqbal, al-Banna, Qutb, Mawdudi and al-Hawa. He also developed close ties with Hasan al-Turabi, attending each of his Popular Arab and Islamic Conferences between 1991 and 1995 and, like the influential Sudanese Islamist, was a vocal supporter of Saddam Hussein's authoritarian regime during the 1990–1991 Gulf Conflict.[13] Yet, Ghannushi came to moderate his stance throughout the 1990s, distancing himself from Saddam as well as the FIS, and articulating a vision of Islamic democracy which, while maintaining that sharia was still preferable to Western laws, accepted the principle of political pluralism. It has been suggested that it was Ghannushi's experiences as a refugee in Western countries that encouraged him to moderate his outlook.

In Algeria, the FIS of Abbasi Madani and Ali Belhadj used the liberalization of the political environment in the late 1980s to launch a more brazen challenge to the regime. Following mounting public anger at its repression of nationwide protests in 1988, the FLN one-party government had been forced to sanction multiparty elections. The result was a landslide victory for the FIS. They won 54.25 per cent of the vote in the council elections, and 47.26 per cent of the vote and 188 out of 340 seats in the national polls.[14] From the perspective of both international and regional observers, the result was alarming because the ideological outlook of the FIS was far less compromising than, for instance, that of their Islamist counterparts in Egypt and Tunisia. The FIS openly campaigned for sharia law and a monolithic Islamic state. In spite of the fact that it was participating in multiparty elections, the constitution of the FIS maintained that the Islamic state they envisaged would not tolerate any form of political pluralism, and one prominent faction of the FIS – led by Belhadj – rejected the notion of democracy outright as a Western colonial innovation.[15] It is a testament to the effectiveness of the religious and cultural messages of the FIS that Algeria's austerity-stricken population voted for it en masse in spite of the fact that its economic policies were neo-liberal rather than left-wing and revolutionary.[16] However, the army would not allow the FIS to take power, and prevented it from doing so by intervening to stop the second round of legislative elections taking place. As a result, the FIS established a military wing, and a bloody civil war ensued. For the more cautious Islamists, the Algerian conflict served as a warning of the dangers inherent in provoking the military regimes too far. For the more ambitious, such as Hasan al-Turabi in Sudan, it confirmed that they would not allow Islamic movements to come to power democratically, and that those who urged use of force instead were vindicated. For the secular authoritarian regimes themselves, as well as their Western backers, the victory of a hard-line Islamist group in free and fair elections appeared to indicate that they had to make a straightforward choice between authoritarianism and Islamist Revolution.

One consequence of the growing popularity of the mainstream Islamist parties in countries such as Egypt and Tunisia was that authoritarian regimes were forced to dilute their own 'secular' character so as to compete for the hearts and minds of the public. In Tunisia, Ben Ali cultivated Sufi orders, funded mosques and helped to establish a religiously orientated radio station.[17] In Egypt, Sadat altered the constitution to make sharia the 'principal source of legislation', while his successor, Hosni Mubarak, promoted conservative religious values through the state-controlled media, targeted the LGBT community and gave considerable latitude to the official religious establishment at al-Azhar to pronounce on what it considered to be irreligious.[18]

In Jordan and Morocco, Islamist parties were willing to cooperate with the monarchical regimes in their efforts to 'Islamize' society, acting as the 'loyal opposition' in the stunted systems of parliamentary democracy obtaining in those countries. Since Nasser's revolution in Egypt in the 1950s, the Jordanian regime had been willing to support the local branch of the Muslim Brotherhood out of a mutual antipathy to Arab socialism, and assisted the charitable enterprises it established. Even after the government outlawed the Brotherhood in 2016, it immediately reincarnated it under a former member who was more friendly to the regime.[19] Meanwhile in Morocco, the Islamist Party of Justice and Development has participated in parliament and continued to express its loyalty to the king, forbidding its members from joining anti-regime protests during the 2011 Arab Spring.[20]

Post-Islamists in Islamist regimes: Iran and Sudan

One of the reasons why it is in Iran that post-Islamism has been at its strongest as a movement is because it is one of the only countries in which an Islamist movement has actually seized power. Witnessing as they did the domination of the political system by the clerical revolutionaries of 1979, both Islamist and non-Islamist intellectuals came to recognize the perils of allowing an ideological movement to control the process of Islamization top–down. Some of the leading 'post-Islamist' intellectuals in the country actually came from the ranks of the revolutionary establishment itself – notably Abolkarim Soroush, a senior member of the Advisory Council of the Cultural Revolution tasked with Islamizing the higher education sector, and Muhammad Khatami, the minister for Islamic Guidance in the 1980s.[21] Both were critical of the manner in which the revolutionary state had transformed Islam into a ruling ideology.[22] Soroush maintained that 'in an ideological society, the government ideologizes the society, whereas in religious societies, the society makes the government religious'.[23] He thus advocated abandoning the effort to construct a religious state by revolutionary means and the reintroduction of democracy so as to enable the many and subjective human interpretations of the nature of Islam to exist and be debated.[24] Both men argued that Islamists needed to develop a more nuanced relationship with the West: one that went beyond the conventional perspective that it was legitimate to appropriate Western scientific and technological achievements while rejecting Western culture as a whole as flawed and godless. They believed in a more substantive intellectual dialogue with the West that would require more openness to Western political ideas, notably the Western understanding of democracy.[25]

The post-Islamist movement in Iran assumed a different character on the university campus. Although the regime made strenuous efforts to ensure that student leaders adhered to Khomeinist ideology, the next generation of students began to reject these efforts.[26] Those of the 1980s and 1990s became more sceptical of Marxist and conventional Islamist rhetoric alike, and were attracted instead to individual rights and freedoms, seeking to defend them in the face of the restrictive ideology of the post-1979 state.[27] Rather than campaigning for outright secularism, the post-Islamist youth attempted to promote readings of Islamist doctrine which they hoped would facilitate social liberalism.[28]

In 1997, Muhammad Khatami was elected president of Iran, polling particularly well among women and the young. He immediately moved to liberalize the press, and encouraged the establishment of independent trade unions as well as a range of new political parties. A number of independent reformist groups, notably the Freedom Movement and the Second Khurdad Group, emerged and began to support Khatami's challenging of the conservative establishment. In 2002, Khatami managed to pass two important reform bills through the Majlis, one of which would have stripped the clerics of their right to veto parliamentary candidates, but they were vetoed by the Council of Guardians.[29] The reformists were frustrated, and Khatami's liberalism gave way to the more hard-line approach of Mahmud Ahmedinejad, president from 2005 until 2013. Ahmedinejad's uncompromising approach to the opposition and the somewhat dubious character of his second election victory in 2009 sparked a wave of mass protest among Iran's disgruntled urban youth, which came to be known as the Green Movement.[30] This subsided in the face of regime repression, although there were hopes in 2013 that Ahmedinejad's more moderate successor, Hassan Rouhani, would act as another Khatami. However, while Rouhani has promoted some moderate measures of reform and furthered diplomatic relations with Western states, unlike Khatami he has been unwilling to challenge the Council of Guardians and Khomeini's successor as Supreme Guide, Ali Khameini.[31]

The Sudanese case highlights many of the ambiguities of 'post-Islamism'. In 1999, Umar al-Bashir ousted his former benefactor, Hasan al-Turabi, and the 'Islamist' character of the Salvation Regime was somewhat diluted. In a bid to prevent the non-Muslim south from seceding, the government signed a peace deal with the secularist rebels in the south and there was no more reference to divine sovereignty in the transitional constitution.[32] In 2013, when al-Bashir dismissed the government's two most prominent Islamists, Ali Uthman Taha and Nafie Ali Nafie, there was much speculation that the regime had abandoned its religious ideology altogether, and was becoming a conventional one-party state just like those of Egypt, Algeria and Syria – albeit one with a façade of political pluralism.[33] However, in the years before al-Turabi's death in 2016, the regime began to fashion a reconciliation with his followers, and members of his Popular Congress Party began to rejoin it.[34] Nevertheless, the regime, busy conducting numerous counter-insurgencies in Darfur, Blue Nile and South Kordofan, has moved away from its revolutionary Islamist ideology. The ruling Islamists or 'post-Islamists' have perhaps turned in a 'neo-fundamentalist' direction, as evidenced by the ongoing prominence of the Public Order Police and its campaigns to regulate women's dress.[35] This is probably the one example of the 'neofundamentalist' turn occurring *after* the Islamist seizure of power.[36]

Islamists who sided with Umar al-Bashir against al-Turabi maintained that they were making a break with the authoritarian approach of the *Shaikh*. For their part, al-Turabi's own supporters maintained that it was his own democratization measures and campaign to decentralize power in marginalized regions such as Darfur that had led to al-Bashir's one-party authoritarianism. Al-Turabi had indeed experimented with a degree of political liberalization before his ouster in 1999, attempting to bring the old parties back into the fold via a system he referred to as *tawali*, or 'mutual allegiance'. He still described these parties – following the radical Islamists – as the 'parties of Satan' at the time and did not promote political pluralism in the Western sense. Nevertheless, after his rift with al-Bashir in 1999 he forged closer relations with the various non-Islamist parties – including, most controversially, the Sudan People's Liberation Army, the secularist rebel movement – and explicitly embraced multipartyism once more.[37] Yet, before his death, he would attempt to make his peace with al-Bashir once more and proposed a 'successor regime' in which all the country's religiously orientated (not necessarily Islamist) parties, and even the Arab nationalists, would form one political bloc – a proposal closer to the old *tawali* model of the 1990s.[38] The various manoeuvrings of both al-Bashir and al-Turabi, therefore, did not mark the emergences of a distinct 'post-Islamist' epoch so much as another series of fluctuations in Sudan's complex political life, which neither heralded the demise of Islamism nor the full realization of its ideological vision.

Hamas and Hizbullah: From militancy to democracy

Of all the militant movements studied in Chapter 11, only Hamas and Hizbullah have been willing to participate in democratic politics. This is probably because, unlike many militant organizations, they made battling Israeli occupation and not unseating 'apostate' regimes their principal objective; the ideological transition to democracy was thus easier for them to make. After the Lebanese Civil War ended in 1990, Hizbullah fully integrated itself into the democratic system in Lebanon, taking part in elections and obtaining control of various ministries in a power-sharing system.[39] It moved further away from an Iranian regime that was beginning to limit its own pan-Islamic ambitions, and adopted (with Israel in mind) the slogan 'The Islamic Resistance in Lebanon' in place of 'The Islamic Revolution in Lebanon'.[40] Like the Muslim Brotherhood and Hamas, and with the assistance of affiliated companies, it began to expand into a mass movement by opening various charities, hospitals and schools.[41]

Like Hizbullah, Hamas was willing to moderate its stance and enter into the formal political arena. In 2006, it participated in legislative elections in the West Bank and Gaza Strip, in spite of the fact that the Palestinian legislature was part of a political framework established under the 1993 Oslo Accords between Israel and the PLO of which it had been intensely critical.[42] During its election campaign, Hamas downplayed religious ideology and stressed socio-economic reform. It did not call for the destruction of Israel, but demanded the 'ending of the occupation' and the establishment of a Palestinian state with Jerusalem as its capital.[43] Was the decision to participate in the democratic process evidence of the 'ideological evolution' of Hamas? The movement had many pragmatic reasons for such a change. It was heavily reliant on funding from donors in Muslim countries that were themselves being criticized for supporting a militant group, and the portrayal of a democratic and moderate image by Hamas relaxed the pressure on these benefactors.[44] It also saw entering into government as a means of keeping its ten thousand-strong military wing intact.[45] Of course, ideology and pragmatism are far from mutually exclusive.

The 'Change and Reform' party of Hamas won a convincing victory in the legislative elections of 2006, obtaining 74 out of 132 possible seats.[46] However, it did not control the Palestinian Authority outright, having boycotted the presidential elections won by Mahmud Abbas of Fatah the previous year. In another sign of apparent ideological moderation, Hamas offered to rule in coalition with the various non-Islamist groups, including Fatah, but this offer was rejected. Meanwhile, together with the majority of Western and regional governments, Israel refused to recognize Hamas's government as legitimate because of its terrorist past. A subsequent embargo ensured that Hamas only stayed in power for one year before civil war broke out with Fatah, and Abbas removed it from the government in the West Bank, leaving it entrenched in the Gaza Strip.[47] Those who believe a 'moderate Islamism' to be possible argue that the Western states missed an opportunity by refusing to recognize Hamas.[48]

Erdogan and the AKP in Turkey: From post-Islamism back to Islamism?

Probably the most notable example of a political party using 'post-Islamist' rhetoric to achieve sufficient popularity to be voted into power is Turkey's Justice and Development Party (AKP). In 2002 it obtained 34.3 per cent of the vote, and increased this share to 46.6 per cent and 49.8 per cent in the elections of 2007 and 2011, respectively.[49] These victories – the first by a purely civilian Islamist party, although Erdogan rejected the label 'Islamist' at the time – are all the more significant because they occurred in a country which since the Turkish Republic was established by Kemal Ataturk in 1923 had been one of the most secular in the region. As in Egypt, Syria and Tunisia secularism had been preserved through military authoritarianism. Two previous iterations of the AKP, the Felicity Party and the Welfare party, had been banned following military interventions in 1980 and 1997 – in the second instance, the Welfare Party leader Necmettin Erbakan was removed from office after obtaining the post of prime minister in a coalition government.[50] Soon after the banning of the Welfare Party in 1997, one of its most prominent members, the mayor of Istanbul Recep Tayyip Erdogan, spent four years in jail for 'inciting hatred based on religious differences'.[51] Yet, as leader of the AKP he was prime minister between 2003 and 2014 and is now the president, with his powers greatly expanded following a referendum on the Turkish Political System in 2017.[52] Since coming to power, the AKP have managed to thwart any further attempts by the military to remove them from power, cracking down on dissidence within the military following alleged coup attempts in 2008, 2013 and 2016.[53]

Is Erdogan really a 'post-Islamist'? After the 2002 election victory there was much optimism that the AKP was turning into a party of conservative democrats, more concerned with economic reform and religion as an individual right than it was with the introduction of sharia.[54] It had close ties to the Hizmet movement of Fethullah Gulen, which follows a liberal interpretation of Islam.[55] Yet, Erdogan himself appeared to switch between Islamist and post-Islamist rhetoric on a regular basis. In 1989, he told his followers to 'salute the customers even in places where alcohol is served', then declared himself in favour of banning alcohol and imposing sharia when he was elected mayor of Istanbul in 1994.[56] He ridiculed the notion of introducing sharia later in the decade, although it has been suggested that this was a tactical adjustment following his imprisonment in 1998 for declaring that 'the mosques are our barracks'.[57] As the AKP rose to power, Erdogan declared that 'we are not an Islamic party', but elsewhere claimed that 'we have only one concern. It is Islam, Islam, Islam.'[58]

In the second decade of its rule, the AKP appears to have shifted in a more authoritarian and more Islamist direction. Its suppression of the 2013 Gezi Park protests led to conflict with the more moderate followers of Fethullah Gulen,[59] whom Erdogan would blame for the most recent coup attempt, in 2016. After this event, he dismissed twenty-one thousand teachers, and over hundred thousand members of the judiciary, military and security forces.[60] These measures recall such purges as those occurring during the phase of *tamkin* or 'enabling' subsequent to the 1989 Islamist coup in Sudan. But is Erdogan attempting to engineer an Islamist revolution in the conventional sense? It has been suggested that his ideology is a form of neo-Ottomanism that positions him as the 'New Sultan'.[61] As of now, he has made few efforts to introduce rule by sharia, which is hardly surprising since a recent survey showed that only 12 per cent of Turks would be happy with 'making sharia the official law of their country', compared with 84 per cent of Pakistanis and 74 per cent of Egyptians.[62] However, Erdogan's government has begun to make strenuous efforts to ensure that the next generation of Turks will be more pious by introducing compulsory courses on Sunni Islam in formerly secular primary schools.[63] Moreover, the AKP allegedly maintains a number of links to extremist groups outside Turkey, particularly in Syria where a number of regional and international media organs have claimed it is funding and training a variety of militant groups, including Islamic State in Iraq and Syria (ISIS).[64] After the 2016 terrorist atrocity in Orlando, the pro-AKP newspaper, Yeni Akit, which has been accused of supporting al-Qa'eda in the past, declared 'Death toll rises to 50 in bar where perverted homosexuals go!'[65]

The Arab Spring

The significance of the Arab Spring of 2011 was that – although it had long been anticipated that the only alternative to secular military authoritarianism was Islamist democracy – dictators were overthrown in Libya, Tunisia and Egypt by civilian protesters who seemed more concerned with issues such as corruption and human rights than they were with rule by sharia. This led to speculation that the Arab Spring would mark an end to the period of 'Middle East exceptionalism' – a prevalent notion which had encouraged Western commentators and Islamists alike to posit the relationship between Islam and governance as the most consequential factor in local political developments.[66]

However, the successes of Islamist parties in post-Arab Spring elections in Tunisia and Egypt appeared to confound these expectations. In Egypt, the Muslim Brotherhood-backed Freedom and Justice Party won 235 seats and 47.2 per cent of the vote,[67] and its candidate for the presidential elections, Muhammad Morsi, emerged victorious after a tight run-off against the last Mubarak-era prime minister, Ahmad Shafiq.[68] In Tunisia, Ennadha emerged as comfortably the largest party in the constituent assembly after acquiring 37 per cent of the votes in the post-uprising elections.[69] Libya's Muslim Brotherhood-backed Justice and Construction party was, however, less successful, receiving only 10 per cent of the vote.[70]

The Ennahda victory was a surprise to many observers, given that the party's cadres in the country had been decimated by two decades of regime repression and its leadership had only officially declared its support for the uprising shortly before Ben Ali's downfall.[71] However, the party drew strength from an electoral campaign in which it appealed effectively to rural Tunisians, whose concerns were very different from those of the urbanites who had brought Ben Ali down.[72] Moreover, it benefited from playing down its Islamist ideology. Two significant decisions made by Ghannushi following the 'Jasmine Revolution' highlighted the 'ideological evolution'[73] of the Tunisian Islamists. First, he indicated a willingness to compromise with secularists by declaring early in 2012 that he did not deem it necessary for any reference to be made to sharia in the country's constitution. Second, he announced that he was prepared to enter a pluralistic political system and govern in coalition with two secularist parties, Ettakatol and the CRP.[74]

Tunisia's coalition parties governed together effectively until July 2013, when Islamist–secularist tensions intensified following the assassination of two prominent leftists, Chokri Belaid and Mohammed Brahmi, by a Salafi–jihadist who later joined ISIS. Many blamed the Islamists in the government for the killings – even though they were also being targeted by Salafi–jihadists – and the Ennahda prime minister, Hamad Jebali, agreed to dissolve the government after the passing of the January 2014 constitution so that fresh elections could be held.[75] This time around, Ennahda came second to the Nida'a Tunis party, but agreed to join another coalition. Ennahda's campaign continued to be marked by its lack of any overt religious references.[76] In May 2016 it announced that it was a 'Muslim Democratic' rather than an Islamist party, and Ghannushi went so far as to say that 'there is no justification for political Islam in Tunisia'.[77] Unlike Erdogan and al-Turabi, therefore, he has been more consistent in his advocacy of 'post-Islamism'.

Like its counterpart in Tunisia, the Egyptian Muslim Brotherhood, having reaped rewards from a more gradualist and educationalist approach in the years preceding the Arab Spring, did not forcefully back the popular uprisings. But as was also the case in Tunisia, numerous members of its youth wing participated as individuals, even cooperating with secular activists, although the organization itself did not declare its support for the uprising until it was well underway. In spite of the victory of the Brotherhood's

Freedom and Justice Party (FJP) in the parliamentary elections, it remained cautious, wary of provoking the army and powerful outsiders. It is true that, in contrast to Tunisia, Egypt seemed fertile ground for an Islamist regime, after decades of ideological proselytizing by the Brotherhood, a regime attempting to bolster its own religious credentials and a variety of transnational Salafi institutions.[78] Liberal secularists did not even represent the second political force in the country. By then, this was the Salafi movement, which had confounded assumptions of it 'neo-fundamentalist' and apolitical character by founding the al-Nur party, which obtained 24.3 per cent of the vote in the parliamentary elections.[79] Yet, the transitional regime was still overseen by the Supreme Council of the Armed Forces, the military body which had helped to usher out Mubarak, and representatives of this body dismissed the significance of the Islamist election victory in their conversations with the international media.[80]

The Muslim Brotherhood initially moved cautiously, wary of provoking an anti-Islamist backlash. The FJP only put forward Muhammad Morsi as a presidential candidate because an independent ex-Brotherhood Islamist and a Salafi candidate had already put themselves forward.[81] The Salafis demanded an alteration to the constitution stipulating that 'sharia law' would be the country's main 'source of legislation', but Morsi – even after his electoral victory – was happy to retain the more ambiguous provision of the Mubarak-era constitution that 'principles of sharia' would merely inform legislation, thereby avoiding the adverse international reaction that implementation of the *hudud* penalties would inevitably invite. In a declaration to the public, Morsi said 'My sharia is freedom, rule of law and social justice.'[82] A conflict with the military resulted nonetheless, and the army's commander-in-chief, Abd al-Fattah al-Sisi, seized the opportunity provided by a wave of secular and liberal protests against Morsi's efforts to end judicial oversight of the presidency to oust him from office and put him in jail. During the ensuing Islamist backlash, in 2013 the army gunned down eight hundred Morsi supporters in Raba'a square in Eastern Cairo.[83] Al-Sisi, who eventually replaced Morsi as president, became in the worldview of the oppressed Islamists the Nasser of the twenty-first century. The massacre also produced divisions within the Brotherhood itself similar to the Qutbist–Hudaybist split of the 1960s, as the more militant youth who had risen to prominence during the 2011 uprising came to question the non-violent approach of the movement's leadership.[84]

Suggested secondary reading

Bayat, Asef, *Making Islam Democratic: Social Movements and the Post-Islamist Turn* (Stanford: Stanford University Press, 2007), Chapter 3 entitled 'The Making of a Post-Islamist Movement'

Questions: How does Bayat define 'post-Islamism'? How did urban transformations facilitate the conditions in which it could flourish? How did the younger generation (including students) experience and drive 'post-Islamism'? What role did women play? How did religious conservatives react to the growth of the 'post-Islamist' phenomenon? What intellectual transformations facilitated the post-Islamist project?

Suggested primary source readings

Mohamed Morsi, 'I have become today the President of all Egyptians', https://www.theguardian.com/commentisfree/2012/jun/25/president-egyptians-mohamed-morsi, *The Guardian*, 25 June 2012

Does Morsi use any rhetoric that could be described as 'Islamist' here? What role does nationalism play in his rhetoric? What are his principle concerns in this speech?

Mohammed Khatami, 'Dialogue of Civilizations', in *Islamism: A Documentary and Reference Guide* (London: Greenwood Press, 2008), pp. 123–7.

To what extent does this speech show Khatami's ideology to be 'post-Islamist'? What roles do post-Islamism and mysticism play in his language here? Is Khatami less critical of Western civilization that other Islamists? What does he believe the purpose of the 'Dialogue of Civilizations' to be?

NOTES

Chapter 1

1 See, for example, Mozaffari, *Islamism*, 22.
2 Denoeux, 'Navigating the Forgotten Swamp'.
3 Choueiri, *Islamic Fundamentalism*, 7.
4 Ruthven, *Islam*, 11.
5 Ibid., 9.
6 Roy, *Failure of Political Islam*.
7 For instance, Mandaville, *Global Political Islam*. Although Mandaville does qualify his use of the term on p. 20 by observing.
8 See, for example, Hartung, *Mawdudi*.
9 Denoeux, 'The Forgotten Swamp'.
10 Ruthven, *Islam*.
11 Choueiri, *Islamic Fundamentalism*, 20–5, 36.
12 Ibid., 38.
13 Peters, *Jihad*.
14 Choueiri, *Islamic Fundamentalism*, 87, 157.
15 Denoeux, 'The Forgotten Swamp', 69–70.
16 Gerges, *The Far Enemy*.
17 Lauzière, *Making of Salafism*, 4–5.
18 See Griffel's discussion of Abduh in 'What We Mean'.
19 Lauzière, *Making of Salafism*, 22–3.
20 Griffel, 'What We Mean'.
21 See Lauzière, *Making of Salafism*, 199–200.
22 Haykel, 'On the Nature of Salafi Thought and Action', 38–40.
23 Lauzière, *Making of Salafism*, 23, 201.
24 Ibid., 11.
25 Denoeux, 'Forgotten Swamp', 62.
26 For Rida, see Lauzière, *Making of Salafism*, Chapter 2. For Muhammad Qutb's introduction of the teachings of his more famous brother Sayyid to Saudi Arabia and their influence on the Salafis, see Calvert, *Qutb*.

27 For this distinction, see Haykel, 'On the Nature of Salafi Thought and Action', 48–9.

28 Denouex, 'Forgotten Swamp', 68.

29 Hegghammer, 'Jihadi-Salafis or Revolutionaries'?

30 Ayubi, *Political Islam*, 231.

31 See Hartung, *Mawdudi*, 6–7. Brown, *Rethinking Tradition*, 3.

32 See, for example, Gallab, *First Islamist Republic*.

33 Berman, *Terror and Liberalism*.

34 Mozaffari, 'The Rise of Islamism', 11.

35 Bernard Lewis, 'The Roots of Muslim Rage', *The Atlantic*, September 1990, https://www.theatlantic.com/magazine/archive/1990/09/the-roots-of-muslim-rage/304643/.

36 Mirsepassi, *Political Islam, Iran, and the Enlightenment*.

37 Choueiri, *Islamic Fundamentalism*, 38.

38 Graeme Wood, 'What ISIS Really Wants', *The Atlantic*, March 2015, https://www.theatlantic.com/magazine/archive/2015/03/what-isis-really-wants/384980/.

39 Dagli, 'The Phony Islam of ISIS', *The Atlantic*, 27 February 2015, https://www.theatlantic.com/international/archive/2015/02/what-muslims-really-want-isis-atlantic/386156/.

40 Milton-Edwards, 'Politics and Religion', 444, 459.

41 Young, *Postcolonialism*.

42 Hudis, *Philosopher of the Barricades*, 134.

43 Said, *Orientalism*, 333.

44 Fanon, *Wretched of the Earth*.

45 Berridge, *Hasan al-Turabi*, Chapters 1 and 4.

46 Bhabha, *Location of Culture*.

47 Mozaffari, *Islamism: A New Totalitarianism*.

Chapter 2

1 Chatterjee, *Shariati*.

2 Mozaffari, *Islamism: A New Totalitarianism*, 58.

3 Silverstein, *Introduction to Islamic History*, 20, 82.

4 Ibid., 84–5.

5 This paragraph is based on Lapidus, *A History of Islamic Societies*, 18–28; Silverstein, *Introduction to Islamic History*, 9–10.

6 Mozaffari, *Islamism: A New Totalitarianism*, 39. Berridge, *Hasan al-Turabi*, 209.

7 See, for example, Mura, 'A Genealogical Inquiry'.

8   For instance, al-Turabi, 'Islam as a pan-National Movement'.

9   Donner, 'The Formation of the Islamic State'.

10 See, for instance, the discussion of ISIS' relationship with the Abbasid Caliphate in Chapter 12.

11 Ruthven, *Islam*, 35.

12 Kenney, *Muslim Rebels*, 36–7.

13 Timani, *Modern Intellectual Readings*, 5, 14–16.

14 Ibid., 20.

15 Ibid., 6–9.

16 Ibid., 95.

17 Kenney, *Muslim Rebels*, 42–3.

18 Timani, *Modern Intellectual Readings*, 21.

19 Ibid., 21.

20 Ibid., 22–3.

21 Ibid., 23.

22 Kenney, *Muslim Rebels*.

23 Ibid., 34.

24 Ibid., 37.

25 Ibid.

26 Ibid., 32.

27 Timani, *Modern Intellectual Readings*, 16.

28 Ibid., 107.

29 Kenney, *Muslim Rebels*, 33.

30 Timani, *Modern Intellectual Readings*, 93–5.

31 Kenney, *Muslim Rebels*, Chapter 5.

32 Lapidus? Black, *The History of Islamic Political Thought*, 18, 21.

33 Black, *The History of Islamic Political Thought*, 54–5.

34 Esposito, *Islam and Politics*, 15, 19.

35 Lapidus, *A History of Islamic Societies*, 68.

36 Black, *The History of Islamic Political Thought*, 53–6, 66–70.

37 Ghazzal, 'The Ulama', in Choueiri (ed.), *A Companion*, 71.

38 Kennedy, 'The Caliphate', in Choueiri (ed.), *A Companion*, 61.

39 Ibid.

40 Berridge, *Hasan al-Turabi*.

41 Mozaffari, *Islamism: A New Totalitarianism*, 40–1.

42 Melchert, *Ahmad Ibn Hanbal*, 85, 93.

43 See Berridge, *Hasan al-Turabi*, 147.

44 See Michael Chamberlain, 'Military Patronage States', 142.

45 Black, *The History of Islamic Political Thought*, 18.

46 Berkey, *The Formation of Islam*, 222.

47 Ruthven, *Islam*.

48 See, for example, Al-Turabi, *Fi al-Fiqh al-Siyasi*.

49 Ruthven, *Islam*, 70–3.

50 Berkey, 'Innovation and Tradition'.

51 Mozaffari, *Islamism: A New Totalitarianism*, 54–5.

52 Berkey, *The Formation of Islam*, 131.

53 Gleave, 'Shi'ism', 90–1.

54 Ibid., 91. For contemporary references see, for example, Chatterjee, *Shariati*, 147.

55 Gleave, 'Shi'ism', 91.

56 Berkey, *The Formation of Islam*, 133–4.

57 Madelung, discussed in Gleave, 'Shi'ism', 89.

58 McCants, *ISIS Apocalypse*, 107.

59 Voll, 'Frontier Fundamentalist', 153.

60 Ibid.

61 Kenney, *Muslim Rebels*.

62 Zollner, *Hudaybi*, 62, 165.

63 See Voll, 'Frontier Fundamentalist'?

64 Lapidus, *A History of Islamic Societies*, 306.

65 Ibid., 306–7.

66 McCants, *ISIS Apocalypse*, 109.

67 Voll, 'Frontier Fundamentalist', 153.

68 Lapidus, *A History of Islamic Societies*, 307.

69 Ibrahim, *Manichaean Delirium*, 339.

70 See, for example, Abu'l-Hasan Nadawi, 'Muslim Decadence and Renewal', 116–20.

71 Waterson, *Sacred Swords*, 89.

72 See Abu'l-Hasan Nadawi, 'Muslim Decadence and Renewal', in *Princeton Readings*, 117.

73 Roy, *Failure*, 74.

74 Kepel, *Jihad*; Schwartz, 'America's Struggle'.

75 Bazzano, 'Ibn Taymiyya'.

76 Ibid.

77 Lauzière, *Making of Salafism*, 7.

78 Rapoport & Shabab, 'Introduction'.

79 Lauzière, *Making of Salafism*, 200.

80 Ukeles, 'The Sensitive Puritan?', 331.

81 Bazzano, 'Ibn Taymiyya', Part II.

82 Tariq al-Jamil, 'Ibn Taymiyya and Ibn Mutahhar al-Hilli', 233.

83 Ibid., 233–4.

84 Bonney, *Jihad*, 119.

85 Ibid.

86 Ibid., 114.

87 Michot, *Muslims Under Non-Muslim Rule*.

88 Hassan, 'Interpretations and Misinterpretations', 358–9.

89 'Extract from a legal ruling by Ibn Taymiyya' cited in Bonney, *Jihad*, 425.

90 Hassan, 'Interpretations and Misinterpretations', 356.

91 'Extract from a legal ruling by Ibn Taymiyya', cited in Bonney, *Jihad*, 425.

92 Faraj, 'Neglected Duty' in Euben and Zaman, *Princeton Readings*. Michot, *Muslims Under Non-Muslim Rule,* 31.

93 As quoted in Bonney, *Jihad*, 115.

94 Michot, *Muslims Under Non-Muslim Rule*.

95 Ibid., 63.

96 Ibid., 11–21.

97 Ibid., 65.

Chapter 3

1 El Moudden, 'The Idea of the Caliphate'.

2 Lapidus, *A History of Islamic Societies*, 189.

3 Ibid.

4 Ibid., 267.

5 El Roauyheb, 'The Myth of "The Triumph of Fanaticism"', 199.

6 Lapidus, *A History of Islamic Societies*, 372.

7 Rafeq, 'A Different Balance of Power', 230–2.

8 M. Athar Ali, 'The Passing of Empire: The Mughal Case'.

9 Choueiri, *Islamic Fundamentalism*, 25.

10 Ibid., 35.

11 Ibid., 33.

12 DeLong-Bas, *Wahhabi Islam*, 42, 46. Where this subversion was intentional is unclear, as DeLong-Bas does to engage explicitly with Choueiri.

13 DeLong-Bas, *Wahhabi Islam*, 205.

14 Ibid., 206–9.

15 Ibid., 18, 208.

16 See, for instance, Dallal, 'Origins and Objectives of Islamic Revivalist Thought', 359.

17 Voll, 'Muhammad Hayat al-Sindi', 33, 37–8.

18 Ibid., 39.

19 For comments on such errors, see Dallal, 'Origins and Objectives of Islamic Revivalist Thought', 342.

20 Dallal, 'Origins and Objectives of Islamic Revivalist Thought', 342.

21 Choueiri, *Islamic Fundamentalism*, 20–1.

22 See, for example. Voll, 'Frontier Fundamentalist'.

23 This argument has advanced by John Voll in 'Frontier Fundamentalist', and 'Foundations for Renewal and Reform', 522–31.

24 Bernard Haykel, 'Western Arabia and Yemen during the Ottoman Period', 437, 446–7.

25 Currie, 'Kadizadeli Ottoman Scholarship', 266–8.

26 Ibid., 266.

27 Ibid., 268–70.

28 Khalil El Rouayheb, 'Changing Views of Ibn Taymiyya', 303–4.

29 Voll, 'Muhammad Hayat al-Sindi and Muhammad Ibn Abd al-Wahhab'.

30 Nafi, 'Tasawwuf and Reform', 326.

31 Gibb, *Mohammedanism*, 171, cited in Voll, 'Frontier Fundamentalist', 155.

32 Choueiri, *Islamic Fundamentalism*, 4.

33 Commins, *The Mission*, 17–19.

34 Ibid., 19.

35 Al-Dakhil, 'Wahhabism as an Ideology of State Formation'.

36 Ibid.

37 Ibid.

38 Abdulaziz H. Al-Fahd. 'The Imama vs the *Iqal*'.

39 Al-Dakhil, 'Wahhabism as an Ideology of State Formation'.

40 Ibid.

41 Abu Hakima, *Lam' al-Shihab fi Sirat*, cited in al-Rasheed, *A History of Saudi Arabia*, 15.

42 DeLong-Bas, *Wahhabi Islam*, 19, 36.

43 Ibid., 17.

44 For instance, see Cook, 'On the Origins of Wahhabism', 200 fn 85 for an extensive list of instances where al-Wahhab references Ibn Taymiyya. The precise content of these references is not analysed.

45 Commins, *The Mission*, 23.

46 Ibid., 15.

47 DeLong-Bas, *Wahhabi Islam*, 52–3.

48 Cook, 'Origins of Wahhabism'.

49 Voll, 'Muhammad Haya al-Sindi'.

50 Currie, 'Kadizadeli Ottoman Scholarship'.

51 Ibid., 286–7.

52 Ibrahim, 'Shaykh Muhammad Ibn Abd al-Wahhab and Shah Wali Allah', 115. Mitchell, *Society of Muslim Brothers?*

53 Bader Ibrahim, 'ISIS, Wahhabism and Takfir'.

54 Schwartz, 'America's Struggle Against the Wahhabi/Neo-Salafi Movement'. Kepel, *Jihad*, 220–1.

55 For example, Bader Ibrahim, 'ISIS, Wahhabism and Takfir'.

56 Commins, *The Mission*, 30.

57 DeLong-Bas, *Wahhabi Islam*, 35–40.

58 Ibid., 58.

59 Ibid., 37–41.

60 Firro, 'Takfir'. Laurent Bonnefoy, review of *Wahhabi Islam*. Stephen Schwartz, review of *Wahhabi Islam*.

61 Firro, 'Takfir', 774–6.

62 DeLong-Bas, *Wahhabi Islam*, 216.

63 Yahya Michot, *Muslims Under Non-Muslim Rule*.

64 Wagemakers, 'Al-Wala wa-l-bara'.

65 Paul Dresch, 'Arabia to the End of the First World War', 149–50.

66 Firro, 'Takfir', 779–82.

67 DeLong-Bas, *Wahhabi Islam*, 263, 273.

68 On this point, see Mostafa Minawi, *The Ottoman Scramble for Africa*.

69 Wagemakers, 'Al-Wala wa-l-bara', 100–1.

70 Ibid.

71 Ibid., 102.

72 Voll, 'Foundations for Renewal and Reform', 519.

73 Choueiri, *Islamic Fundamentalism*, 23.

74 Voll, 'Foundations for Renewal and Reform', 533.

75 Choueiri, *Islamic Fundamentalism*, 23.

76 Reid, *A History of Modern Africa*, 97.

77 These last two are among the central characteristics of Revivalism discussed by Choueiri, *Islamic Fundamentalism*, 24–5.

78 Voll, 'Foundations for Renewal and Reform', 531.

79 Voll, 'Frontier Fundamentalist', 155.

80 Voll, 'Foundations for Renewal and Reform', 532.

81 Voll, 'Frontier Fundamentalist', 164.

82 Holt, *Mahdist State*, 39–40.

83 Holt and Daly, *History of Sudan*.

84 Holt, *Mahdist State*, 98–9.

85 Ibid., 101.

86 Ibid.
87 Warburg, 'Mahdiyya and Wahabiyya', 670.
88 Voll, 'Frontier Fundamentalist', 156.
89 Slatin, *Fire and Sword*, 230.
90 Daly, *Empire on the Nile*.
91 Ibrahim, 'Shaykh Muhammad Ibn Abd al-Wahhab and Shah Wali Allah', 106.
92 Ibid., 105, 113.
93 Ibid.
94 Ibid., 113.
95 Ibid.
96 Ibid., 107.
97 Ibid., 107–8.
98 Voll, 'Renewal and Reform', 525.
99 Ibid.
100 Dobbin, 'Islamic Revivalism'.
101 Van Dijk, 'Islam and Socio-Political Conflicts', 10.
102 Dobbin, 'Islamic Revivalism', 337.
103 Van Dijk, 'Islam and Socio-Political Conflicts', 10.
104 Ibid., 11.
105 Reid, *History of Modern Africa*, 170–3.
106 Reynolds, 'Good and Bad Muslims', 603.
107 Warburg, 'British Policy towards the Ansar', 679.
108 Warburg, *Islam, Nationalism and Communism*, 32.
109 Al-Rasheed, *A History of Saudi Arabia*, 40–1, 87–96.
110 Firro, 'Takfir', 785.

Chapter 4

1 Choueiri, *Islamic Fundamentalism*, 33–50.
2 For the concept of 'informal' Empire, see Robinson and Gallagher, 'The Imperialism of Free Trade'.
3 Inal, 'Eighteenth and Nineteenth Century Ottoman Attempts'.
4 Ayubi, *Political Islam*.
5 Choueiri, *Islamic Fundamentalism*, 37, 43.
6 Kedourie, *Afghani and Abduh*.
7 Sedgwick, *Abduh*, 125–6.
8 Anscombe, 'Islam in the Age of Ottoman Reform'.
9 Euben, *Enemy in the Mirror*. See also Keddie, *Islamic Response*, 36–45.

10 DeLong-Bas, *Wahhabi Islam*, 235.

11 See, for example, Weismann, 'Genealogies of Fundamentalism', Badawi, *Reformers*. Zaman, *Radical Age*, 7.

12 Lauzière, *Making of Salafism*, 22–3.

13 Ayubi, *Political Islam*.

14 Voll, 'Foundations for Renewal and Reform'.

15 Washbrook, 'India 1818-1860' and Moore, 'Imperial India, 1858-1914'.

16 Robinson, 'South Asia to 1919', 233.

17 Ahmad, *Islamic Modernism*, quoted in Esposito, *Islam and Politics*, 55.

18 Malik, 'Sir Sayyid Ahmad Khan Progress', 235–6.

19 Ibid., 236.

20 Brown, *Rethinking Tradition*.

21 Esposito, *Islam and Politics*, 56.

22 Malik, 'Sir Sayyid Ahmad Khan's Doctrines', 240.

23 Ibid., 227.

24 Malik, 'Sir Sayyid Ahmad Khan's Contribution', 137.

25 Malik, 'Sir Sayyid Ahmad Khan's Doctrines', 227.

26 Gelvin, *The Modern Middle East*.

27 Findley, *Turkey, Islam, Nationalism and Modernity*, 33.

28 Hanioglu, 'Modern Ottoman Period', in *Routledge Handbook of Modern Turkey*.

29 Hanioglu, 'Modern Ottoman Period'.

30 Ibid.

31 Ibid.

32 Ibid.

33 Anscombe, 'Islam', 184.

34 Hanioglu, 'Modern Ottoman Period'.

35 Cain and Hopkins, *British Imperialism*.

36 Robinson and Gallagher, 'Imperialism of Free Trade'.

37 Hanioglu, 'Modern Ottoman Period'.

38 Findley, 'The Ottoman Lands', 45.

39 Ibid.

40 Ibid., 55–6.

41 Perkins, *Tunisia*, 32–6.

42 Bennison, 'New Order', 600.

43 Ibid., 602.

44 Lauzière, *Making of Salafism,* 150–3.

45 Bennison, 'New Order', 596–7.

46 Choueiri, *Islamic Fundamentalism*, 57.

47 Keddie, *Islamic Response*, 5–8.

48 Ibid., 9–11.

49 Ibid., 12.

50 Voll, 'Impact of the Wahhabi Tradition'.

51 Keddie, *Islamic Response*, 17.

52 Sedgwick, *Abduh*, 50.

53 Keddie, *al-Afghani*, 82.

54 Sedgwick, *Abduh*, 1–8.

55 Ibid., 11.

56 Ibid., 13.

57 Ibid., 26–35.

58 Ibid., 72–7.

59 Ibid., 79–81, 103–4.

60 Ibid., 108.

61 Ibid., 101–2.

62 For the influence on Arab nationalism, see Dawisha, *Arab Nationalism*.

63 Kedourie, *Afghani and Abduh*, 15.

64 Ibid., 44.

65 Ibid., 45.

66 Sedgwick, *Abduh*, 45.

67 Holt, Review of Kedourie, *Afghani and Abduh*.

68 Keddie, *Islamic Response*.

69 Keddie, *Political Biography*, 100.

70 Sedgwick, *Abduh*, 16.

71 Keddie, *Political Biography*, 95, 179.

72 Scharbrodt, 'Salafiyya and Sufism', 102–3.

73 Ibid., 103.

74 Keddie, *Political Biography*, 70.

75 Scharbrodt, 'Salafiyya and Sufism', 111.

76 Wood, *Christian Proofs*, 27.

77 Ibid.

78 Ibid.

79 Lauzière, *Making of Salafism*, 41, 251 (fn 56). Sedgwick, *Abduh*, 64.

80 Sedgwick, *Abduh*, 64.

81 Lauzière, *Making of Salafism*, 1–19.

82 Ibid., 39.

83 Ibid., 38.

84 Ibid., 31.

85 Ibid., 22, 39–40.

86 Griffel, 'What We Mean', 198–9.

87 Ibid., 186.

88 Lauzière, 'What We Mean', 92.

89 Lauzière, *Making of Salafism*, 35.

90 Ibid., 23, 70–5, 219–22.

91 Ibid., 149–52.

92 Choueiri, *Islamic Fundamentalism*, 50.

93 Brown, *Rethinking Tradition*, 22. Choueiri, *Islamic Fundamentalism*, 50. Scharbrodt, 'Salafiyya and Sufism', 94. Wood, *Christian Criticisms*, 23.

94 Scharbrodt, 'Salafiyya and Sufism', 92–3.

95 Wood, *Christian Criticisms*, 23.

96 Keddie, *Political Biography*, 17–18.

97 Scharbrodt, 'Salafiyya and Sufism', 98.

98 Ibid.

99 Ibid., 95.

100 Choueiri, *Islamic Fundamentalism*, 46–7.

101 Cited in Sedgwick, *Abduh*, 33.

102 Kayali, 'Elections in the Ottoman Empire', 266–7.

103 Choueiri, *Islamic Reformism*, 46–7.

104 Malik, 'Sir Sayyid Ahmad Khan's Contribution to the Development of Muslim Nationalism', 143–5.

105 Esposito, *Islam and Politics*, 35. Khatab and Bouma, *Democracy in Islam*, 57.

106 Khatab and Bouma, *Democracy in Islam*, 58.

107 Sedgwick, *Abduh*, 22. Keddie, *Islamic Response*, 55–8.

108 Keddie, *Islamic Response*, 58.

109 Ibid., 26.

110 See, for example, Peters, *Jihad*, 6–7.

111 See, for example, Mawdudi, *Jihad in Islam*.

112 Peters, *Jihad*, 6.

113 Ibid.

114 Al-Afghani, 'The Materialists in India', cited in Keddie, *Islamic Response*, 176.

115 Keddie, *Political Biography*.

116 Kedourie, *Afghani and Abduh*.

117 See Kedourie's comments regarding al-Afghani's adulation of the Mahdi in Kedourie, *Afghani and Abduh*, 48–55.

118 Sedgwick, *Abduh*, 23.

119 Ibid., 54.

120 Ibid.

121 Umar Ryad, 'Islamic Reformism and Great Britain', 264–6.

122 Ibid., 270.

123 The quote is from Rida (1929), 772, cited in Ryad, 'Islamic Reformism and Great Britain', 271. See also Wood, *Christian Criticisms*.

124 Provence, 'Ottomanism', 208–9.

125 Peters, *Jihad*, 59.

126 See, for example, Calvert, *Qutb,* 153–4, 163–4.

127 Mitchell, *Society of Muslim Brothers*, 321.

128 Martin, *Khomeini.* Jackson, *Mawdudi*, 105–6.

129 See, for example, Kramer, *Hasan al-Banna.*

Chapter 5

1 See, for example, Shadi Hamid's critique of Mitchell, *Illiberal Democracy*, 16.

2 For a useful critique of 'Modernization Theory', see Peng, 'Modernization Theory'.

3 Mitchell, *Society*.

4 For a good discussion of how this paradigm emerged in the previous literature on the Brotherhood, see Munson, 'Islamic Mobilization', 491.

5 See, for example, Mura, 'Genealogical Inquiry'.

6 Lia, *Muslim Brothers*, 279–80.

7 Ayubi, *Political Islam*, 231.

8 Mura, 'Genealogical Inquiry', 71.

9 Choueiri, *Islamic Fundamentalism*, 58.

10 Soage, 'Continuity or Rupture'.

11 Ryad, 'Islamic Reformism and Great Britain', 270.

12 Mozaffari, 'The Rise of Islamism'.

13 Mitchell, *Society*, 40.

14 Gilbert Achar, 'Fascism in the Middle East and North Africa'.

15 Soage, 'Hasan al-Banna or the Politicisation of Islam', 36.

16 Baron, *Orphan Scandal*. Reid, *Cairo University*, Chapter 5.

17 Gershoni and Janksowi, *Egypt, Islam and the Arabs.* See also Kaufman, *Reviving Phoenecia*.

18 Gershoni and Jankowski, *Redefining the Egyptian Nation*.

19 Mitchell, *Society*, 1.

20 Lia, *Society*, 23.

21 Ibid., 25.

22 Ibid., 26.

23 Kramer, *Hasan al-Banna*, 9.

24 Mitchell, *Society*, 4.

25 Kramer, *Hasan al-Banna,* 18.

26 Mitchell, *Society*, 7.

27 Ibid., 16.

28 Ibid., 15.

29 Ibid., 9.

30 Lia, *Society*, 111.

31 Ibid.

32 Munson, 'Islamic Mobilization', 501, 504–6.

33 Mitchell, *Society*, 8.

34 Lia, *Society*, 236–7.

35 Ibid., 239–41. Gershoni.

36 Lia, *Society*, 236.

37 Gellner, Kepel.

38 Munson, 'Islamic Mobilization', 490–1.

39 Ibid., 491.

40 Ibid., 492.

41 Mitchell, *Society*, 328.

42 Lia, *Society*, 279.

43 Soage, 'Politicisation of Islam'.

44 Mitchell, *Society*, 172–3.

45 Lia, *Society*, 103.

46 Ibid.

47 Mitchell, *Society*, 166–7.

48 Ibid.

49 Munson, 'Islamic Mobilization', 497.

50 Lia, *Society*, 115.

51 Mitchell, *Society,* 195.

52 Ibid., 296

53 Ibid., 105, 116.

54 Stemmann, 'The Crossroads of Muslim Brothers in Jordan', 57.

55 Choueiri, *Islamic Fundamentalism*, 75.

56 Lia, *Society*, 257.

57 Ibid., 254–5.

58 Mitchell, *Society*, 26.

59 Ibid. Lia, *Society*, 264–5.

60 Mitchell, *Society*, 37–8.

61 Ibid., 38.

62 Ibid.

63 Kramer, *Hasan al-Banna*, 74.

64 See Soage, 'Politicisation of Islam', for a reading of events that follows the latter interpretation.

65 Mitchell, *Society*, 62. Kramer, *Society*, 77.

66 Mitchell, *Society*, 71.

67 Kramer, *Hasan al-Banna*, 80.

68 Ibid.

69 Al-Banna, 'On Jihad', in Wendell, *Five Tracts*, 156.

70 Ibid, 159.

71 Ibid., 139, 142.

72 Levy, 'Jihad'.

73 Kramer, *Society*, 103. For Qutb's views, see Chapter 7.

74 Kramer, *Society*, 103.

75 Lia, *Society*, 83.

76 Mitchell, *Society*, 321.

77 Ibid., 325.

78 Lia, *Society*, 142–3.

79 Kramer, *Hasan al-Banna*, 7.

80 Cited in Lia, *Society*, 140.

81 Ibid., 142–3.

82 Ibid., 59.

83 Ibid., 59–60.

84 Quoted in Kramer, *Hasan al-Banna*, 43.

85 Ibid., 96.

86 Ibid.

87 Mitchell, *Society*, 214–16.

88 Lia, *Society*, 38.

89 Kramer, *Hasan al-Banna*, 38.

90 Mitchell, *Society*, 214–15.

91 Kramer, *Society*, 41–2.

92 Ibid., 61.

93 Ibid.

94 Al-Banna, *Towards the Light*.

95 Soage, 'Hasan al-Banna or the Politicisation of Islam'.

96 Ibid.

97 Ibid.

98 See, for example, Kuntzel, *Jihad and Jew-Hatred: Islamism, Nazism and the Roots of 9/11* (New York: Telos Press, 2007)
99 Gershoni and Jankowski, *Confronting Fascism*, 211.
100 Al-Banna, *Towards the Light.*
101 Gershoni and Jankowski, *Confronting Fascism*, 211–12.
102 Al-Banna, *Towards the Light.*
103 Gershoni and Jankowski, *Confronting Fascism*, 219.
104 Ibid., 217–21.
105 Hasan al-Banna, 'Peace in Islam'.
106 Ibid.
107 Al-Banna, *Towards the Light.*
108 Lia, *Society*, 246.
109 Mitchell, *Society*, 278–9.
110 Gershoni and Jankowski, *Confronting Fascism*, 224.
111 Lia, *Society*, 246.
112 Ibid.
113 Choueiri, *Islamic Fundamentalism*, 73.
114 Al-Banna, *Towards the Light.*
115 Lia, *Society*, 82.
116 Al-Banna, *Towards the Light.*
117 As is implied by Choueiri in *Islamic Fundamentalism*, 72–3.
118 Lia, *Society*, 208–12.
119 Mitchell, *Society*, 172–3.
120 Munson, 'Islamic Mobilization', 497–8.
121 Ibid., 500.
122 Simms, 'Islam is Our Politics'.
123 Soage, 'Politicisation of Islam'.
124 Mura, 'A Genealogical Inquiry'.
125 Ibid., 72.
126 Mitchell, *Society*, 265.
127 Ibid.
128 Ibid.
129 Al-Banna, *Towards the Light.* See discussion in Mura, 'A Genealogical Inquiry', 75.
130 Al-Banna, *Towards the Light.*
131 Al-Banna, *Message of the Teachings*, as quoted in Mura, 'A Genealogical Inquiry', 77.
132 Mura, 'A Genealogical Inquiry', 78.
133 Baron, *Orphan Scandal*, 197.

Chapter 6

1   Choueiri, *Islamic Fundamentalism*, 157.

2   Jackson, *Mawdudi*, 48.

3   For example, Bale, 'Islamism and Totalitarianism'

4   Nasr, *Mawdudi*, 28.

5   This section is largely based on Nasr, *Mawdudi*, 10–20 and Jackson, *Mawdudi*, 1–47.

6   Sana Haroon, 'The Rise of Deobandi Islam', 48.

7   Sana Haroon, 'The Rise of Deobandi Islam', 48. Ingram, 'Sufis, Scholars and Scapegoats', 479.

8   Sana Haroon, 'The Rise of Deobandi Islam'. Ingram, 'Sufis, Scholars and Scapegoats'.

9   Ira Lapidus, *History of Islamic Societies*, 627.

10 Ingram, 'Crises of the Public', 404–5.

11 Lapidus, *History of Islamic Societies*, 626.

12 Jackson, *Mawdudi*, 47.

13 Ibid., 48.

14 Nasr, *Mawdudi*, 28.

15 This section draws heavily on Jackson, *Mawdudi*, 42–68 and Nasr, *Mawdudi*, 21–8.

16 Lapidus, *History of Islamic Societies*, 631.

17 Ibid., 636.

18 Nasr, *Mawdudi*, 22.

19 Lapidus, *A History of Islamic Societies*, 638.

20 See last chapter.

21 This section draws heavily on Jackson, *Mawdudi* and Nasr, *Mawdudi*.

22 Jackson, *Mawdudi*, 97.

23 Ibid., 106.

24 Hartung, *Mawdudi*, 163.

25 Mawdudi, *The Battle between Islam and Capitalism*, cited in Choueiri, *Islamic Fundamentalism*, 123–4.

26 Nasr, *Mawdudi*.

27 Mawdudi, *Islam Today*.

28 Mawdudi, *Jihad in Islam*.

29 Maududi, *Islamic Law and Constitution*, 144–5, as discussed by Jeffrey Bale, 'Islamism and Totalitarianism', 73.

30 Jackson, *Mawdudi*.

31 Ibid., 65.

32 Mawdudi, *The Islamic Movement*, 77.

33 For this concept, see Scott, 'Colonial Governmentality'.

34 Ahmad, 'Genealogy'.

35 Mawdudi in *Tarjuman*, March 1938, as quoted in Ahmad, 'Genealogy', 5154.

36 Ahmad, 'Genealogy', 5153.

37 Hartung, *Mawdudi*, 64.

38 Choueiri, *Islamic Fundamentalism*.

39 Nasr, *Mawdudi*, 60.

40 Cited in Hartung, *Mawdudi*, 65.

41 Jackson, *Mawdudi*, 118.

42 Calvert, *Qutb*, 259.

43 Osman, 'Mawdudi's Contribution', 480–1.

44 See, for instance, Mawdudi's discussion of nationalism in 'Nations Rise and Fall and Why'.

45 Jackson, *Mawdudi*, 59.

46 Ibid.

47 Nasr, *Mawdudi*, 22.

48 Mawdudi, *Jihad in Islam*.

49 Ibid.

50 Ibid.

51 Nasr, *Mawdudi*, 70–9.

52 Ibid., 74.

53 Nasr, *Mawdudi*, 93. Jackson, *Mawdudi*, 71.

54 Nasr, *Mawdudi*, 71.

55 Ibid., 94.

56 Jackson, *Mawdudi*, 131–2.

57 Quoted in Jackson, *Mawdudi*, 131.

58 Ibid., 131.

59 This section is based on Jackson, *Mawdudi*, 70–80, 161–76, and Nasr, *Mawdudi*, 41–6.

60 Nasr, *Mawdudi*, 76.

61 Ahmad, 'Theorizing Islam and Democracy', 894.

62 Ibid.

63 Ibid., 895.

64 Ibid., 894–6.

65 Euben and Zaman, *Princeton Readings,* 108–9. See also Calvert, *Qutb*, 158, 217.

66 See Nadwi, 'Muslim Decadence and Renewal', in Euben and Zaman, *Princeton Readings*, 114–15.

67 Euben and Zaman, *Princeton Readings*, 111.

68 Ibid., 110.
69 Hossein and Siddiquee, 'Islam in Bangladesh Politics', 386.
70 Ibid., 387–9.
71 Osman, 'Transnational Islamism'. Othman, 'The Role of Egyptian Influences'.
72 Formichi, 'Islam and the Making of the Nation', 52, 70.
73 Ibid., 44.
74 Ibid., 2, 65–6.
75 Ibid., 66.
76 Osman, 'Transnational Islamism', 44.
77 Ibid., 45.
78 Ibid., 46.
79 Ibid., 46. Voll and Esposito, *Makers*.
80 Voll and Esposito, *Makers*.
81 Ibid.
82 Ibid., 182.

Chapter 7

1 Alex Mitchell, *Come the Revolution*, 329.
2 Roy, *Failure of Political Islam*, 3.
3 Gallab, *Their Second Republic*, 15.
4 Kepel, *Jihad*. Ayubi, *Political Islam*. Mozaffari, *Islamism*, 44–50.
5 Milton-Edwards, 'Politics and Religion'.
6 See, for example, Kenney, *Muslim Rebels*, 13.
7 Chatterjee, *Shariati*, 89.
8 Munson, 'Islamic Mobilization', 500.
9 This definition is provided by Walker and Gray, *Historical Dictionary of Marxism*, 286.
10 Walker and Gray, *Historical Dictionary of Marxism*.
11 Ibid.
12 Renton, *Classical Marxism*.
13 Ibid.
14 Smith, *Oxford Handbook*.
15 Walker and Gray, *Historical Dictionary of Marxism*.
16 Ibid., 187.
17 Ibid., 188.
18 Ali, *Suqut*, 22.
19 Young, *Postcolonialism*, 108–9.

20 Ibid., 129.

21 Ibid., 138.

22 Ibid., 134–13.

23 Walker and Grey, *Historical Dictionary of Marxism*, 302–6.

24 Young, *Postcolonialism*.

25 Walker and Grey, *Historical Dictionary of Marxism*, 317–20.

26 Ibid., 125–6.

27 Butko, 'Revelation or Revolution'.

28 Walker and Gray, *Historical Dictionary of Marxism*, 202–6.

29 Rabaka, 'Revolutionary Fanonism'.

30 Fanon, 'French Intellectuals and Democrats and the Algerian Revolution', in *Toward the African Revolution*.

31 Fanon, 'French Intellectuals'. Fanon, *Wretched of the Earth*, 86.

32 Fanon, *Wretched of the Earth*, 47.

33 Ibid., 103.

34 Choueiri, *Islamic Fundamentalism*, 73.

35 Roy, *Failure of Political Islam,* 39–40.

36 This was notably the case, for instance, in Sudan and Egypt. See Berridge, *Civil Uprisings*.

37 Bale, 'Islamism and Totalitarianism', 73.

38 Choueiri, *Islamic Fundamentalism*.

39 Calvert, *Qutb*, 210. See also Toth, *Qutb*, 147.

40 Butko, 'Revelation or Revolution', 46.

41 Choueiri, *Islamic Fundamentalism*, 152–3.

42 Lefevre, *Ashes of Hama*, 36.

43 Ibid.

44 Rabil, 'Syrian Muslim Brotherhood', 75.

45 Choueiri, *Islamic Fundamentalism*, 78.

46 Voll and Esposito, *Makers*, 75–6.

47 Ibid., 83.

48 Except where otherwise noted, the following is based on Chatterjee, *Shariati*, 75–93; Rahnema, *Islamic Utopian*, 24–34, 120–7, 200–4, 277–9, 339–49, 369; Abrahamian, *Iran Between Two Revolutions*, 467–8.

49 Shariati, 'The Philosophy of History', 98.

50 Ibid., 109.

51 Ibid., 104.

52 Chatterjee, *Shariati*, 91–3.

53 Shariati, 'Reflections of a Concerned Muslim', 39–40.

54 Ibid., 36.

55 Abrahamian, *Khomeinism*, 47.

56 Mirsepassi, *Political Islam, Iran and the Enlightenment*, Chapter 4.

57 Hudis, *Philosopher of the Barricades*, 134.

58 Yahya al-Awad, 'Makr al-Tarikh wa Maharat Tamziq al-Rumuz', *al-Rakoba*, 9 November 2011, https://www.alrakoba.net/articles-action-show-id-11936.html.

59 El-Affendi, *Turabi's Revolution*.

60 Ghassan Ali Uthman interview with Abdullah Zakariyya, 13 September 2009, *Muthagafa,* http://muthagafa.blogspot.co.uk/2009/11/blog-post_4375.html.

61 Vandewalle, *Libya: A Modern History,* 87.

62 Vandewalle, *Libya Since Independence*, 64–5.

63 Muhammad (ed.), *Babikir Karrar*, 47.

64 Ibid., 61.

65 Vandewalle, *Libya Since Independence*, 92.

66 These are the Palestinian journalist Ahmad Abu Matar in 'Diktator Muluk Ifriqiyya fi Muwajiha al-Sahafa al-Maghribiyya', *al-Libya al-Mustaqbal*, 7 July 2009, http://archive.libya-al-mostakbal.org/articles0709/dr_ahmad_abumatar_070709.html (accessed 22 June 2017) and the Sudanese attorney Abd al-Aziz Shiddu – see al-Awad, 'Makr al-Tarikh'.

67 Nasir al-Sid, interview with *Akhir Lahza*, 15 December 2016.

68 Vandewalle, *Libya Since Independence,* 93–4.

69 Al-Qathafi, *Green Book*, 17–21, 47–52.

70 Ibid., 29.

71 Bearman, *Qadhafi's Libya*, 164.

72 Ibid., 162.

73 Vandewalle, *Libya Since Independence*.

74 Ibid., 95.

75 Ibid., 99.

76 Ibid., 100–2.

77 Ibid., 99.

78 Berridge, *Civil Uprisings*, 91.

79 Berridge, *Hasan al-Turabi*. See also Abdullah Zakariyya's interview with Muzammil Abd al-Ghaffar, *al-Intibaha*, 19 July 2017, http://www.alintibaha.net/index.php/ (accessed 10 March 2018).

80 See, for example Munson, 'Islamic Mobilization', 500–1.

81 Behrooz, *Rebels with a Cause*.

82 Milani, *The Making of Iran's Islamic Revolution*, 190–4.

83 Kepel, *Roots*.

84 Roy, *Failure of Political Islam*, 75.

85 Roy, *Globalized Islam*, 234–47.

Chapter 8

1 Soage, 'Continuity or Rupture', 295–6.

2 Musallam, *From Secularism to Jihad*, 202.

3 Calvert, *Qutb*, 7.

4 Euben, *Enemy in the Mirror*, 12–15.

5 Soage, 'Hasan al-Banna'.

6 For the former perspective, see Soage, 'Continuity or Rupture', 295–6. For the latter perspective, see Calvert, *Qutb*, 17–18, 212–13.

7 This section draws heavily on Calvert, *Qutb*, 40–104; Toth, *Qutb*, 12–19; Musallam, *From Secularism to Jihad*, 41–69.

8 Calvert, *Qutb*, 41. Qutb was speaking in the third person.

9 Botman, 'Liberal Age'.

10 Toth, *Qutb*, 21 and fn 58.

11 Calvert, *Qutb*, 72.

12 This section is particularly based on Calvert, *Qutb*, 104–263.

13 See, for example, Martin Amis, 'The Age of Horrorism', *The Guardian*, 10 September 2006.

14 Calvert, *Qutb*. Musallam, *From Secularism to Jihad*, 93.

15 Calvert, *Qutb*, 133.

16 Sayyid Qutb, 'The America I have Seen'.

17 Gordon, *Nasser's Blessed Movement*, 53–5.

18 Elie Podeh and Onn Winckler, *Rethinking Nasserism: Revolution and Historical Memory in Egypt* (Gainesville: University Press of Florida, 2004), 14.

19 Zollner, *Hudaybi*.

20 See, Fanon, *Wretched of the Earth*, Chapter 3.

21 Calvert, *Qutb*, 226.

22 Ibid., 240–1. Zollner, *Hudaybi*, 40.

23 Calvert, *Qutb*, 229.

24 Ibid.

25 Ibid., 261–3.

26 Ibid., 257.

27 Kenney, *Muslim Rebels*, Chapter 3.

28 Calvert, *Qutb*, 235.

29 Zollner, *Hudaybi*.

30 Kenney, *Muslim Rebels*, 122. Calvert, *Qutb*, 274–5.

31 Toth, *Qutb*, 84.

32 Kenney, *Muslim Rebels*, 120.

33 Calvert, *Qutb*, 235, 257–8.

34 Qutb, 'Signposts along the Road', in Euben and Zaman, *Princeton Readings*, 143.

35 Calvert, *Qutb*, 274.

36 Osman, 'Mawdudi's Contribution', 480.

37 Ibid.

38 As quoted in Bergesen, 39–40.

39 Calvert, *Qutb*, 221–2.

40 Bonney, *Jihad*, 217–20.

41 Schwarz, 'America's Struggle', 121.

42 Qutb, *In the Shade of the Quran*.

43 Maher, *Salafi-Jihadism*, 87.

44 Toth, *Qutb*, 89.

45 Maher, *Salafi-Jihadism*, 87.

46 Ibid., 181.

47 Calvert, *Qutb*, 226–7.

48 Qutb, 'Signposts', in Euben and Zaman.

49 Qutb, 'In the Shade of the Quran', in Euben and Zaman, 145.

50 Qutb, 'In the Shade of the Quran', 149.

51 See *Milestones* quotes in Bergesen, 38. Calvert, *Qutb*.

52 For example, Soage, 'Continuity or Rupture'.

53 Berman, *Terror and Liberalism*.

54 Quoted in Choueiri, *Islamic Fundamentalism*, 190.

55 Ibid., 186–92.

56 Ibid., 191–3.

57 Stoica, 'Do Modern Radicals Believe their Mythologies'.

58 Calvert, *Qutb*, 169–71. See also Berridge, 'Islamism and the Instrumentalization of Conspiracism'.

59 Choueiri, *Islamic Fundamentalism*, 153–4.

60 Bonney, *Jihad*, 217.

61 Calvert, *Qutb*, 215.

62 Ibid., 217.

63 Toth, *Qutb*.

64 Toth, *Qutb*, 208.

65 Choueiri, *Islamic Fundamentalism*, 215.

66 Toth, *Qutb*, 194–5.

67 Ibid., 195.

68 Choueiri, *Islamic Fundamentalism*, 145–6.

69 Toth, *Qutb*, 208.

70 Khatab and Bouma, *Democracy in Islam*, 7, 16–17.

71 Euben, *Enemy in the Mirror*, 62.

72 As quoted in Euben, *Enemy in the Mirror,* 62.

73 Calvert, *Qutb*, 216.

74 Peters, *Islamic Criminal Law.*

75 Hassan, 'Modern Interpretations and Misinterpretations', 338–66.

76 Toth, *Qutb*, 227.

77 Calvert, *Qutb*, 219.

78 Toth, *Qutb*. 203.

79 Calvert, *Qutb*, 276.

80 Ibid.

81 Ibid.

82 Ibid., 286–7.

83 Ibid., 291–2.

84 Soage, 'Continuity or Rupture', 295.

85 Calvert, *Qutb*, 282.

Chapter 9

1 Lapidus, *History of Islamic Societies*, 33–48.

2 Silverstein, *Islamic History*, 41, 55–6.

3 Lapidus, *History of Islamic Societies*.

4 Ibid., 234.

5 Ibid.

6 Voll, 'Foundations for Revival and Reform', 515–16.

7 Keddie, *A Political Biography*.

8 Voll, 'Foundations for Revival and Reform', 515–16.

9 Martin, *Khomeini*, 5–6.

10 Ibid., 104.

11 The next three paragraphs are largely based on Axworthy, *Revolutionary Iran*, 36–59.

12 Zia-Ebrahimi, 'Arab Invasion'.

13 Axworthy, *Revolutionary Iran*, 79.

14 Martin, *Khomeini*, 129–32. Mozaffari, *Islamism: A New Totalitarianism*, 125–8.

15 Mozaffari, *Islamism: A New Totalitarianism*, 125–8.

16 Chatterjee, *Shariati*, 61.

17 Mirsepassi, *Political Islam, Iran, and the Enlightenment*, 117.

18 Chatterjee, *Shariati*, 58.
19 Ibid., 80.
20 Martin, *Khomeini*, 29. Abrahamian, *Iran Between Two Revolutions*, 425.
21 Brumberg, 'Islamic Rule and Islamic Social Justice', 23.
22 Abrahamian, *Iran Between Two Revolutions*, 425.
23 Ibid.
24 Martin, *Khomeini*, 29.
25 Abrahamian, *Iran Between Two Revolutions*, 475.
26 Chatterjee, *Shariati*, 179.
27 Martin, *Khomeini*, 62.
28 Ibid., 21, 62.
29 Mozaffari, *Islamism: The New Totalitarianism*, 90.
30 Abrahamian, *Iran Between Two Revolutions*, 425.
31 Martin, *Khomeini*, 64.
32 Brumberg, 'Social Justice', 30–1.
33 Martin, *Khomeini*, 111.
34 Quoted in Abrahamian, *Iran Between Two Revolutions*, 476.
35 Martin, *Khomeini*, 476.
36 Quoted in Abrahamian, *Iran Between Two Revolutions*, 477.
37 Jackson, *Mawdudi*, 2. Martin, *Khomeini*, 144.
38 Martin, *Khomeini*, 102.
39 Ibid., 144.
40 Ibid., 144–6.
41 Mozaffari, *Islamism: A New Totalitarianism*, 125.
42 Khomeini, *Islam and Government*, 28.
43 Ibid., 36.
44 Ibid., 38.
45 Martin, *Khomeini*, 64.
46 Khomeini, *Islam and Government*, 33, 38.
47 Abrahamian, *Khomeinism*. Gray, *Conspiracy Theories in the Arab World*.
48 Martin, *Khomeini*, 31–3.
49 Ibid.
50 Ibid., 44.
51 Ibid.
52 Ibid., 31–2, 44.
53 Ibid.
54 Abrahamian, *Iran Between Two Revolutions*.
55 Ibid., 498–501.

56 Ibid., 504.

57 Axworthy, *Revolutionary Iran*, 99–100.

58 Ibid., 101.

59 Abrahamian, *Iran Between Two Revolutions*, 505.

60 Ibid., 522. Martin, *Khomeini*, 151–2.

61 Abrahamian, *Iran Between Two Revolutions*, 517.

62 Martin, *Khomeini*.

63 Abrahamian, *Iran Between Two Revolutions*, 498.

64 Ibid.

65 Ibid., 528.

66 Ibid., 528–9.

67 Ibid., 525–7.

68 Martin, *Khomeini*, 156–7.

69 Axworthy, *Revolutionary Iran*, 145.

70 Ibid., 146.

71 Ibid., 146–7.

72 Martin, *Khomeini*, 158.

73 Ibid.

74 Ibid., 158–9.

75 As quoted in Martin, *Khomeini*, 160.

76 Abrahamian, *Khomeinism*. Mozaffari, *Islamism*, 120.

77 Martin, *Khomeini*, 162.

78 Ibid., 163.

79 Quoted in Axworthy, *Revolutionary Iran*, 212.

80 Ibid.

81 As cited in Brumberg, 'Islamic Rule and Islamic Social Justice', 42–3.

82 Ibid.

83 Ibid., 60.

84 Axworthy, *Revolutionary Iran*, 274.

85 Roy, *Failure of Political Islam*, 173.

86 Ibid., 174.

87 Ibid., 179.

88 As quoted in Mo'addel, 'Class Struggle', 321.

89 Axworthy, *Revolutionary Iran*, 146–7.

90 Moaddel, 'Class Struggle', 323–4.

91 Ibid., 325–8.

92 Ludwig, 'Iranian Nation', 202.

93 Axworthy, *Revolutionary Iran*, 188–9.

94 Roy, *Failure of Political Islam*, 180.

95 Ludwig, 'Iranian Nation', 210–11.

96 Abrahamian, *Khomeinism*, 15.

Chapter 10

1   Mazrui, *Violence and Thought*, 163–83.

2   Mozaffari, *Islamism*, 143.

3   Tonneson, *Hasan al-Turabi's Search*, 14.

4   See discussion of el-Affendi's views in Magdi Gizouli, 'Hasan al-Turabi: Praying to the State', *Still Sudan*, 25 May 2016, http://sudantribune.com /spip.php?iframe&page=imprimable&id_article=59080.

5   Voll and Esposito, *Makers*, 149. Tonneson, *Hasan al-Turabi's Search*, 14.

6   See, for example, statements quoted in *Sudan Tribune*, 25 March 2012.

7   Woodward, 'Hasan al-Turabi'. See also statements by Bona Malwal quoted in Washington Post, April 1988.

8   El-Affendi, *Turabi's Revolution*, 179.

9   Gallab, *First Islamist Republic*, 102. Moussalli, 'Hasan al-Turabi's Islamist Discourse', 53–5.

10 De Waal and Abdel Salaam, 'Islamism, State Power and Jihad'.

11 Gallab, *First Islamist Republic*, 114.

12 Berridge, *Hasan al-Turabi*, Chapters 1 and 4.

13 Salomon, *For Love of the Prophet*, 175.

14 Ibrahim, *Manichaean Delirium*, 101.

15 Ibid., 350.

16 Ibid., 330.

17 Berridge, *Hasan al-Turabi*, 41–3, 56, 94.

18 Ibid., 48.

19 Ibid.

20 Ibrahim, *Manichaean Delirium*, 348–50.

21 This section is largely based on Chapter 2 of W. J. Berridge, *Hasan al-Turabi*.

22 Al-Turabi interview in al-Ayyam 9 January 1984, cited in Berridge, *Hasan al-Turabi*.

23 This section is largely based on Chapters 4 and 5 of Berridge, *Hasan al-Turabi*.

24 Hasan Makki Muhammad Ahmad, Interview with *al-Sahafa*, 28 November 2004.

25 Abdullahi Ali Ibrahim, 'Al-Turabi Bolsheviki ... Awad Abd al-Raziq Mensheviki', *al-Sahafa*, 20 September 2012.

26 Berridge, *Hasan al-Turabi*. Smith, 'Oxford Handbook'.

27 Al-Turabi, *al-Usul al-Fikr al-Siyasi al-Islami* (1984), reproduced in *Fi al-Fiqh al-Siyasi*, 181. See also Al-Turabi, *Qadaya al-Tajdid*, 27.

28 I owe this concept to Abdullahi Gallab, *First Islamist Republic*, 79–80.

29 Ghasan Sharbal, Interview with Al-Turabi, *al-Wasat*, 1 February 1999.

30 This term was coined by Roger Griffin in *The Nature of Fascism*, 32–6. For the argument, see Mubarak, *Turabi's 'Islamist' Venture*, 103.

31 Mubarak, *Turabi's 'Islamist' Venture*, 101–3.

32 Al-Turabi interview in al-Ayyam 9 January 1984, cited in Berridge, *Hasan al-Turabi*.

33 For the concept of colonial/postcolonial ambivalence, see Bhabha, *Location of Culture*.

34 Cited in Berridge, *Hasan al-Turabi*.

35 Al-Turabi, *Fi al-Fiqh al-Siyasi*, 286.

36 Ibid., 76.

37 Al-Turabi, *The Islamic Movement*, 140.

38 Hasan al-Turabi, 'The Islamic State', 247.

39 This section and the next one are largely based on Chapters 7 and 8 of Berridge, *Hasan al-Turabi*.

40 See al-Turabi's statements quoted in *al-Mithaq*, 24 August 1967, as discussed in Berridge, *Al-Turabi*.

41 Al-Turabi, 'Islam as a Pan-national Movement', 618.

42 Al-Turabi, *al-Shura wa'l-Dimuratiyya*, 15–26. See Berridge, *Hasan al-Turabi* for the questionable historical evidence behind al-Turabi's claims.

43 Al-Turabi, *al-Shura wa'l-Dimuratiyya*, 26.

44 Al-Turabi, 'Islam as a Pan-National Movement', 610.

45 The following section is largely based on Chapters 3 and 7 of Berridge, *Hasan al-Turabi*.

46 Lesch, *Sudan*, 124–5.

47 This section is largely based on Chapter 6 of Berridge, *Hasan al-Turabi*.

48 Burr, *Terrorist Internationale*.

49 Westerlund, 'Action and Reaction', 328.

50 Turner, 'These Young Men'.

51 Westerlund, 'Action and Reaction', Solomon, 'Combatting Islamist Radicalisation in South Africa', 23.

52 Alex De Waal, 'Politics of Destabilization on the Horn', 196–201.

53 Scorgie-Porter, 'Militant Islamists or Borderland Dissidents'.

54 Alex De Waal, 'Politics of Destabilization on the Horn', 204.

55 Westerlund, 'Action and Reaction'.

56 Ibid., 327.

57 Hansen, 'Boko Haram'.

58 Ibid., 561–2.

59 Marchal, 'Islamic Political Dynamics', 125–9, 139.

60 Walker, *Eat the Heart of the Infidel*, 118. Turner, 'These Young Men'.

61 Westerlund, 'Reaction and Action', 317.

62 Ibid., 313.

Chapter 11

1 See Ayubi, *Political Islam*, 35.

2 Moallem, *Warrior Brother, Veiled Sister*, 19–20.

3 'Badriyya Suleiman wa Qawanin September', *al-Rakoba*, 10 March 2018, https://www.alrakoba.net/news-action-show-id-86133.htm (accessed 10 March 2018).

4 Sharabi, *Neo-Patriarchy*.

5 Moallem, *Warrior Brother, Veiled Sister*, 177–9.

6 Ayubi, *Political Islam*, 36.

7 Lapidus, *A History of Islamic Societies*, 852.

8 Lapidus, for instance, argues along these lines. See *A History of Islamic Societies*, 852–3. For a similar Islamist narrative see Al-Turabi, *Emancipation of Women*.

9 Lapidus, *A History of Islamic Societies*, 852–3.

10 DeLong-Bas, *Wahhabi Islam* 187–9. For a similar point with regard to inheritance, see al-Dakhil.

11 El-Fadl, *Speaking in God's Name*, and Doumato, *Getting God's Ear*, as discussed in Al-Rasheed, *A Most Masculine State*, 46.

12 DeLong-Bas, *Wahhabi Islam*, 31.

13 Ibid.

14 Madawi al-Rasheed, *A Most Masculine State*, 48.

15 Qasim Amin, 'The Emancipation of Women and the New Woman', in Kurzmann (ed.), *Modernist Islam*, 64.

16 Kaler, 'Inscribing Gender', 341–2.

17 Ibid., 342–3.

18 El-Ali, *Secularism, Gender and the State*, 54.

19 See, for example, Moallem, *Veiled Sister*. For Algeria, see Fanon, 'Algeria Unveiled', in *A Dying Colonialism*.

20 Mawdudi, *Purdah and the Status of Women in Islam*, 15.

21 Al-Ashari introduction to Mawdudi, *Purdah and the Status of Women in Islam*, iii.

22 Ibid. See also Jackson, *Mawdudi*.

23 Calvert, *Qutb*, 85.

24 See Calvert, *Qutb*, 85 and Jackson, *Mawdudi*, 134. For a good example of the role of colonialism in spreading medicalized sexism to Egypt, see Abugideiri.

25 Mawdudi, *Purdah and the Status of Women in Islam*.

26 Qutb, *Social Justice*, cited in Calvert, *Islamism*, 69.

27 Qutb, *Social Justice* and Mawdudi, *Purdah and the Status of Women in Islam*.

28 Ibid.

29 Mawdudi, *Purdah and the Status of Women in Islam*.

30 Qutb, *Social Justice*, cited in Calvert, *Islamism*, 70.

31 Jackson, *Mawdudi*, 74.

32 Ibid., 50.

33 Shariati, 'Expectations'.

34 Fanon, 'Algeria Unveiled', in *A Dying Colonialism*.

35 Shariati, 'Expectations'.

36 Ibid.

37 Ibid.

38 Ibid.

39 Moallem, *Warrior Brother*, 93.

40 See Chapter 9.

41 Khomeini, 'Address to a Group of Women in Qum'.

42 Ferdows, 'Women and the Islamic Revolution', 292–3. Calvert, *Qutb* and Mawdudi, *Purdah and the Status of Women in Islam*.

43 Afshar, 'Khomeini's Teachings'.

44 Burki, 'Regime Consolidation', 210; Paidar, *Women and the Political Process*, 278.

45 Al-Turabi, *Islamic Movement*, 150–1.

46 Al-Turabi, *Emancipation of Women*, 43.

47 Ibrahim, *Fasad Nazariyya*, 33.

48 *Al-Wasat*, 13 December 1993.

49 Mubarak Tayyib al-Zain, 'Bayna al-Fikr al-Jumhuri wa'l Sha'abi', in *al-Sahafa*, 22 March 2013.

50 Hasan al-Turabi, Interview with *al-Sharq al-Awsat*, 24 April 2006.

51 Ibid.

52 Al-Turabi, *Emancipation of Women*, 52.

53 Ibid.

54 Paidar, *Women and the Political Process*.

55 Burki, 'Regime Consolidation', 215–16.

56 Paidar, *Women and the Political Process*, 342.

57 Burki, 'Regime Consolidation', 210.

58 Berridge, 'Public Order Police'.

59 Berridge, *Hasan al-Turabi*, 306.

60 Al-Rasheed, *A Most Masculine State*.

61 Ibid., 20–3.

62 Shalinsky, 'Women's Roles'.

63 Moghadam, 'Patriatchy, the Taliban, and Politics of Public Space', 19–31.

64 Ibid., 25–6.

65 Ibid., 26.

66 Benazir Bhutto observed of the United States, Saudi and Pakistani backing of the *mujahidin* that 'you are creating a veritable Frankenstein'. See Unger, *House of Bush*, 111.

67 See the arguments of, for example, Miriam Cooke, 'Zaynab al-Ghazali'. This paragraph and the next two are largely based on Cooke as well as Euben and Zaman, *Princeton Readings*, 275–82 and Calvert, *Qutb*, 231, 251–8.

68 Cooke, 'Zaynab Al-Ghazali', 18–20.

69 Shalinsky, 'Women's Roles', 665.

70 Cited in Cooke, 'Zaynab Al-Ghazali', 3.

71 Willemse, 'A Room of One's Own'.

72 Berridge, *Hasan al-Turabi*, 229.

73 Hale, 'Mothers and Militias', 379.

74 Ibid., 380.

75 Hasan al-Turabi, Interview with *al-Sudan al-Hadith*, 2 October 1996.

76 Hale, *Gender Politics in Sudan*, 216.

77 Moallem, *Warrior Brother*, 179.

78 Ibid.

79 Paidar, *Women and the Political Process*, 308.

80 Moallem, *Warrior Brother*, 179.

81 Ibid., 167, 181.

82 Ibid.

83 Ibid.

Chapter 12

1 Gerges, *The Far Enemy*.

2 Roy, *Failure of Political Islam*.

3 For an analysis of the 'near enemy' and 'far enemy' concepts, see Gerges, *The Far Enemy*.

4 Gerges, *The Far Enemy*.

5 Schulze, *A Modern History*, 226.

6 Ibid., 225–9.

7 Kepel, *Jihad*, 63.

8 Zollner, *Muslim Brotherhood*.

9 Gerges, *The Far Enemy*, 91.

10 See, for example, Lia, 'Islamist Uprising', 547.

11 Gerges, *The Far Enemy*, 88.

12 Kepel, *Jihad*, 122–5.

13 Ibid., 131–2. See also Chapter 10.

14 Ibid., 130–3. See also Berridge, *Hasan al-Turabi*.

15 Ibid., 73, 119–20.

16 Hegghammer and Lacroix, 'Rejectionist Islam', 112–13. Schulze, *A Modern History*, 227.

17 Ibid., 114, 117.

18 Ochsenwald, 'Saudi Arabia and Islamic Revival', 276.

19 Musallam, *Qutb*.

20 Kepel, *Jihad*, 75.

21 This paragraph and the next are based on Kepel, *Roots*, 70–92.

22 Faraj, 'Neglected Duty' in Euben and Zaman, *Princeton Readings*, 337.

23 Faraj, 'Neglected Duty'.

24 Gerges, *The Far Enemy*, 89–90.

25 Kepel, *Roots*, 220–1.

26 Gerges, *The Far Enemy*, 141–3.

27 Fandy, 'Egypt's Islamic Group', 611.

28 Kepel, *Roots*, 132, 137.

29 Ibid., 138–43.

30 Ibid., 153–75.

31 Gerges, *The Far Enemy*, 153.

32 Fandy, 'Egypt's Islamic Group', 623.

33 Gerges, *The Far Enemy*, 153–8.

34 Lia, 'Islamist Uprising', 544. Rabil, 'The Syrian Muslim Brotherhood', 77.

35 Rabil, 'The Syrian Muslim Brotherhood', 77–8.

36 Lia, 'Islamist Uprising', 549.

37 Rabil, 'The Syrian Muslim Brotherhood', 78.

38 Ibid. Conduit, 'The patterns of Syrian Uprising', 75.

39 Stora, *Algeria*, 209–11.

40 Hafez, 'Armed Islamist Movements', 573–5.

41 Ibid., 580–91.

42 Calvert, *Islamism*, 162.

43 Stora, *Algeria*, 205–6.

44 Hafez, 'Armed Islamist Movements', 588. Stora, *Algeria*, 206.

45 Hafez, 'Armed Islamist Movements', 587. Turshen, 'Militarism and Islamism', 125.

46 Hudis, *Philosopher of the Barricades*, 133.

47 Hafez, 'Armed Islamist Movements', 587–8.

48 Ibid., 588–9.

49 Calvert, *Islamism*, 163.

50 Gerges, *The Far Enemy*, 2.

51 See Hegghammer, 'Jihadi-Salafis or Revolutionaries?', 259.

52 Gerges, *The Far Enemy*, 81.

53 Ibid., 81–2.

54 Ibid., 136.

55 Calvert, *Islamism*, 205.

56 Bonney, *Jihad*, 350.

57 Ibid.

58 Weinbaum, 'The Afghan Factor in Pakistan's India Policy'. Gerges, *The Far Enemy*, 53–4.

59 Agbiboa, 'Ties that Bind'.

60 Bonney, *Jihad*.

61 Weinbaum, 'The Afghan Factor'.

62 Fredholm, 'Kashmir, Pakistan, India and Beyond'.

63 Cedric Barnes and Harun Hassan, 'The Rise and Fall of Mogadishu's Islamic Courts', *Journal of Eastern African Studies* 1 (2007), 151.

64 Commander Abu Aziz 'Barbaros', 'We Were Looking for Jihad', in Calvert, *Islamism*, 203.

65 Calvert, *Islamism*, 205.

66 Agbiboa, 'Ties that Bind', 588–9, 593.

67 'Profile: Lashkar-e-Taiba', *BBC News*, 3 May 2010, http://news.bbc.co.uk/1/hi/world/south_asia/3181925.stm (accessed 7 March 2018).

68 Bonney, *Jihad*, 350–1.

69 Sluglett and Farouk-Sluglett, *Iraq since 1958*, 196.

70 Ibid., 200.

71 ICG, 'Shi'ite Politics in Iraq', 2–3.

72 Ibid., 4.

73 Sluglett and Farouk-Sluglett, *Iraq Since 1958*.

74 ICG, 'Shi'ite Politics in Iraq', 5–6.

75 Dawisha, *Iraq: From Independence to Occupation*.

76 Ibid., 203.

77 Ibid., 187–91.

78 Bonney, *Jihad*, 295. Saouli, 'Hizbullah and the Civilizing Process', 932.

79   Bonney, *Jihad*, 295–300.

80   Saouli, 'Hizbullah and the Civilizing Process', 932–6.

81   Bonney, *Jihad*, 304.

82   Gerges, *The Far Enemy*, 43–79.

83   Hroub, *Hamas: A Beginner's Guide*, 11–13.

84   Dunning, 'Islam and Resistance', 290–1.

85   Hamas Covenant (1988), available at *The Avalon Project*, http://avalon.law.yale.edu/20th_century/hamas.asp.

86   Hroub, *Hamas: A Beginner's Guide*, 29–33.

87   Litvak, 'Martyrdom is Life', 716, 719. Hroub, *Hamas: A Beginner's Guide*.

88   Dunning, 'Islam and Resistance', 302.

89   Zollner, *Hudaybi*, 45.

90   Litvak, 'Martyrdom is Life', 718.

91   Ibid., 719.

92   Ibid., 725–6.

93   Ziad Abu Amr, 'Shaikh Ahmad Yassin'.

94   Hroub, *Hamas*, 53–6.

95   See, for example, Hroub, *Hamas*, 34.

96   Zia-Ibrahimi, 'Arab Invasion'.

97   The Hamas Covenant (1988), available at the *Avalon Project*, http://avalon.law.yale.edu/20th_century/hamas.asp (accessed 7 March 2018).

98   Hroub, *Hamas*, 24.

99   Litvak, 'The Anti-Semitism of Hamas', 43.

100 Except where otherwise noted, this section is based on Roy, 'Islamic Radicalism in Afghanistan and Pakistan' and Rashid, *Taliban*.

101 Roy, 'Islamic Radicalism in Afghanistan and Pakistan', 6. One senior member of the Hizb-i-Islami went as far to observe that 'Islam does not present a blueprint for an Islamic government'.

102 Mahendrarajah, 'Saudi Arabia, Wahhabism and the Taliban', 383. Roy, 'Islamic Radicalism in Afghanistan and Pakistan'.

103 Such as the practice of women being required to marry their brothers-in-law after the deaths of their husbands. See Euben and Zaman, *Princeton Readings*, 412.

104 Bonney, *Jihad*, 340.

105 Brahimi, 'The Taliban's Evolving Ideology', 6.

106 Ahmed, *Taliban*.

107 Brahimi, 'The Taliban's Evolving Ideology', 5.

108 Ibid., 6.

109 Ibid., 7–12.

110 Ibid., 7–8.

111 Kenney, *Muslim Rebels*.

112 Ibid., 126–31.

113 Ibid., 129.

114 Hegghammer, 'Jihadi-Salafis or Revolutionaries'?, 246–8.

115 Kenney, *Muslim Rebels*, 136.

116 As quoted in Kenney, *Muslim Rebels*, 137–8.

117 Hassan, 'Modern Interpretations and Misinterpretations', 356–7; Michot, *Muslims Under Non-Muslim Rule*, 49.

118 As quoted in Kenney, *Muslim Rebels*, 138.

119 Hassan, 'Modern Interpretations and Misinterpretations', 356; Michot, *Muslims Under Non-Muslim Rule*, 38, 49.

120 See Abd al-Salam Faraj, 'The Neglected Suty', cited in *Princeton Readings*, 328.

121 Hassan, 'Ibn Taymiyya', 356–7.

122 Michot and Taymiyya, *Muslims Under Non-Muslim Rule*.

123 Ibid., 38.

124 Ibid., 61.

125 Abdullah Azzam. 'The Entire Islamic Land', in Calvert, *Islamism*, 196.

126 Bonney, *Jihad*, 344.

127 Roy, 'Islamic Radicalism in Afghanistan and Pakistan', 7.

128 Hegghammer, 'Jihadi-Salafis or Revolutionaries?'

Chapter 13

1 Wood, 'What ISIS Really Wants'.

2 Byman, *Al-Qaeda, Islamic State*, 4. Gerges, *The Far Enemy*, 81.

3 Gerges, *The Far Enemy*, 68–70, 83–4.

4 Ibid., 80–4.

5 Byman, *Al-Qaeda, Islamic State*, 5. Gerges, *The Far Enemy*, 83–4.

6 Byman, *Al-Qaeda, Islamic State*, 7.

7 Gerges, *The Far Enemy*, 75–6.

8 Ibid., 84–7.

9 Ibid., 88.

10 Byman, *Al-Qaeda, Islamic State*, 7.

11 Gerges, *The Far Enemy*, 135–6.

12 Byman, *Al-Qaeda, Islamic State*, 8–9. Gerges, *The Far Enemy*, 131–7.

13 Gerges, *The Far Enemy*, 121.

14 Byman, *Al-Qaeda, Islamic State*, 16.

15 Ibid., 10.

16 Gerges, *The Far Enemy*, 148.

17 Byman, *Al-Qaeda, Islamic State*, 16.

18 Gerges, *The Far Enemy*, 130–1.

19 Bin Laden, 'Jihad against Jews and Crusaders', in Calvert, *Islamism*, 227.

20 Byman, *Al-Qa'eda, The Islamic State*, 25.

21 Ibid., 30.

22 Ibid., 31–5.

23 Bin Laden, 'Letter to America'.

24 Bin Laden, 'Jihad against Jews and Crusaders' in Calvert, *Islamism*, 227.

25 Hegghammer, *Jihad in Saudi Arabia*, 228–9.

26 Gerges, *The Far Enemy*, 203.

27 Ibid., 128.

28 Ibid., 126–7.

29 Byman, *Al-Qa'eda, The Islamic State*, 41–2.

30 Ibid., 42–3.

31 Ibid., 43–4.

32 Hegghammer, *Jihad in Saudi Arabia*.

33 See last chapter.

34 Maher, *Salafi-Jihadism*, 105.

35 McCants, *ISIS Apocalypse*, 10–11.

36 See Chapter 10.

37 McCants, *ISIS Apocalypse*, 12–13.

38 Ibid., 13.

39 Ibid., 14.

40 Ibid., 15.

41 Ibid., 19.

42 Ibid., 45.

43 Roy, *Jihad and Death*, 80.

44 Ibid.

45 McCants, *ISIS Apocalypse*, 79–80, 136.

46 Graeme Wood, *Way of Strangers*, 54.

47 Byman, *Al-Qa'eda, Islamic State*, 173.

48 Hamdan, 'Breaker of Barriers'.

49 Ibid.

50 Fawaz A. Gerges, 'The Strategic Logic of the Islamic State', *The Strategist*, 11 August 2016, https://www.aspistrategist.org.au/strategic-logic-islamic-state/ (accessed 27 February 2018).

51 See, for example, Stephen Schwartz and Irfan al-Alawi, 'No Saudi Surprise in 9/11 Commission's '28 Pages', *The Huffington Post*, 20 July 2017, https://www.huffingtonpost.com/stephen-schwartz/no-saudi-surprises-in-911_b_11051460.html (accessed 27 February 2018).

52 Byman, *Al-Qaeda, The Islamic State and the Global Jihadi Movement*.

53 Gerges, *The Far Enemy*, 135.

54 Hegghammer, *Jihad in Saudi Arabia*, 28, 37.

55 Maher, *Salafi-Jihadism*, 136–7.

56 Ibid., 135–40.

57 Firro, 'Takfir', 784.

58 Ibid.

59 Al-Ibrahim, 'ISIS, Wahhabism and Takfir', 409–10.

60 DeLong-Bas, *Wahhabi Islam*, 262–4.

61 Ibid., 265.

62 Gerges, *The Far Enemy*, 4–5.

63 Ibid., 114, 205.

64 Safar al-Hawali, 'Mu'amira ala al-Islam, *alhawali.com*, [no date], goo.gl/gwMr87.

65 Maher, *Salafi-Jihadism*, 131–2.

66 Ibid., 140–1.

67 Gerges, *ISIS*, 38.

68 Bin Laden, 'Jihad against Jews and Crusaders', 227.

69 Gerges, *ISIS*, 83.

70 Michot, views cited in Wood, *Way of Strangers*, 240.

71 Wood, *Way of Strangers*, 242.

72 McCants, *ISIS Apocalypse*, 131–3.

73 Ibid., 102–11.

74 Ibid., 8–9.

75 Roy, *Jihad and Death*, 63.

76 Roy, *Globalized Islam*, 43.

77 Ibid., 46.

78 Bin Laden, 'Letter to America'.

79 Graeme Wood, 'What ISIS Really Wants'.

80 Ibid.

81 Maher, *Salafi-Jihadism*, 5.

82 Dagli, 'Phony Islam of ISIS'.

83 Ibid.

84 Ibid.

85 Gerges, *ISIS*, 26–7.

86 Berridge, *Hasan al-Turabi*, 206.

87 Wood, *Way of Strangers*, 67.

88 Maher, *Salafi-Jihadism*, 209.

89 Wood, *Way of Strangers*, 67.

90 Ibid., 47–8.

91 McCants, *ISIS Apocalypse*, 127.

92 Mehdi Hasan, 'How Islamic is Islamic State?', *New Statesman*, 10 March 2015, https://www.newstatesman.com/world-affairs/2015/03/mehdi-hasan-how-islamic-islamic-state (accessed 6 March 2018).

93 Gerges, *ISIS*, 156.

94 Ibid., 141–2, 153–5.

95 Atwan, *Secret History*, 90.

96 Antony Barnett, 'Suicide Bombs are a Duty, says Islamic Scholar', *The Guardian*, 28 August 2005, https://www.theguardian.com/politics/2005/aug/28/uk.terrorism (accessed 28 February 2018).

97 Atwan, *Secret History*, 86.

98 Ibid., 86–7.

99 Vidino, 'Islamism and the West'.

100 Ibid.

101 Roy, *Jihad and Death*, 8.

102 Ibid., 20–7.

103 Ibid., 3–4, 9.

104 Francois Burgat, 'A Response to Olivier Roy's "Islamisation of Radicalism"', *The New Arab*, 15 December 2015, https://www.alaraby.co.uk/english/comment/2015/12/15/a-response-to-olivier-roys-islamisation-of-radicalism.

105 Adam Nossiter, 'That Ignoramus: 2 French Scholars of Radical Islam Turn Bitter Rivals', *New York Times*, 12 July 2016, https://www.nytimes.com/2016/07/13/world/europe/france-radical-islam.html (visited 6 March 2016). See also Robert F. Worth, 'The Professor and the Jihadi', *The New York Times Magazine,* 5 April 2017, https://www.nytimes.com/2017/04/05/magazine/france-election-gilles-kepel-islam.html (visited 10 June 2018).

Chapter 14

1 Roy, *Failure of Political Islam*.

2 Bayat, *Making Islam Democratic*, 11.

3 Cavatorta and Merone, 'Post-Islamism'.

4 For this term, see Wolf, *Political Islam*, 95.

5 Brumberg, 'The Trap of Liberalized Autocracy'.

6 Soage and Franganillo, 'The Muslim Brothers in Egypt', 44.

7 Ibid., 46.

8 El-Ghobashy, 'Metamorphosis', 385.

9 Ibid.

10 Ibid.

11 Bayat, *Making Islam Democratic*, 186.

12 Except where noted, the following paragraphs are based on Wolf, *Political Islam in Tunisia*, 65–72, 93–4; Voll and Esposito, *Makers*, 93–5.

13 Wolf, *Political Islam in Tunisia*, 95. Berridge, *Hasan al-Turabi*, 308.

14 Sebastian, 'Islamist Movements Engaging with Democracy', 263.

15 Ibid., 262.

16 Ibid., 263.

17 Wolf, *Political Islam*, 111–12.

18 Bayat, *Making Islam Democratic*, 167–74.

19 Wiktorowicz, 'Islamists, the State and Co-operation in Jordan'.

20 Lefèvre, 'Balancing Act', 627.

21 Valla Valkili, 'Abolkarim Soroush', 152; Chatterjee, *Shariati*, 186.

22 Chatterjee, *Shariati*. Valla Valkili, 'Abolkarim Soroush'.

23 Valla Valkili, 'Abolkarim Soroush', 157.

24 Ibid.

25 Chatterjee, *Shariati*.

26 Bayat, *Making Islam Democratic*, 68.

27 Ibid., 69.

28 Ibid., 62–3.

29 Ibid., 109–12, 127–30.

30 Afshari and Underwood, 'The Green Wave'.

31 Grinberg, 'Iranian Reformists: Between Moderation and Revolution'.

32 Berridge, *Hasan al-Turabi*, 230.

33 Magdi Gizouli, 'Bashir, the ICC, and Jirtig', *Sudan Tribune*, 21 June 2015.

34 'Sudan's PCP Expects Three Ministers and Seven Seats in New Government', *DabangaSudan*, 4 May 2017, https://www.dabangasudan.org/en/all-news /article/sudan-s-pcp-expects-three-ministers-and-seven-seats-in-new-govt.

35 Berridge, 'Ambiguous Role'.

36 Berridge, *Hasan al-Turabi*, 305.

37 Ibid., 302.

38 Abdullah Hussein al-Attar, 'Al-Nizam al-Khalif ... Utruha al-Turabi al-Jadida li-hall mashakil al-Sudan', *Al-Rakoba*, 26 April 2015.

39 Saouli, 'Hizbullah and the Civilizing Process'.

40 Ibid.

41 Joseph Daher, 'Reassessing Hizbullah's Socioeconomic Policies in Lebanon'.

42 Hroub, *Hamas*.

43 Ibid., 140–1.

44 Bhasin and Hallward, 'Hamas as a Political Party'.

45 Hroub, *Hamas*, 138.

46 CRS report for Congress, 'Palestinian Elections', https://fas.org/sgp/crs/mideast/RL33269.pdf.

47 Hroub, *Hamas*.

48 See, for example, Bhasin and Hallward, 'Hamas as a Political Party'.

49 The next two paragraphs are mainly based on Phillips, *An Uncertain Ally*. Phillips, *An Uncertain Ally*.

50 Phillips, *An Uncertain Ally*, 8–9.

51 Ibid., 10.

52 BBC News, 'Recep Tayyip Erdogan: Turkey's Pugnacious President', 17 April 2017, http://www.bbc.co.uk/news/world-europe-13746679.

53 Phillips, *An Uncertain Ally*, 27, 166–72.

54 Hale and Ozbudun, *Islamism, Democracy and Liberalism in Turkey*.

55 Phillips, *An Uncertain Ally*, 21.

56 Halil Karaveli, 'Erdogan's Journey', 122.

57 Ibid.

58 Phillips, *An Uncertain Ally*, 22.

59 Azeri, 'The July 15 Coup Attempt in Turkey'.

60 Phillips, *An Uncertain Ally*, 171.

61 Cagaptay, *The New Sultan*.

62 Mustafa Akyol, 'Does Erdogan Want His Own Islamic State?', *Al-Monitor*, 15 April 2016.

63 Cagaptay, *The New Sultan*, 129.

64 Phillips, *An Uncertain Ally*, 138.

65 Chris York, 'Turkish Newspaper Calls Orlando Shooting Victims "Perverts"', *Huffington Post*, 13 June 2016, http://www.huffingtonpost.co.uk/entry/yeni-akit-orlando-mass-shooting_uk_575e5dc1e4b041514369e4b1.

66 Laurence Louer, 'A Decline of Identity Politics', *International Journal of Middle Eastern Studies* 43 (2011), 389–90.

67 'Egypt's Islamist Parties win Elections to Parliament', *BBC News*, 21 January 2012, http://www.bbc.co.uk/news/world-middle-east-16665748.

68 David D. Kirkpatrick, 'Named Egypt's Winner, Islamist Makes History', *New York Times*, 24 June 2012, http://www.nytimes.com/2012/06/25/world/middleeast/mohamed-morsi-of-muslim-brotherhood-declared-as-egypts-president.html.

69 Wolf, *Political Islam*, 133.

70 Larbi Sadiki, 'Libya's Arab Spring', 309.

71 Wolf, *Political Islam*, 130–1.

72 Ibid., 133–4.

73 Cavatorta and Merone, 'Post-Islamism'.

74 Wolf, *Political Islam*, 152–6.

75 Ibid., 156.

76 Ibid., 156–7.

77 Hamid, McCants and Dar, 'Islamism after the Arab Spring'.

78 Hamid, *Temptations of Power*, 167–74.

79 'Egypt's Islamist Parties'.

80 Hamid, *Temptations of Power*, 150.

81 Ibid., 153–4.

82 Shahira Amin, 'For Fear of Morsi, Egypt's Secularists got Something far Worse', *Middle East Eye*, 26 June 2015, http://www.middleeasteye.net/columns/fear-morsi-egypt-s-secularists-got-something-worse-1258985653 (accessed 1 July 2017).

83 Patrick Kingsley, 'How Mohamed Morsi, Egypt's First Elected President, End up on Death Row', *The Guardian*, Monday 1 June 2015, https://www.theguardian.com/world/2015/jun/01/mohamed-morsi-execution-death-sentence-egypt.

84 Hamid, McCants and Dar, 'Islamism after the Arab Spring'.

BIBLIOGRAPHY

Abduh, Muhammad, *The Theology of Unity*, trans. Ishaq Musa'ad and Kenneth Cragg (Kuala Lumpur: Islamic Book Trust, 2004).

Abrahamian, Ervand, 'Ali Shariati: The Ideologue of the Iranian Revolution,' *MERIP Reports* 102 (January 1982), 24–8.

Abrahamian, Ervand, *Iran Between Two Revolutions* (Princeton: Princeton University Press, 1982).

Abrahamian, Ervand, *Khomeinism: Essays on the Islamic Republic* (London: I.B. Tauris, 1993).

Abu Amr, Ziad, 'Shaykh Ahmad Yasin and the Origins of Hamas', in R. Scott Appleby (ed.), *Spokesmen for the Despised: Fundamentalist Leaders of the Middle East* (Chicago: Chicago University Press, 1997), 225–56.

Abu Rabi, Ibrahim, *Intellectual Origins of Islamic Resurgence in the Modern Arab World* (Albany: SUNY Press, 1995).

Abugideiri, Hibba, 'The Scientisation of Culture: Colonial Medicine's Construction of Egyptian Womanhood, 1893-1929', *Gender & History* 16 (2004), 83–98.

Achar, Gilbert, 'Fascism in the Middle East and North Africa', in Amal Ghazzal and Jens Hansen (eds), *The Oxford Handbook of Contemporary Middle Eastern and North African History* (Oxford: Oxford University Press, 2015), http://www.oxfordhandbooks.com/view/10.1093/oxfordhb/9780199672530.001.0001/oxfordhb-9780199672530-e-30

Afshar, Haleh, 'Khomeini's Teachings and their Implications for Women', *Feminist Review* 12 (1982), 59–72.

Afshari, Ali and Underwood, H. Graham, 'The Green Wave', *Journal of Democracy* 20 (2009), 6–10.

Agbiboa, Daniel E., 'Ties that Bind: The Evolution and Links of al-Shabab', *Round Table: The Commonwealth Journal of International Affairs* 103 (2014), 581–97.

Ahmad, Irfan, *Islamism and Democracy in India: The Transformation of Jamaat-e-Islami* (Princeton: Princeton University Press, 2009).

Ahmad, Irfan, 'Theorizing Islam and Democracy: Jamaat-e-Islami in India', *Philosophy and Social Criticism* 37 (2011), 459–70.

Ahmed, Rashid, *Taleban: The Power of Militant Islam in Afghanistan and Beyond* (London: I.B. Tauris, 2010).

Al-Azm, Sadik, 'Orientalism, Occidentalism and Islamism: A Keynote Address to "Orientalism and Fundamentalism in Islamic and Judaic Critique: A Conference Honouring Sadik al-Azm', *Comparative Studies of Asia, South Africa and the Middle East* 30 (2010), 6–13.

Al-Banna, Hasan, 'Peace in Islam' (1948), translated at http://www.t.islamicbulletin.org/free_downloads/resources/peace_in_islam.pdf

Al-Banna, Hasan, *Risalat al-Jihad* (n.d.), available at http://www.ikhwanwiki.com/
index.php?title=%D8%B1%D8%B3%D8%A7%D9%84%D8%A9_%D8%A
7%D9%84%D8%AC%D9%87%D8%A7%D8%AF

Al-Gaddafi, Mu'ammar, *The Green Book* (London: Martin Brian & O'Keefe, 1976).

Ali, M. Athar, 'The Passing of Empire: The Mughal Case', *Modern Asian Studies* 9
(1975), 385–96.

Al-Ibrahim, Bader, 'ISIS, Wahhabism and Takfir', *Contemporary Arab Affairs* 8
(2015), 408–15.

Ali, Haydar Ibrahim, *Suqut al-Mashroua al-Hadari* (Khartoum: Markaz al-Dirasat
al-Sudaniyya, 2004).

Al-Jamil, Tariq, 'Ibn Taymiyya and Ibn Mutahhar al-Hilli: Shi'i Polemics and the
Struggle for Religious Authority in Medieval Islam', in Yossef Rapoport and
Shahab Ahmed (eds), *Ibn Taymiyya and his Times* (Oxford: Oxford University
Press, 2010).

al-Mawdudi, Abu'l-Ala, *Islamic Law and Constitution* (Delhi: Taj Company, 1986).

al-Mawdudi, Abu'l-Ala, *Islam Today* (n.d.), accessed via https://www.muslim-
library.com/dl/books/English_Islam_Today.pdf (accessed February 26 2018).

al-Mawdudi, Abu'l-Ala, *Jihad in Islam* (Lahore: Islamic Publications, 1980).

al-Mawdudi, Abu'l-Ala, *Purdah and the Status of Woman in Islam*, trans. al.Ash'ari
(Delhi: Markazi Maktaba Islami, 1974).

Al-Rasheed, Madawi, *A History of Saudi Arabia* (Cambridge: Cambridge
University Press, 2010).

Al-Rasheed, Madawi, *A Most Masculine State: Gender, Politics and Religion in
Saudi Arabia* (Cambridge: Cambridge University Press, 2013).

al-Turabi, Hasan, *Emancipation of Women: An Islamic Perspective*, 2nd edition,
(London: Muslim Information Centre, 2000).

al-Turabi, Hasan, *Fi al-Fiqh al-Siyasi* (Beirut: Dar al-Arabiyya li'l-Ulum, 2010).

al-Turabi, Hasan, 'Islam as a Pan-national Movement and Nation-states: An
Islamic Doctrine of Human Association', *Royal Society of Arts Journal* (August/
September 1992).

al-Turabi, Hasan, trans. Abdelwahab El-Affendi, *The Islamic Movement in Sudan*
(Beirut: Arab Scientific Publishers, 2009).

al-Turabi, Hasan, *al-Shura wa'l-Dimuqratiyya* (Khartoum: Alam al-'Alaniyah,
2000).

al-Turabi, Hasan, *Tajdid al-Fikr al-Islami* (Al-Ribat: Dar al-Qarafi, 1993).

al-Turabi, Hasan, *Tajdid Usul al-Fiqh al-Islami* (Tunis: Dar al-Ra'id, 1981).

Anscombe, Frederick F., 'Islam in the Age of Ottoman Reform', *Past and Present*
208 (2010), 159–89.

Atwan, Abdel Bari, *The Secret History of al-Qa'ida* (London: Abacus, 2007).

Axworthy, Michael, *Revolutionary Iran: A History of the Islamic Republic*
(London: Penguin Books, 2014).

Ayubi, Nazih N., *Over-stating the Arab State: Politics and Society in the Middle
East* (London: I.B. Tauris, 1996).

Ayubi, Nazih J., *Political Islam: Religion and Politics in the Arab World* (London:
Routledge, 1991).

Azeri, Siyaves, 'The July 15 Coup Attempt in Turkey: The Erdogan–Gulen
Confrontation and the Fall of "Moderate" Political Islam', *Critique* 44 (2016),
465–78.

Badri, Malik, 'A Tribute to Mawlana Mawdudi from an Autobiographical Point of
View', *Muslim World* 93 (2003), 487–502.

Bakhash, Shaul, *The Reign of the Ayatollahs: Iran and the Islamic Revolution* (London: Unwin, 1986).

Bale, Jeffrey M., 'Islamism and Totalitarianism', *Totalitarian Movements and Political Religions* 10 (2009), 73–96.

Barnes, Cedric and Hassan, Harun, 'The Rise and Fall of Mogadishu's Islamic Courts', *Journal of Eastern African Studies* 1 (2007), 151–60.

Baron, Beth, *The Orphan Scandal: Christian Missionaries and the Rise of the Muslim Brotherhood* (Palo Alto, CA: Stanford University Press, 2014).

Baroudi, Sami E., 'The Islamic Realism of Sheikh Yusuf Qaradawi (1926-) and Sayyid Mohammad Hussein Fadlallah (1935-2010)', *Middle Eastern Studies* 43 (2016), 94–114.

Bayat, Asef, *Making Islam Democratic: Social Movements and the Post-Islamist Turn* (Stanford: Stanford University Press, 2007).

Bazzano, Elliott A., 'Ibn Taymiyya, Radical Polymath, Part I: Scholarly Perceptions', *Religion Compass* 9 (2015), 100–16.

Bazzano, Elliott A., 'Ibn Taymiyya, Radical Polymath, Part II: Intellectual Contributions', *Religion Compass* 9 (2015), 117–39.

Bearman, Jonathon, *Qadhafi's Libya* (London: Zed Books, 1986).

Behrooz, Maziar, *Rebels with a Cause: The Failure of the Left in Iran* (London: I.B. Tauris, 1994).

Bennison, Amira K., 'The "New Order" and Islamic Order: The Introduction of the Niẓāmī Army in the Western Maghrib and Its Legitimation, 1830-73', *International Journal of Middle East Studies* 36 (2004), 591–612.

Bergesen, Albert, *The Sayyid Qutb Reader: Selected Readings on Politics, Religion and Society* (London: Routledge, 2008).

Berkey, Jonathan Porter, *The Formation of Islam: Religion and Society in the Near East, 600-1800* (New York: Cambridge University Press, 2003).

Berman, Paul, *Terror and Liberalism* (London: W.W. Norton, 2003).

Berridge, W. J., 'The Ambiguous Role of the Popular, Society and Public Order Police in Sudan, 1983-2011', *Middle Eastern Studies* 49 (2013), 528–46.

Berridge, W. J., *Civil Uprisings in Modern Sudan: The 'Khartoum Springs' of 1964 and 1985* (London: Bloomsbury, 2015).

Berridge, W. J., *Hasan al-Turabi: Islamist Politics and Democracy in Sudan* (Cambridge: Cambridge University Press, 2017).

Berridge, W. J., 'Islamism and the Instrumentalization of Conspiracism', in Absjorn Dyrendal, David Robertson and Egil Asprem (eds), *Handbook of Conspiracy Theory and Contemporary Religion* (Brill: forthcoming).

Bhasin, Tavishi and Hallward, Maia, 'Hamas as a Political Party: Democratization in the Palestinian Territories', *Terrorism and Political Violence* 25 (2013), 75–83.

Black, Anthony, *The History of Islamic Political Thought: From the Prophet to the Present* (Edinburgh: Edinburgh University Press, 2012).

Bodansky, Yossef, *Bin Laden: The Man who Declared War on America* (New York: Forum, 1999).

Bonnefoy, Laurent, Review of DeLong-Bas, Natana, J., *Wahhabi Islam: from Revival and Reform to Global Jihad* (Oxford: Oxford University Press, 2004), *Journal of Islamic Studies* 17 (2006), 371–2.

Bonney, Richard, *Jihad: From the Qu'ran to Bin Laden* (Basingstoke: Palgrave Macmillan, 2007).

Brahimi, Alia, 'The Taliban's Evolving Ideology' (LSE local governance, 2010), http://www.lse.ac.uk/globalGovernance/publications/workingPapers/WP022010.pdf

Browers, M., 'Rethinking Post-Islamism and the study of changes in Islamist ideology', *Project on Middle East Political Science* 24 (2014), 16–19.

Brown, Daniel W., *Rethinking Tradition in Modern Islamic Thought* (Cambridge: Cambridge University Press, 1999).

Brumberg, Daniel, 'Democratization in the Arab World? The Trap of Liberalized Autocracy', *Journal of Democracy* 13 (2002), 56–68.

Brumberg, Daniel, 'Khomeini's Legacy: Islamic Rule and Islamic Social Justice', in R. Scott Appleby (ed.), *Spokesmen for the Despised: Fundamentalist Leaders of the Middle East* (Chicago: Chicago University Press, 1997), 16–82.

Burgat, François, *Face to Face with Political Islam* (London: I.B. Tauris, 2003).

Burke, Jason, *Al-Qaeda*, 3rd edition (London: Penguin, 2007).

Burki, Shireen Khan, 'Regime Consolidation and Female Status in a Fledgling Theocracy: Khomeini's Vilayat-e-Fiqh, 1979-1989', *Middle Eastern Studies* 51 (2015), 208–33.

Burr, J. Millard, *The Terrorists' Internationale: The Khartoum Venue* (Arizona: American Centre for Democracy, 2009).

Burr, J. Millard and Collins, Robert O., *Sudan in Turmoil: Hasan al-Turabi and the Islamist State, 1989-2003* (Princeton, NJ: Markus Wiener, 2010).

Butko, Thomas J., 'Revelation or Revolution: a Gramscian Approach to the Rise of Political Islam', *British Journal of Middle Eastern Studies* 31 (2004), 141–62.

Byman, Daniel, *Al-Qaeda, the Islamic State and the Global Jihadist Movement: What Everyone Needs to Know* (New York: Oxford University Press, 2015).

Cagaptay, Soner, *The New Sultan: Erdogan and the Crisis of Modern Turkey* (London: I.B. Tauris, 2017).

Cain, P. J. and Hopkins, A. G., *British Imperialism: 1688-2000* (Harlow: Longman, 2001).

Calvert, John, *Sayyid Qutb and the Origins of Radical Islamism* (London: Hurst and Company, 2013).

Calvert, John, *Islamism: A Documentary and Reference Guide* (Westport: Greenwood Press, 2008).

Cavatorta, Francesco and Merone, Fabio, 'Moderation through Exclusion? The Journey of the Tunisian *Ennahda* from Fundamentalist to Conservative Party', *Democratization* 20 (2013), 857–75.

Cavatorta, Francesco and Merone, Fabio, 'Post-Islamism, Ideological Evolution and "La *Tunisianité*" of the Tunisian Islamist Party *Ennahda*', *Journal of Political Ideologies* 20 (2015), 27–42.

Chamberlain, Michael, 'Military Patronage States and the Frontier', in Youssef M. Choueiri (ed.), *A Companion to the History of the Middle East* (Oxford: Blackwell, 2008), 135–53.

Chamkhi, Tarek, 'Neo-Islamism in the post-Arab Spring', *Contemporary Politics* 20 (2014), 453–68.

Chatterjee, Kingshuk, *'Ali Shari'ati and the Shaping of Political Islam in Iran* (New York: Palgrave Macmillan, 2011).

Choueiri, Youssef M., *Islamic Fundamentalism: The Story of Islamist Movements*, 3rd edition (London: Continuum, 2010).

Choueiri, Youssef M. (ed.), *A Companion to the History of the Middle East* (Oxford: Blackwell, 2008).

Commins, David Dean, *The Mission and the Kingdom: Wahhabi Power behind the Saudi Throne* (London: I.B. Tauris, 2016).

Conduit, Dara, 'The Patterns of Syrian Uprising: Comparing Hama in 1980-1982 and Homs in 2011', *British Journal of Middle Eastern Studies* 44 (2017), 73–87.

Cook, Michael, 'On the Origins of Wahhabism', *The Royal Asiatic Society* 2 (1992), 191–202.

Cooke, Miriam, 'Zaynab al-Ghazali: Saint or Subversive?', *Die Welt des Islams* 34 (1994), 1–20.

Currie, James Muhammad Dawud, 'Kadizadeli Ottoman Scholarship, Muhammad Ibn Abd al-Wahhab, and the Rise of the Saudi State', *Journal of Islamic Studies* 26 (2015), 265–88.

Daher, Joseph, 'Reassessing Hizbullah's Socioeconomic Policies in Lebanon', *The Middle East Journal* 70 (2016), 339–418.

Dakhil, Khalid S., 'Wahhabism as an Ideology of State Formation', in Mohammed Ayoob and Hasan Kosebalaban (eds), *Religion and Politics in Saudi Arabia: Wahhabism and the State* (London: Lynne Rienner Publishers, 2009), 23–38.

Dallal, Ahmad, 'The Origins and Objectives of Islamic Revivalist Thought, 1750-1850', *Journal of the American Oriental Society* 113 (1993), 341–59.

Daly, M. W., *Empire on the Nile: The Anglo-Egyptian Sudan, 1898-1934* (Cambridge: Cambridge University Press, 2002).

Dawisha, Adeed, *Arab Nationalism in the Twentieth Century: From Triumph to Despair* (Princeton: Princeton University Press, 2003).

Dawisha, Adeed, *Iraq: A Political History from Independence to Occupation* (Oxford: Princeton University Press, 2009).

DeLong-Bas, Natana J., *Wahhabi Islam: from Revival and Reform to Global Jihad* (Oxford: Oxford University Press, 2004).

Denouex, Guilian, 'The Forgotten Swamp: Navigating Political Islam', in Frédéric Volpi (ed.), *Political Islam: A Critical Reader* (New York: Routledge, 2011), 55–79.

Denouex, Guilian, *Urban Unrest in the Middle East: A Comparative Study of Informal Networks in Egypt, Iran and Lebanon* (Albany: SUNY Press, 1993).

Devji, Faisal, 'ISIS: Haunted by Sovereignty', *Sp!ked Review* December 2015, http://www.spiked-online.com/spiked-review/article/isis-haunted-by-sovereignty/17680#.V7dRlTV7xDo/

De Waal, Alex, 'The Politics of Destabilization in the Horn, 1989-2001', in Alex De Waal (ed.), *Islamism and its Enemies in the Horn of Africa* (London: Hurst, 2004), 182–230.

De Waal, Alex and Abdel Salam, A. H., 'Islamism, State Power and *Jihad* in Sudan', in Alex de Waal (ed.), *Islamism and Its Enemies in the Horn of Africa* (London: Hurst and Company, 2004), 71–113.

De Waal, Alex and Salam, Abdel, 'On the Failure and Persistence of Jihad', in Alex De Waal (ed.), *Islamism and its Enemies in the Horn of Africa* (London: Hurst, 2004), 21–70.

Dobbin, Christine, 'Islamic Revivalism in Minangkabua at the Turn of the Nineteenth Century', *Modern Asian Studies* 8 (1974), 319–45.

Donner, F. M., 'The Formation of the Islamic State', *Journal of the American Oriental Society* 106 (1986), 283–96.

Doumato, Eleanor, *Getting God's Ear: Women, Islam and Healing in Saudi Arabia and the Gulf* (New York: Columbia University Press, 2000).

Dresh, Paul, 'Arabia till the end of the First World War', in Francis Robinson (ed.), *The New Cambridge History of Islam Volume 5: The Islamic World in the Era of Western Dominance* (Cambridge: Cambridge University Press, 2010), 134–53.

Dunning, Tristan, 'Islam and Resistance: Hamas, Ideology and Islamic Values in Palestine', *Critical Studies on Terrorism* 8 (2015), 284–305.

Edwards, Beverly Milton, 'Politics and Religion', in Youssef M. Choueiri (ed.), *A Companion to the History of the Middle East* (Oxford: Blackwell, 2008), 444–61.

El-Affendi, Abdelwahab, *Turabi's Revolution: Islam and Power in the Sudan* (London: Grey Seal, 1991).

El Fadl, Khaled Abou, *Speaking in God's Name: Islamic Law, Authority, and Women* (Oxford: Oneworld Publications, 2014).

El-Ghobashy, Mona, 'Metamorphosis of the Egyptian Muslim Brothers', *International Journal of Middle East Studies* 37 (2005), 373–95.

El Moudden, Abderrahmane, 'The Idea of the Caliphate between Moroccans and Ottomans: Political and Symbolic Stakes in the 16th and 17th Century Maghrib', *Studia Islamica* 92 (1995), 103–12.

El Rouayheb, Khalil, 'The Myth of the "Triumph of Fanaticism" in the Seventeenth Century Ottoman Empire', *Die Welt Des Islams* 48 (2008), 196–221.

El Rouayheb, Khalil, 'From Ibn Hajar al-Haytami to Khayr al-Din al-Alusi: Changing Views of Ibn Taymiyya amongst non-Hanbali Sunni scholars', in Yossef Rapoport and Shahab Ahmed (eds), *Ibn Taymiyya and his Times* (Oxford: Oxford University Press, 2010), 269–318.

Esposito, John L., *Islam and Politics* (Syracuse: Syracuse University Press, 1998).

Esposito, John L. and Voll, John O., *Islam and Democracy* (Oxford: Oxford University Press, 1996).

Esposito, John L. and Voll, John O., *Makers of Contemporary Islam* (Oxford University Press, 2001).

Esposito, John L. and Shahin, Emad el-Din (eds), *The Oxford Handbook of Islam and Politics* (Oxford University Press, 2013).

Esposito, John L. (ed.), *The Oxford History of Islam* (Oxford: Oxford University Press, 1999).

Euben, Roxanne, 'A Counternarrative of Shared Ambivalence: some Muslim and Western Perspectives on Science and Reason', *Common Knowledge* 9 (2003), 50–77.

Euben, Roxanne L., *Enemy in the Mirror: Islamic Fundamentalism and the Limits of Modern Rationalism: A Work of Comparative Political Theory* (Princeton: Princeton University Press, 1999).

Euben, Roxanne L. and Zaman, Qasim (eds), *Princeton Readings in Islamist Thought* (Princeton: Princeton University Press, 2009).

Fandy, Mamoun, 'Egypt's Islamic Group: Regional Revenge?', *Middle East Journal* 48 (1994), 607–25.

Fanon, Frantz, 'Algeria Unveiled', in *A Dying Colonialism* (London: Writers and Readers Publishing, 1980).

Fanon, Frantz, *A Dying Colonialism* (New York: Grove, 1965).

Fanon, Frantz, *Toward the African Revolution* (Harmondsworth: Penguin, 1970).

Fanon, Frantz, *The Wretched of the Earth* (London: Penguin, 1990).

Farouk-Sluglett, Marion and Sluglett, Peter, *Iraq Since 1958: From Revolution to Dictatorship* (London: I.B. Tauris, 2001).

Ferdows, Adele K., 'Women and the Islamic Revolution', *International Journal of Middle East Studies* 15 (1983), 283–98.

Findley, Carter V., *Turkey, Islam, Nationalism and Modernity: A History, 1789-2007* (New Haven: Yale University Press, 2010).

Findley, Carter V., 'The Ottoman Lands to the post-World War Settlement', in Francis Robinson (ed.), *The New Cambridge History of Islam Volume 5: The Islamic World in the Era of Western Dominance* (Cambridge: Cambridge University Press, 2010), 31–78.

Firro, Tarik K., 'The Political Context of the Early Wahhabi Discourse of Takfir', *Middle Eastern Studies* 49 (2013), 770–89.

Formichi, Chiara, *Islam and the Making of the Nation: Kartosuwiyro and Political Islam in 20th Century Indonesia* (Leiden: KITLV Press, 2012).

Fredholm, Michael, 'Kashmir, Afghanistan, India and Beyond: A Taxonomy of Islamic Extremism and Terrorism in Pakistan', *Himalayan and Central Asian Studies* 15 (2011), 24–80.

Gallab, Abdullahi A., *The First Islamist Republic: Development and Disintegration of Islamism in the Sudan* (Aldershot: Ashgate, 2008).

Gallab, Abdullahi A., *Their Second Republic: Islamism in the Sudan from Disintegration to Oblivion* (Farnham: Ashgate, 2014).

Gallagher, John and Robinson, Ronald, 'The Imperialism of Free Trade', *Economic History Review* 6 (1953), 1–15.

Gelvin, James, *The Modern Middle East: A History* (New York: Oxford University Press, 2005).

Gentile, Emilio, 'Fascism, Totalitarianism and Political Religion: Definitions and Critical Reflections on Criticism of an Interpretation', *Totalitarian Movements and Political Religions* 5 (2004), 326–75.

Gerges, Fawaz A., *The Far Enemy: Why Jihad Went Global* (Cambridge: Cambridge University Press, 2005).

Gerges, Fawaz, A. *ISIS: A History* (Princeton: Princeton University Press, 2016).

Gerges, Fawaz A., 'The Strategic Logic of the Islamic State', *The Strategist*, 11 August 2016.

Gershoni, Israel and Jankowski, James, *Confronting Fascism in Egypt: Dictatorship versus Democracy in the 1930s* (Stanford: Stanford University Press, 2010).

Gershoni, Israel and Jankowski, James, *Egypt, Islam and the Arabs: the Search for Egyptian Nationhood, 1900-1930* (New York: Oxford University Press, 1986).

Gershoni, Israel and Jankowski, James, *Redefining the Egyptian Nation, 1930-1945* (Cambridge: Cambridge University Press, 1995).

Ghazzal, Zouhair, 'The Ulama: Status and Function', in Youssef M. Choueiri (ed.), *A Companion to the History of the Middle East* (Oxford: Blackwell, 2008).

Gleave, Robert, "Shi'ism", in Youssef M. Choueiri (ed.), *A Companion to the History of the Middle East* (Oxford: Blackwell, 2008).

Gibson, Nigel C., *Fanon: The Postcolonial Imagination* (Cambridge: Polity, 2003).

Gordon, Joel, *Nasser's Blessed Movement: Egypt's Free Officers and the July Revolution* (New York: Oxford University Press, 1992).

Gray, Matthew, *Conspiracy Theories in the Arab World* (London: Routledge, 2010).

Griffel, Frank, 'What do We Mean by "Salafi"? Connecting Muhammad Abduh with Egypt's Nur Party in Islam's Contemporary Intellectual History', *Die Welt Des Islams* 55 (2015), 186–220.

Griffin, Roger (ed.), *Fascism* (Oxford University Press, 1995).

Griffin, Roger, *The Nature of Fascism* (London: Routledge, 1993).

Grinberg, Alex, 'Iranian Reformists: Between Moderation and Revolution', *Middle East Review of International Affairs* 20 (2016), 14–21.

Guha, Ranajit, *Dominance Without Hegemony: History and Power in Colonial India* (London: Harvard University Press, 1997).

Hafez, Mohammed M., 'Armed Islamist Movements and Political Violence in Algeria', *Middle East Journal* 54 (2000), 572–91.

Hale, Sondra, *Gender Politics in Sudan* (Boulder: Westview Press, 1996).

Hale, Sondra, 'Mothers and Militias: Islamic State Construction of the Women Citizens of Northern Sudan', *Citizenship Studies* 3 (1999), 373–86.

Hale, William and Ozbudun, Ergun, *Islamism, Democracy and Liberalism in Turkey: the Case of the AKP* (London: Routledge, 2009).

Hamdan, Ali Nehme, 'Breaker of Barriers? Notes on the Geopolitics of Islamic State in Iraq and Sham', *Geopolitics* 21 (2016), 1–23.

Hamdi, Mohamed E., *The Making of an Islamic Political Leader: Conversations with Hasan al-Turabi* (Oxford: Westview Press, 2008).

Hamid, Shadi, *Temptations of Power: Islamists and Illiberal Democracy in a New Middle East* (Oxford: Oxford University Press, 2014).

Hamid, Shadi, McCants, William and Dar, Rashid, 'Islamism after the Arab Spring: between the Islamic State and the Nation State' (Brookings Project on US relations with the Islamic World, 2017), https://www.brookings.edu/wp-content/uploads/2017/01/islamism-after-the-arab-spring_english_web_final.pdf

Hanioglu, M. Sukru, 'Modern Ottoman Period', in Metin Heper and Sabri Sayari (eds), *The Routledge Handbook of Modern Turkey* (Routledge: Abingdon, 2012), 15–25.

Hansen, William, 'Boko Haram: Religious Radicalism and Insurrection in Northern Nigeria', *Journal of Asian and African Studies* (2017), 551–69.

Haroon, Sana, 'The Rise of Deobandi Islam in the North-West Frontier Province and its Implications in Colonial India and Pakistan, 1914-1996', *Journal of the Royal Asiatic Society* 18 (2008), 47–70.

Harrison, Ross, *Democracy* (London: Routledge, 1993).

Hartung, Jan-Peter, *A System of Life: Mawdudi and the Ideologisation of Islam* (Oxford University Press, 2014).

Hassan, Mona, 'Modern Interpretations and Misinterpretations of a Medieval Scholar: Apprehending the Medieval Thought of Ibn Taymiyyah', in Yossef Rapoport and Shahab Ahmed (eds), *Ibn Taymiyya and his Times* (Oxford: Oxford University Press, 2010), 338–66.

Hawting, Gerald R., 'The Rise of Islam', in Youssef M. Choueiri (ed.), *A Companion to the History of the Middle East* (Oxford: Blackwell, 2008), 9–28.

Haykel, Bernard, 'On the Nature of Salafi Thought and Action', in Roel Meijer (ed.), *Global Salafism: Islam's New Religious Movement* (New York: Columbia University Press, 2009), 33–51.

Haykel, Bernard, 'Western Arabia and Yemen in the Ottoman Period', in Maribel Fierro (ed.), *The New Cambridge History of Islam Volume 2: The Western Islamic World, Eleventh to Eighteenth Centuries* (Cambridge: Cambridge University Press, 2010), 436–49.

Hegghammer, Thomas, *Jihad in Saudi Arabia: Violence and Pan-Islamism since 1979* (Cambridge: Cambridge University Press, 2010).

Hegghammer, Thomas, 'Jihadi-Salafis or Revolutionaries? On Religion and Politics in the Study of Militant Islamism', in Roel Meijer (ed.), *Global Salafism: Islam's New Religious Movement* (New York: Columbia University Press, 2009), 244–66.

Hegghammer, Thomas and Lacroix, Stephane, 'Rejectionist Islam in Saudi Arabia: the Story of Juhaynam al-Utaybi Revisited', *International Journal of Middle East Studies* 39 (2007), 103–22.

Holt, P. M., *The Mahdist State in Sudan: a Study of its History, Origins and Overthrow* (Oxford: Clarendon Press, 1970).

Holt, P. M., Review of Elie Kedourie, *Afghani and Abduh: An Essay on Religious Unbelief and Political Activism in Modern Islam* (London: Frank Cass, 1966) and Muhammad Abduh, trans. Ishaq Musa'ad and Kenneth Cragg, *The Theology of Unity* (London: George Allen and Unwin, 1966), published in *Bulletin of the School of Oriental and African Studies* 30 (1967), 190–4.

Hossein, Ishtiaq and Siddiquee, Noore Alam, 'Islam in Bangladesh Politics: The Role of Ghulam Azam of Jama'at-i-Islami', *Inter-Asia Cultural Studies* 5 (2004), 384–99.

Hroub, Khaled, *Hamas: A Beginner's Guide* (London: Pluto Press, 2010).

Hudis, Peter, *Frantz Fanon: Philosopher of the Barricades* (London: Pluto Press, 2015).

Ibrahim, Abdullahi Ali, *Manichaean Delirium: Decolonizing the Judiciary and Islamic Renewal in the Sudan, 1898-1985* (Boston: Brill, 2008).

Ibrahim, Abdullahi Ali, 'A Theology of Modernity: Hasan al-Turabi and Islamic Renewal in Sudan', *Africa Today* 46 (1999), 195–222.

Ibrahim, Abd al-Fattah Mahjub, *al-Duktur Hasan al-Turabi wa Fasad Nazariyyat Tatwir al-Din* (al-Qahira: Bayt al-Hikmah, 1995).

Ibrahim, Hassan Ahmad, 'Shaikh Muhammad Ibn Abd al-Wahhab and Shah Walliallah: A Preliminary Comparison of some aspects of their lives and careers', *Asian Journal of Science* 34 (2006), 103–19.

Inal, Vedit, 'Eighteenth and Nineteenth Century Ottoman Attempts to Catch up with Europe', *Middle Eastern Studies* 47 (2011), 725–56.

Ingram, Brannon D., 'Crises of the Public in Muslim India: Critiquing "Custom" at Aligarh and Deoband', *South Asia: Journal of South Asian Studies* 38 (2015), 403–18.

Ingram, Brannon D., 'Sufis, Scholars and Scapegoats: Rashid Ahmad Ganoghi (d. 1905) and the Deobandi Critique of Sufism', *The Muslim World* 99 (2009), 478–501.

Irfan, Ahmad, 'Genealogy of the Islamic State: Reflections on Mawlana Maududi's Political Thought and Islamism', *The Journal of the Royal Anthropological Institute* 15 (2009), 145–62.

Jackson, Roy, *Mawlana Mawdudi and Political Islam: Authority and the Islamic State* (London: Routledge, 2011).

Kaler, Helena J., 'Inscribing Gender in the Imperial Context: the "Woman Question" in Nineteenth Century Egypt', *Hawwa* 4 (2006), 328–55.

Karaveli, Halil, 'Erdogan's Journey', *Foreign Affairs* 95 (2016), 121–5.

Kaufman, Asher, *Reviving Phoenicia: The Search for Identity in Lebanon* (London: I.B. Tauris, 2014).

Kayali, Hasan, 'Elections and the Electoral Process in the Ottoman Empire, 1876-1919', *International Journal of Middle East Studies* 27 (1995), 265–86.

Keddie, Nikki R., *An Islamic Response to Imperialism: Political and Religious Writings of Sayyid Jamal ad-Din 'al-Afghani'* (London: University of California Press, 1983).

Keddie, Nikki R., *Jamal al-Din al-Afghani: A Political Biography* (New York: American Council of Learned Societies, 2008).

Kedourie, Elie, *Afghani and 'Abduh: An Essay on Religious Unbelief and Political Activism in Modern Islam* (London: Frank Cass, 1997).

Kennedy, Hugh, 'The Caliphate', in Youssef M. Choueiri (ed.), *A Companion to the History of the Middle East* (Oxford: Blackwell, 2008).

Kenney, Jeffrey T., *Muslim Rebels: Kharijites and the Politics of Extremism in Egypt* (Oxford University Press, 2006).

Kepel, Gilles, *Jihad: The Trail of Political Islam*, trans. Anthony F. Roberts (London: I.B. Tauris, 2002).

Kepel, Gilles, *The Roots of Radical Islam* (London: Saqi, 2005).

Khatab, Sayed, *The Power of Sovereignty: The Political and Ideological Sovereignty of Sayyid Qutb* (London: Routledge, 2006).

Khatab, Sayed and Bouma, Gary D., *Democracy in Islam* (London: Routledge, 2011).

Khomeini, Ayatollah Ruhollah, *Islam and Revolution: Writings and Declarations of Imam Khomeini,* ed. Hamid Algar (Berkeley: Mizan Press, 1980).

Kramer, Gudrun, *Hasan al-Banna* (Oxford: Oneworld, 2010).

Kuntzel, Matthias, *Jihad and Jew-Hatred: Islamism, Nazism and the Roots of 9/11* (New York: Telos Press, 2007).

Kurzman, Charles, *Modernist Islam: 1840-1940: A Sourcebook* (Oxford: Oxford University Press, 2002).

Lapidus, Ira, *A History of Islamic Societies* (Cambridge: Cambridge University Press, 2002).

Lauzière, Henri, 'The Construction of Salafiyya: Reconsidering Salafism from the Perspective of Conceptual History', *International Journal of Middle Eastern Studies* 42 (2010), 369–89.

Lauzière, Henri, *The Making of Salafism: Islamic Reform in the Twentieth Century* (New York: Columbia University Press, 2016).

Layish, Aharon and Warburg, Gabriel R., *The Reinstatement of Islamic Law in Sudan under Numayri* (Leiden: Brill, 2002).

Lefèvre, Raphaël, *Ashes of Hama: The Muslim Brotherhood in Syria* (Cary: Oxford University Press, 2014).

Lefèvre, Raphaël, 'Balancing Act: Islamism and the Monarchy in Morocco', *The Journal of North African Studies* 18 (2013), 626–9.

Lesch, Ann Mosely, *The Sudan: Contested National Identities* (Oxford: James Currey, 1998).

Levy, Ran A., 'The Idea of Jihad and its Evolution: Hasan al-Banna and the Society of Muslim Brothers', *Die Welt des Islams* 54 (2014), 139–58.

Lia, Brynjar, 'The Islamist Uprising in Syria, 1976-1982: The History and Legacy of a Failed Revolt', *British Journal of Middle Eastern Studies* 43 (2016), 541–59.

Lia, Brynjar, *The Society of the Muslim Brothers in Egypt: The Rise of an Islamic Mass Movement, 1928-1942* (Reading: Ithaca Press, 2006).

Litvak, Meir, 'The Anti-Semitism of Hamas', *Palestine-Israel Journal of Politics, Economics and Culture* 12 (2005), 41–6.

Litvak, Meir, '"Martyrdom is Life": Jihad and Martyrdom in the Ideology of Hamas', *Studies in Conflict and Terrorism* 33 (2010), 716–34.

Louer, Laurence, 'A Decline of Identity Politics', *International Journal of Middle East Studies* 43 (2011), 389–90.

Madelung, Wilferd, *The Succession to Muhammad: A Study of the Early Caliphate* (Cambridge: Cambridge University Press, 1997).

Mahendrarajah, Shivan, 'Saudi Arabia, Wahhabism, and the Taliban of Afghanistan: "Puritannical Reform" as Revolutionary War program', *Small Wars & Insurgencies* 26 (2015), 383–407.

Maher, Shiraz, *Salafi-Jihadism: The History of an Idea* (London: Hurst & Company, 2016).

Malik, Hafeez, 'Sir Sayyid Ahmad Khan's Doctrines of Muslim Nationalism and National Progress', *Modern Asian Studies* 2 (1968), 221–44.

Malik, Hafeez, 'Sir Sayyid Ahmad Khan's Contribution to the Development of Muslim Nationalism in India', *Modern Asian Studies* 4 (1970), 129–47.

Mandaville, Peter G., *Global Political Islam* (London: Routledge, 2007).

Marchal, Roland, 'Islamic Political Dynamic in the Somali Civil War: Before and After September 11', in Alex de Waal (ed.), *Islamism and Its Enemies in the Horn of Africa* (London: Hurst and Company, 2004), 114–45.

Martin, Vanessa, *Creating an Islamic State: Khomeini and the Making of a New Iran* (London: I.B. Tauris, 2003).

Mazrui, Ali, *Violence and Thought: Essays on Social Tension in Africa* (London: 1969), 163–83.

McCants, William Faizi, *The ISIS Apocalypse: The History, Strategy and Doomsday Vision of the Islamic State* (New York: St Martin's Press, 2015).

Melchert, Christopher, *Ahmad Ibn Hanbal* (Oxford: Oneworld, 2006).

Miller, Judith, 'Faces of Fundamentalism: Hasan al-Turabi and Muhammad Fadlallah', *Foreign Affairs* 73 (1994), 123–42.

Miller, Judith, 'Global Islamic Awakening or Sudanese Nightmare?', in R. Scott Appleby (ed.), *Spokesmen for the Despised: Fundamentalist Leaders of the Middle East* (Chicago: Chicago University Press, 1999), 182–224.

Minawi, Mostafa, *The Ottoman Scramble for Africa: Empire and Diplomacy in the Sahara and the Hijaz* (Stanford: Stanford University Press, 2016).

Mirsepassi, Ali, *Political Islam, Iran, and the Enlightenment: Philosophies of Hope and Despair* (Cambridge: Cambridge University Press, 2010).

Mitchell, Alex, *Come the Revolution: A Memoir* (Sydney: New South, 2014).

Mitchell, Richard P., *The Society of the Muslim Brothers* (Oxford University Press, 1993), 294–300.

Moaddel, Mansoor, 'Class Struggle in Post-Revolutionary Iran', *International Journal of Middle East Studies* 23 (1991), 317–43.

Moallem, Minoo, *Between Warrior Brother and Veiled Sister: Islamic Fundamentalism and the Politics of Patriarchy in Iran* (London: University of California Press, 2005).

Moghadam, Valentine, 'Patriarchy, the Taleban, and Politics of Public Space in Afghanistan', *Women's Studies International Forum* 25 (2002), 19–31.

Moore, Robin J., 'Imperial India, 1858-1914', in Andrew Porter (ed.), *The Oxford History of the British Empire Vol III: The Nineteenth Century* (Oxford: Oxford University Press, 1999), 422–46.

Moussalli, Ahmad S., 'Hasan al-Turabi's Islamist Discourse on Democracy and Shura', *Middle Eastern Studies* 30 (1994), 52–63.

Moussalli, Ahmad S., *Moderate and Radical Islamic Fundamentalism: The Quest for Modernity, Legitimacy and the Islamic State* (Gainesville: University Press of Florida, c.1999).

Mozaffari, Mehdi, *Islamism: A New Totalitarianism* (Boulder: Lynne Rienner, 2017).

Mozaffari, Mehdi, 'The Rise of Islamism in the Light of European Totalitarianism', *Totalitarian Movements and the Rise of Political Religions* 10 (2009), 1–13.

Mubarak, Khalid, *Turabi's 'Islamist' Venture: Failure and Implications* (Cairo: Dar al-Thaqafia, 2001).

Muhammad, Ahmad Abd al-Rahman (ed.), *Takhlid Dhikra al-Mufakkir al-Arabi al-Islami Babikir Karrar* (Khartoum: Dar al-Sudaniyya li'l-Kutub, 2008).

Munson, Ziad, 'Islamic Mobilization: Social Movement Theory and the Egyptian Muslim Brotherhood', *Sociological Quarterly* 42 (2001), 487–510.

Mura, Andrea, 'A Genealogical Inquiry into Early Islamism: The Discourse of Hasan al-Banna', *Journal of Political Ideologies* 17 (2012), 61–85.

Musallam, Adnan A., *From Secularism to Jihad: Sayyid Qutb and the Founding of Radical Islamism* (Westport: Praeger, 2005).

Nafi, Basheer, 'Tasawwuf and Reform in Pre-Modern Islamic Culture: In Search of Ibrahim al-Kurani', *Die Welt des Islams* 42 (2002), 307–55.

Nasr, Seyyed Vali Reza, *Mawdudi and the Making of Islamic Revivalism* (Oxford University Press, 1997).

Ochsenwald, William, 'Saudi Arabia and the Islamic Revival', *International Journal of Middle East Studies* 13 (1981), 271–86.

Osman, Fathi, 'Mawdudi's Contribution to the Development of Modern Islamic Thinking in the Arabic-Speaking World', *Muslim World* 93 (2003), 465–85.

Osman, Mohamed, 'Transnational Islamism and its Impact in Malaysia and Indonesia', *Middle East Review of International Affairs* 15 (2011), 42–52.

Othman, Mohammad Redzuan and Haris, Abu Hanifah, 'The Role of Egyptian Influences on the Religious Dynamics and the Idea of Progress of Malaya's Kaum Muda (Young Faction) before the Second World War', *British Journal of Middle Eastern Studies* 42 (2015), 465–80.

Paidar, Parvin, *Women and the Political Process in Twentieth-Century Iran* (Cambridge: Cambridge University Press, 1995).

Paul, Ludwig, '"Iranian Nation" and Iranian-Islamic Revolutionary Ideology', *Die Welt Des Islams* 39 (1999), 183–217.

Peng, Yuan, 'Modernization Theory', *Chinese Studies in History* 43 (2009), 37–45.

Perkins, Kenneth J., *A History of Modern Tunisia* (Cambridge: Cambridge University Press, 2004).

Peters, Rudolph, *Crime and Punishment in Islamic Law: Theory and Practice from the Sixteenth to the Twenty-First Century* (Cambridge: Cambridge University Press, 2005).

Peters, Rudolph, *Jihad in Classical and Modern Islam: A Reader* (Princeton: Markus Wiener, 2005).

Phillips, David L., *An Uncertain Ally: Turkey under Erdogan's Dictatorship* (London: Routledge, 2017).

Podeh, Elie and Winckler, Onn, *Rethinking Nasserism: Revolution and Historical Memory in Modern Egypt* (Gainesville: University Press of Florida, 2004).

Provence, Michael, 'Ottoman Modernity, Colonialism and Insurgency in the Interwar Arab East', *International Journal of Middle East Studies* 43 (2011), 205–25.

Qutb, Sayyid, 'The America I have Seen: In the Scale of Human Values', in K. Abdel-Malek and Mouna El Kahla (eds), *America in an Arab Mirror: Images of America in Arab Travel Literature: An Anthology 1895-1995* (New York: Palgrave, 2000).

Rabaka, Reiland, 'Revolutionary Fanonism: On Frantz Fanon's Modification of Marxism and the Decolonization of Democratic Socialism', *Socialism and Democracy* 25 (2011), 126–45.

Rabil, Robert G., 'The Syrian Muslim Brotherhood', in Barry Rubin (ed.), *The Muslim Brotherhood: The Organization and Policies of a Global Islamist Movement* (Basingstoke: Palgrave Macmillan, 2010), 73–88.

Rafeq, Abdul-Karem, 'A Different Balance of Power: Europe and the Middle East in the Eighteenth and Nineteenth Centuries', in Youssef M. Choueiri (ed.), *A Companion to the History of the Middle East* (Oxford: Blackwell, 2008), 229–247.

Rahnama, Ali, *An Islamic Utopian: A Political Biography of Ali Shariati* (London: I.B. Tauris, 1998).

Randal, Jonathan, *Osama: The Making of a Terrorist* (New York: Alfred A. Knopf, 2004).

Rapoport, Yossef and Ahmed, Shahab (eds), *Ibn Taymiyya and his Times* (Oxford: Oxford University Press, 2010).

Reid, Donald Malcolm, *Cairo University and the Making of Modern Egypt* (Cambridge: Cambridge University Press, 1990).

Reid, Richard, *A History of Modern Africa* (Malden: Wiley-Blackwell, 2009).

Renton, Dave, *Classical Marxism: Socialist Theory and the Second International* (Cheltenham: New Clarion, 2002).

Reynolds, Jonathon T., 'Good and Bad Muslims: Islam and Indirect Rule in Northern Nigeria', *The International Journal of African Historical Studies* 34 (2001), 601–18.

Rida, Muhammad Rashid and Wood, Simon A., *Christian Criticisms, Islamic Proofs: Rashid Rida's Modernist Defense of Islam* (Oxford: Oneworld Publications, 2007).

Robinson, Francis, 'South Asia to 1919', in Francis Robinson (ed)., *The New Cambridge History of Islam Vol V: The Islamic World in the Age of Western Dominance* (Cambridge: Cambridge University Press, 2011), 212–39.

Ronen, Yehudit, 'Rise and Fall of Hasan Abdullah al-Turabi: A Unique Chapter in Sudan's Political History (1989-1999)', *Middle Eastern Studies* 50 (2014), 992–1005.

Roy, Olivier, *The Failure of Political Islam*, trans. Carol Volk, Cambridge, MA: Harvard University Press 1994).

Roy, Olivier, *Globalized Islam: The Search for a New Ummah* (London: C Hurst, 2002).

Roy, Olivier, 'Islamic Radicalism in Afghanistan and Pakistan', Paper No. 6/2001, http://www.refworld.org/pdfid/3c6a3f7d2.pdf

Roy, Olivier, *Jihad and Death: The Global Appeal of Islamic State* (London: Hurst and Company, 2017).

Rubin, Barry (ed.), *The Muslim Brotherhood: The Organization and Policies of a Global Islamist Movement* (Basingstoke: Palgrave Macmillan, 2010).

Ruthven, Malise, *Islam: A Very Short Introduction* (Oxford University Press, 2012).

Ryad, Umar, 'Islamic Reformism and Great Britain: Rashid Rida's Image as Reflected in the Journal al-Manar in Cairo', *Islam and Christian-Muslims Relations* 21 (2010), 263–85.

Sadiki, Larbi, 'Libya's Arab Spring', *International Studies* 49 (2012), 285–314.

Said, Edward, *Orientalism* (London: Penguin, 1995).

Salomon, Noah, *For Love of the Prophet: An Ethnography of Sudan's Islamic State* (Princeton: Princeton University Press, 2016).

Saouli, Adham, 'Hizbullah in the Civilising Process: Anarchy, Self-Restraint and Violence', *Third World Quarterly* 32 (2011), 925–42.

Scharbrodt, Oliver, 'The Salafiyya and Sufism: Muhammad Abduh and his Risala al-Waridat', *Bulletin of the School of Oriental and African Studies* 70 (2007), 89–115.

Scheuer, Michael, *Osama Bin Laden* (Oxford University Press, 2011).

Schulze, Reinhard, *A Modern History of the Islamic World* (London: I.B. Tauris, 2000).

Schwartz, Benjamin E., 'America's Struggle Against the Wahhabi/Neo-Salafi Movement', *Orbis* 51 (2007), 107–28.

Schwartz, Stephen, Review of Natana DeLong-Bas, *Wahhabi Islam: From Revival and Reform to Global Jihad* (New York: Oxford University Press, 2004), in *The Middle East Quarterly* 12, 2005, http://www.meforum.org/1517/wahhabi-islam-from-revival-to-global-jihad

Scorgie-Porter, Lindsay, 'Militant Islamists or Borderland Dissidents? An Exploration into the Allied Democratic Forces' Recruitment Practises and Constitution', *The Journal of Modern African Studies* 53 (2015), 1–25.

Sebastian, N., 'Islamist Movements Engaging in Democracy: Front Islamique du Salut (FIS) and the Democratic Experiment in Algeria', *India Quarterly* 71 (2015), 225–71.

Sedgwick, Mark, *Muhammad Abduh* (Oxford: Oneworld, 2009).

Shalinsky, Audrey C., 'Women's Roles in the Afghanistan Jihad', *International Journal of Middle East Studies* 25 (1993), 661–75.

Sharabi, Hisham, *Neo-Patriarchy: A Theory of Distorted Change in Arab Society* (Oxford: Oxford University Press, 1988).

Shariati, Ali, 'Expectations from the Muslim Woman', available from *Shariati.com*, http://www.shariati.com/kotob.html (accessed 11 March 2018).

Shariati, Ali, 'Reflections of a Concerned Muslim on the Plight of Oppressed People' (translated and introduced by Mansour Farhang), *Race and Class* 21 (1979), 31–40.

Shariati, Ali, *On the Sociology of Islam: Lectures* (Berkeley: Mizan Press, 1979).

Silverstein, Adam, *Islamic History: A Very Short Introduction* (Oxford: Oxford University Press, 2010).

Simms, Rupe, '"Islam is Our Politics": A Gramscian Analysis of the Muslim Brotherhood', *Social Compass* 49 (2002), 563–82.

Slatin, Rudolf and Wingate, F. R., *Fire and Sword in Sudan; a Personal Narrative of Fighting the Dervishes, 1879-1895* (London: E. Arnold, 1896).

Soage, A. B., 'Hasan al-Banna and Sayyid Qutb: Continuity or Rupture?', *Muslim World* 99 (2009), 294–311.

Soage, A. B., 'Hasan al-Banna or the Politicisation of Islam', *Totalitarian Movements and Political Religions* 9 (2008), 21–42.

Soage, A. B. and Franganillo, J. F., 'The Muslim Brothers in Egypt', in Barry Rubin (ed.), *The Muslim Brotherhood: The Organization and Policies of a Global Islamist Movement* (Basingstoke: Palgrave Macmillan, 2010).

Solomon, Hussein, 'Combating Islamist Radicalisation in South Africa', *African Security Review* 23 (2001) 17–33.

Stemmann, Juan José Escobar, 'The Crossroads of the Muslim Brotherhood in Jordan', in Barry Rubin (ed.), *The Muslim Brotherhood: The Organization and Policies of a Global Islamist Movement* (Basingstoke: Palgrave Macmillan, 2010), 57–72.

Stoica, Dragos, 'Do Modern Radicals Believe in their Mythologies? A Comparison Between the Muslim Brotherhood and the Legion of the Archangel Michael in the Light of Four Political Mythologies', *Politics, Religions & Ideology* 15 (2014), 103–35.

Stora, Benjamin, *Algeria 1830-2000* (London: Cornell University Press, 2001).

Strindberg, Anders and Wärn, Mats, *Islamism: Religion, Radicalization and Resistance* (Cambridge: Polity, 2011).

Taylor, Max and Elbushra, Mohamed E., 'Research Note: Hassan al-Turabi, Osama bin Laden, and Al Qaeda in Sudan', *Terrorism and Political Violence* 18 (2006), 449–64.

Timani, Hussam S., *Modern Intellectual Readings of the Kharijites* (New York: Peter Lang, 2008).

Tønnesson, Liv, *Hasan al-Turabi's Search for Islamist Democracy* (Bergen: Chr. Michelsen Institute: CMI Working Paper WP 12, 2006).

Toth, James, *Sayyid Qutb: the Life and Legacy of a Radical Islamic Intellectual* (New York: Oxford University Press, 2013).

Turner, Simon, '"These Young Men Show No Respect for Local Customs" – Globalisation and Islamic Revival in Zanzibar', *Journal of Religion in Africa* 39 (2009), 237–61.

Turshen, Meredeth, 'Islamism and Militarism in Algeria', *Journal of Asian and African Studies* 39 (2004), 119–32.

Ukeles, Raquel M., 'The Sensitive Puritan? Revisiting Ibn Taymiyya's Approach to Law and Spirituality in Light of 20th Century Debates on the Prophet's Birthday (*mawlid al-nabi*)', in Yossef Rapoport and Shahab Ahmed (eds), *Ibn Taymiyya and his Times* (Oxford: Oxford University Press, 2010), 319–37.

Unger, Craig, *House of Bush, House of Saud: The Secret Relationship between the World's Two Most Powerful Dynasties* (London: Gibson Square, 2006).

Valkili, Valla, 'Abolkarim Soroush', in John L. Esposito and John O. Voll (eds), *Makers of Contemporary Islam* (Oxford University Press, 2001).

Vandewalle, Dirk, *A History of Modern Libya* (Cambridge: Cambridge University Press, 2012).

Vandewalle, Dirk, *Libya Since Independence: Oil and State Building* (London: I.B. Tauris, 1998).

Van Dijk, Cees, 'Islam and Socio-Political Conflicts in Indonesian History', *Social Compass* 31 (1984), 5–25.

Verhoeven, Harry, 'The Rise and Fall of Sudan's Ingaz Revolution: the Transition from Militarised Islamism to Economic Salvation and the Comprehensive Peace Agreement', *Civil Wars* 15 (2) (2013), 118–40.

Vidino, Lorenzo, 'Islamism and the West: Europe as a Battlefield', *Totalitarian Movements and Political Religions* 10 (2009), 165–76.

Voll, John, 'Foundations for Renewal and Reform: Islamic Movements in the Eighteenth and Nineteenth Centuries', *Oxford History of Islam* (Oxford: Oxford University Press 1999), 509–48.

Voll, John, 'Muḥammad Ḥayya al-Sindi and Muḥammad ibn 'Abd al-Wahhab: An Analysis of an Intellectual Group in Eighteenth-century Madina', *Bulletin of the School of Oriental and African Studies* 38 (1975), 32–9.

Voll, John O., 'The Impact of the Wahhabi Tradition', in Mohammed Ayoob and Hasan Kosebalaban (eds), *Religion and Politics in Saudi Arabia* (Boulder: Lynne Rienner, 2009), 149–68.

Voll, John, 'The Sudanese Mahdi: Frontier Fundamentalist', *International Journal of Middle East Studies* 10 (1979), 145–66.

Wagemakers, Joas, 'The Enduring Legacy of the Second Saudi State: Quietist and Radical Wahhabi Contestations of Al-Wala wa-l-Bara', *International Journal of Middle Eastern Studies* 44 (2012), 93–110.

Walker, Andrew, *Eat the Heart of the Infidel: The Harrowing of Nigeria and the Rise of Boko Haram* (London: Hurst & Co, 2016).

Walker, David M. and Gray, Daniel, *Historical Dictionary of Marxism* (Lanham, MD: Scarecrow Press, 2002).

Warburg, Gabriel, 'British Policy towards the Ansar in Sudan: A Note on a Historical Controversy', *Middle Eastern Studies* 33 (2007), 675–92.

Warburg, Gabriel, *Islam, Sectarianism and Politics in Sudan since the Mahdiyya* (London: Hurst, 2003).

Warburg, Gabriel, 'From Sufism to Fundamentalism: the Mahdiyya and the Wahhabiyya', *Middle Eastern Studies* 45 (2009), 661–72.

Washbrook, D. A., 'India, 1818-1860: The Two Faces of Colonialism', in Andrew Porter (ed.), *The Oxford History of the British Empire Vol III: The Nineteenth Century* (Oxford: Oxford University Press, 1999), 395–421.

Waterson, James, *Sacred Swords: Jihad in the Holy Land 1097-1295* (London: Frontline Books, 2010).

Weinbaum, Marvin, 'The Afghan Factor in India's Foreign Policy', *Himalayan and Central Asian Studies* 1 (1997), 3–17.

Weisman, Itzchak, 'Genealogies of Fundamentalism: Salafi Discourse in Nineteenth Century Baghdad', *British Journal of Middle Eastern Studies* 36 (2009), 267–80.

Wendell, Charles and al-Banna, Hasan, *Five Tracts of Hasan al-Banna (1906-1949): A Selection from the Majmu'at Rasa'il al-Imam al-Shahid Hasan al-Banna* (Berkeley: University of California Press, 1978).

Westerlund, David, 'Reaction and Action: Accounting for the Rise of Islamism', in David Westerlund and Eva Evers Rosander (eds), *African Islam and Islam in Africa: Encounters between Sufis and Islamists* (London: Hurst & Company, 1997), 308–34.

Westerlund, David and Rosander, Eva Evers, *African Islam and Islam in Africa: Encounters between Sufis and Islamists* (London: Hurst & Company, 1997).

Wiktorowicz, Quintain, 'Islamists, the State and Co-operation in Jordan', *Arab Studies Quarterly* 21 (1999), 1–18.

Willemse, Karin, '"A room of one's own": Single Female Teachers negotiating the Islamist Discourse in Sudan', *Northeast African Studies* 8 (2001), 99–127.

Wolf, Anne, *Political Islam in Tunisia: The History of Ennahda* (London: Hurst, 2017).

Wood, Graeme, *The Way of Strangers: Encounters with the Islamic State* (London: Allen Lane, 2017).

Wright, Lawrence, *The Looming Tower: Al-Qaeda and the Road to 9/11* (New York: Knopf, 2006).

Young, Robert J. C., *Postcolonialism: An Historical Introduction* (Oxford: Blackwell, 2001).

Zia-Ebrahimi, Reza, '"Arab Invasion" and Decline, or the Importation of European Racial Thought by Iranian Nationalists', *Ethnic and Racial Studies* 37 (2014), 1043–61.

Zollner, Barbara H. E., *The Muslim Brotherhood: Hasan al-Hudaybi and Ideology* (London: Routledge, 2009).

Zubaida, Sami, *Islam, the People and the State: Political Ideas and Movements in the Middle East* (London: I.B. Tauris, 1989).

INDEX